Thomas Hoccleve's Collected Shorter Poems

EXETER MEDIEVAL TEXTS AND STUDIES

Series Editors: Vincent Gillespie and Richard Dance

Founded by M.J. Swanton and later co-edited by Marion Glasscoe

THOMAS HOCCLEVE'S COLLECTED SHORTER POEMS

A Critical Edition of the Huntington Holographs

Edited By

SEBASTIAN J. LANGDELL

LIVERPOOL UNIVERSITY PRESS

First published in 2023 by
Liverpool University Press
4 Cambridge Street
Liverpool
L69 7ZU

Copyright © 2023 Sebastian J. Langdell

Sebastian J. Langdell has asserted the right to be identified as the author of this book in accordance with the Copyright, Designs and Patents Act 1988.

All rights reserved. No part of this book may be reproduced, stored in a retrieval system, or transmitted, in any form or by any means, electronic, mechanical, photocopying, recording, or otherwise, without the prior written permission of the publisher.

British Library Cataloguing-in-Publication data
A British Library CIP record is available

ISBN 978-1-83764-425-4

Typeset by Carnegie Book Production, Lancaster

CONTENTS

ACKNOWLEDGMENTS	vii
CHRONOLOGY	viii
LIST OF MANUSCRIPTS & SIGLA	ix
INTRODUCTION	xi
NOTE ON EDITORIAL PRACTICES	xxix

HUNTINGTON LIBRARY, MS HM 111		1
1.	COMPLAINT PARAMOUNT	3
2.	TO SIR JOHN OLDCASTLE	13
3.	LA MALE REGLE	31
4.	FOR HENRY V AT KENNINGTON	45
5–6.	KNIGHTS OF THE GARTER	48
7.	MOTHER OF LIFE	52
8.	THE BONES OF RICHARD II	57
9.	BALADE TO EDWARD, DUKE OF YORK	60
10.	MOTHER OF GOD	64
11.	BALADE TO JOHN, DUKE OF BEDFORD	70
12.	BALADE TO THE CHANCELLOR	73
13.	BALADE AND ROUNDEL TO HENRY SOMER	75
14.	REGIMENT OF PRINCES ENVOI	78
15.	VICTORIOUS KING	80
16.	BALADE TO JOHN CARPENTER	83
17.	THE COURT OF GOOD COMPANY	85
18.	BALADE FOR ROBERT CHICHELE	89

HUNTINGTON LIBRARY, MS HM 744		95
1.	INUOCACIO AD PATREM	97
2.	AD FILIUM	103
3.	AD SPIRITUM SANCTUM	107
4.	WORSHIPFUL MAIDEN	111
5.	MOTHER OF GRACE	114
6.	THE MONK WHO CLAD THE VIRGIN	120
7.	THE EPISTLE OF CUPID	126
8.	HENRY V'S LAST RETURN	143
9.	THREE ROUNDELS	146
10.	LEARN TO DIE	150

OCCURRENCES OF SHORTER POEMS BEYOND HM 111/744   181
TEXTUAL VARIANTS   184
BIBLIOGRAPHY   198

ACKNOWLEDGMENTS

This project has been supported at every stage by generous funding from the Huntington Library and the National Endowment for the Humanities, as well as Baylor University summer sabbatical awards and URC funding. This book would not have been possible without this generous support, which facilitated research travel, archival work, and each phase of writing and revision.

Several individuals lent their expertise and intelligence to this enterprise along the way. I wish to thank Jenni Nuttall for her ongoing collegial input and idea-exchange, and for demonstrating how wide-ranging Hoccleve's neologisms are; Jane Griffiths for guidance, encouragement, and enriching dialogue, especially on 'To Sir John Oldcastle' (and its thorny glosses); Ruen-chuan Ma, my partner at the helm of the Hoccleve Society, for his friendship and insight; David Watt, for his continued encouragement and input; Misty Schieberle, for her expert input, enthusiasm, and support; Daniel Wakelin, Steve Rozenski, and Philip Knox, for helpful suggestions; my esteemed editors in the Exeter Medieval Texts and Studies Series, Vincent Gillespie and Richard Dance; Clare Litt at Liverpool University Press, and Lucy Frontani at Carnegie; my Baylor English colleagues; and my intrepid graduate research assistants: Olivia Taylor, Elizabeth Travers Parker, Becky Presnall, and Madelyn Dyk.

I would also like to thank the 'Hoccleve at Home' community for offering over two years of especially energizing discussions on Hoccleve. The lecture series began in June 2020, just months after the onset of the pandemic, and the routine of gathering monthly to talk Hoccleve with scholars worldwide warmed the heart, steadied the mind, and inspired new avenues of research. I would also like to thank my fellow members of the Hoccleve Society, and the godfather of the modern Hoccleve community, John Burrow: while we never met in person, I have benefited greatly from his fruitful toiling in the field of Hoccleve.

Finally, I thank my wonderful family – Anna, Oliver, and Athena – for their support, encouragement, and companionship over the five-year period of creation.

CHRONOLOGY

Life Events		Works	
c. 1367:	Hoccleve born		
c. 1387 (Easter):	Hoccleve begins at Privy Seal		
1399:	coronation of Henry IV		
1400:	Chaucer dies		
		1402:	Epistle of Cupid
		1405–6:	La Male Regle
		c. 1406–7:	Balade to the Chancellor
		1408–9:	Balade and Roundel to Henry Somer
		1410–11:	Regiment of Princes
1413:	death of Henry IV & coronation of Henry V	1413:	For Henry V at Kennington
		1413:	The Bones of Richard II
1414:	death of Archbishop Arundel & elevation of Archbishop Henry Chichele	<1414:	Balade to John, Duke of Bedford
		<1414:	Complaint Paramount
1414–18:	Council of Constance	1414 or 1416:	Knights of the Garter
		<1415:	Balade to Edward, Duke of York
1415:	Battle of Agincourt	1415:	To Sir John Oldcastle
		c. 1415–16:	Victorious King
1417:	Sir John Oldcastle executed		
1420:	Treaty of Troyes		
		1421:	The Court of Good Company
		1421:	Henry V's Last Return
1422:	death of Henry V & accession of Henry VI		
1422–6:	production of Durham Series, HM 111 & 744, Formulary	c. 1419–26:	The Series (including Learn to Die)
1426:	Hoccleve dies		
		Note: several works, including almost all Marian poems, are not listed here, because we have no indication of date.	

LIST OF MANUSCRIPTS & SIGLA

A   = British Library MS Arundel 38
Ad   = British Library MS Additional 18632
Ad2 = British Library MS Additional 17492
Ad3 = British Library MS Additional 34193
Ar   = British Library MS Arundel 59
As   = Bodleian Library MS Ashmole 40
B   = Bodleian Library MS Bodley 221
B2   = Bodleian Library MS Bodley 638
B3   = Bodleian Library MS Bodley 770
Ba   = National Library of Scotland MS Advocates 1.1. 6
C   = Coventry City Record Office MS Acc. 325/1
Ca   = Canterbury Cathedral Archives, Register O
Cc   = Corpus Christi College, Cambridge, MS 496
Ch   = Christ Church, Oxford, MS 152
Co   = Corpus Christi College, Oxford, MS 237
D   = Durham University MS Cosin V.III.9
D1   = Bodleian Library MS Digby 181
D2   = Bodleian Library MS Digby 185
D3   = Durham University MS Cosin V.II.13
Do   = Bodleian Library MS Douce 158
Du   = Bodleian Library MS Dugdale 45
Eg   = British Library MS Egerton 615
F   = Bodleian Library MS Fairfax 16
Fi1 = Fitzwilliam Museum, Cambridge, MS McClean 182
Fi2 = Fitzwilliam Museum, Cambridge, MS McClean 185
G   = Gonville and Caius College, Cambridge, MS 124/61
Ga   = Princeton University, MS Garrett 137
Gg   = Cambridge University Library MS Gg. vi. 17
H   = Hatfield House MS Cecil 270
H1   = San Marino, Huntington Library, MS HM 111
H2   = San Marino, Huntington Library, MS HM 744
H3   = San Marino, Huntington Library, MS EL 26 A 13
Ha   = British Library MS Harley 172
Ha1 = British Library MS Harley 116
Ha2 = British Library MS Harley 372
Ha3 = British Library MS Harley 4826
Hh   = Cambridge University Library MS Hh. iv. 11
Kk   = Cambridge University Library MS Kk. i. 3, part 10–12

L	=	Bodleian Library MS Laud Misc. 735
M	=	Melbourne, Victoria State Library MS 096/G94
N	=	New York Public Library MS Spencer 19
Na	=	National Library of Scotland, MS Advocates 19. I. II, part 3
Na2	=	National Library of Scotland, MS Advocates 18.2.8
Ne	=	Chicago, Newberry Library MS 33.7
Qu	=	Queens' College, Cambridge, MS 24 (James 12)
R	=	British Library MS Royal 17 D. vi
R2	=	British Library MS Royal 17 C. xiv
R3	=	British Library MS Royal 17 D. xviii
R4	=	British Library MS Royal 17 D. xix
Ra1	=	Bodleian Library MS Rawlinson Poet. 10
Ra2	=	Bodleian Library MS Rawlinson Poet. 168
Ro	=	Philadelphia, Rosenbach Foundation MS 1083/30
S	=	Bodleian Library MS Selden supra 53
S2	=	Bodleian Library MS Arch Selden B 24
Sl1	=	British Library MS Sloane 1212
Sl2	=	British Library MS Sloane 1825
So	=	Society of Antiquaries of London MS 134
T	=	Bodleian Library MS Tanner 346
Tr1	=	Trinity College, Cambridge, MS R.3.20 (600)
Tr2	=	Trinity College, Cambridge, MS R.3.21 (601)
Tc	=	Trinity College, Cambridge, MS R.3.22 (602)
U	=	Cambridge University Library MS Ff i. 6
U2	=	Cambridge University Library Kk.i.7
Un	=	University College, Oxford, MS 181
Y	=	Yale University, Beinecke Library MS 493
*H	=	agreement of non-H1/H2 witnesses

INTRODUCTION

Thomas Hoccleve (c. 1367–1426) copied Huntington Library MSS HM 111 and 744 during the last four years of his life (1422–6). These two manuscripts, often referred to as the 'Huntington holographs', contain all of his shorter poems – his entire poetic output save his two longer projects: the *Regiment of Princes* (c. 1410–11) and the *Series* (c. 1419–26). These final four years appear to have been a time of vigorous scribal activity for Hoccleve: in addition to creating the Huntington holographs, he was copying the 'Durham *Series*' (another autograph verse manuscript), and he was completing the massive Formulary, a collection of specimen administrative documents for use by future clerks in the Office of the Privy Seal.[1]

The contents of the Huntington manuscripts span Hoccleve's poetic career: the earliest and latest datable items are from 1402 ('Epistle of Cupid') and 1421 ('Henry V's Last Return'; 'Court of Good Company'), respectively. Prayers for Henry V's soul in headings included in both manuscripts indicate that both were copied after Henry's death in August 1422. Other undated items may have been completed at any point before Hoccleve's death in early 1426. (See 'Dates and Manuscript Descriptions')

It is hard to overstate how valuable the Huntington holographs are to the late medieval scholar: the majority of the writer's shorter poems (nineteen) exist only in these collections. Without these manuscripts, they would be lost to time entirely. At times, a poem exists in only a few other manuscripts, and is identifiable as Hoccleve's only because it appears in the holographs – as is the case with 'Mother of God', which had been classed as Chaucer's for centuries, or 'The Monk Who Clad the Virgin', which was interpolated into one manuscript of the *Canterbury Tales* (Oxford, Christ Church, MS 152) as the 'Ploughman's Tale'. 'Knights of the Garter' and 'Epistle of Cupid' were included in Thynne's edition of Chaucer (1532), and remained in subsequent editions of Chaucer's works through 1721.[2] Even 'Complaint Paramount', which exists in ten manuscripts beyond the autograph copy, making it one of Hoccleve's most widely disseminated poems, is not identifiable as Hoccleve's anywhere else, because it is integrated seamlessly into the Middle English translation of Guillaume Deguileville's *Pèlerinage de l'Âme*. We only know it was written by Hoccleve because it appears (as item 1) in HM 111.

A study of variant witnesses of the shorter poems reveals much about the relative popularity of some poems, and the relative obscurity of others – even those that we prize most today. Hoccleve's 'Epistle of Cupid' remains popular today – and it was evidently relatively widely read in the fifteenth century. It ties for first place with 'Complaint Paramount', in terms of most manuscript witnesses, with ten witnesses beyond the holographs. By comparison,

---

[1] Durham, University Library, MS Cosin V. III. 9 and London, British Library, MS Additional 24062. For the dating of these manuscripts (and the Huntington manuscripts), see Burrow and Doyle 2002 (*Facsimile of the Autograph Verse Manuscripts*): xx–xxi, and Burrow 1994: 26–8. While Hoccleve oversaw the creation of the Formulary and copied many of its contents, his is not the only hand found therein: see Sobecki 2021: 267–8.

[2] Burrow 1994: 54.

xii INTRODUCTION

Hoccleve's *Series* exists in full in only six manuscripts. 'Learn to Die' exists, beyond HM 744, in eight manuscripts: the six full *Series* manuscripts; another 'quasi-*Series*' arrangement (British Library MS Royal 17 D. vi), where it is joined by the two *Gesta* tales, but not the 'Complaint' and 'Dialogue'; and, finally, collected with other devotional texts (without any other *Series* items) in British Library MS Harley 172. All other shorter poems that exist elsewhere survive in only one or two other manuscripts.

Two of these poems are notable for being among the most widely read Hoccleve poems today – and yet they offer little by way of witnesses and, hence, little trace of popularity: 'La Male Regle' and 'To Sir John Oldcastle'. 'Male Regle' survives outside HM 111 in only one manuscript: it is included in Register O of the Canterbury Cathedral archives, amidst the business affairs of the cathedral, and it is found there in a much different form: it is shorn of its London particulars, and of the 'autobiographical' elements that so excite critics today. Hoccleve's own name and place of work (embedded within the poem) are also edited out. What remains distills the poem to its moral core: a less personalized meditation on moderation – following a 'mene reule', a virtuous middle path. 'To Sir John Oldcastle' is much studied today, not least for what it tells us about orthodox–heterodox tensions in the period; but it has no contemporary witnesses – only a seventeenth-century transcription (likely done from the HM 111 version), with introduction and notes, by Richard James (1592–1638), extant in two manuscripts: Bodleian Library MS James 34, and British Library MS Add. 33785.[3]

The Huntington holographs, taken together, have the distinction of being the first author-curated 'collected poems' in the English language. Hoccleve certainly had French precedents for an author-curated collected poems, but no one in England had ventured the same feat prior to Hoccleve. We do not know who the manuscripts were created for – or, indeed, whether Hoccleve had created them as his personal copies. It is also possible that Hoccleve's Formulary offers an analogue for the type of collection Hoccleve conceived: as the Formulary showcases a range of *forms*, different types of documents for which future clerks of the Privy Seal would need exemplars, the Huntington holographs include poetic forms that could be emulated by others. The holographs may have served to collect the various *types* of verse (drawn from French models; see 'Sequencing, Form, & the Question of Design') that Hoccleve had learned over a lifetime. He suggests that he himself was taught by Chaucer as a young man, and it is possible he played a similar tutelary role for others. The poems herein showcase a range of poetic forms, such as rhyme royal, experiments in the double croisée stanza, and roundel. They also showcase a mixture of genres: complaint, poems of Marian devotion, miracles of the Virgin, petitionary poems, envoi, dedicatory verse, invocations to the Trinity, and *ars moriendi*. And they showcase his aptitude with Latin and French translation: 'Complaint Paramount' is translated from Guillaume Deguileville's French *Pèlerinage Jhesucrist*; 'Learn to Die' from Henry Suso's Latin *Horologium sapientiae*; 'Balade for Robert Chichele' from an anonymous French balade; 'Epistle of Cupid' from Christine de Pizan's 'Epistre au dieu d'amours'; and the latter part of 'Mother of God' is translated from a popular Latin prayer. (It is also possible that other short poems are translations, with as-yet undiscovered sources.)

The inclusion of a revised version of Hoccleve's envoi to the *Regiment of Princes* – like the inclusion of dedicatory verses to John, Duke of Bedford and Edward, Duke of York – offers an 'accompanying text' without the 'main text', per se. While such texts stand alone as

---

3 Burrow and Doyle 2002: xii. See Perkins 2018 on James and these manuscripts.

witty, compelling compositions, they also show the reader *how* one might write an envoi, or dedicatory stanzas that prove humble, stylish, and adequately obsequious. (What is more, the *Regiment* envoi connects these collections – and Hoccleve's name therein, recorded in both manuscripts – to his most popular work, which survives in over 40 manuscripts.) 'Balade to John Carpenter', on the other hand, functions as a playful kind of form letter: as John Burrow has noted, Carpenter appears not to have been the original recipient of the poem: his surname is written over an erasure, and the three syllables in his name disrupt the meter.[4] Hoccleve's marginal gloss, 'A de B et C de D etc.' – facing the text that mentions debts – shows the reader where the names of creditors would have appeared: e.g., 'John de Bedford and Joan de Westmorland, etc'. The poem exists now, stripped somewhat of its initial coordinates, yet nonetheless useful in form.

And yet to limit these poems to their status *as forms* would be an injustice. The writing here is virtuosic, and in keeping with the standards set by Hoccleve's longer works, the *Regiment* and the *Series*. We witness herein the evolution of themes, wordplay, and style across decades. The collections are invaluable for the devotional works alone, and for the way they showcase Hoccleve's role as a religious writer – as in 'Complaint Paramount', 'Learn to Die', and the Trinity poems that open HM 744. They bear witness, equally, to the kingship of Henry V, his rise and fall, and to Hoccleve's attempts to help shape the interplay between church and state, heterodoxy and orthodoxy, during this tumultuous period. Steeped only in the Hoccleve criticism of our time, we might be forgiven for thinking Hoccleve himself would be the main star in these poems – or that the question of heresy or madness might rule the day. In fact, if anything, the Virgin Mary is the most consistent presence: the manuscripts are replete with Marian devotion and miracles of the Virgin; they are then punctuated with politics, the Trinity, Hoccleve's colleagues, and fleeting glimpses of the man himself.

The present edition is the first to present the entire contents of both Huntington manuscripts in full, in the same sequence in which Hoccleve collected them, and with the same versions included in the holographs – and it is the first edition to offer full variant readings for all manuscript witnesses of the poems, as well as up-to-date notes for each of the poems.

Dates and Manuscript Descriptions

Both HM 111 and HM 744 are dated to the final four years of Hoccleve's life: 1422–6. Both manuscripts include prayers for Henry V's soul, making August 31, 1422 (the date of Henry's death) the *terminus post quem* for the manuscripts. Hoccleve's death – between March 4 and May 8, 1426 – naturally provides the *terminus ante quem*.[5]

The dates of the poems themselves range across decades: the datable items are from 1402–21, but it is possible that undatable poems predate and/or postdate this period. When it is possible to give a date or date range for a poem, I have done so in the individual introductions found at the head of each piece. (See also 'Chronology')

As mentioned above, Hoccleve was also copying his autograph 'Durham *Series*' during this period. Orthographical and marginalia-based evidence suggests that the Huntington

---

[4] Burrow 1994: 16.
[5] Burrow 1994: 29.

xiv INTRODUCTION

manuscripts likely pre-date the Durham *Series*. We can track a progression between the
Huntington manuscripts, the 'Variant Original' from which the scribal copies of the *Series*
derive, and the Durham *Series*, most evident in two respects: Hoccleve's use of mid-line *y* vs.
I for the first-person singular subject pronoun; and a movement towards using paraphs to
denote speaker change within a poem, rather than scribal **cc** and marginal name-markers. The
evidence suggests that Hoccleve moved in the direction of using *y* for the personal pronoun,
in mid-line instances, and towards using paraphs to signal speaker change, later in life.[6]

Given the rarity of these manuscripts, and the value they hold for the late-medieval scholar,
it bears noting that they are but simple, unornate, relatively small productions – each is light,
and easy to hold in a single hand. Other, non-autograph copies of Hoccleve's works – such
as British Library MSS Harley 4866 and Arundel 38 (both early *Regiment* manuscripts) or
Bodleian Library MS Selden supra 53 (including both the *Regiment* and the *Series*) – are finer
productions, both larger and more ornate: all include vivid illuminations, for instance, and
intricate decoration throughout, the likes of which are missing from HM 111 and 744.

HM 111 and HM 744 appear to have been made as complementary collections: they follow
the same layout, writing style, and decoration, are of similar sizes (though HM 111 has been
cropped to be shorter; it is hard to say when this cropping was done), and they do not repeat any
poems – and of course they both date to the same period, and collect poems from throughout
Hoccleve's career (rather than just newer compositions). While they may not have been made
to be bound together, it seems likely that they were made as part of the same broader project.[7]

HM 111

HM 111 consists entirely of Hoccleve's poems, whereas HM 744 includes a mixture of
Hoccleve's poems and non-Hocclevian material bound in at a later date. The present binding
(not original) dates to the early seventeenth century and bears 'the arms supposedly of Prince
Henry, son of King James I of Great Britain'.[8] The leaves (likely sheepskin) are trimmed to
21 cm × 15.5 cm. HM 111 comprises 47 leaves total, 'originally as five quires of eight and one
of ten leaves', but now missing the first folio of the first poem, 'Complaint Paramount'.[9]
This loss results in the absence of lines 1–42 of the poem; and the beginning of 'To Sir John
Oldcastle', the second poem in the collection, has been bound in instead at the beginning
of the collection, perhaps to cover up this lacuna. (To remedy this, I copy the first lines of
'Complaint' from BL MS Egerton 615, and relegate 'Oldcastle' to its rightful place.)

The writing space on each page measures roughly 17 cm × 10 cm (with slight variation).
Hoccleve writes in a clear secretary script and separates his stanzas with a short line. For much
of the collection, Hoccleve is able to include exactly three stanzas per page. He diverts from
this layout when a heading takes the place of a stanza (e.g., 16v) or when longer stanzas make
the layout difficult to maintain (e.g., 32v–34r, 39v).

---

[6] Burrow 1999: 111–18; Langdell 2012. See also Burrow and Doyle 2002: xx–xxi.
[7] See Burrow and Doyle 2002: xxvii for a convincing refutation of John Bowers' argument that the two manuscripts may have been bound together at one time, in the order 744–111 (for which see Bowers 1989).
[8] Burrow and Doyle 2002: xxiii.
[9] Burrow and Doyle 2002: xxi.

Latin glosses appear throughout 'To Sir John Oldcastle', also in Hoccleve's hand (in lighter ink), offering textual citation. Hoccleve also adds shorter clarifying glosses elsewhere (e.g., 25v) and interlinear glosses (e.g., 26v). The catchwords are also in Hoccleve's hand.

Only rarely does Hoccleve offer a title, in the modern sense, before the beginning of a poem. Most often, he includes a heading, most often in French and in a larger set script, offering context or a description.[10] The titles given for the poems in the present edition take into account the information given in these headings, as well as popular names for the poems in modern criticism. Often, a poem will have several names by which it is known in Hoccleve scholarship; or (as in the case of 'Ad beatam virginem') the same heading may be used for several poems. In the running text, I include both Hoccleve's headings (when given) and editorial titles. Often, though not always, Hoccleve ends a given poem with 'Cest tout' (That's all). Red and blue decorated initials are used to begin a new poem, or mark a new section in a poem (e.g., 11v, 16v). Otherwise, the manuscript is relatively sparse and undecorated.

The arms of Prince Henry (lived 1594–1612; son of King James I) on the book's cover suggest that it once belonged either to him or Prince Charles.[11] At some point thereafter it was acquired by Anthony Askew (1722–74). George Mason (1735–1806) then acquired it at auction in 1785, and published selections from it in his edition, *Poems by Thomas Hoccleve* (1796). It was then sold, in turn, to Richard Heber (1773–1833) in 1799; and Sir Thomas Phillipps (1792–1872) in 1836; and then A.S.W. Rosenbach in 1923, who acquired it for the Huntington Library.[12]

Thomas Tyrwhitt made notes regarding the 'disorder of the first leaves' of the manuscript, in a letter dated April 4, 1785, which is 'now affixed to the first pastedown'.[13] The manuscript was in Mason's possession at this time; and indeed Mason added to the notes himself. Frederick Furnivall worked from the manuscript directly when creating his edition (1892), at which time it was still in Phillipps' collection. Furnivall's own notes, added to the front of the volume, are dated September 22, 1882.[14]

For further details on the manuscript, refer to the description in the facsimile edition by J.A. Burrow and Ian Doyle (2002): pp. xxi–xxiii.

HM 744

HM 744 is comprised of two disparate parts bound together. The part including Hoccleve's poems forms the latter portion of the manuscript: ff. 25–68. The first part (ff. 1–24) is comprised of a table for determining Easter Day between 1387 and 1527, memoranda of the Fyler family for the years 1424–73, and a range of devotional texts, including 'Erthe upon erthe', two texts on the Ten Commandments, at least one work by John Wyclif, and a 'form of absolution by a confessor to a penitent'.[15] Burrow and Doyle surmise that the two parts were bound together in the third quarter of the fifteenth century. A household inventory (dated 1463) is included at the end of the volume, written by one of the hands found in the Fyler family memoranda

---

[10] Burrow and Doyle 2002: xxii, xxx, xxxvii.
[11] See note by Burrow and Doyle 2002, xxiii.
[12] Huntington Library Catalogue: 'HM 111. The Huntington Library, San Marino, CA.'; Burrow and Doyle 2002: xxiii.
[13] Huntington Library Catalogue: 'HM 111'.
[14] Ibid.
[15] Huntington Library Catalogue: 'HM 744. The Huntington Library, San Marino, CA.'; Burrow and Doyle 2002: xxiii.

xvi INTRODUCTION

earlier in the volume.[16] One of the more notable aspects of this first portion of HM 744 is the presence of shorthand, possibly dated to the mid-seventeenth century (the years 1648 and 1651 appear in the marginalia), on ff. 1r, 16r, and 18r.

In contrast to the solid, regal binding of HM 111, HM 744 is bound in 'old limp leather […] much repaired', dating to the sixteenth or seventeenth century (perhaps earlier).[17] The binding measures 23 cm × 16 cm. There are 44 leaves (six quires) in the Hocclevian section of HM 744, similar in material (likely sheepskin) to those in HM 111. The leaves are slightly more variable in size – measuring 23–23.5 cm × 15.5–16 cm – and slightly longer. The fourth gathering is smaller, suggesting Hoccleve intended to finish copying on f. 52v (just after 'Three Roundels'), but then changed his mind, and continued on with 'Learn to Die'.[18] The connecting couplet at the bottom of 52v is written slightly below the standard writing space, and it, in itself, seems to admit to the jarring tonal shift between 'Three Roundels' (light-hearted) and 'Learn to Die' (very serious). (Note also that the second line of the couplet is written over an erasure.) HM 744 lacks the final folios of 'Learn to Die'; it ends on folio 68v, leaving 35 stanzas absent. (In the present edition, I substitute the final stanzas from the Durham *Series* rendition of 'Learn to Die' for the missing portion. A binding error in HM 744 also mixes up the order of stanzas in this poem; I rectify this, restoring the original order.)

The writing space in HM 744 measures 15–16 cm × 10–10.5 cm. Again, Hoccleve writes in a clear secretary script, and separates his stanzas with a short line, averaging three full stanzas per page. In fact, this three-stanza-per-page format is much more regular here than in HM 111, in large part because almost all items are in rhyme royal. Hoccleve even endeavors to squeeze headings in between stanzas, so as not to surrender a full stanza space: see ff. 30r, 31v, 36r. (It helps that most of the headings are much shorter than those in HM 111.) 'Three Roundels' is the sole departure from rhyme royal here, but Hoccleve manages to squeeze the whole piece into 52r–v, with the heading just fitting (in all its verbosity) at the bottom of 51v (see 51v–52v).

As HM 111 has 'To Sir John Oldcastle', its own relatively heavily glossed text, HM 744 has 'Learn to Die', which features both speaker-glosses (e.g., sapientia, discipulus) and Latin glosses taken from Hoccleve's source, Henry Suso's *Horologium sapientiae*. Unlike the glosses in 'Oldcastle', these are not rendered in lighter ink – in fact, they sometimes appear darker than the main text. There is also one gloss in 'The Monk Who Clad the Virgin' (indicating its patronage) and another aside the linking couplet following 'Three Roundels'; and there are interlinear glosses, also in Hoccleve's hand – e.g., 32r, last stanza; 44v, first stanza. The catchwords are also in Hoccleve's hand.

The headings are more concise in HM 744, often closer to titles in the modern sense. They are, again, rendered in a larger angular set script. (The one exception here is 'Honor et Gloria', which follows the title to the second piece, 'Ad filium' – written in slightly more elaborate script, with an exaggerated 'H'. It is possible that Hoccleve merely wanted to fill space here; he had given himself a full stanza-space for the title, so that he might begin 'Ad filium' on the next page.) 'Henry V's Last Return' and 'Three Roundels' both get longer, descriptive headings, but all other poems have short headings. (Hoccleve was possibly attempting to save space in this volume, and therefore limited the amount of contextual information. He notes that 'The

---

[16] Burrow and Doyle 2002: xxiii. On a 'textual network' linking the texts herein to the Birgittine Syon Abbey, Carthusian Sheen, Benedictine Barking Abbey and Dominican Dartford Priory, see Cré 2018: 414–16.

[17] Huntington Library Catalogue: 'HM 744'; Burrow and Doyle 2002: xxvi.

[18] Burrow and Doyle 2002: xxiii–xxiv.

Monk Who Clad the Virgin' was translated at the request of Thomas Marleburgh in a gloss, for instance, rather than including it in the heading to that poem.) Hoccleve uses 'explicit' to mark the end of certain poems or sections in HM 744 ('Epistle of Cupid'; 'Monk Who Clad the Virgin' – both at the end of the prologue and at the very end); whereas, the word is not used in HM 111, where instead 'Cest tout' or 'Amen' (or both) is the preferred ending. 'Cest tout' is also used in HM 744: e.g., in 'Henry V's Last Return' and 'Three Roundels'.[19] The same decoration scheme is present in HM 744: red and blue decorated initials used to mark the beginnings of poems, or new sections. Otherwise, there is no decoration.

On ff. 49r–v, there is the trace of red liquid. On ff. 50–51, the bottoms of the leaves have been cut, just under the last written portion on each page (even trimming off some of Hoccleve's dividing lines) – 'presumably for some nonce utilisation in the fifteenth or sixteenth century', suggest Burrow and Doyle.[20]

The volume appears to have been owned by the Fyler family (see description above) in the late fifteenth century – whether in part or whole. Ownership between then and the nineteenth century is a mystery; but the book ended up in the collection of the earl of Ashburnham (1797–1878), and was sold thereafter to Henry Yates Thompson (1838–1928) in 1897, and then shortly after – in 1899 – to Leighton, a London bookseller. It was sold again in 1913 to the London bookseller Maggs and then came into the possession of Sir Israel Gollancz (1863–1930), who edited the poems therein for the Early English Text Society (published 1925). It was acquired that same year (1925) for the Huntington Library – reuniting at long last (after five centuries) with HM 111, which had been acquired by the library two years prior.[21]

For further details on the manuscript, refer to the description in the facsimile edition by J.A. Burrow and Ian Doyle (2002): pp. xxiii–xxvi.

Punctuation, Abbreviations, and Meter

Punctuation

The present edition updates Hoccleve's punctuation to help make the poems more accessible to the twenty-first-century reader. It also, of course, takes into account Hoccleve's own punctuation, and aims to align the medieval with the modern as nearly as possible: the selection of punctuation for this edition necessitated a detailed examination of Hoccleve's own punctuation practices in the holographs. I detail the fundamentals of Hoccleve's punctuation below.

Hoccleve's two main punctuation marks are the *virgula suspensiva* (otherwise just known as 'virgule') and the *punctus elevatus*. The virgule (/) is used most frequently. It can denote a comma- or period-like break (shorter or longer pauses), mark a medial pause in a line of verse, or otherwise mark the rhythm of a given line.[22]

The *punctus elevatus* looks like an upside-down semicolon (⁏) or an S-shaped mark, dotted or undotted. Hoccleve uses this mark similarly to a colon or dash – that is, when what follows resolves or completes what has come before. It can also be used in any instance where one's

---

[19] The first five pieces in 744 do not have any such word at the end, perhaps indicating a continuity between them.
[20] Burrow and Doyle 2002: xxiv.
[21] Huntington Library Catalogue: 'HM 744'; Burrow and Doyle 2002: xxvi.
[22] Cf. Burrow and Doyle 2002: xxxix.

voice might naturally rise – such as, to punctuate a question. The *punctus elevatus* is particularly used, in interrogative instances, when marking a yes/no type question ('Are you okay?'), where intonation tends to rise more than with an open question. It can also be used in other, non-interrogatory (and 'non-final') instances where the voice naturally rises.[23]

A third, as-yet unnamed group of punctuation – a small curved line, reminiscent of a virgule – functions more like the *elevati*, albeit in a 'fragmentary form'. They 'commonly point forward to what follows after initial dependent clauses, fronted objects, and the like' (e.g., HM III: 24v, line 21; 26r, line 1) – or they may be used interchangeably with *elevati*.[24]

In the holographs, Hoccleve sometimes uses the scribal **cc** (a miniature 'cc' with a line) and/or marginal name markers ('Sapientia'; 'discipulus') to mark speech, similar to our present-day use of quotation marks. In the Durham *Series*, Hoccleve will transition to using paraphs (¶) for this purpose.[25] See 'Dates and Manuscript Descriptions' for information on how this shift affects our understanding of manuscript dates.

Abbreviations & Meter

Hoccleve uses several abbreviations in his verse. The most common include: $þ^t$ (=þat); w^t (=with); suprascript a (=ra); hi with a horizonal line over it (=him); and a '2' shaped suprascript 'r' (=ur).[26] I have silently expanded these, for sense, in the present edition. I wish to flag one abbreviation mark in particular that affects the way we read Hoccleve's syllable count, and hence meter: ll with a horizontal stroke through it, indicating addition of a final -e (=lle). Hoccleve uses such extra strokes – whether a horizontal line through an ascender, or hooked strokes – on several other letters and letter-groups: f, g, k, r, and the letter-groups gh and ssh. These extra strokes do *not* appear to denote expansion in any of these cases, with the exception of the (crossed) ll and (hooked) r. Expanding these other letters or letter-groups (f, g, k, gh, ssh) with a final -e disrupts Hoccleve's norms and metrical patterns.[27] I do, however, expand the ll with a horizontal stroke (-lle) and the hooked r (-re) in this edition.

In general, each line of verse in Hoccleve's poems has ten syllables (in rare circumstances, eleven); and Hoccleve holds to this rule doggedly.[28] Final -e (e at the end of a word) is not always sounded, however; one needs to know the rules to determine when to count the -e syllabically. The 'deletion rules' are as follows:[29]

- Final (unstressed) -e is not sounded when preceding a word beginning with a vowel or h. (This rule does not hold up across a line break – meaning that a final -e may be sounded if occurring at the end of a line, even if the next line begins with a vowel or h.)
- Words that end in a consonant + *le*, *ne*, *re*, or *we* often elide. E.g.: 'Yit Thomas herkne a word and be souffrable' (*Series* 2.369), where 'herkne' elides.

---

[23] For a comprehensive analysis of this mark, see Burrow 2002 and 2013.

[24] Burrow and Doyle 2002: xl.

[25] See Langdell 2012.

[26] Burrow and Doyle give a comprehensive list of abbreviations on pp. xxxvii–xxxviii of their facsimile edition (2002).

[27] See further Burrow and Doyle 2002: xxxviii.

[28] In this he is following his French contemporaries: see Burrow 1997: 38–9.

[29] This guide is indebted to Burrow's helpful list, which it summarizes, and which I encourage the reader to consult for further details and examples: Burrow 1999 (*Complaint and Dialogue*): xxx–xxxi. The quotations below are drawn from this list.

– 'The word-ending <ye> or <ie>, when unstressed, counts for only one syllable [...] but for two when it carries some degree of metrical emphasis.'
– 'Words ending in vocalic <y> may delete that syllable when the sound combines with a following vowel.' (E.g., 'many a' often counts as two syllables, rather than three.)
– 'Words with two unstressed vowels separated by a liquid or nasal consonant delete one syllable. So euele (adverb), euene, euere, euery, and neuere have two syllables only, reduced to one where the final /e/ elides.' Hoccleve also treats forms of the verb 'considere' as having three, rather than four, syllables (e.g., considereth).

Hoccleve and 'Hoccleve'

Hoccleve's use of a quasi-autobiographical 'Hoccleve' (or 'Thomas') narrator in given poems has invited a fair amount of comparison – at times, equation – between persona and person. While the Hoccleve persona sees its fullest development in the longer poems – specifically, in the opening section of the *Regiment of Princes*, and the opening two sections of the *Series* – the shorter poems also see the emergence of 'Hoccleve', both as a persona and as a voice.

'La Male Regle' (1405–6) sees the earliest incorporation of a 'Hoccleve' narrator. He records his name twice within that poem – once in the heading, and once in the body of the text. Here, Hoccleve takes on a 'Geffrey' type of narrator (à la *House of Fame*), the loveless bookish type,[30] and maps it onto his own coordinates in London and Westminster: we hear of the Privy Seal, his misadventures in the Paul's Head Tavern, harsh mornings after revelry, and his amblings about town. Two other shorter poems feature less developed iterations of a named Hoccleve: he names himself (alongside three Privy Seal colleagues) in the 'Balade and Roundel to Henry Somer' – a collective begging poem – and in the playful 'Three Roundels', where Lady Money chides him by name.

There is also the question of voice. Even in poems where Hoccleve is not named, there might be a 'Hoccleve presence'. This is most obvious in the balades to York and Bedford, 'Balade to the Chancellor', and 'Court of Good Company'. In each case, internal referents point to a historical Hoccleve as the voice speaking, even if he does not record his name. With his Henry V-oriented poetry, similarly, we assume the speaker is Hoccleve, and that the requests made – or lessons imparted – are done from Hoccleve's mouth. 'To Sir John Oldcastle' sees Hoccleve at his most fervent, orthodox, beseeching. We might think of this as a voice that he 'tries on' – the stern admonisher – first under the guise of the old man in the *Regiment*, and then from the seat of his own (unnamed, newly strident) first person.[31]

We should keep in mind, however, that our fascination with the 'Hoccleve' persona, and with Hoccleve's advancements in a genre we now think of as 'autobiography', appears to be one of the ways in which our contemporary tastes are somewhat at odds with the tastes of Hoccleve's fifteenth-century readers and editors.[32] We have our own canon of Hoccleviana today, and our privileging of works like 'Male Regle', 'To Sir John Oldcastle', and the 'Complaint' (from the *Series*) is at odds with what manuscript count tells us was actually widely disseminated

---

[30] E.g., *House of Fame* ll. 620–8.
[31] The old man serves as Hoccleve's interlocutor for the opening section of the *Regiment*. His tone is at once solicitous, stern, orthodox, and well-meaning.
[32] For Hoccleve's advancements in a vein of proto-autobiography, see especially Knapp 1999, 2001.

xx INTRODUCTION

and read. We are drawn to 'Male Regle' in part because it is Hoccleve's earliest experiment in incorporating aspects of his historical person into his poetry. But the only early copy of the poem that exists outside of the Huntington holographs undoes what we so cherish: it removes the historical particularity of the 'Hoccleve' narrator, vanquishes all traces of 'Hoccleve', and leaves us with what J.A. Burrow and Marian Trudgill call a 'general moral ballade'. This version is found in Register O of the Canterbury Cathedral archives, written 'on blank leaves towards the end of a volume otherwise largely devoted to the business affairs of the monastery'.[33] The Canterbury version is shorn of the original's geographical particulars, having edited out Hoccleve's references to precise locations in London and Westminster, drinking haunts, people, perambulations home. Perhaps most tellingly, the writer omits Hoccleve's own name at one point: where the autograph version has 'Bewaar, Hoccleue, I rede thee therfore, / And to a mene reule thow thee dresse' (351–2), the Canterbury version omits 'Hoccleue' and rewrites the lines so that they merely prescribe the 'mene reule' [moderate lifestyle] that comes across in the autograph version as a pleasing meta-literary moment (and redolent of Mary's own self-address, just two poems earlier in HM 111: 'Bewaar, Hoccleue' following on the heels of 'Poore Marie, thy wit is aweye' (217)).[34] Peter Brown argues against the notion that the Canterbury version exists as a 'facile redaction' of Hoccleve's original; he underscores that the type of moral lesson being advertised in the 'Male Regle' (which is perhaps to us overshadowed by the novelty of Hoccleve's pseudo-autobiographical narrator), namely the virtue of moderation, would have appealed to the Canterbury monks. Brown offers that the Canterbury version of 'Male Regle' fits well within the bounds of the records in which it is found, records which similarly encourage the eschewing of excess, and into which Hoccleve's playful admonishment fits readily.[35] What might seem integral to the poem for us (Hoccleve; his biographical particulars; his London whereabouts) may have been of less use to some contemporary readers than the moral content.

This is also the case with manuscripts of the *Series* and its assorted elements, including 'Learn to Die' (the final item in HM 744): editors did not see the 'autobiographical' sections of the *Series* as indivisible from the whole. London, BL MS Royal 17 D. vi includes the other three items in the *Series* – the two *Gesta Romanorum* tales and 'Learn to Die' – without the 'Complaint' and 'Dialogue'. 'Learn to Die' travels on its own in BL MS Harley 172, and, of course, in HM 744; whereas the *Gesta* tales travel unaccompanied in Oxford, Bodleian Library MS Digby 185. (Fragments of the *Gesta* tales are also found, without the other three items in the *Series*, in Oxford, Bodleian Library, MS Eng. Poet. d. 4.) This is to say that the 'Complaint' and 'Dialogue' survive the *least* out of the five components of the *Series*. 'Learn to Die' – the centerpiece of the *Series* – is found the most. Where fifteenth-century readers might have found the Hoccleve persona useful as a parallel devotional medium, or as a playful organizing device in collecting sundry poems, they by no means saw the 'Hoccleve' persona, and the texts that we now think of under the grand banner of 'autobiography', as inseparable from the other items in the *Series*. It is perhaps closer to the then-contemporary understanding to think of the 'Hoccleve' persona in either work – *Series* and 'Male Regle' – as a spectacle: useful for

---

[33] Trudgill and Burrow 1998: 180.

[34] David Watt suggests that the balade may have traveled to Canterbury in the hands of Hoccleve's one-time colleague, Thomas Felde, who left the Privy Seal in 1414 or 1415 to serve as an official to archbishop of Canterbury Henry Chichele (Watt 2012: 4).

[35] See Brown 2014.

animating and illustrating the moral messaging of the greater work, but by no means the main focus of the work as a whole.

It is also useful to keep in mind the points at which persona does not necessarily map onto person – and to take a lesson from this. As John Burrow points out, 'The Court of Good Company' (HM III, no. 17) dates to the same period as Hoccleve's 'Complaint' and 'Dialogue', the opening texts of the *Series* – and yet, these poems could not be more tonally disparate: we encounter entirely different 'Hoccleves'.[36] Whereas the *Series*-Hoccleve is disparaged, dejected, and somber, the Hoccleve in 'Good Company' eagerly awaits a dinner party: the mood is convivial, lively.[37] On the other hand, mentions of Hoccleve's wife in both the *Series* and the *Regiment* have the effect of momentarily pulling the veil back on the Hoccleve persona: he works for the first 1,000 lines or so of each text to present a solitary 'Hoccleve', and when it is revealed that he is married, later in the respective dialogues, the effect is jarring: 'Hoccleve' and Hoccleve clash. The information rises and fades; the solitary Hoccleve marches on.[38]

Still, we can home in on the particulars of a historical Hoccleve. We believe he was born around 1367–8, a date we deduce based on his reference to being 'fifty wintir and three' in the 'Dialogue' (*Series*: 2.246), thought to have been completed in early 1421. In the *Regiment*, he mentions having worked for the Privy Seal for 'twenti yeer / And foure come Estren' (804–5). Given a completion year of 1411 for that work, Hoccleve would have started his bureaucratic career at the Privy Seal around 1387. The fact that Hoccleve was indeed married (as mentioned in both longer poems) is corroborated by mention of Hoccleve's wife in the will of his colleague, John Bailey. The will also reveals that Hoccleve owned land in the Bedfordshire village of Hockliffe – the location previous critics had pinpointed as the probable original of his surname.[39] We know that Hoccleve worked steadily for the Privy Seal until his death: indeed, one of his last tasks was the copying of the massive Formulary, a collection of specimen administrative documents for use by future clerks (copied in the same period as the Huntington holographs: 1422–6). We know that his claim to have been 'acquainted' with Chaucer – lodged in the *Regiment* – is not a vain boast: two requests in Hoccleve's hand, for payment due to Chaucer, indicate that the two writers were at least acquainted.[40] He claims to have been trained for the priesthood, only to have abandoned that course when he decided to take a wife; and indeed his poetry suggests a heightened level of biblical literacy and clerical training. And finally we know that Hoccleve died between March 4 and May 8, 1426: we have record of a March 4 payment made to Hoccleve; and a document dated May 8 indicates that his corrody (a supplemental form of income derived from the priory of Southwick, Hampshire) was transferred to an Alice Penfold – from 'Thomas Ocle ja trespasse' ['Thomas Hoccleve now deceased'].[41]

---

[36] Burrow 1994: 28–9; cf. Nuttall 2015: 3.

[37] Sebastian Sobecki has recently suggested another layer of meaning in the somber *Series*: he notes that 'Thomas' may be mourning his recently departed friend and colleague John Bailey. See Sobecki 2019: Chapter 2.

[38] On this dynamic, see Langdell 2023.

[39] See Sobecki 2019: Chapter 2. Stubbs and Mooney also recently suggested an identification of Hoccleve's father as a William Hoccleve, a draper in London (see Stubbs and Mooney 2011). This suggests that, while Hoccleve's surname derives from Hockliffe, he was raised in London. Mooney also recently discovered Hoccleve's personal seal; and Green and Knapp decipher his personal motto: 'va ma voluntee' ('go my will'). See Mooney 2007: 317; Green and Knapp 2008: 319.

[40] Mooney 2007: 312; Killick 2010: 30–1. The requests are dated November 9, 1399 and February 9, 1400, respectively.

[41] Burrow 1994: 29.

We can also trace Hoccleve's position within a London-based network of scribes copying works of vernacular poetry at the turn of the fifteenth century. Hoccleve's hand is found in the Cambridge, Trinity College, MS R.3.2 copy of Gower's *Confessio amantis*, alongside Doyle and Parkes' Scribe D, who also copied the Ilchester manuscript of the *Piers Plowman* C-Text (London, University Library, MS SL V.88) and two copies of the *Canterbury Tales*. This manuscript – the 'Trinity Gower' – also contains the hand of Scribe B, responsible for copying the Ellesmere and Hengwrt manuscripts of the *Canterbury Tales*.[42] Critics have also noted similarities in format and textual practice between Ellesmere and the two earliest, most authoritative manuscripts of Hoccleve's *Regiment*; and Simon Horobin has suggested that Hoccleve would have been well positioned to serve as editor for Ellesmere and Hengwrt.[43] Misty Schieberle has recently identified Hoccleve's hand in British Library MS Harley 219, which includes Christine de Pizan's *Epistre Othea* (in Hoccleve's hand), *Gesta Romanorum* tales, and the French *Secretum secretorum* (one of the sources for Hoccleve's *Regiment of Princes*).[44] Sebastian Sobecki suggests that the other hands found in the manuscript are all Privy Seal colleagues, and that Hoccleve likely served as overseer of the project.[45] Such a case study indicates moments of literary crossover from within Hoccleve's immediate professional network, with Hoccleve himself at the helm.

Recent criticism has also opened up Hoccleve's role as a religious writer – and his involvement in orthodox–heterodox dialogues – and it is telling that many of these studies reach beyond the longer texts, into the shorter poems. Vincent Gillespie's reading of the *Series* in the context of the Council of Constance probes the presence of Emperor Sigismund in 'Knights of the Garter', while also highlighting nods to heresy in 'Balade for Robert Chichele', translated for the brother of Archbishop Henry Chichele – a main actor at Constance.[46] Laurie Atkinson's work on memory and 'remembrance' spans the entirety of Hoccleve's shorter devotional verse.[47] David Lawton's work on the Psalmic voice in Hoccleve centers mainly on the *Regiment* and (particularly) the *Series*, but the argument is especially potent in relationship to 'Learn to Die', and Hoccleve's use of Psalms therein.[48] Shannon Gayk's exploration of optics and theology in Hoccleve's work considers the writer's complaints of languishing eyesight in the dedicatory poems to York and Bedford, and the use of 'spectacles' as spiritual metaphor in 'To Sir John Oldcastle'.[49] Andrew Cole focuses on 'Oldcastle', too, indicating the potentially mediatory role Hoccleve fashions for himself in that poem.[50] Jenni Nuttall's evaluation of

---

[42] Doyle and Parkes 1991. Linne Mooney and Estelle Stubbs' suggested identifications of Scribe B and Scribe D – as Adam Pinkhurst and John Marchaunt, respectively – center the activity for such copying in the context of the London Guildhall. Such identifications have been called into question in recent years, and the conversation on scribal attribution is evolving rather than conclusive. Mooney 2006; Mooney and Stubbs 2013: Chapters 3–4 (on Hoccleve's potential role with regard to the Guildhall scribes, see pp. 123–31); in response, see especially Roberts 2011, Warner 2015.

[43] Burrow 1994: 18; Horobin 2015; cf. Pearsall 1992: 338 n. 9. Doyle and Parkes had ventured the suggestion that Hoccleve offered corrections in Hengwrt as Hand F (see 1979: xlvi); Horobin expands on this suggestion.

[44] Schieberle 2019.

[45] Sobecki 2021. In this article, Sobecki identifies the handwriting of Privy Seal clerks William Alberton, Henry Benet, John Claydon, John Hethe, John Offord, and Richard Priour. On Harley 219, including the suggestion that Hoccleve served as overseer, see pp. 263–4.

[46] Gillespie 2011.

[47] Atkinson 2019.

[48] Lawton 2017: Chapter 4.

[49] Gayk 2010: Chapter 2.

[50] Cole 2008: Chapter 5.

'anti-occasional verse' points up the middle ground between 'political poem' and 'ecclesiastical poem' in much of Hoccleve's shorter verse for Henry V. Nuttall argues that Hoccleve spends much of his career advocating for the rights of the church – and rallying the crown to uphold its duties to the church – rather than functioning as a Lancastrian spokesman, as had previously been thought.[51] Hoccleve's investment in the orthodox church is evident; but it is also true that the poet betrays anxiety in the wake of the church's newly militant guise – his poetry can be cautious and wary, even as it means to do well.[52]

It should be noted how many of the shorter poems are in fact *prayers*. Poems that might otherwise be deemed 'political' end on 'Amen', indicating their status as prayers (HM III: nos. 4, 5–6, 8). HM III nos. 7 and 10 are prayers to Mary (the latter ending with 'Amen'). Items 1–5 in HM 744 are invocations or prayers to the persons of the Trinity and to Mary. It is worth noting that the last third of 'Mother of God' is translated from a Latin prayer; whereas 'Learn to Die' is replete with vernacular translation of biblical verse – woven into the fabric of the treatise, and present in his source text, but troubling Arundelian waters nonetheless. 'Learn to Die' is present, of course, in the *Series* as well – but it is HM III and 744 that offer the most convincing case for Hoccleve as an innovative writer of vernacular spiritual works.

Earlier Editions

Editions of Hoccleve's shorter poems date back to the late eighteenth century. The first scholarly edition appears in 1796, when George Mason edited six poems from HM III (nos. 3, 9, 13, 15–17), which was then in his possession. (See 'Dates and Manuscript Descriptions') In 1882, L. Toulmin Smith edited 'To Sir John Oldcastle' for the journal *Anglia*. In 1892, Furnivall published his edition of HM III (then 'the Phillipps MS'), along with the *Series* poems and 'Epistle of Cupid', for the first volume of the EETS *Hoccleve's Works*. This was joined, in 1925, by Israel Gollancz's edition of the poems from HM 744 ('the Ashburnham MS'), minus 'Learn to Die'. (These were revised by Jerome Mitchell and A.I. Doyle as *Hoccleve's Works: The Minor Poems* in 1970.) Vol. VII of W.W. Skeat's *Works of Chaucer* includes HM III nos. 5–6 and HM 744 no. 7. Two editions of Hoccleve's 'selected poems' were published in the early 1980s: M.C. Seymour's *Selections from Hoccleve* (1981) and Bernard O'Donoghue's *Thomas Hoccleve: Selected Poems* (1982). Seymour's edition includes HM III nos. 1–5, 9–11, 13–17, and HM 744 no. 9, alongside excerpts from the *Series* and *Regiment*. O'Donoghue's edition includes HM III nos. 3, 9–11, 13, and HM 744 no. 9, alongside excerpts from the *Series* and *Regiment*. Fenster and Erler edit Hoccleve's 'Epistle of Cupid' alongside its source, Christine de Pizan's 'Epistre au dieu d'amours' (in *Poems of Cupid*, 1990). And Ellis's edition of the *Series* (2001) contains six shorter poems: HM III nos. 1, 3, 13, 18, and HM 744 nos. 6–7.

The shorter poems contained in HM III and 744 have never been edited in their entirety and with Hoccleve's own sequencing in a single volume. Furnivall and Gollancz came closest to achieving this with their complementary editions of HM III and 744 (1892; 1925). Their editions lack HM 744's version of 'Learn to Die'. It is omitted because Furnivall prints the contents of the *Series* (including that version of 'Learn to Die'), from the Durham manuscript, following the items in HM III and 'Epistle of Cupid'. The present edition differs thus: it offers all poems

---

[51] Nuttall 2015.
[52] See Langdell 2018 for a comprehensive appraisal of Hoccleve's role as religious writer.

in a single collection, in the same order in which they appear in HM 111 and 744; it provides a full list of textual variants; it corrects errors in transcription and dating from previous editions, as well as misidentification of poetic forms and sources; and it provides an up-to-date notes matrix for the poems, taking into account all recent codicological and archival discoveries, as well as the wealth of current scholarship on Hoccleve, given the efflorescence in Hoccleve Studies over the past two decades. It also clarifies the text by avoiding a dual-punctuation system: Furnivall and Gollancz offer a mixture of Hoccleve's own punctuation (mainly his virgules) and their own additions, including a preponderance of semicolons and exclamation marks. The system proves faulty for several reasons: the punctuation often has the effect of making the poems *sound* more forceful than they are on the manuscript page; and it can often be confusing to balance Hoccleve's virgules against the parallel modern punctuation. I opt for less intrusive modern punctuation in the present edition, and refer the reader to the EETS facsimile edition for reference when discerning Hoccleve's original marks of punctuation. (It should be noted that Hoccleve is not by any means regular in his use of punctuation; and Furnivall and Gollancz do not themselves always accurately relay Hoccleve's own punctuation in their editions.) I also eschew the earlier practice of including summarizing glosses, as in the Furnivall–Gollancz editions. Instead, I offer the reader difficult-word glosses throughout, and modern English translations for difficult phrases in the notes, where necessary. I also provide translations of all French and Latin headings and glosses in the notes.

The *Series* poems are included in Furnivall under the aegis of 'minor poems' – an interesting choice in itself, and at odds with our contemporary acceptance of the *Series* as a relatively major poem, or at least a longer work, set apart from the sundry shorter poems in the Huntington manuscripts. (Ellis nods to this in his edition – *'My Compleinte' and Other Poems* – by collecting six of the shorter poems under the heading 'minor verse', and then including the *Series* in a subsequent section, under its own heading, suggesting its status as 'non-minor' verse.) It is also telling that Furnivall chose to include 'Epistle of Cupid', on its own, after the items from HM 111 – indicating that text's special status and presumed interest to the reader.[53] Furnivall's collection thus offers its own sequence, divergent from Hoccleve's: 'Epistle' is seen to be of sufficient interest to be included with the poems of HM 111; and the *Series* poems follow in their own section – still 'minor', but self-contained.

Beyond Furnivall and Gollancz, editors have used their respective editions to construct alternatives of sorts to the holographs: they have offered their own collections of the shorter poems, dictated by personal taste, and owing to what the given editor feels is most relevant or interesting about Hoccleve. George Mason (1796) launches a centuries-long penchant for showcasing the shorter poems that feature the Hoccleve persona: 'Male Regle' and 'Balade and Roundel to Henry Somer' appear here, and are among the most commonly collected shorter poems in the editions listed above – and both record Hoccleve's name. Mason also offers up poems that shed light on Hoccleve's social context, such as 'Balade to John Carpenter' and 'Court of Good Company'. He admits that 'To Sir John Oldcastle' might seem an ideal poem to print – 'But the editor has rejected it, as too great an imposition on the patience of his readers.'[54] Ellis and O'Donoghue also leave 'Oldcastle' out – although Ellis admits to regretting

---

[53] Furnivall used MS Fairfax 16 as the base text for his edition of the 'Epistle', but re-sequenced the stanzas according to the order in HM 744.

[54] Mason 1796 (*Poems by Thomas Hoccleve*): 11.

that choice.[55] O'Donoghue admits a preference for Hoccleve's 'autobiographical' poetry, and a distaste for his religious poetry, and his selections follow suit.[56] He even includes 'Three Roundels', the third shorter poem to include Hoccleve's name. Seymour's choices stand out if only because he includes large swaths of HM 111, and only 'Three Roundels' from HM 744 (but not 'Epistle of Cupid' or 'Learn to Die').[57] 'Epistle of Cupid' is included in Ellis, but largely missing elsewhere. It is, however, collected in some early editions of Chaucer, beginning with Thynne's 1532 edition.[58] Ellis also prints HM 111 no. 18 ('Balade for Robert Chichele') and HM 744 no. 6 ('The Monk Who Clad the Virgin'), both underrepresented in Hoccleve editions.

Editors often found themselves up against the problem of critical distaste for Hoccleve – sometimes on the defensive against it, and sometimes embodying that distaste themselves. (Furnivall greets the work before him so grudgingly, we almost feel we should apologize on Hoccleve's behalf.) Mason – Hoccleve's earliest editor, and among the most careful – spends pages defending Hoccleve against Thomas Warton, who had dismissed Hoccleve in his *History of English Poetry* (1774).[59] Bernard O'Donoghue follows Mason in responding to critics, and mounting a defense of Hoccleve, before presenting the poems.[60] Furnivall equates the Hoccleve persona thoroughly with the historical Hoccleve, and finds both wanting. He commends Hoccleve for his closeness to Chaucer, and treats him with equal amounts of pity, scorn, and mild sympathy.[61] Seymour at times emblematizes a strain of Hoccleve criticism that assumes much about Hoccleve, and makes editorial leaps as a result. He assigns poems to time periods on the basis of nothing more than a vague impression of the writer's mood at that given time. So, for instance, Seymour admits the 'Carpenter' poem is 'without any indication of date, but it clearly belongs to Hoccleve's free-spending bachelor days'.[62] 'Mother of God' is said to be 'before 1405' without any evidence supporting this suggestion, as is 'Complaint Paramount'.[63] The tendency to group religious poems early, to align them with his priestly training perhaps, and to assign jovial material to the years roughly around 'Male Regle', ladles too much weight upon supposition.

We have a better idea now of chronology, thanks to the wealth of Hoccleve scholarship in the intervening years – and I do my best to give as accurate dates as possible for the poems (see 'Chronology', and the individual introductions to the poems); I also indicate where a given date is probable rather than definite.

Sequencing, Form, & the Question of Design

It is clear that the Huntington manuscripts do not follow the same type of intentional design as the *Series* – a similar collection, made during roughly the same period, that also collects

---

[55] Ellis 2001 (*My Compleinte*): 7–8.

[56] O'Donoghue 1982 (*Selected Poems*): 17, 11. It should be noted, however, that he includes 'Mother of God'.

[57] See Seymour 1981 (*Selections from Hoccleve*). Despite drawing heavily on HM 111, Seymour groups those poems according to type or common affinity (e.g., Henry V or Henry Somer poems grouped together; 'Mother of God' with 'Complaint Paramount'), rather than using Hoccleve's own sequencing.

[58] The poem is first ascribed to Hoccleve in Speght's 1598 Chaucer edition (Burrow and Doyle 2002: xvi).

[59] 1796: 6–9.

[60] 1982: 7–12.

[61] E.g., pp. xxxiv–xxxix.

[62] 1981: 110.

[63] Ibid.: 104, 103.

xxvi INTRODUCTION

otherwise disparate texts, but that makes a clear attempt to bind the texts together with the help of the 'Complaint', 'Dialogue', and other interlinking conversations. That said, the sequences used in HM 111 and 744 are not entirely random: some measure of design can be deduced. While it is possible that Hoccleve was at times copying with an eye towards filling the available quire-space (and fitting the poems in according to length), at times we see evidence of more concrete thematic and/or formal consistencies.

HM 744 offers the greatest opportunities to discuss design. The first three poems are part of a discrete unit – invocations in turn to the three persons of the Trinity. Hoccleve marks the end of the third poem in the sequence with three lines that underscore the joint nature of these three poems; this final flourish ends, 'O Trinitee, haue vs in remembrance' ('Ad spiritum sanctum', lines 68–70). The following three poems in HM 744 are bound, similarly, by their focus on the Virgin Mary: the first two are prayers to Mary, and the third is a 'miracle of the Virgin' tale, prefaced with a prologue (à la Prioress's Tale) indicating that it was written in honor of the Virgin. These six opening poems therefore form a devotional sequence, beginning with the Trinity and then extending to the Virgin Mary. 'Epistle of Cupid' would seem a swerve after this devotional run, until one remembers that that poem (in Hoccleve's hands) builds its way to a climactic contemplation of holy women – Mary foremost – in its final stanzas. The 'Epistle of Cupid', written in 1402, subtly channels the atmosphere of political upheaval and treachery circa 1399–1402 (the time between Christine's original and Hoccleve's translation), and, as such, forms an interesting link with 'Henry V's Last Return' – these are Henrician bookends: one poem written at the (murky) dawn of Henry IV's reign, and the other at the very end of Henry V's reign. (The latter poem is among the latest datable pieces in the collections, dated to 1421, but by the time Hoccleve was actually copying these poems (post-August 1422), Henry V had died.) The 'Three Roundels' do interrupt the sequence both formally and tonally: all poems in the manuscript, except this one, are written in rhyme royal.[64] Hoccleve acknowledges the tonal shift between that poem and 'Learn to Die' with the linking couplet found in between. This is the only overt instance (other than the final lines of 'Ad spiritum sanctum', above) of Hoccleve attempting a link between the poems.[65] 'Learn to Die' – an *ars moriendi* treatise, translated from Henry Suso's *Horologium sapientiae* – returns to the thematic concerns with which HM 744 began, and allows the collection to be bookended with serious, somber devotional material. On one end, there is Christ's death and a reminder of our redemption – and on the other end, a reminder that we are also mortal, and that we can better honor the fruits of this redemption by living and dying well.

As noted above, all poems but one in HM 744 are rendered in rhyme royal. In HM 111, conversely, variety abounds. Some consistent themes and subjects should be noted, however: this manuscript includes all Hoccleve's poems concerning Henry V (4, 5–6, 8, 14, 15), save the latest-written one, 'Henry V's Last Return'. It also includes all dedicatory verses (nos. 9, 11, 14) and all petitionary ('begging') poems (nos. 3, 12, 13, 15, 16, 17). Four are poems of

---

[64] It should be noted, however, that 'Three Roundels' provides an opportunity for Hoccleve's authorial signature: his name is written several times within that poem (just as it appears in 'Male Regle' and 'Balade and Roundel to Henry Somer', in HM 111). Its placement in 'Three Roundels' ensures that the name occurs in the middle of HM 744, where it is less likely to be lost due to the breaking away of opening and/or closing leaves.

[65] The closest other instances would be the twin balades in 'Knights of the Garter'; and 'The Monk Who Clad the Virgin', which includes prologue and tale, each ending with an explicit, and which Gollancz counts as two separate pieces (but which I count as one).

Marian devotion (nos. 1, 7, 10, 18). Two poems are addressed to Henry Somer (nos. 13 and 17). In general, the collection is flush with the names of recipients, benefactors, and dedicatees (see nos. 1, 9, 11, 13, 16–18), whereas HM 744 includes only one such case – a gloss in 'The Monk Who Clad the Virgin' indicating that it was written at the request of 'T. Marleburgh'. (Relatedly, only a couple of items in HM 744 are firmly datable, whereas most of the poems in HM 111 can be dated because of these useful referents.)

HM 111 features a range of forms and poetic types, perhaps offered (in part) so that Hoccleve could preserve foreign forms he had mastered, and perhaps so that others might emulate them. But the collection stands out for its showcasing of Hoccleve's experiments with the balade, specifically variations on the balade derived from the French 'double croisée'[66] and 'balade de vii bastons' forms. The latter of these is better known to us as rhyme royal. While Chaucer and Hoccleve both used this form for longer works (e.g., *Troilus and Criseyde, Regiment of Princes*), it was mainly used for shorter poems in France.[67] In his headings and glosses, Hoccleve identifies ten poems in the holographs as 'balades' (HM 111 nos. 4, 5–6, 8, 13, 14, 16, 17, 18; HM 744 no. 8). The majority of these (all save 111 nos. 16–17 and 744 no. 8) use the eight-line double croisée stanza, which rhymes ababbcbc.[68] Five other poems in HM 111 also use the double croisée stanza (nos. 2, 3, 7, 12, 15), making it the predominant form in HM 111. As John Burrow shows, Hoccleve uses the term 'balade' rather loosely. Contrary to the traditional French balade (and contrary to Chaucer's precedents in English), Hoccleve does not follow the rules: the French balade included three stanzas with a refrain, and with the 'same rhyme-sounds in the same order'.[69] None of Hoccleve's balades have a refrain, and often he incorporates interlocking rhyme between stanzas, which means the rhyme order cannot remain constant. This use of interlocking rhyme between double croisée stanzas seems to have been a signature form for Hoccleve, and his own invention. It is found in six of the poems in HM 111: nos. 4, 8, 12, 13, 14, 15. In this variation of the double croisée, the first line of the second stanza rhymes with the last line of the first stanza. The rhyme scheme then adapts to suit this interlocking rhyme, hence: ababbcbc cbcbbaba, etc. Hoccleve's choice not to include refrains in these balades allows for this form to take shape.

It is worth noting, when considering sequencing within the holographs, that nos. 12–15 in HM 111 all showcase this unusual interlocking double croisée. As such, this run of four poems constitutes an implicit unit, akin to the first six items in HM 744. Interestingly, all four poems require a degree of submission and humility from Hoccleve: two are addressed to Henry V (nos. 14–15); and three are 'begging' poems, requesting intercession for a payment, addressed to Thomas Langley, Henry Somer, and Henry V, respectively (nos. 12–13, 15). It is possible that Hoccleve enjoyed using these instances of ritual submission to showcase (paradoxically) his most virtuosic adaptations of a French *forme fixe* – a form that would have been recognizable to at least some of Hoccleve's learned readers.[70] We can even pinpoint a relatively precise

---

[66] Also known as the 'Monk's Tale stanza', following Chaucer's use of the form.

[67] Burrow 1997: 38.

[68] On the 'double croisée', see Burrow 1997: 38, Nuttall 2016: 63–5. Note that Seymour misidentifies this form as the virelai; see Nuttall for disambiguation between the two.

[69] Burrow 1997: 40. As Burrow notes, the twin balades in 'Knights of the Garter' come closest to following the archetype: they have the same rhymes in the same order, but each is four – rather than three – stanzas, and neither has a refrain.

[70] Immersed as we are in the French formal contexts of the poems collected here, we should also note that the very project that HM 111 and 744 constitute – an authorial collected works – is itself adapted from French models (Burrow 1997: 40–3).

xxviii INTRODUCTION

time period for these experiments: the three more firmly datable poems in this sequence were written between 1406 and 1411 (nos. 12–14). The other two poems in HM 111 to use this form (nos. 4 and 8) were both written in 1413.[71]

For Hoccleve, evidently the goal was not adherence to the thrall of a fixed form, but rather the thrill of departure – of experimentation within and beyond those confines. A parallel could be drawn here to Hoccleve's translation of three French poems in the holographs: all three are adapted, rather than translated directly – with the most contemporary of the three sources (that is, the one whose context Hoccleve was arguably closest to), Christine's 'Epistre au dieu d'amours', receiving the most thorough and transformative treatment. He demonstrated his skill by indicating how radically or inventively a source could be transformed – not by how closely he conformed to precedent.

Form and content interact in other ways, too: Hoccleve's dedicatory verses to York and Bedford (HM 111 nos. 9 and 11; both written before 1415) not only closely resemble each other in terms of use and content, but also both use a nine-line stanza – the only two among his poems to do so. Hoccleve's devotional poems[72] tend overwhelmingly to be written in rhyme royal (see HM 111 nos. 1, 10; HM 744 nos. 1–6, 10). The two exceptions to this are found in HM 111: nos. 7 ('Mother of Life') and 18 ('Balade for Robert Chichele'). It should also be noted that Hoccleve names himself in both manuscripts, and takes care to position the name away from the very beginning and very end of the respective manuscripts (where leaves would most likely be (indeed, *were*) lost): his name appears in 111, nos. 3 and 13, and 744, no. 9.[73] Both manuscripts are also bookended with devotional verse, and both manuscripts end with poems that serve as *memento mori*.

---

[71] Item 15, 'Victorious King', may have been written shortly after, to commemorate Henry V's achievements at Agincourt (1415).

[72] That is, poems written to or about the Virgin Mary, and/or the Trinity, or *ars moriendi*.

[73] This is also the case in *Regiment of Princes*: Hoccleve's most overt instance of self-naming occurs at lines 1864–5, about a third of the way through the poem's total 5463 lines (cf. line 4360).

NOTE ON EDITORIAL PRACTICES

I have transcribed each of the poems, in their original order, from HM 111 and HM 744. Where necessary, I have amended errors, taking into account readings from variant witnesses to the given poems. (For reference, a list of textual variants is found at the end of the volume.) Where HM 111 lacks the beginning of 'Complaint Paramount', I substitute the relevant text from British Library MS Egerton 615. Where HM 744 lacks the end of 'Learn to Die', I substitute the relevant text from the Durham *Series*.

I maintain Hoccleve's original spelling throughout. Punctuation and capitalization have been modernized. I have silently expanded all relevant abbreviations. Where final -e is concerned, I only expand ll with horizontal stroke, and hooked r. (See discussion under 'Punctuation, Abbreviations, and Meter'.) Occasionally, two words in Hoccleve will be rendered as one, in accordance with modern usage: e.g., vn to (=vnto); ther of (=therof).

I include difficult-word glosses throughout, as a helping tool; I also include occasional summaries or translations in the notes. I include all French headings and Latin and French glosses, original to Hoccleve, in the places where they appear in the holographs. Translations are given in the notes.

All substantial textual variants for the poems are found in the appendix. Note that a majority reading among variants does not necessarily change the main text. I privilege the versions of the poems given in the Huntington holographs – so, while I will correct an error for sense, I will not revert to another version of the text. The aim is to preserve the poems as Hoccleve himself saw fit to revise and present them in the final years of his life. For instance, in the *Regiment of Princes* envoi (HM 111, no. 14), Hoccleve has clearly revised the text, substituting three words in particular, in disagreement with all extant witnesses to the envoi. I offer the text as given in HM 111 in the main text, but include the variant readings in the textual variants list. I correct the main text only where there is a lacuna or error.

HUNTINGTON LIBRARY, MS HM 111

ᴄᴈ

COMPLAINT PARAMOUNT
Date: in or before 1413

୧୭

This poem was long believed to be a translation of a portion of Guillaume Deguileville's *Pèlerinage de l'Âme* (c. 1358). It is incorporated (without attribution) into the full Middle English translation of Deguileville's text (*The Pilgrimage of the Soul*) in all surviving ten manuscripts. The Middle English *Soul* is dated (in a colophon) to 1413. Hoccleve's excerpted poem is not otherwise extant outside HM 111 – and this is the only instance in which it exists, excerpted, on its own. (In that respect, it shares common ground with the *Regiment* envoi, which exists autonomously only in HM 111.)

Josephine Houghton has recently argued convincingly that Hoccleve translated his poem not from *Pèlerinage de l'Âme*, but from a similar section in *Le Pèlerinage Jhesucrist*, the third part of Deguileville's *Pèlerinage* trilogy (see Houghton 2013). The two relevant sections are very close, but changes once thought original to Hoccleve, as recently as in Ellis's edition, are now known to be Deguileville's own revisions. A main difference between the two texts is setting: whereas *Âme* grounds the crucifixion within a greater arboreal allegory (dry versus blooming tree; death and rebirth), *Jhesucrist* simply depicts the crucifixion at Golgotha.

The compiler of the Middle English *Pilgrimage of the Soul* clearly had access to Hoccleve's translation, but may not have known that it was translated from *Jhesucrist*, not *Âme*. The suggestion has been made that Hoccleve might have been responsible for translating the entire Middle English *Soul* or other lyrics therein. Burrow argues convincingly against it, and Houghton's discovery all but eliminates the possibility. (Doyle 1987: 16; Burrow 1994: 24; Houghton 2013: 266)

The poem is told from the point of view of Mary, mother of Jesus. She recounts her former joy in carrying Jesus in her womb and giving birth; and then the focus of the poem turns to Jesus's crucifixion and death, and her subsequent sorrow and pain. The complaint belongs to a tradition of *planctus Mariae*, made popular by Bernard of Clairvaux, but reaching back to the sixth century and earlier (Bryan 2002: 1175). This poem ends at the moment of Jesus's death and Mary's greatest despair; it denies us resurrection. As such, our shared sorrow with Mary is deepened, and the moral is offered with a sharper edge: all this was done – all this sorrow incurred – for your sake.

As previously noted ('Editorial Practices'), I substitute the relevant text from British Library MS Egerton 615 where HM 111 lacks the first six stanzas (lines 1–42). When transcribing from Egerton, I update the spelling to accord with Hoccleve's own practice (e.g., thow for Egerton's thu, my/thy/why for mi/thi/whi, thee for the, syn for sith).

Comparisons to the originals below are taken from *Le Pèlerinage de l'Âme* (ed. Stürzinger 1895) and *Le Pèlerinage Jhesucrist* (ed. Stürzinger 1897).

COMPLAINT PARAMOUNT

O fadir God, how fers° and how cruel, — fierce
In whom thee list or wilt°, canst thow thee make°. — wish or desire, you can act against
Whom wilt thow spare, ne wot° I neuere a deel°, — nor know, not at all
Syn thow thy sone hast to the deth betake°, — since you sent your son to die
5 That thee offendid neuere° ne dide wrake°, — who never offended you, exact vengeance
Or mystook him to thee° or disobeyde, — committed an offense against you
Ne° to noon othir dide he harme or seide. — nor

I had ioye entiere° and also gladnesse — complete joy
Whan thow betook him me° to clothe and wrappe — entrusted him to me
10 In mannes flesch°. I wend°, in soothfastnesse°, — man's flesh, thought, truthfully
Haue had foreuere ioye by the lappe°. — in my grasp
But now hath sorwe° caught me with his trappe. — has sorrow
My ioye hath made a permutacioun° — an exchange
With wepyng and eek° lamentacioun. — also

15 O holy gost, þat art alle confortoure° — comforter
Of woful hertes that wofull be,
And art hire verray° helpe and counceyloure°, — their true, counselor
That of hy vertu° shadowist° me — high power, overshadowed
Whan þat the cleernesse of thy diuinite
20 So shynyng in my feerful gost° alight, — spirit
Which that me sore agasted and affright°, — scared and frightened

Why hast thow me not in thy remembraunce
Now at this tyme, right as thow had tho°? — then
O, why is it noght to thyn pleasaunce
25 Now for to schadwe° me as weel also, — shade/protect
That hid from me myght be my sones wo?
Wherof if þat I may no counfort haue,
From dethis strok° ther may nothyng me saue. — death's blow

8–10. Cf. Luke 1:47, 2:6–7. As Houghton points out, these lines betray the poem's source in *Pèlerinage Jhesucrist*, rather than *Pèlerinage de l'Âme*. Deguileville makes important revisions en route to *Jhesucrist*, which Hoccleve follows here. The notion of 'clothing and wrapping' Jesus in human flesh has its roots in *Âme*'s arboreal metaphor, where Mary remembers being given Jesus to clothe and cover in human bark (*escore*) so that he might become an apple (*pomme*) – lines changed in *Jhesucrist* to human flesh (*char*) and man (*homme*, not *pomme*). See *Âme*, lines 6359–63; *Jhesucrist*, lines 9157–60; and Houghton's comment, 2013: 261.

13–14. Cf. as possible inversions: Psalms 29:12; Jeremiah 31:16; John 16:20.

18. See Luke 1:34–5.

21. See Luke 1:28–30.

22–3. Cf. Psalms 21:2–3, 12:1; Matthew 27:46; 'Learn to Die', lines 744–5. Cf. *Jhesucrist*, lines 9172–3: 'Que ne m'obumbres tu ausi / Maintenant … '

COMPLAINT PARAMOUNT 5

	O Gaubriel, whan þat thow come aplace°	when you appeared
30	And madest vnto me thy salewyng°,	your greeting
	And seidist thus: 'Heil Mary, ful of grace',	
	Why ne had thow youen° me warnyng	didn't you give
	Of þat grace that veyn° is and faylyng,	vain
	As thow now seest°, and sy° it weel beforne?	you now see, saw
35	Syn° my ioye is me rafte°, my grace is lorne°.	since, taken from me, lost

	O thow Elizabeth, my cosyn° dere,	cousin
	The word[es] þat thow spak° in the mowntayne°	you spoke, mountain
	Be ended al in anothir maner	
	Than thow had wened°. My blissyng into peyne°	thought, pain
40	Retorned is. Of ioye am I bareyne°.	barren
	I song to sone°, for I sang by the morwe°,	sang too soon, in the morning
	And now at evene° I wepe and make sorwe°.	evening, sorrow

	O womman þat among the peple speek,	
	How þat the wombe blessid was þat beer°,	bore
45	And the tetes° þat yaf to sowken eek°,	breasts, gave suck also
	The sone of God, which on hy hangith heer,	
	What seist thow now? Why comest thow no neer°?	nearer
	Why nart° thow heere? O womman, where art thow	aren't
	That nat ne seest° my woful wombe now?	who doesn't see

50	O Simeon, thow seidest me ful sooth°,	spoke the truth
	The strook that perce shal my sones herte,	
	My soule thirle° it shal, and so it dooth.	pierce
	The wownde of deeth ne may I nat asterte°.	escape
	Ther may no martirdom me make smerte°	cause me pain
55	So sore as this martire smertith° me.	pains
	So sholde he seyn þat myn hurt mighte see.	

---

29. Gabriel is the angel who informed Mary that she would carry Jesus in her womb.

31. See Luke 1:28. This also forms the beginning of the 'Ave Maria'.

36–42. For Mary's visit to Elizabeth while both were pregnant (with Jesus and John, respectively), see Luke 1:39–45. The words that Elizabeth spoke (line 37) begin: 'Blessed art thou among women, and blessed is the fruit of thy womb … ' Mary's 'song' (line 41), known as 'the Magnificat', gives thanks and is a song of joy; it follows after this exchange, at Luke 1:46–55. Mary's phrase 'Of ioye am I bareyne' (40) inverts Elizabeth's sentiment at Luke 1:44, 'as soon as the voice of thy salutation sounded in my ears, the infant in my womb leaped for joy'. Also cf. 'Male Regle', 14–15: 'And now my body empty is, and bare / Of ioie'. Lines 41–2, thought by Ellis to be an original addition, are in fact found in *Jhesucrist*, lines 9194–6. (Houghton 2013: 264)

43. Here begins the portion of the poem found in Hoccleve's hand, in HM 111. The 'womman' in question here is seen in Luke 11:27: she calls up to Jesus from the crowd, saying, 'Blessed is the womb that bore thee'.

50–2. See Luke 2:25–35. Mary and Joseph go to Jerusalem to make a sacrifice for Jesus, their firstborn son, as is the custom. They meet Simeon, who prophesies Jesus's death: 'Behold this child is set for the fall … *And thy own soul a sword shall pierce*, that, out of many hearts, thoughts may be revealed'.

6 COMPLAINT PARAMOUNT

O Joachim, O deere fadir° myn,   _father_
And Seint Anne, my modir° deere also,   _mother_
To what entente°, or to what ende or fyn°,   _aim, purpose_
60 Broghten yee me foorth þat am greeued° so?   _pained_
Mirthe is to me become a verray fo°.   _true enemy_
Your fadir Dauid, þat an harpour° was,   _harper_
Conforted folk þat stood in heuy cas°.   _a sad condition_

Me thynkith yee nat doon to me aright
65 Þat° were his successours, syn° instrument   _who, since_
Han yee noon° left wherwith me make light°,   _you have none, to cheer me up_
And me conforte in my woful torment.
Me to doon ese° han yee no talent°,   _give comfort, ability_
And knowen° myn confortelees distresse.   _though you know_
70 Yee oghten weepe for myn heuynesse.

O blessid sone, on thee wole I out throwe
My salte teeres, for oonly on thee
My look is set. O thynke how many a throwe°   _time_
Thow in myn armes lay, and on my knee
75 Thow sat and haddist many a kus° of me.   _kiss_
Eek° thee to sowke° on my brestes yaf° Y,   _also, suck, offered_
Thee norisshyng faire° and tendrely.   _sweetly_

Now thee fro me withdrawith bittir deeth
And makith a wrongful disseuerance°.   _separation/severing_
80 Thynke nat, sone, in me þat any breeth
Endure may þat feele al this greuance°.   _grief_
My martirdom° me hath at the outrance°.   _suffering, at the utmost (pain)_
I needes sterue moot syn° I thee see   _I must die since_
Shamely° nakid, strecchid on a tree°.   _shamefully, i.e., the cross_

85 And this me sleeth°, þat in the open day   _this kills me_
Thyn hertes wownde shewith him° so wyde   _shows itself_
Þat alle folk see and beholde it may,
So largeliche opned is thy syde.
O wo is me, syn° I nat may it hyde.   _since_
90 And among othre of my smerte greeues°,   _painful griefs_
Thow put art also, sone, amonges theeues°,   _thieves_

57–60. Mary's parents are Joachim and Anna. Mary is asking them why she was born – why would they have given birth to Mary, only to have her experience such pain?

62. Jesus is described as descended from David (on Joseph's side). (See Luke 1:26–7, 3:23–31; Matthew 1:1–16.) David was a young shepherd known as a musician (for his role as harp player, see 1 Samuel 16:23), then known for slaying Goliath. He later became king. On song, cf. line 41 above.

78–9. 'Now bitter death takes you from me, and makes a wrongful separation.'

83–4. See Matthew 27:31, 35; Mark 15:20, 24; John 19:23–25.

85–8. See John 19:33–4, 37; cf. Zechariah 12:10.

90–1. Jesus is crucified between two thieves. See Matthew 27:38; Mark 15:27–8, 32; Luke 23:33; John 19:19.

COMPLAINT PARAMOUNT   7

As thow° were an euel and wikkid wight.   as though you
And lest þat somme folk par auenture°   perhaps
No knowleche hadde of thy persone aright,
95 Thy name Pilat hath put in scripture°,   in writing
Þat knowe mighte it euery creature,
For thy penance sholde nat been hid.
O wo is me þat al this see betid°.   happen

How may myn yen° þat beholde al this   my eyes
100 Restreyne hem° for to shewe°, by weepynge,   themselves, from showing
Myn hertes greef? Moot° I nat weepe? O yis.   must
Sone, if thow haddist a fadir lyuynge
That wolde weepe and make waymentynge°,   wail
For þat he hadde paart of° thy persone,   had a (physical) part in
105 That were a greet abreggynge° of my mone°.   would be a great lessening, woe

But thow in eerthe fadir haddist neuere.
No wight° for thee swich° cause hath for to pleyne°   person, such, lament
As þat haue I. Shalt thow fro me disseuere°   separate
Þat aart al hoolly° myn? My sorwes deepe   wholly
110 Han al myn hertes ioie leid to sleepe°.   joy laid to sleep (quashed)
No wight with me, in thee, my sone, hath part.
Hoolly of my blood, deere chyld, thow art.

That doublith al my torment and my greef.
Vnto myn herte it is confusion°   destruction
115 Thyn harm to see, þat° art to me so leef°.   who, dear
Mighte nat, sone, the redempcioun
Of man han bee° withoute effusioun°   have been (possible), spilling
Of thy blood? Yis, if it had been thy lust° –   will
But what thow wilt be doon°, souffre me must.   what you will to happen

---

95–6. Matthew and John report Pilate displaying Jesus's name with the title, 'King of the Jews'. Luke and Mark have just the title (no name). See Matthew 27:37; Mark 15:26; Luke 23:38; John 19:18–19.

102–9. Mary points out that Jesus has never had an earthly father (Joseph has only served as a surrogate), and so no one can truly share the magnitude of this pain with her. God is presented as Jesus's father – but in this instance, God cannot seem to help Mary, and neither can anyone else. She is alone in experiencing Jesus's death as she does.

112. There is a possible pun in 'hoolly' here – wholly and holy. A double resonance also possible in line 109. In a literal sense, Jesus comes 'wholly' from Mary's flesh – because there is no earthly father, he proceeds (in a fleshly, if not a spiritual sense) from her alone.

116–19. Cf. Matthew 26:38–9; Mark 14:35–6; Luke 22:41–2; Hebrews 9:22. Jesus prays in Gethsemane that the 'chalice' might 'pass from him' – i.e., that he might be spared this fate. But he accepts that God's will – not his own – will be done. The concession is the same as the one that Mary makes here, but she is addressing Jesus as God. In *Âme*, this passage abounds with arboreal connotations – the life of apple and tree alike are implicated in Jesus's choice. These references are removed in *Jhesucrist*, and Hoccleve follows that version – bare of the tree/apple metaphor – in his translation. See *Âme*, lines 6469–76; *Jhesucrist*, lines 9271–4; cf. Houghton 2013: 261–2.

8 COMPLAINT PARAMOUNT

120	O deeth, so thow kythist° thy bittirnesse	show
	First on my sone, and aftirward on me.	
	Bittir art thow and ful of crabbidnesse°	wickedness
	That my sone hast slayn thurgh thy crueltee	
	And nat me sleest°. Certein, nat wole I flee.	don't slay me
125	Come of, come of, and slee° me heere as blyue°.	slay, at once
	Departe from him wole I nat alyue.	

O moone, O sterres°, and thow firmament°,   stars, sky
How may yee fro wepynge yow° restreyne   yourselves
And seen° your creatour in swich° torment?   when you see, such
130 Yee oghten troublid been in euery veyne
And his despitous° deeth with me conpleyne.   cruel
Weepeth, and crieth as lowde as yee may –
Our creatour with wrong° is slayn this day.   wrongfully

O sonne°, with thy cleere bemes° brighte,   sun, beams
135 Þat seest my child nakid this nones tyde°,   noontide
Why souffrest thow him, in the open sighte
Of the folk heere, vnkeuered abyde°?   (to) remain exposed
Thow art as moche or more holde him to hyde
Than Sem° þat helid° his Fadir Noe°   Shem, covered, Noah
140 Whan he espyde° þat nakid was he.   saw

If thow his sone be, do lyk° therto –   the same
Come of, withdrawe thy bemes brightnesse.
Thow art to blame but if° thow so do.   unless
For shame, hyde my sones nakidnesse.
145 Is ther in thee no sparcle of kyndenesse?
Remembre he is thy lord and creatour.
Now keuere° him, for thy worsship and honour.   cover

127–33. Cf. Psalms 148:1–12. For other examples of the elements interacting with divinity, cf. Psalms 18:2–5, 95:11–13, 96:1–6; Luke 19:36–40.

138–40. See Genesis 9:20–7.

141. There is a pun on 'sone' here, meaning both son and sun. Hoccleve has just evoked Shem, son of Noah, and his act of covering his father. The sun is in some ways 'son' of Jesus (as God), as are all created things. *Jhesucrist* has a similar dynamic, although the son/sun pun is absent (given French), and so it is less ambiguous; see line 9298: 'Se bon fil es, si fai ausi'.

142–3. Interestingly, the sun obeys, according to the Gospels – light recedes and darkness descends: see Matthew 27:45–6; Mark 15:33–5; Luke 23:45–6.

145. There is a possible pun in 'kyndenesse' here – meaning both kindness and naturalness in Middle English. (I.e., can you not do what is natural and good?) The idea of a 'sparkle' of kindness is appropriate when speaking to the sun. This is not present in *Jhesucrist*, although cf. lines 9299b–300: 'couvert sera / Rien plus il ne te coustera'.

COMPLAINT PARAMOUNT 9

O eerthe, what lust° hast thow to susteene°	desire, support
The crois on which he þat thee made and it	
150 Is hangid, and aourned° thee with greene,	furnished
Which þat thow werist°? How hast thow thee qwit°	you wear, justified yourself
Vnto thy lord? O do this for him yit:	
Qwake for doel°, and cleue° thow in two,	quake for sorrow, crack
And al þat blood restore me vnto	
155 Which thow hast dronke. It myn is and nat thyn.	
Or elles thus withouten taryynge°,	delay
Tho° bodyes dede, whiche in thee þat lyn°,	those, that lie in you
Caste out, for they by taast of swich dewynge°	such moisture
Hem oghte clothe ageyn in hir clothynge°.	ought clothe themselves again (in flesh)
160 Thow Caluarie°, thow art namely	(Mount) Calvary
Holden for to do so. To thee speke Y.	
O deere sone, myn deeth neighith° faste,	nears
Syn° to anothir thow hast youen° me	since, given
Than° vnto thee. And how may my lyf laste	rather than
165 Þat me yeuest° any othir than thee?	when you give me to
Thogh he whom thow me yeuest° maiden° be,	give, virgin
And thogh by iust° balance thow weye° al,	just, weigh
The weighte of him and thee nat is egal°.	equal
He a disciple is, and thow art a lord.	
170 Thow al away art gretter than he is.	
Betwixt your mightes is ther greet discord°.	incongruity
My woful torment doublid is by this.	
I needes mourne moot° and fare amis°.	I must mourn, go astray/suffer
It seemeth þat thow makist departynge	
175 Twixt° thee and me for ay°, withoute endynge°.	between, forever, endlessly
And namely, syn° thow me 'womman' callist,	since
As I to thee straunge were and vnknowe°,	unknown

148–50. ' … what desire do you have to continue supporting the cross on which Jesus (he that made you) is hanged … ' In *Âme* (line 6520), Jesus hangs on an 'arbre sec' (dry tree) – changed to 'aspre croiz' (harsh/painful cross) in *Jhesucrist* (line 9302). Cf. 'aourned … with greene' (line 149) with *Jhesucrist*'s 'de verdures aourna' (line 9304).

153–9. On the image of the earth drinking blood, cf. Genesis 4:9–11. On the earth quaking and the dead rising at the time of Jesus's death, see Matthew 27:51–3. As with the sun retreating (see note to lines 142–3, above), these lines and their Gospel counterparts give the effect of the elements listening to Mary as she cries out: her complaint has real power.

160. Mount Calvary is the location where Christ is crucified. See Matthew 27:33; Mark 15:22; Luke 23:33; John 19:17.

162–70. See John 19:25–7. Jesus (calling Mary 'woman') offers his disciple John to his mother as a surrogate son, and offers Mary to John as a surrogate mother. The 'disciple who Jesus loved', as he is described in the Gospel account, is interpreted as John through Christian tradition. See also 'Mother of God', lines 99–105.

176. See note to lines 162–70.

10 COMPLAINT PARAMOUNT

Therthurgh, my sone, thow my ioie appallist°.   you dim my joy
Wel feele I þat deeth his vengeable° bowe   vengeful
180 Hath bent, and me purposith doun to throwe.
Of sorwe talke may I nat ynow°,   not enough
Syn° fro my name 'I' doon° away is now.   since, taken

Wel may men clepe° and calle me Mara   name
From hennesforward. So may men me calle.
185 How sholde I lenger clept be° Maria   any longer be called
Syn° 'I', which is Ihesus, is fro me falle°.   since, fallen from me
This day al my swetnesse is into galle°   bitterness
Torned, syn þat 'I', which was the beautee
Of my name, this day bynome is me°.   is taken from me

190 O Iohn, my deere freend, thow haast receyued
A woful modir, and an heuy sone
Haue I of thee. Deeth hath myn othir weyued°.   removed
How may we two the deeth eschue or shone°?   flee
We drery wightes° two, wher may we wone°?   people, dwell
195 Thow art of confort destitut I see,
And so am I. Ful careful° been wee.   sorrowful

Vnto oure hertes deeth hath sent his wownde.
Noon of vs may alleggen° othres peyne.   lighten (the)
So manye sorwes in vs two habownde°.   abound
200 We han no might° fro sorwe vs restreyne.   power
I see noon othir – die moot we tweyne°.   must we two
Now let vs steruen° heer par conpaignie°:   die, together
Sterue thow° there, and heere wole I die.   you die

O angels, thogh yee mourne and waile and weepe,
205 Yee do no wrong. Slayn is your creatour
By tho° folk þat yee weren wont to keepe   those
And gye° and lede. They to dethes shour°   guide, storm
Han put him. Thogh yee han wo and langour°,   suffering
No wondir is it – who may blame yow? –
210 And yit ful cheer he had hem° þat him slow°.   he had true affection for those, slew

---

182–9. See Ruth 1:19–20. There Noemi asks to be called 'Mara' [bitter], as she is filled with bitterness. Here, the wordplay is extended: Maria loses the 'I' in her name (which is 'Ihesus'), becoming Mara (bitter) with the loss of her son. The wordplay is also present in Hoccleve's source; see lines 9336–42 (9339b–40: 'quar i, c'est Ih*esus* / M'est hui osté et n'i est plus').

190–2. See note to lines 162–70.

194–6. On this binding of John and Mary, cf. 'Mother of God', lines 99–140.

203. Cf. 'Learn to Die', line 740.

210. Cf. Luke 23:34, where Jesus begs God's forgiveness for his tormentors.

COMPLAINT PARAMOUNT 11

O special loue°, þat me ioyned haast   *i.e., divine love*
Vnto my sone, strong is thy knyttynge.
This day therin fynde I a bittir taast,
For now the taast I feele and the streynynge°   *pressure*
215 Of deeth. By thy deeth, feele I deeth me stynge.
O poore modir, what shalt thow now seye?
Poore Marie, thy wit is aweye.

Marie? Nay, but 'marred' I thee calle.
So may I wel, for thow art, wel I woot°,   *I know well*
220 Vessel of care° and wo and sorwes° alle.   *sorrow, sorrows*
Now thow art frosty cold, now fyry hoot,
And right as þat a ship or barge or boot°   *boat*
Among the wawes° dryueth steerelees°,   *waves, rudderless*
So doost thow, woful womman confortlees°.   *comfortless*

225 And of modir° haast thow eek° lost the style°.   *mother (the title), also, status*
No more maist thow clept° be by thy name.   *called*
O sones of Adam, al to long whyle
Yee tarien° hens; hieth hidir° for shame.   *delay, hurry here*
See how my sone for your gilt and blame
230 Hangith heer al bybled° vpon the crois.   *bloodied*
Bymeneth° him in herte and cheere and vois.   *pity*

His blody stremes see now and beholde.
If yee to him han any affeccioun,
Now for his wo your hertes oghten colde°.   *ought to feel remorse/pity*
235 Shewith your loue and your dileccioun°.   *adoration*
For your gilt makith he correccioun
And amendes right by his owne deeth.
Þat yee nat reewe° on him, myn herte it sleeth°.   *not have pity, slays*

---

215. Cf. 1 Corinthians 15:55–6.

217. This phrase is original to Hoccleve (not found in *Jhesucrist*: cf. lines 9369–71). Cf. 'Balade and Roundel for Henry Somer', line 28: 'our wit is aweye'; and 'Complaint' (*Series*), lines 59 and 64, in which Hoccleve's wit is personified and goes away, only to return 'hoom … aȝein'.

218. The wordplay with Mary's name continues – from Maria to Mara (bitter) to 'marred'. See lines 182–9, above. Cf. *Jhesucrist*, line 9371: 'Non Marie, mez marrie'.

222–4. The nautical reference here has a loose anchor in the source text: in a series of puns (lines 9371–8), Deguileville takes Marie to 'marrie' (marred), from 'mere' (mother) to 'amere' (bitterness), so that 'de mer a mer' (from sea to sea) one cannot find one so bitter, all because Love ('amour', line 9365) has caused her to love ('amer') Jesus so. Hoccleve substitutes the metaphor of a ship adrift, likely drawing upon the raw material of a 'mere' sent 'de mer a mer'.

226. That is, no longer will you be called mother.

227. 'sones of Adam'. That is, everyone. Cf. *Jhesucrist*: 'filz Adam' (line 9379).

230–1. These lines, and the two stanzas following, are flush with apple and tree metaphors in *Âme* (see lines 6599–620), wherein Jesus is a broken apple with juices flowing out. In *Jhesucrist*, the crushed apple becomes a broken body, with blood streaming out – and it is this (human) version that Hoccleve follows. For a comparison of the three passages, see Houghton 2013: 261–3.

12 COMPLAINT PARAMOUNT

A modir þat so soone hir cote taar°   coat tore
240   Or rente°, sy° men neuere noon or° this,   ripped, saw, before
For chyld which þat shee of hir body baar°   bore
To yeue hir tete°, as my chyld þat heere is.   give her breast
His cote hath torn° for your gilt, nat for his,   his coat has torn (he has died)
And hath his blood despent° in greet foysoun°,   spilled, abundance
245   And al it was for your redempcioun.

C'est tout.

Ceste conpleynte paramont feust translatee
au commandement de ma dame de Hereford,
que Dieu pardoynt

232–8. Cf. 'Inuocacio ad Patrem', lines 105–13. Line 235: 'dileccioun': cf. use in 'Mother of God', line 122 (see note); *Regiment*, line 851. In 'Mother of God', the word is translated from the Latin 'dilectionis'. In *Jhesucrist*, Deguileville invites the reader here to get drunk on the 'grant amour' of Christ (by drinking his blood). Hoccleve turns this around somewhat, inviting the reader to show love and adoration for Christ. Lines 236–7: cf. 1 Peter 2:24; Isaiah 53:3–6; Galatians 3:13; 1 John 2:2; Acts 5:30–31.

239–40. The Bible offers several instances of people tearing their garments as a sign of grief. Cf., for instance, 2 Samuel 1:11–12; Job 1:20–1; Genesis 37:34–5. In Hoccleve's poem, Mary's torn garment gives way to Jesus's torn 'cote' (figurative for body) in line 243. The metaphor – and the way it passes from Mary to Jesus – makes more sense when we consider its original grounding (in *Âme*) in the tree/apple metaphor. In *Âme*, the crucified Jesus is imagined as a broken apple (*pomme entemmee*), with peel pierced so that mankind can suck the juice, and thereby taste his love for us ('son escorce trespercier / Pour vous faire son jus succier'). In *Jhesucrist*, the peel/apple metaphor is removed, with Jesus merely being pierced (and bleeding). Both *Âme* and *Jhesucrist* reference Mary's torn 'cote' [tunic/coat], with the implication being in *Âme* that her own bark/flesh is sundered at the sight of her apple pierced and split. See *Âme*, lines 6599–620; *Jhesucrist*, lines 9381–98.

Closing dedication: 'This superlative complaint was translated at the request of my lady of Hereford, may God pardon her'

[Joan Fitzalan, countess of Hereford, to whom the poem is dedicated, was the mother of Henry IV's wife, Mary Bohun. She died in 1419.]

TO SIR JOHN OLDCASTLE

Date: summer 1415

❧

John Oldcastle, a knight and sometime comrade of Henry V, was by summer 1415 a criminal at large, an ardent supporter of Lollardy. Oldcastle had been arrested in September 1413 and imprisoned in the Tower, but escaped on October 19, 1413. He remained at large until November 1417, and was executed on December 14, 1417. Hoccleve's heading helps to date his poem: it tells us that the poem was written while Henry V (and his troops) was at Southampton, awaiting his 'first passage to Harfleur'. This dates the poem between July and early August 1415. (Seymour 1981: 129) At the time the poem was written, then, Oldcastle was still in hiding, and Henry V was still holding out an offer of reconciliation and pardon, should Oldcastle renounce his errors – hence the mixture of hortatory preaching and a more mediatory, conciliatory tone in the poem. Oldcastle also had family connections to John Prophete, who served as Keeper of the Privy Seal from 1406–15; and it has been suggested that that connection may have spurred Hoccleve to write the poem, and to write it in the manner he did. (See Burrow 1994: 21)

In its form, an open letter, 'Oldcastle' recalls Hoccleve's 'Epistle of Cupid' (written thirteen years earlier) and 'The Court of Good Company' (six years later) – albeit with decidedly more at stake. It also resonates with the *Regiment of Princes* itself, insofar as that poem is written for the 'ear' of Prince Henry, but obviously circulated much more widely.

'Oldcastle' does not have any medieval witnesses beyond HM 111, but it was twice copied by the scholar Richard James in the early seventeenth century (Oxford, Bodleian Library, MS James 34; London, British Library, MS Add 33785). James supplied ample notes for the poem, claiming a position for Oldcastle as a 'proto-protestant martyr'. (See Perkins 2018; cf. Nuttall–Watt 2022: 10)

TO SIR JOHN OLDCASTLE

Ceste feust faicte au temps que le .R. .H. le .V^t. que dieu pardoint feust a Hampton sur son primer passage vers Harflete

The laddre of heuene, I meene charitee,
Commandith vs, if our brothir be falle° — has fallen
Into errour, to haue of him pitee
And seeke weyes in our wittes alle
5   How we may him ageyn to vertu calle.
And in gretter errour ne knowe I noon° — I know none
Than thow, þat dronke haast heresies galle°, — poison
And art fro Crystes feith twynned and goon°. — departed and gone

Allas, þat thow þat were a manly knyght,
10   And shoon° ful cleer in famous worthynesse, — shone
Standynge in the fauour of every wight°, — person
Haast lost the style° of Cristenly prowesse° — manner, Christian strength
Among alle hem° þat stande in the cleernesse — those
Of good byleeue°, and no man with thee holdith, — i.e., orthodoxy
15   Sauf cursid caitifs°, heires of dirknesse. — except cursed scoundrels (heretics)
For verray routhe° of thee myn herte coldith°. — pity, grows cold

Thow haast maad a fair permutacion°, — exchange
Fro Crystes lore° to feendly° doctryne, — teaching, devilish
From honour and fro dominacion° — power/control
20   Vnto repreef and mescheuous ruyne,
Fro Cristen folk to hethenly couyne°, — heathendom
Fro seuretee° vnto vnsikirnesse°, — security, insecurity
Fro ioie and ese° vnto wo and pyne°, — joy and ease, woe and pain
Fro light of trouthe vnto dirk falsnesse.

25   O Oldcastel, allas, what eilid thee° — what was wrong with you
To slippe into the snare of heresie,
Thurgh which thow foo° art to the Trinitee, — foe
And to the blissid virgyne Marie,
And to the innumerable holy conpaignie° — holy company
30   Of heuene, and to al holy chirche? Allas!
Too° longe haast thow bathid in þat folie. — too
Ryse vp, and pourge thee of thy trespas!

Heading: This was made when King Henry V, may God pardon him, was at Hampton for his first passage to Harfleur.

1–5. Cf. James 5:19–20; 2 Thessalonians 3:14–15; Galatians 6:1.
9. Cf. Hoccleve's use of 'manly' in 'Male Regle' – the next poem in HM III, written a decade earlier – lines 174, 360.
26. Cf. Psalms 118:110.

TO SIR JOHN OLDCASTLE 15

Seint Austyn seith, whiles a man abydith
In heresie or scisme°, and list° nat flee   *schism, desires*
35 Therfro, his soule fro God he diuidith,
And may nat saued been, in no degree;
For what man holdith nat the vnitee
Of holy chirche, neithir his bapteeme°   *baptism*
Ne his almesse°, how large þat it be,   *nor his alms*
40 To helthe° him profyte, ne God qweeme°.   *(spiritual) health, nor God please*

> Augustinus de fide, ad Petrum: 'Firmissime tene, et nullatenus dubites, quemlibet hereticum etc. qui ecclesie catholice non tenet vnitatem, neque baptismus, neque elemosina quantumcumque copiosa, neque mors pro Christi nomine suscepta, proficere poterit ad salutem.'

And yit, moreouer, he seith thus also:
Thogh þat an heretyk for Crystes name
Shede his blood, and his lyf for Cryst forgo°,   *lose (i.e., die for Christ)*
Shal nat him saue. Allas, the harm and shame.
45 May nat thy smert° thy sturdy° herte attame°?   *grief, stubborn, tame*
Obeie, obeie, in the name of Ihesu.
Thow art of merit and of honur lame;
Conquere hem° two, and thee arme° in vertu.   *those, arm yourself*

If thyn hy herte, bolnynge° in errour,   *swelling*
50 To holy chirche can nat buxum° be,   *obedient*
Beholde Theodosius Emperour,
How humble and buxum vnto God was he.
No reward took he of his dignitee,
But as a lamb to holy chirche obeide.
55 In the scripture may men rede and se
How meekly of the bisshop grace he preide°.   *he asked for grace*

> De Theodosij illustris Imperatoris obedienciali humilitate respice in historia tripartita, libro ix°, vbi narrat, 'Cum apud Thesolonicam Ciuitatem', etc.

33–40. gloss: In *De fide ad Petrum*, Augustine says: 'Hold most firmly in mind and you shall not doubt at all that for whatever heretics, etc., who do not believe in one Catholic church, neither baptism, nor alms as copious as possible, nor death undergone in the name of Christ can be an aid to (spiritual) health.' [Translation by Jane Griffiths]

While attributed to Augustine by Hoccleve, this work – *De fide ad Petrum* – is actually by Fulgentius. Hoccleve translates the passage quite closely in lines 33–44. (See Fraipont 1968: 757)

47–8. Hoccleve begins to use the language of knighthood to appeal to Oldcastle ('conquere'). The two things he is being compelled to conquer, however, are intangible: merit and honor.

51–6. gloss: Of Theodosius the illustrious emperor's humility to the rule, see *Historia Tripartita*, Book IX, where it is said: 'When at the city of Thessalonica,' etc. [Translation by Jane Griffiths] The named source here is *Historia ecclesiastica tripartita* (Epiphanius–Cassiodorus; sixth-century). Hoccleve's actual source (as with the Constantine gloss at lines 225–32) would appear to be Rufinus's continuation (402 AD) of Eusebius's *Historia ecclesiastica* (Book 11, Chapters 18–19). (See Nuttall 2015: 10; Schwartz and Mommsen 1999: 1022–4) Hoccleve uses Theodosius as an example of obedience to the church and humility – willingness to admit wrongdoing and reform oneself accordingly: 'following his tyrannical slaughter of both guilty and innocent in the Thessaloniki massacre, [he] submitted to the rebukes of Ambrose, bishop of Milan, and obeyed the bishop's calls for repentance' (Nuttall 2015: 10).

16 TO SIR JOHN OLDCASTLE

Th'offense which þat he ageyn° God wroghte°   against, made
Was nat so greet as thyn by many fold,
And yit ful heuy° he was, and it forthoghte°,   sorrowful, regretted
60 Obeyyng as þat holy chirche hath wolde°.   as Holy Church would have it
Thow þat thy soule to the feend° haast sold,   devil
Bye° it agayn thurgh thyn obedience.   buy
Thyn heresie is al to hoor° and old;   too gray
Correcte thee° at Crystes reuerence.   reform yourself

65 And for thy soules helthe, do eek so°:   also thus
Thy pryde qwenche° and thy presumpcioun.   quench
Wher thow hast been to Crystes feith a fo,
Plante in thyn herte a deep contricioun°,   contrition
And hennesfoorth be Crystes champioun.
70 The welle of mercy renneth al in brede° –   flows generously
Drynke therof, syn° ther is swich foysoun°.   since, such abundance
Thyn hertes botel° thereof fille, I rede°.   heart's bottle, advise

Thow haast offendid God wondirly sore°,   severely
And nathelees°, if thow thee wilt amende°,   nevertheless, will amend yourself
75 Thogh thy gilt were a .ml.° tymes more,   thousand
Axe him° mercy and he wole it thee sende.   ask him (for)
Thow art vnwys, thogh thow thee wys pretende°,   you claim to be wise
And so been alle of thyn opinoun°.   i.e., it's the same with other Lollards
To God and holy chirche thow thee bende°.   supplicate
80 Caste out thy venym thurgh confessioun.

Thow seist confessioun auriculeer°   oracular confession
Ther needith noon°, but it is the contrarie.   is unnecessary
Thow lookist mis°; thy sighte is nothyng cleer.   amiss
Holy Writ therin is thyn aduersarie,   Scriptum est
85 And clerkes alle fro thy conceit° varie   belief   'Ostendite vos
Þat Crystes partie holden and maynteene.   sacerdotibus'
Leue° þat conceit, lest þat thow miscarie°.   abandon, come to grief (or death)
Waar° of the swerd of God, for it is keene°.   beware, sharp

---

68. Cf. Psalms 50:19.
70–2. Cf. John 4:10, 13–14; Jeremiah 2:13.
73–80. Cf. 2 Chronicles 7:14, 30:9; Ecclesiasticus 18:20.
81–2. After his opening salvo, Hoccleve turns to a point-by-point refutation of Lollard arguments, starting here. His first target is oracular (spoken) confession: Lollards hold that confession to a priest is not necessary to salvation, whereas orthodox belief considers it central. Line 81: 'auriculeer': an apparent neologism, derived from Latin.
83. Cf. lines 417–24.
84–5. gloss: It is written, 'Show yourselves to the priests' [See Luke 17:14. Jesus is greeted by ten lepers; he tells them to show themselves to the priests and, when they do, they are healed.]

TO SIR JOHN OLDCASTLE   17

Heere, in this lyf, vnto God mercy crie,

90   And with the ax or hamer of penance

Smyte° on the stoon. Slee° thyn obstinacie. — *strike, slay*

Haue of thy synnes heuy remembrance.

Rowne° in the preestes ere°, and the greuance — *whisper, priest's ear*

Of thy soule meekly to him confesse –

95   And in the wal of heuene, is no doutance°, — *without a doubt*

Thow shalt a qwik stoon° be for thy goodnesse. — *living stone*

O Oldcastle, how hath the feend° thee blent°? — *devil, blinded you*

Where is thy knyghtly herte? Art thow his thral°? — *slave*

Thow errest° foule eek° in the Sacrament — *stray, also*

100   Of the Auter°, but how in special — *Sacrament of the Altar (Eucharist)*

For to declare it needith nat at al° – — *it is unnecessary*

It knowen is in many a regioun.

Now syn° the feend hath youen thee a fal°, — *since, has brought you down*

Qwyte° him, let see – ryse vp and slynge him doun. — *take revenge on*

105   Ryse vp a manly knyght out of the slow° — *slough*

Of heresie. O lurkere° as a wrecche, — *skulker*

Whereas thow erred haast, correcte it now.

By humblesse° thow mayst to mercy strecche°. — *humility, reach for mercy*

To holy chirche go and there fecche° — *fetch*

110   The holsum oyle of absolucion°. — *oil of absolution (sacrament of penance)*

If thow of soules hurt ne shame recche°, — *don't take heed*

Thow leesist° heuene and al knyghtly renoun. — *lose*

Augustinus de visitatione infirmorum dicit, 'In muro Ciuitatis superne apponendus es lapis viuus, in cuius edificio non auditur securis aut malleus. Hic perferendus est strepitus, hic adiciendus est lapidi malleus, hic conterendum est totum lapidis superuacuum, strepitus [sit] peccatorum tuorum recordatio super quibus perstrepat in aure sacredotis humillima tua confessio', etc.

89–96. gloss: Augustine says in *De visitatione infirmorum*: 'You must be added as a living stone to the wall of the heavenly city, in the building of which no axe or hammer is heard. Here noise must be undergone; here the hammer must be struck on the stone; here everything superfluous about the stone must be destroyed. [Let] the memory of your sins [be] the noise above which your very humble confession sounds in the ear of the priest', etc. [Translation by Martine van Kassen] Taken from Pseudo-Augustine, *De visitatione infirmorum*. (*Patrologia Latina* 40, 1147–8) Hoccleve translates the passage loosely in the corresponding stanza (lines 89–96). His decision to end (rather than begin) with the image of being a stone in the wall of heaven makes for a firmer landing to the stanza.

89–96. Cf. Jeremiah 23:29; Psalms 33:19; Ecclesiasticus 20:4.

97–8. Cf. John 12:40.

99–100. Here begins Hoccleve's second subject for refutation: Lollard arguments against the Eucharist (the Sacrament of the Altar). Orthodox thought held that transubstantiation occurred when the priest performed the Sacrament of the Altar (i.e., that the bread was transformed into the body of Christ); whereas, at least some Lollards argued that the bread remained bread, and should be seen only symbolically as Christ's body. Orthodox belief centralized the role of the priest (in that he held the unique power to perform the sacrament), whereas Lollard belief challenged the centrality of the priesthood, and thus priestly powers. In the *Regiment*, Hoccleve underscores the role that rejection of transubstantiation played in the execution of John Badby: see lines 281–322.

110. In encouraging Oldcastle to seek the oil of absolution, Hoccleve is encouraging him to engage in the formal process of penance and absolution.

TO SIR JOHN OLDCASTLE

Par cas° thow to thyself shame it arettist°   *perhaps, you consider it shameful*
Vnto prelatz° of holy chirche obeie.   *authorities*
115 If it so be, thy conceit thow missettist°.   *you are mistaken*
What man aright can in his herte weye°   *weigh*
The trouthe of that? To Ihesu Cryst, I seye,
Principally is þat obedience.
God hath ordeyned preestes to purueye°   *provide*
120 Salue of penance for mannes offense.

Vnto Seint Petir and his successours°   *successors (i.e., priests)*
And so foorth doun°, God hath his power lent°.   *down, granted*
Go to the preest. Correcte thyn errours
With herte contryt vnto God ybent.
125 Despute no more of the sacrament.
As holy chirche biddith°, folwe it.   *prescribes*
And hennesforward, as by myn assent,
Presume nat so mochil of thy wit°.   *intellectual capacity*

I putte cas° a prelat° or a preest   *take as an example, prelate*
130 Him viciously° gouerne in his lyuynge –   *who immorally*
Thow oghtist reewe on it° whan thow it seest°,   *pity it, see it*
And folwe him nat; but aftir his techynge
Thow oghtest do, and for thyn obeyynge
Thow shalt be sauf°. And if he teche amis,   *saved*
135 Toforn° God shal he yeue° a rekenynge,   *before, have*
And, þat a streit°, the greet peril is his.   *in so dire a case*

Lete holy chirche medle of° the doctryne   *occupy itself with*
Of Crystes lawes and of his byleeue.
And lete alle othir folk therto enclyne°,   *follow (the church)*
140 And of our feith noon argumentes meeue°.   *propose*   **Fides non habe[t] meritum etc.**
For if we mighte our feith by reson preeue,
We sholde no meryt of our feith haue.

113–20. Cf. Hebrews 13:17.

121–2. See Matthew 16:15–20. Jesus names Saint Peter (one of the twelve apostles) as the 'rock' of the Christian Church, the first leader in a long succession of priests.

125–8. For lines 125–6, cf. *Regiment*, lines 379–85: 'Of our feith wole I nat despute at al, / But at o word, I in the sacrament / Of the auter fully byleeve and shal ... '; for line 128, cf. *Regiment*, lines 375–8.

132–6. That is, you should not follow his immoral lifestyle, but should follow his teaching – and by following his teaching you will be saved. If his teaching is amiss, God will be the one to judge (and he will be punished by God alone). Lines 134–6: cf. James 3:1.

140. gloss: Faith has no merit, etc.
    This gloss accompanies lines 141–2 of the text: if we could prove everything we believe through reason, our faith would have no merit. The source is Gregory the Great's *Homilies on the Gospels* (homily 26), *Patrologia Latina* 76, 1197C (translated in Hurst 1990: 201). Cf. *Regiment*, lines 351–2 (and lines 344–57, broadly): 'Our feith nat were unto us meritorie / If that we mighten by reson it preeve', also accompanied by a marginal gloss: 'Fides non capit meritum ubi ratio praebet experimentum' (see Blyth, note to line 350). Cf. also *Piers Plowman* B.X.250a: 'Fides non habet meritum ubi humana racio prebet experimentum'; and John 20:29.

TO SIR JOHN OLDCASTLE 19

But nowadayes, a baillif° or reeue°	administrative official, officer
Or man of craft° wole in it dote° or raue.	craftsman, speak foolishly (on such matters)

145 Some wommen eek°, thogh hir wit° be thynne, — *also, their intelligence*
Wole argumentes make in holy writ.
Lewde calates°, sittith doun and spynne° — *ignorant women, weave (make clothes, etc.)*
And kakele° of sumwhat elles, for your wit — *chatter*
Is al to feeble° to despute of it. — *too weak*
150 To clerkes° grete appartenteth° þat aart. — *scholars/ecclesiasts, belongs*
The knowleche of þat, God hath fro yow shit°. — *shut*
Stynte° and leue of°, for right sclendre° is your paart°. — *cease, leave it, slender, role*

Oure fadres° olde and modres° lyued wel, — *fathers, mothers*
And taghte hir° children as hemself taght were° — *their, as they were themselves taught*
155 Of holy chirche, and axid nat a del°, — *asked not at all*
'Why stant this word° heere? And why this word there? — *does this word fall*
Why spak God thus, and seith thus elleswhere?
Why dide he this wyse°, and mighte han do thus?' — *way*
Our fadres medled nothyng of swich gere°. — *such affairs*
160 Þat oghte been a good mirour to vs.

If land to thee be falle of heritage°, — *i.e., if you inherit land*
Which þat thy fadir heeld in reste and pees°, — *peace*
With title° iust° and treewe in al his age°, — *legal right, just, throughout his life*
And his fadir before him brygelees°, — *undisputed*
165 And his and his, and so foorth, doutelees,
I am ful seur, whoso wolde it thee reue°, — *take it from you*
Thow woldest thee deffende and putte in prees°. — *defend yourself and fight*
Thy right thow woldest nat, thy thankes, leue°. — *you wouldn't willingly abandon your right*

Right so, whereas our goode fadres olde
170 Possessid were and hadden the seisyne° — *possession*
Peisible° of Crystes feith, and no man wolde — *peaceable*
Inpugne° hir° right, it sit vs° to enclyne — *oppose, their, it is fitting for us*

143–4. That is, now anyone (from any station) presumes to debate matters of the faith. John Badby would have offered a recent example: he was a craftsman – likely either a tailor or smith. Cf. *Regiment*, lines 292–4. For Badby's treatment in the *Regiment*, see lines 281–329.

147–9. Cf. 1 Timothy 2:12; 1 Corinthians 14:34. 'Calate' seems to serve here as a derogatory term for a woman. (The only prior reference in the *MED* is from *Piers Plowman* – 'kalote my douȝter' (18.426) – where, by contrast, it seems to be used as a name.) Julian of Norwich and Margery Kempe of course provide two contemporaneous counterarguments – proof that women in late medieval England did produce transformative religious writing, despite obvious prejudice.

160. Cf. 'Epistle of Cupid', line 179.

161–76. Hoccleve uses a legal metaphor, saying one's rightfully inherited title should not be called into question – so it is with the inheritors of orthodox Christianity: we have inherited our fathers' version of Christianity, and need to preserve it with all our might. On the notion of Christianity as an inheritance, see Acts 20:32; 1 Peter 1:4; Hebrews 9:15. As in 'Epistle of Cupid', Hoccleve's training as a bureaucrat (who creates official royal/legal documents for a living) is on display here.

20 TO SIR JOHN OLDCASTLE

Therto. Let vs no ferthere° ymagyne   *further*
But° as þat they dide, occupie° our right,   *than, take control of*
175 And in oure hertes fully determyne
Our title good, and keepe it with our might.

Whoso hath right and nat wole it deffende°,   *won't defend it*
It is no manhode – it is cowardyse.
And, as in this cas, he shal God offende
180 So greuously þat he shal nat souffyse°   *shall not be able*
The maugree for to bere° in no wyse°.   *to bear the wrath (of God), way*
Fro Cryst þat right first greew, and if þat we
Nat shuln susteene° it, we been ful vnwyse.   *shall not sustain*
Himself° is feith, right, trouthe, and al bontee°.   *He himself (i.e., Christ), goodness*

185 The Cristen Emperour Justinian,
As it is writen, whoso list it see°,   *wishes to see it*
Made a lawe deffendyng euery man,
Of what condicion or what degree°   *of whichever status or rank*
Þat he were of, nat sholde hardy° be   *bold*
190 For to despute of the feith openly;
And therevpon sundry peynes° sette he,   *various punishments*
Þat° peril sholde eschued be° therby.   *so that that, be avoided*

Bewar, Oldcastel, and for Crystes sake
Clymbe no more in holy writ so hie°.   *high*
195 Rede the storie of Lancelot de Lake,
Or Vegece°, Of the Art of Chiualrie,   *Vegetius*
The Seege° of Troie or Thebes. Thee applie°   *Siege, apply yourself*

Lege Nemo. 'Nemo Clericus vel militar[is] vel cuiuslibet alteri[us] condicionis de fide christiana publice turbis coadunatis e[t] audientibus tractar[e] conetur in posteru[m] ex hoc tumultus et perfidie occasionem requirens' etc. et ib[i] expressatur pena in huiusmodi causis exequendis.

182–3. Cf. lines 121–2. In both cases, Hoccleve highlights power given directly by Christ and passed down; preserving the status quo means preserving what was originally given by Christ.

184. Cf. John 6:35, 14:6.

185–92. gloss: *Lege Nemo.* 'No clergyman or member of the imperial service, or any person of any status, shall hereafter attempt to lecture on the Christian faith before crowds assembled to listen, thereby seeking to foment disorder and treachery' [Translation from Frier 2016: 19], etc., and there the punishment to be enforced in such cases as this is expressed.

    Taken from the beginning of Justinian's *Codex* (I. I. 4) – 'Marcian's imperial decree that neither the clergy nor the laity should debate the faith in public'. (Nuttall 2015: 10; Frier 2016: 18–19) Justinian was a sixth-century Byzantine emperor (cf. lines 433–40; 'Knights of the Garter', line 3). Hoccleve seems to use the decree here to suggest that Oldcastle should wish to follow the leader's example: he should refrain from disputing the faith openly. Archbishop Thomas Arundel's *Constitutions* (1407–9) put severe restrictions on unauthorized translation of Scripture, and unauthorized preaching – but Hoccleve notably does not mention that more recent example.

193–200. This section, in which Hoccleve recommends secular texts as a corrective balm, and as more suitable reading for a knight, has drawn much critical attention. See e.g., Nissé 1999: 294–5, Nall 2012: 1–2. The Arthurian legends of Lancelot du Lac are clearly correlated to chivalry, as was Vegetius's late fourth-century *De re militari*, which Ruth Nissé describes as a 'blunt how-to manual for winning a war with the Roman army' (1999: 295). Hoccleve uses it in his *Series* (see 2.561–2), where he suggests it as a work that Duke Humphrey might like to read. Both there and here it serves as metonymic of 'orthodox chivalry'. The 'Siege of Troy or Thebes' mentioned here is vague, and might refer to any number of texts related to the fall of Troy or siege of Thebes (such as

TO SIR JOHN OLDCASTLE 21

To thyng þat may to th'ordre of knyght longe°. (material) more fitting for a knight
To thy correccioun° now haaste and hie°, self-amendment, hasten
200 For thow haast been out of ioynt° al to longe. out of joint (straying)

If thee list° thyng rede of auctoritee°, wish to, (biblical) authority
To thise stories sit it° thee to goon: it is fitting
To Iudicum, Regum, and Iosue°, Judges, Kings, Joshua
To Iudith° and to Paralipomenon°, Judith, Chronicles
205 And Machabe°. And as sikir as stoon°, Maccabees, sure as stone
If þat thee list in hem bayte thyn ye°, feast your eye on them
More autentik° thyng shalt thow fynde noon true/authoritative
Ne° more pertinent to chiualrie°. nor, chivalry

Knyghtes so dide in tymes þat be past,
210 Whan they had tendrenesse of° hire° office. care for, their
In Crystes feith they stooden stidefast°. steadfast
And as þat the preest hir° soules norice°, their, nourished
Hem goostly fedde°, and yaf hem° the notice spiritually fed them, gave them
Of Crystes lore°, with obedience Christ's teachings
215 They° took it. But now regneth swich° malice i.e., knights, such
That buxumnesse° is put in abstinence°. obedience, on hold

O Constantyn°, thow prince of hy nobleye°, Constantine, high nobility
O Cristen emperour, whos worthynesse
Desdeyned nat to holy chirche obeye,
220 But didest al thy peyne and bisynesse° labor and hard work
With wel disposid spirit of meeknesse°, humility
The ministres of God for to honure,
How thow wroghtist hast thow so strong witnesse°, you've created such a strong model
That lyue it shal whil the world wole endure°. as long as the world lasts

---

Chaucer's own *Troilus and Criseyde*). Nissé offers Benoit de Ste.-Maure's *Roman de Troie* and *Roman de Thèbes*, suggesting that Hoccleve may be offering 'the cultural unity of France and England as an alternative to heresy' – noting the popularity of the prose *Lancelot*, and that Jean de Meun translated *De re militari* (1999: 294). Lydgate, author of the *Troy Book* and *Siege of Thebes*, can be seen to be self-positioning to cater to such literary tastes.

201–8. One of the more perplexing moments in the poem: after demanding that Oldcastle avoid reading 'holy writ' (line 194), Hoccleve then includes several books of the Bible in his 'recommended reading' list. It bears noting that these are all drawn from the Old Testament, perhaps indicating that they are far enough removed from the life of Christ to merit being read by the likes of Oldcastle. There is also a fair amount of action therein; so Hoccleve's note about them being pertinent to chivalry is not entirely disingenuous. See Nissé 1999: 295–8.

212–14. Cf. John 21:15.

TO SIR JOHN OLDCASTLE

225 Thow took nat on thee hir° correccioun,   *their*

Ne° vpon hem° thow yaf° no iugement,   *nor, them, gave*

Swich° was to God thy good affeccioun.   *such*

Thow seidest they been goddes to vs sent,

And þat it is nothyng conuenient°   *not at all appropriate*

230 That a man sholde goddes iuge° and deeme.   *judge*

Thow were a noble and a worthy regent°.   *ruler*

Wel was byset° on thee thy diadeeme°.   *bestowed, crown*

Blessid be God, fro whom deryued° is   *descended*

Al grace, our lige lord which þat is now

235 Our feithful Cristen prince and kyng°, in this   *i.e., Henry V*

Folwith thy steppes. O, for shame, thow

Oldcastel, thow haast longe tyme ynow°   *enough*

Folwed the feend°. Thogh thow° no lenger do,   *devil, although/even if you*

Do by my reed°: it shal be for thy prow° –   *follow my advice, benefit*

240 Flee fro the feend, folwe tho° princes two°.   *those, i.e., Constantine and Henry V*

Reward had and consideracioun°   *pay attention and consider*

Vnto the dignitees of tho° persones.   *those*

Thow art of a scars° reputacioun.   *slight*

A froward° herte haast thow, for the nones°.   *unruly/deviant, indeed*

245 Bowe and correcte thee. Come of at ones°!   *come on now*

Foule haast thow lost thy tyme° many a day.   *wasted your time*

For thyn vnfeith° men maken many mones°.   *lack of faith, are distraught*

To God retourne, and with his feith dwelle ay°.   *always*

Thogh God thee haue souffrid regne a whyle,

250 Be nat too° bold. Bewar of his vengeance.   *too*

He tarieth for° thow sholdist reconsyle   *delays (retribution) so that*

Thee to him, and leue thy mescreaunce.

Holsum° to thee now were a variaunce°   *advisable, change of course*

Fro the feend to our lord God, and fro vice

[right margin gloss, 225–32:] De admirabili honore quem Constantinus Imperator exhibuit ecclesie Ministris ita scribitur, 'Deus vos constituit sacerdotes, et potestatem dedit vobis iudicandi et ideo nos a vobis iudicamur; vos autem non potestis ab hominibus iudicari', etc.

225–32. gloss: Of the wonderful honor that the emperor Constantine showed to the ministers of the church, it is written thus, 'God made you priests and gave you power to judge, and so too we are judged by you; you however cannot be judged by men', etc. [Translation by Jane Griffiths/ Ruen-chuan Ma] Hoccleve's source here is Rufinus's continuation (402 AD) of Eusebius's *Historia ecclesiastica* (Book 10, Chapter 2). (Nuttall 2015: 10; Schwartz and Mommsen 1999: 961) Constantine was a fourth-century Roman emperor (d. 337), the first Roman emperor to convert to Christianity. Cf. 'Knights of the Garter', line 10.

228–30. One reading of these lines would be: 'You [Constantine] said they [ministers, line 222] were God's, sent to us, / And that it's not at all appropriate / That a man should judge what is God's.' The fact that 'goddes' can mean either 'God's' or 'gods' adds a complication, however: the lines can also mean: 'You said they were gods, sent to us, / And that it's not at all appropriate / That a man should judge gods.'

234–6. Immediately after gesturing towards Constantine as an emperor capable of being respectful of sacerdotal authority, Hoccleve gives thanks that Henry V follows in Constantine's footsteps. For the notion that Hoccleve is speaking to the king on behalf of the church (rather than acting as a spokesman for the Lancastrian regime), see Nuttall 2015: 10–11.

TO SIR JOHN OLDCASTLE   23

255 Vnto vertu. Þat wereº his hy plesaunceº,   would be, great pleasure
And his modres, mankyndes mediatriceº.   mankind's mediator (i.e., Virgin Mary)

Some of thy fetheres weren plukkid late,
And mo shuln beº. Thow shalt it nat asterteº.   more shall be, not stop it
Thow art nat wys ageynº God to debate.   against
260 The flood of pryde caste out of thyn herte.
Grace is alyue – to God thee conuerte!
Thow maist been his, if thee list him obeieº.   desire to obey him
If thow nat wilt so, sorrerº shalt thow smerteº   sorer, be pained
Than herte of man may thynke, or tonge seye.

265 Almighty God, thow lord of al, and syreº,   father
Withouten whom is no goodnesse wroghtº,   made
This knyght of thyn habundant grace enspyre.
Remembre how deere þat thow haast him boght.
He is thyn handwerkº, lord – refuse him noght.   handiwork
270 Thogh he thee haue agilt outrageouslyº,   he has sinned (against) you excessively
Thow, þat for mercy deidestº, change his thoght.   died
Benigne lord, enable him to mercy.

YEE þat peruerted him – yee folk dampnableº,   damnable
Yee heretikes þat han him betrayed
275 That manly was, worthy and honurable,
Or þatº he hadde of your venym assayedº –   before, tasted
I doute it nat your wages shal be payedº   you will be repaid (punished)
Sharply, butº yee correcte your trespas.   unless
In your fals errour, shul yee been outrayedº   overcome
280 And been enhabited with Sathanasº.   Satan

Yee, with your sly colouredº argumentes   deceitful
Which þat contenenº nothyng but falshode,   contain
Han on this knyght put so feendly ententesº   such diabolical ideas
Þat he is ouerchargedº with the lodeº   overburdened, load
285 Which yee han leid on his good old knygthode,
That now a wrecchid knyght men calle may.
The lak of feith hath qwenchidº his manhode.   destroyed
His force ageynº God naght is at assayº.   against, is nothing at all

'Prynce of preestes' our lige lord yee calle
290 In scorn, but it is a styleº of honour.   title

---

264. Cf. 1 Corinthians 2:9.
265–6. Cf. John 15:5; Romans 7:18.
268. Cf. 1 Corinthians 6:20; 7:23.
269–72. Cf. Job 14:15; Isaiah 45:9, 11–12; Galatians 1:4.
273. Hoccleve uses a large initial to set off this stanza, marking a new section. Hoccleve's address pivots here from 'thow' (Oldcastle) to 'yee', as he addresses Lollards more broadly, as a group.
289–96. See 1 Peter 5:1–5. This title – prince of priests (line 289) – was apparently used by Lollards against Henry V, to suggest he was overly accommodating of priests.

24   TO SIR JOHN OLDCASTLE

Auctoritee of preest excedith alle
Eerthely powers, thogh it seeme sour
To the taast of your detestable errour.
They þat in the feith been constaunt and sad°   steadfast
295   In Seint Petres wordes han good fauour,
And fayn been° to fulfille þat he bad°.   are happy/willing, what he bade

Alle eerthely princes and othir men
Bisshops to obeie commandid he.
Yee han no ground to holde ther ayen°.   against
300   Spirituel thynges passe° in dignitee   surpass
Alle the thynges temporel° þat be,   temporal/worldly
As moche as dooth the soule the body.
In the scriptures serche and yee shul see
Þat it no lees° at al is, hardily°.   lie, indeed

305   Two lightes God made in the firmament
Of heuene – a more made he, and a lesse°.   a greater and a lesser
The gretter light to the day hath he lent°   granted
It for to serue in his cleer brightnesse.
The smaller to the nyght, in soothfastnesse°,   in truth
310   He lente also, to helpe it with his light.
Two dignitees they toknen° in liknesse: symbolize
Auctoritee papal°, and kynges might.   papal authority

Looke how moche and how greet dyuersitee°   a difference
Betwixt the sonne ther is and the moone.
315   So moche is a popes auctoritee
Aboue a kynges might. Good is to doone
Þat yee aryse out of your errour soone
Þat therein walwid han°, goon is ful yore°.   have wallowed, recently
And but yee do, God I byseeche a boone°   I say a prayer to God
320   Þat in the fyr yee feele may the sore°.   pain

Yee þat nat sette by° preestes power   you that don't value
'Crystes rebels and foos' men may yow calle.
Yee waden in presumpcioun to fer°.   overconfidence too far
Your soules to the feend yee foule thralle°.   sinfully submit
325   Yee seyn, 'A preest in deedly synne falle°,   who has fallen into deadly sin
If he so go to messe°, he may nat make   mass
Crystes body°.' Falsly yee erren° alle   i.e., transubstantiate the host, err
Þat holden so. To° deepe yee ransake°.   too, probe/inquire

300–4. Cf. James 1:17; John 3:31; 2 Corinthians 4:17–18.
305–6. That is, he made a sun and a moon. See Genesis 1:16–18.
311–12. That is, papal authority should be understood as the sun; whereas regal (kingly) authority is moon-like, lesser.
324–7. Lollards questioned the efficacy of a sinful priest, with some arguing that a sinful priest did not have the power to 'make' Christ's body – to effect transubstantiation, whereby the communion bread is transformed into Christ's living body.

                                                    TO SIR JOHN OLDCASTLE   25

As wel may a preest þat is vicious°   an immoral priest can just as well
330 Þat precious body° make day by day   i.e., Christ's body (in the Eucharist)
As may a preest þat is ful vertuous,
But waar° the preest his soule it hurte may   be aware that
And shal, but he be cleene, it is no nay°.   there is no doubt
Be what he be, the preest is instrument
335 Of God, thurgh whos wordes – trustith this ay° –   always
The preest makith the blessid sacrament.

Yee medle of al thyng, yee moot shoo the goos°.   you're wasting your time (lit. putting shoes on a goose)
How knowen yee what lyf° a man is ynne?   what manner of life
Your fals conceites° renne aboute loos°.   false ideas, run amok
340 If a preest synful be and fro God twynne°,   depart
Thurgh penitence he may ageyn God wynne°.   return to God
No wight may cleerly knowen it or gesse
Þat any preest, beynge in deedly synne,
For awe of God dar° to the messe him dresse°.   dare, perform mass

345 Yee seyn also, 'Ther sholde be no pope,
But° he the beste preest were vpon lyue°.'   unless, alive
O wherto graspen yee so fer° and grope   far
Aftir swich° thyng? Yee mowe it neuere dryue   such
To the knowleche°. Nothyng thereof stryue.   i.e., never find the answer
350 Medle nat therwith. Let al swich thyng passe,
For if þat° yee do, shul yee neuere thryue.   for unless
Yee been therin as lewde as is an asse°.   as dumb as an ass

Many man outward° seemeth wondir° good,   outwardly, extraordinarily
And inward is he wondir fer° therfro.   extraordinarily far
355 No man be iuge° of þat, but he be wood°.   judge, unless he's crazy
To God longith° þat knowleche and no mo°.   belongs, and no others
Thogh he be right synful, sooth is also°   it is also true
The hy power þat is to him committid
As large as Petres is, it is right so.
360 Amonges feithful folk, this is admittid.

What is the lawe the werse° of nature°   worse, in itself
If þat a iuge vse it nat aright°?   if a judge misuses it
Nothyng°, God woot°. Auyse him þat the cure   not at all (worse), knows
Therof hath take, looke he do but right.
365 Waar° þat he nat stonde in his owne light.   be aware
Good is þat he his soule keepe and saue.
Your fals conceites puttith to the flight,
I rede°, and Crystes mercy axe and haue.   advise

353–6. Cf. 1 Kings 16:7; 3 Kings 8:39.
357–9. 'Even if he is truly sinful, it is still true that the power vested in him (by God) is just as strong as that of St. Peter.'
361–3a. 'In what way is a law (in itself) worse when a judge misuses it? It isn't, God knows.'

26 TO SIR JOHN OLDCASTLE

Yee, þat pretenden folwers for to be
370 Of Crystes disciples, nat lyue sholde
Aftir the flesshly lustes, as doon yee,
Þat rekken° nat whos wyf yee take and holde.   *care*
Swich° lyf the disciples nat lyue wolde,   *such*
For cursid is the synne of aduoutrie°.   *adultery*
375 But yee therin so hardy° been and bolde,   *daring*
Þat yee no synne it holden ne folie°.   *nor foolishness*

If yee so holy been as yee witnesse°   *attest*
Of yourself, thanne in Crystes feith abyde.
The disciples of Cryst had hardynesse°   *courage*
380 For to appeere; they nat wolde hem hyde°   *hide themselves*
For fere of deeth, but in his cause dyde°.   *died in his name*
They fledden nat to halkes ne to hernes°,   *to nooks nor to corners*
As yee doon, þat holden the feendes syde,
Whiche arn of dirknesse the lanternes.

385 Ne° neuere they in forcible maneere   *nor*
With wepnes roos° to slee folk and assaille,   *weapons rose*
As yee diden late° in this contree heere,   *recently*
Ageyn° the kyng stryf to rere° and bataille°.   *against, to raise strife, battle*
Blessid be God, of your purpos yee faille
390 And faille shuln°; yee shuln nat foorth° therwith.   *will continue to fail, advance*
Yee broken meynee°, yee wrecchid rascaille°,   *you fractured multitude, rascal*
Been al to weyk° – yee han therto no pith°.   *too weak, strength*

Also yee holden ageyn° pilgrimages –   *argue against*
Whiche arn ful goode if þat folk wel hem vse° –   *if people use them well*
395 And eek° ageyns the makyng of ymages°.   *also, i.e., religious icons*

369–76. Cf. Romans 2:22.

379–80. For evidence of such 'hardynesse', see, e.g., Acts 5:40–2. But Christ's followers did indeed flee or hide at times to avoid danger: see, e.g., Acts 14:5–6; Matthew 26:56; Mark 14:50; John 19:38, 20:19.

382. 'halkes ne to hernes': cf. 'Franklin's Tale', line 1121; 'Canon Yeoman's Prologue', line 658.

384. A possible pun on (and inversion of) *Lanterne of Light*, a Lollard text written just prior to 'Oldcastle' (c. 1409–15). The book was found among the possessions of John Claydon, a London currier who was executed for heresy in September 1415.

385–8. The violent incident in question was the unsuccessful St Giles' Fields uprising, January 1414.

391. Possibly a dual address to Lollards in general ('meynee') and Oldcastle specifically ('rascaille').

393–5. The Bible does note instances of pilgrimage (to Jerusalem), without recommending it explicitly for followers (e.g., Luke 2:41–2). On the biblical admonition against making graven images, see the second commandment: Exodus 20:4–5.

TO SIR JOHN OLDCASTLE 27

What, al is nat worth° þat yee clappe and muse°. — it's all worthless, chatter and brood over
How can yee by reson yourself excuse
Þat yee nat erren, whan yee folk excite° — move people
To vice, and stire hem° vertu to refuse? — encourage them
400 Waar° Goddes strook: it peisith nat a lyte°. — beware, it isn't a light blow

For to visite seintes° is vertu° — visiting saints, virtuous
If þat it doon be° for deuocioun, — is done
And elles good is be therof eschu°. — otherwise it's good to avoid it
Meede° wirkith in good entencioun. — (spiritual) reward
405 Be cleene of lyf and be in orisoun°. — prayerful
Of synne talke nat in thy viage°. — speak not of sin on your journey
Let vertu gyde thee fro toun to toun.
And so to man profitith pilgrimage°. — pilgrimage benefits man

And to holde ageyn° ymages makynge, — against
410 Be they maad in entaille or in peynture°, — in sculpture or painted
Is greet errour, for they yeuen stirynge° — inspire
Of thoghtes goode, and causen men° honure — compel men to
The seint aftir whom maad is that figure,
And nat worsshipe it, how gay° it be wroght°. — (no matter) how beautifully, made
415 For this knowith wel euery creature
Þat reson hath: þat a seint is it noght°. — that it isn't (itself) a saint

Right° as a spectacle° helpith feeble° sighte — just, an eyeglass, weak
Whan a man on the book redith or writ°, — reads or writes
And causith him to see bet° than he mighte, — better
420 In which spectacle his sighte nat abit°, — doesn't stop
But gooth thurgh, and on the book restith it,
The same may men of ymages seye:
Thogh the ymage nat the seint be°, yit — the image isn't the saint
The sighte vs myngith to the seint to preye°. — reminds us to pray to the saint

425 Ageyn° possessions yee holden eek° — against, you argue also
Of holy chirche, and that is eek errour.
Your inward ye° is ful of smoke and reek°. — inner eye, fumes
While heere on eerthe was our sauueour,
Whom angels diden seruice and honour,
430 Purses had he – why? For his chirche sholde
So haue° eek aftir, as seith myn auctour°. — have (money), author/scriptural authority
Yee goon al mis; al is wrong þat yee holde.

417–24. Hoccleve uses a spectacle metaphor to argue in favor of the use of icons: as a spectacle sharpens one's sight (of a book), but is not an end in itself, only a medium passed through, so too is an icon a medium through which the spiritual sight passes, reminding the person to pray to a given saint.
425–6. That is, you argue against possessions held by the church.
430. There is biblical support for the idea that Jesus had a purse – indeed, it was kept by Judas: see John 12:4–6, 13:26–9.

28 TO SIR JOHN OLDCASTLE

Iustinian Emperour had swich cheertee°   *such charity*
To holy chirche, as þat seith the scripture,
435 Þat of goodes how large or greet plentee°   *abundance*
It hadde of yifte° of any creature°,   *gift, person*
Him thoghte it youe° in the beste mesure°   *given, best amount*
Þat mighte been, his herte it loued so.
Yee neuere yaf hem° good, par auenture.   *gave them*
440 What title° han yee aght for to take hem fro°?   *right, to take anything from them*

And if yee had aght youe hem or° this tyme,   *given them something before*
Standynge in the feith as yee oghten stonde,
Sholden they now for your change and your cryme
Despoillid been° of þat they haue in honde?   *be deprived*
445 Nay, þat no skile is°. Yee shul vndirstonde,   *that isn't logical*
They nyght and day labouren in prayeere
For hem° þat so yaf°. Styntith° and nat fonde°   *those, gave, cease, don't attempt*
To do so, for first boght wole it be deere°.   *dearly*

Presumpcion° of wit and ydilnesse°   *arrogance, sloth*
450 And couetyse° of good, tho° vices three,   *greediness, those*
Been cause of al your ydil bysynesse°.   *futile/idle activity*
Yee seyn eek°, 'Goodes commune oghten be°.'   *also, ought to be shared*
Þat ment is° in tyme of necessitee°,   *is meant, (inescapable) necessity*
But nat by violence or by maistrie°   *force*
455 My good to take of me, or I of thee,
For þat is verray wrong and robberie.

If þat a man the soothe° telle shal   *truth*
How þat your hertes in this cas been set,
For to ryfle° is your entente final°.   *steal, ultimate goal*
460 Yee han be° bisy longe aboute a net°,   *have been, i.e., fishing net*
And fayn wolde han it in the watir wet
The fissh to take, which yee han purposid°,   *had intended (to do)*
But God and our lord lige hath yow let°;   *prevented*
It nis ne shal been° as yee han supposid.   *it wasn't nor will be*

465 Men seyn yee purpose° hastily appeere   *plan to*
The worm for to sleen in the pesecod°.   *to slay the worm in the peapod*

---

433. Hoccleve's second mention of Justinian as an exemplary leader, especially charitable to the church. See lines 185–92. Cf. 'Knights of the Garter', line 3.

452–6. Cf. Acts 4:32; Exodus 20:15. Hoccleve responds to the idea that goods should be held in common: this should be done only when totally necessary; otherwise, taking what is not yours is theft.

465–6. Possibly referring to rumors of another imminent attack.

TO SIR JOHN OLDCASTLE 29

Come on whan yow list°; yee shul reewe° it deere.
The feend° is your cheef°, and oure heed is God.
Thogh we had in oure handes but a clod
470 Of eerthe at your heedes to slynge or caste,
Were wepne ynow°, or a smal twig or rod,
The feith of Cryst stikith in vs so faste°.

We dreden° nat, we han greet auantage°
Whethir we lyue or elles° slayn be we
475 In Crystes feith, for vp to heuenes stage°,
If we so die, our soules lift shul be;
And on þat othir part yee feendes, yee,
In the dirk halke° of helle shul descende.
And yit with vs abit° this charitee:
480 Our desir is þat yee yow wolde amende°.

Yee holden many anothir errour mo°
Than may be writen in a litil space,
But lak of leisir° me commandith ho.
Almighty God byseeche I of his grace
485 Enable yow to seen his blessid face,
Which þat is o° God, and persones three°.
Remembre yow: heuene is a miry° place,
And helle is ful of sharp aduersitee.

Yit, Oldcastel, for him þat his blood shadde°
490 Vpon the crois, to his feith torne agayn°.
Forgete nat the loue he to vs hadde –
Þat blisful lord þat for alle vs was slayn.
From hennesforward trouble nat thy brayn,
As thow hast doon ageyn° the feith ful sore°.
495 Cryst of thy soule glad be wolde and fayn°;
Retourne knyghtly now vnto his lore°.

Repente thee, and with him make accord.
Conquere meryt and honour. Let see –
Looke how our Cristen prince°, our lige lord,
500 With many a lord and knyght beyond the see°,
Laboure in armes°. And thow hydest thee
And darst nat come and shewe thy visage°.
O fy, for shame. How can a knyght be
Out of th'onur° of this rial viage°?

come when you like, regret
devil, leader

it would be weapon enough
is set so firmly in us

fear, advantage
else
heaven

dark recesses
remains
change (reform yourself)

many other errors

lack of time

one, the Trinity
blissful

who shed his blood (i.e., Christ)
return to his faith

against, grievously
joyful
teachings/guidance

Henry V
sea (in France)
wage war
show your face

the honor, royal expedition

469–72. 'Even if we only had a clod of dirt, or mere twigs, that would be weaponry enough, because the faith of Christ is set so firmly in us that we will prevail.'

473–6. Cf. Philippians 1:21–3.

499–501. These lines suggest that Henry is already fighting in France, not awaiting departure from England as the poem's heading indicates. Seymour suggests that the second part of the poem (or the whole poem) may have been written 'after Henry's arrival in Normandy [...] on 13 August' (129).

30 TO SIR JOHN OLDCASTLE

505 Sum tyme° was no knyghtly turn° nowhere,
Ne° no manhode shewid in no wyse°,
But° Oldcastel wolde, his thankes°, be there.
How hath the cursid feend changid thy gyse°!
Flee from him, and alle his wirkes° despyse.
510 And þat ydoon°, vnto our Cristen kyng
Thee hie° as faste as þat thow canst dyuyse°,
And humble eek thee to him for anythyng.

C'est tout.

at one time, expedition
nor, way
except that, willingly
your manner
acts
done
hurry, devise

---

505. 'Sum tyme'. Hoccleve ends by gesturing to Oldcastle's illustrious history as a knight, and by summoning to mind legends of his manhood. It harkens back to the early years of Henry IV's reign, when Prince Henry and Oldcastle fought alongside each other against the Welsh. (Epstein 2002: 24)

LA MALE REGLE

Date: late 1405–March 1406

❧

'La Male Regle' is Hoccleve's earliest attempt at absorbing his autobiographical persona into one of his poems. The *Regiment of Princes* (c. 1410–11) and the *Series* (c. 1419–26) see this persona developed further, but in 'Male Regle' 'Hoccleve' is at his most youthful, playful, and sociable. This poem proves intrepid not only for its accomplishments in the context of his other poems, but also for its place in the development of English literature: Hoccleve is seizing on the type of pseudo-autobiographical narrator we see, for instance, in Chaucer's *House of Fame*, and imbuing it further with the fully fleshed-out details of his own life: his drinking haunts, his social life, the very itinerary of his walks home, his friends in Westminster (both in and beyond the Privy Seal). It all glints with the contours of classical myth – to the extent that his ramblings evoke the odyssey of Ulysses, and the pub sign shines with the lure of Bacchus.

The poem itself is hard to classify. It is true that it ends with a request for money, but to call the poem as a whole petitionary verse would seem delimiting. It is, no doubt, a very early entry into what we might now class as a genre of 'autobiography' – or, more accurately, autofiction; but that comes with the caveat that those terms are necessarily anachronistic. The sole other witness to 'Male Regle', found in the Canterbury Cathedral archives (Register O), gives some indication of how it may have been received by Hoccleve's contemporaries. That version preserves the moral lesson at the heart of the poem – an illustration of temperance and moderation, spoken in the voice of one who has lived long enough, and experienced enough, to *know*. Interestingly, the London particulars – and the particulars of Hoccleve's own life and person – are edited down considerably, allowing the moral message itself to be distilled. (For more discussion, see General Introduction, and note to lines 351–2, below.) This points towards what Hoccleve achieves in the poem: the moral message is not secondary nor is it incidental: Hoccleve is placing himself at the center, and mining the details of his own life (however embellished) in order to exact moral meaning and inspire others to virtue. In this respect, this poem sets the tone for his very similar experiments in the *Regiment* and the *Series*.

It should also be noted that the London/Westminster environs at the heart of 'Male Regle' function almost as a main character in their own right: one would be hard pressed to find another late-medieval poem in which one feels so fully immersed in the daily flow of London life.

On the poem's date (late 1405–March 1406), see note to lines 423–4, below.

32 LA MALE REGLE

LA MALE REGLE

Cy ensuyt la male regle de T. Hoccleue

O precious tresor° inconparable, — *treasure*
O ground and roote of prosperitee,
O excellent richesse° commendable, — *splendor*
Abouen alle þat in eerthe° be, — *on earth*
5 Who may susteene thyn aduersitee°? — *opposition*
What wight° may him auante° of worldly welthe — *person, boast*
But if° he fully stande in grace of thee, — *unless*
Eerthely god, piler° of lyf, thow Helthe? — *pillar (supporter)*

Whil thy power and excellent vigour°, — *strength*
10 As was plesant vnto thy worthynesse,
Regned in me, and was my gouernour,
Than was I wel, tho° felte I no duresse°. — *then, distress*
Tho farsid° was I with hertes gladnesse, — *then stuffed*
And now my body empty is, and bare
15 Of ioie°, and ful of seekly° heuynesse, — *joy, sickly*
Al poore of ese and ryche of euel fare.

If þat thy fauour twynne° from a wight, — *departs*
Smal is his ese and greet is his greuance.
Thy loue is lyf. Thyn hate sleeth° doun right. — *slays*
20 Who may conpleyne thy disseuerance° — *about your departure*
Bettre than I, þat of myn ignorance
Vnto seeknesse am knyt, thy mortel fo?
Now can I knowe feeste° fro penaunce, — *feast*
And whil I was with thee, kowde I nat so.

25 My grief and bisy smert° cotidian° — *intense pain, daily*
So me labouren and tormenten sore
Þat what thow art now wel remembre I can,
And what fruyt° is in keepynge of thy lore°. — *benefit, lessons*
Had I thy power knowen or this yore°, — *long ago*
30 As now thy fo conpellith° me to knowe, — *compels*
Nat sholde his lym° han cleued° to my gore°, — *lime, have stuck, clothing*
For al his aart°, ne° han me broght thus lowe. — *cunning, nor*

But I haue herd men seye longe ago,
Prosperitee is blynd and see ne may,

Heading: Here follows the unruly life of T. Hoccleve

1–8. Hoccleve employs the 'delayed signified' here, whereby lines 1–7 tease a supreme recipient – perhaps God or Christ – and line 8 playfully resolves the ambiguity: the object of address is the less august, less overtly Christian 'earthly god', Health. Cf. Hoccleve's build-up to revealing Chaucer as 'firste fyndere of our fair langage' in the *Regiment*, lines 4978–84.

14–15. 'bare / Of ioie': cf. 'Complaint Paramount', line 40: 'Of ioye am I bareyne'.

LA MALE REGLE   33

35 And verifie I can wel it is so,
     For I myself put haue it in assay°.   to the test
     Whan I was weel°, kowde I considere it? Nay,   well/healthy
     But what me longed aftir nouelrie°,   I longed after novelty
     As yeeres yonge yernen° day by day,   as younger people yearn
40 And now my smert accusith my folie°.   my pain reveals my folly

     Myn vnwar° yowthe kneew nat what it wroghte°,   careless, did
     This woot I wel°, whan fro thee twynned° shee.   I know well, departed
     But of hire ignorance hirself shee soghte°   she considered herself (alone)
     And kneew nat þat shee dwellyng was with thee,
45 For to a wight° were it greet nycetee°   person, foolishness
     His lord or freend wityngly for t'offende,
     Lest þat the weighte of his aduersitee
     The fool oppresse° and make of him an ende.   overpowers

     From hennesfoorth wole I do reuerence
50 Vnto thy name and holde of thee in cheef,
     And werre° make and sharp resistence   war
     Ageyn° thy fo and myn, þat cruel theef,   against
     Þat vndir foote me halt° in mescheef,   holds
     So° thow me to thy grace reconcyle.   so that
55 O now thyn help, thy socour and releef,
     And I for ay° misreule° wole exyle.   forever, disorderly living

     But° thy mercy excede myn offense,   unless
     The keene assautes° of thyn aduersarie   fierce attacks
     Me wole oppresse with hir° violence.   their
60 No wondir thogh thow° be to me contrarie: no wonder though that you
     My lustes blynde han causid thee to varie
     Fro me thurgh my folie and inprudence,
     Wherfore I, wrecche, curse may and warie°   damn
     The seed and fruyt of chyldly sapience°.   unripened wisdom

65 As for the more paart, youthe is rebel
     Vnto reson, and hatith hir doctryne,
     Regnynge which, it may nat stande wel
     With yowthe, as fer as wit can ymagyne.
     O yowthe, allas, why wilt thow nat enclyne,
70 And vnto reuled resoun bowe thee,
     Syn° resoun is the verray streighte lyne   since
     Þat ledith folk vnto felicitee°.   happiness

37–40. The tone of the 'Hoccleve' speaker – who only knows well-being because he has fallen into its
antithesis – resembles the 'Hoccleve' of the *Series*: a voice arriving after the crash and looking back,
gaining perspective in retrospect.

57–9. Cf. Psalms 24:7; Ephesians 6:16.

71–2. Cf. The 'Complaint' (*Series*) where the figure of Reason in the borrowed text (Isidore of Seville's
Synonyma) leads Thomas from dejection to relief: 1.309–71.

34 LA MALE REGLE

Ful seelde° is seen þat yowthe takith heede — seldom
Of perils þat been likly for to falle°, — occur
75 For haue he° take a purpos, þat moot neede° — once he has, must needs
Been execut. No conseil wole he calle.
His owne wit he deemeth best of alle,
And foorth therwith he renneth brydillees°, — runs without a guide
As he þat nat betwixt hony° and galle° — honey, gall (sweet vs. bitter)
80 Can iuge°, ne° the werre° fro the pees°. — judge, nor, war, peace

Alle othir mennes wittes he despisith.
They answeren nothyng to his entente°. — don't correspond with his understanding
His rakil° wit only to him souffysith°. — impetuous, suffices
His hy presumpcioun nat list° consente — deigns not
85 To doon as þat Salomon wroot and mente,
Þat redde° men by conseil for to werke. — who advised
Now, youthe, now thow sore shalt repente
Thy lightlees wittes dulle, of reson derke.

My freendes seiden vnto me ful ofte
90 My misreule° me cause wolde a fit, — disorderly living
And redden° me in esy wyse° and softe° — advised, way, gently
A lyte and lyte° to withdrawen it – — bit by bit
But þat nat mighte synke into my wit,
So was the lust yrootid in myn herte.
95 And now I am so rype vnto my pit° — so near death
Þat scarsely I may it nat asterte°. — escape

Whoso cleer yen° hath, and can nat see, — eyes/vision
Ful smal of ye° auaillith the office°. — the eye, use
Right so°, syn° reson youen° is to me — similarly, since, given
100 For to discerne a vertu from a vice,
If I nat can with resoun me cheuice°, — conduct myself
But wilfully fro reson me withdrawe,
Thogh° I of hire° haue no benefice°, — that, her, receive no kindness
No wondir, ne° no fauour in hir lawe. — nor

105 Reson me bad and redde° as for the beste, — advised
To ete and drynke in tyme attemprely°, — temperately
But wilful youthe nat obeie leste° — does not like to obey
Vnto þat reed°, ne sette nat° therby. — advice, nor value it
I take haue of hem° bothe outrageously° — them, excessively
110 And out of tyme°. Nat two yeer or three, — at inappropriate times

---

77–80. Cf. Isaiah 5:20.

84–6. The need to take counsel is prevalent in Proverbs: see Proverbs 3:21, 13:16, 19:20.

95–6. Unlike similar lines in the *Series*, written relatively close to Hoccleve's actual death, this type of 'approaching death' sentiment comes across as largely exaggerated, rhetorical.

97–8. 'Whoever has working eyes, but cannot see – little good are eyes to him.' The speaker is likening this to having been given reason (to discern virtue from vice), but not using it correctly.

106–7. Cf. Ecclesiasticus 31:32.

LA MALE REGLE   35

But xx^{tio} wyntir past continuelly, *twenty*
Excesse at borde° hath leyd his knyf° with me. *at the table, dined (colloq.)*

The custume° of my repleet abstinence°, *habit, abstaining only when full*
My greedy mowth, receite of swich outrage°, *receiver of such excess*
115 And hondes° two, as woot° my negligence, *hands, knows*
Thus han me gyded and broght in seruage° *brought (me) into the service*
Of hire° þat werreieth° euery age – *she, who attacks*
Seeknesse°, Y meene, riotoures whippe, *sickness*
Habundantly þat° paieth me my wage°, *who has abundantly, i.e., punished me*
120 So þat me neithir daunce list° ne skippe°. *wish to dance, nor skip*

The outward signe of Bachus° and his lure, *Bacchus*
Þat at his dore hangith day by day,
Excitith° folk to taaste of his moisture° *entices, refreshments*
So often þat men can nat wel seyn nay°. *say no*
125 For me, I seye I was enclyned ay° *always*
Withouten daunger° thidir for to hye° me *resistance, hasten*
But if° swich charge° vpon my bak lay *unless, such a burden*
That I moot it forbere° as for a tyme, *must forego it*

Or but° I were nakidly bystad° *unless, plainly overtaken*
130 By force of the penylees maladie°, *lack of money (as an illness)*
For thanne° in herte kowde I nat be glad, *then*
Ne° lust had noon to Bachus hows° to hie°. *nor, house, hasten*
Fy! Lak of coyn departith conpaignie°, *drives away company*
And heuy purs with herte liberal° *generous spirit*
135 Qwenchith° the thristy hete of hertes drie, *quenches*
Wher chynchy° herte hath therof but smal. *whereas a miserly*

I dar nat telle how þat the fressh repeir° *throng*
Of Venus femel lusty children° deere *Venus's pleasing young girls*
Þat so goodly, so shaply were, and feir°, *pretty*
140 And so plesant of port° and of maneere, *demeanor*
And feede cowden al a world with cheere,
And of atyr° passyngly wel byseye°, *apparel, dressed*
At Poules Heed° me maden° ofte appeere *Paul's Head, (they) made me*
To talke of mirthe and to disporte and pleye.

---

111. The 'Hoccleve' narrator claims to have eaten and drunken excessively for the last twenty years. If we equate 'Hoccleve' and a historical Hoccleve here, he would be talking about ages (roughly) 18–38.
121–2. Bacchus (equivalent to the Greek Dionysus) is the Roman god of wine and festivity. Seymour notes on the 'outward signe'/'lure': 'the long pole or ale-stake projecting above the door of a medieval tavern and surmounted by a "bush", a garland or bunch of evergreen' (107).
132. 'Bachus hows': the tavern.
133–136. Cf. Proverbs 19:4.
137–44. After mention of Bacchus (121, 132), Venus, the Roman goddess of love and beauty, makes an appearance: the beautiful women 'Hoccleve' would encounter at Paul's Head Tavern (line 143) are imagined as fair children of Venus. Seymour notes that Paul's Head 'stood on the east side of Paul's Wharf Hill, just south of the Cathedral and opposite Paul's bakehouse' (107).

36   LA MALE REGLE

145	Ther was sweet wyn° ynow° thurghout the hous	wine, enough
	And wafres thikke°, for this conpaignie	thick wafers
	Þat I spak of been sumwhat likerous°.	gluttonous
	Whereas° they mowe° a draght of wyn espie° –	wherever, might, see
	Sweete and in wirkynge hoot for the maistrie°	warming in its effects
150	To warme a stommak with – therof they drank.	
	To suffre hem° paie had been no courtesie°.	them, would not be courteous
	That charge I took°, to wynne loue and thank.	i.e., he paid the bill
	Of loues aart yit touchid I no deel°.	not at all
	I cowde nat, and eek° it was no neede.	also
155	Had I a kus°, I was content ful weel,	kiss
	Bettre than I wolde han be° with the deede°.	have been, i.e., sex
	Theron can I but smal°, it is no dreede°.	I know only a little, surely
	Whan þat men speke of it in my presence,	
	For shame I wexe as reed° as is the gleede°.	grew as red, a live coal
160	Now wole I torne ageyn to my sentence°.	story/lesson
	Of him þat hauntith tauerne of custume°,	frequents the tavern regularly
	At shorte wordes°, the profyt is this:	in short
	In double wyse° his bagge° it shal consume,	doubly, wallet
	And make his tonge speke of folk amis,	
165	For in the cuppe seelden° fownden is	seldom
	Þat any wight° his neigheburgh° commendith.	person, neighbor
	Beholde and see what auantage is his	
	Þat God, his freend, and eek° himself offendith.	also
	But oon auauntage° in this cas° I haue.	one advantage, situation
170	I was so ferd° with any man to fighte	afraid
	Cloos° kepte I me, no man durste I depraue°,	(that) quiet, dared I speak against
	But rownyngly° I spak, nothyng on highte°.	whisperingly, too loud
	And yit my wil was good, if þat I mighte°,	if I could
	For lettynge° of my manly cowardyse	save for the impediment
175	Þat ay of strokes° impressid the wighte°,	always for fear of blows, oppressed me
	So þat I durste medlen° in no wyse°.	dared not fight, way

145–50. There's a Eucharistic undertone to the sharing of wine and bread (or 'wafres'). See Matthew 26:26–9; cf. Proverbs 12:11, 23:20–1; Ecclesiasticus 19:2.

153. The persona's self-distancing from 'loues aart' is reminiscent of Chaucer's 'Geffrey' persona in *House of Fame*: cf. lines 620–8.

161–8. See Ecclesiasticus 31:38–42.

165–6. 'It is seldom found "in the cup" [i.e., when one has been drinking] that one compliments his neighbor'. That is, you are more likely to say the wrong thing when drinking.

167–8. 'What advantage is it to him to offend God, his friend, and himself?'

174–6. 'save for the impediment of my manly cowardice, which always made me freeze for fear of blows, so that I dared not fight under any circumstances.'

LA MALE REGLE 37

Wher was a gretter maistir eek° than Y? — *also*
Or bet aqweyntid° at Westmynstre yate°, — *better acquainted, Westminster gate*
Among the tauerneres namely
180 And cookes, whan I cam, eerly or late? — *wasn't stingy with them, purchases*
I pynchid nat at hem° in myn acate°, — *them, would ask*
But paied hem° as þat they axe wolde°, — *always*
Wherfore I was the welcomere algate°, — *true, held*
And for a verray° gentilman yholde°.

185 And if it happid on the someres° day — *summer's*
Þat I thus at the tauerne hadde be°, — *had been*
Whan I departe sholde and go my way
Hoom to the Priuee Seel°, so wowed° me — *home to the Privy Seal, courted (wooed)*
Hete and vnlust° and superfluitee° — *laziness, excess*
190 To walke vnto the brigge° and take a boot° — *bridge, boat*
Þat nat durste° I contrarie hem° alle three, — *dared, them*
But dide as þat they stired me, God woot°. — *knows*

And in the wyntir, for the way was deep,
Vnto the brigge° I dressid me° also, — *bridge, went*
195 And ther the bootmen took vpon me keep,
For they my riot° kneewen fern ago°. — *extravagance, long since*
With hem° I was itugged to and fro, — *them*
So wel° was him þat I with wolde fare°, — *happy, would travel with*
For riot° paieth largely° eueremo, — *extravagance, generously*
200 He styntith° neuere til his purs be bare. — *stops*

Othir than maistir callid was I neuere
Among this meynee° in myn audience. — *crowd (of boatmen)*
Me thoghte I was ymaad° a man foreuere, — *made*
So tikelid° me þar nyce reuerence — *delighted*
205 Þat it me made largere of despense° — *more generous*
Than þat I thoghte han been. O flaterie,
The guyse of thy traiterous diligence
Is folk to mescheef haasten and to hie.

Albeit° þat my yeeres be but yonge, — *although*
210 Yit haue I seen in folk of hy degree
How þat the venym of faueles° tonge — *flattery's*
Hath mortified hir° prosperitee — *destroyed their*
And broght hem° in so° sharp aduersitee — *them, such*
Þat it hir° lyf hath also throwe adoun. — *their*

---

188. 'Hoom to the Priuee Seel'. Hoccleve worked as a clerk in the Office of the Privy Seal. In situating 'home' at the Privy Seal, he may be referring to one of the inns – such as Chester's Inn (*Regiment*, line 5) – that housed clerks.
189–92. Heat, laziness, and excess all encouraged him to take a boat home – and he didn't want to contradict them, but instead did as they commanded.
201–2. The boatmen called him 'master' to flatter him (so he would pay them more).
206–8. Flattery hastens people into a state of misfortune. Cf. Proverbs 29:5.

38 LA MALE REGLE

215 And yit ther can no man in this contree
Vnnethe eschue° this confusioun.   hardly escape

Many a seruant vnto his lord seith
Þat al the world spekith of him honour,
Whan the contrarie of þat is sooth° in feith°,   true, in fact
220 And lightly leeued° is this losengeour°.   easily believed, flatterer
His hony° wordes, wrappid in errour°,   sweet, falseness
Blyndly conceyued° been, the more harm is°. believed, more harmful they are
O, thow fauele°, of lesynges auctour°,   flattery, author of lies
Causist al day thy lord to fare amis.

225 Tho combreworldes° clept° been enchantours   those trouble-makers, called
In bookes, as þat I haue or° this red –   before
That is to seye sotil° deceyuou[r]s,   cunning
By whom the peple is misgyed and led
And with plesance so fostred° and fed   nourished
230 Þat they forgete hemself° and can nat feele   themselves
The soothe° of the condicion in hem bred°,   truth, developed for them
No more than hir wit° were in hire° heele.   (if) their brains, their

Whoso þat list° in the book Of Nature   whoever wishes
Of Beestes rede, therin he may see,
235 If he take heede vnto the scripture°,   writing
Where it spekth° of meermaides in the see°,   speaks, sea
How þat so inly mirie° syngith shee   intensely pleasant
Þat the shipman therwith fallith asleepe
And by hire° aftir deuoured is he.   her
240 From al swich° song is good men hem to keepe°.   such, to guard themselves

Right so the feyned wordes of plesance
Annoyen aftir, thogh they plese a tyme,
To hem° þat been vnwyse of gouernance.   to those
Lordes, beeth waar: let nat fauel° yow lyme°.   flattery, ensnare
245 If þat yee been enuolupid° in cryme,   enveloped (wrapped)
Yee may nat deeme° men speke of yow weel.   judge (how)
Thogh° fauel peynte° hir tale in prose or ryme,   (even) though, spins
Ful holsum° is it trust hir nat a deel°.   truly advisable, not at all

Holcote seith vpon the book also
250 Of Sapience°, as it can testifie,   Wisdom
Whan þat Vlixes° saillid to and fro   Ulysses
By meermaides, this was his policie:

225–32. Cf. Ecclesiasticus 12:13–15; Psalms 57:4–6. Line 225, 'combreworldes': cf. *Regiment* line 2091. Likely drawn in both instances from *Troilus*, 4.279.

233–40. The book in question is believed to be Theobaldus, *Physiologus de naturis duodecim animalium*; see Seymour 108.

249–57. Likely referring to Robert Holcot's account of Ulysses and the sirens in *Super sapientiam Salomonis* (see Seymour 108).

LA MALE REGLE 39

	Alle eres° of men of his conpaignie°	ears, company
	With wex° he stoppe leet, for þat they noght	wax
255	Hir° song sholde heere, lest the armonye°	their, harmony
	Hem° mighte vnto swich° deedly sleep han broght,	them, such
	And bond° himself vnto the shippes mast.	tied
	Lo, thus hem alle saued his prudence°.	his prudence saved them all
	The wys man is of peril sore agast°.	truly afraid
260	O flaterie, O lurkyng pestilence!	
	If sum man dide his cure° and diligence	took care
	To stoppe his eres fro thy poesie,	
	And nat wolde herkne° a word of thy sentence°,	would not hear, remarks
	Vnto his greef it were° a remedie.	would be
265	A, nay. Althogh° thy tonge were ago°	even if, lost
	Yit canst thow glose° in contenance° and cheere°.	deceive, expression, behavior
	Thow supportist with lookes eueremo	
	Thy lordes wordes in eche mateere°,	on each subject
	Althogh þat they a myte be to deere°;	are worth little
270	And thus thy gyse is, priuee and appert°,	privately and openly
	With word and look among our lordes heere	
	Preferred be°, thogh ther be no dissert°.	to be preferred, it isn't deserved
	But whan the sobre, treewe, and weel auysid°,	prudent (person)
	With sad visage° his lord enfourmeth pleyn°	serious expression, explains plainly
275	How þat his gouernance is despysid	
	Among the peple, and seith him as they seyn,	
	As man treewe oghte° vnto his souereyn,	ought (to do)
	Conseillynge him amende° his gouernance,	(to) change
	The lordes herte swellith for desdeyn°	swells with hatred
280	And hir° him voide blyue° with meschance°.	commands, leave quickly, good riddance
	Men setten nat by° trouthe nowadayes.	care not about
	Men loue it nat. Men wole it nat cherice°.	cherish
	And yit is trouthe best at alle assayes°.	in all instances
	Whan þat fals fauel°, soustenour° of vice,	false flattery, sustainer
285	Nat wite shal° how hire to cheuyce°,	shall not know, to defend herself
	Ful boldely shal trouthe hire heed vp bere°.	raise up her head
	Lordes, lest fauel° yow fro wele tryce°,	flattery, take well-being from you
	No lenger souffre hire° nestlen in your ere°.	her, ear
	Be as be may, no more of this as now,	
290	But to my misreule° wole I refeere°,	disorderly living, return
	Wheras I was at ese weel ynow	
	Or° excesse vnto me leef° was and deere,	before, beloved
	And, or° I kneew his ernestful maneere,	before

273–80. When the honest man tells his lord (honestly) that he is despised among the people, and counsels him to change the way he governs, he is asked to leave at once.

My purs of coyn had resonable wone° –   use
295 But now therin can ther but scant appeere.
Excesse hath ny° exiled hem echone°.   nearly, each and every coin

The feend° and excesse been conuertible°,   devil, interchangeable
As enditith° to me my fantasie°.   dictates, imagination
This is my skile°, if it be admittible: reasoning
300 Excesse of mete and drynke is glotonye;
Glotonye awakith malencolie;
Malencolie engendrith werre° and stryf;   war
Stryf causith mortel° hurt thurgh hir folie.   deadly
Thus may excesse reue° a soule hir lyf.   deprive

305 No force° of al this. Go we now to wacche°   no matter, staying awake
By nyghtirtale° out of al mesure°,   at night, immoderately
For as in þat fynde kowde I no macche°   match
In al the Priuee Seel with me to endure –
And to the cuppe° ay° took I heede and cure°,   i.e., my drink, always, attention
310 For þat the drynke apalle° sholde noght.   grow stale
But whan the pot emptid was of moisture,
To wake aftirward cam nat in my thoght.

But whan the cuppe had thus my neede sped°,   satisfied
And sumdel more than necessitee,
315 With repleet° spirit wente I to my bed   sated
And bathid there in superfluitee°.   excess
But on the morn was wight of no degree°   (there) was no one of any kind
So looth° as I to twynne° fro my cowche°,   loath, depart, bed
By aght I woot°. Abyde° – let me see –   by anything I know, wait
320 Of two as looth°, I am seur° kowde I towche.   loath, sure

I dar nat seyn° Prentys and Arondel   dare not say
Me countrefete° and in swich wach° go ny° me,   copy me, such wakefulness, near
But often they hir° bed louen so wel   their
Þat of the day it drawith ny the pryme°   i.e., near 9 am
325 Or° they ryse vp. Nat telle I can the tyme   before

----

296. Excessive spending has exiled every coin (from his purse).

307–8. The suggestion is that his fellows in the Privy Seal were drinking companions – yet none so excessive as Hoccleve.

321. Ellis refers to these figures as 'younger colleagues'. However, Prentys and Arondel served not as scribes in the Privy Seal, but rather as clerks of the King's Chapel. Prentys was later appointed Dean of St. Stephen's, Westminster, in 1418; and Arondel became Dean of St. George's, Windsor, in 1419. (Nuttall 2007: 69) Hoccleve suggests they were as lively at night as he was, and so were equally reluctant to leave their beds in the morning.

324. 'Pryme' is the period between 6am and 9am. Since Hoccleve is accusing them of sleeping late, he is likely referring to them rising towards the end of the period. Cf. 'Squire's Tale', line 360: 'They slepen til that it was pryme large.'

Whan they to bedde goon; it is so late.
O Helthe, lord, thow seest hem° in þat cryme,   see them
And yit thee looth is° with hem° to debate.   you are loath, them

And why? I not°. It sit nat vnto me°,   I don't know, it isn't suitable for me
330 Þat mirour am of riot° and excesse°,   extravagance, intemperance
To knowen of a goddes pryuetee°,   a god's secrets
But thus I ymagyne and thus I gesse°:   guess
Thow meeued art°, of tendre gentillesse°,   are moved, graciousness
Hem to forbere°, and wilt hem° nat chastyse,   to endure them, them
335 For they in mirthe and vertuous gladnesse
Lordes reconforten° in sundry wyse°.   comfort, various ways

But to my purpos. Syn° þat my seeknesse°,   since, sickness
As wel of purs° as body, hath refreyned°   wallet, restrained
Me fro tauerne and othir wantonnesse,
340 Among an heep° my name is now desteyned°.   a group of people, sullied
My greuous hurt ful litil is conpleyned°,   lamented
But they the lak conpleyne of my despense°.   spending
Allas, þat euere knyt I was and cheyned°   chained
To excesse, or him dide obedience.

345 Despenses° large enhaunce a mannes loos°   expenses, reputation
Whil they endure, and whan they be forbore°   abstained from
His name is deed. Men keepe hir° mowthes cloos°,   their, closed
As° nat a peny had he spent tofore°.   as if, before
My thank° is qweynt°, my purs his stuf hath lore°,   regard, gone, has lost
350 And my carkeis° repleet with heuynesse°.   body, full of sorrow
Bewaar, Hoccleue, I rede° thee therfore,   advise
And to a mene reule° thow thee dresse°.   moderate lifestyle, direct yourself

Whoso passynge mesure desyrith°   desires excessively
(As þat witnessen olde clerkes wyse)
355 Himself encombrith oftensythe° and myrith°,   encumbers often, ensnares
And forthy° let the mene° thee souffyse.   therefore, moderation
If swich° a conceit° in thyn herte ryse   such, thought

329–31. Cf. 'Miller's Prologue', lines 3163–4: 'An housbonde shal nat been inquisityf / Of Goddes pryvetee, nor of his wyf'. Hoccleve's 'god' is of course the 'earthly god' Health, rather than God.

337–8. The personification of his purse, to the extent that purse and man alike can be 'sick', recalls Chaucer's 'Complaint to His Purse'. See also Hoccleve's 'Three Roundels'.

341–2. 'My pain is lamented but little, but they do lament how little I now spend.'

351–2. Cf. 393–4. One of three instances in the shorter poems in which Hoccleve names himself. For the others, see 'Balade and Roundel to Henry Somer' (line 25) and 'Three Roundels' (line 16). The self-address also resonates with Mary's meta-moment in 'Complaint Paramount', line 217 ('Poore Marie, thy wit is aweye'). The Canterbury Cathedral Archives version of 'Male Regle', the sole other witness, omits 'Hoccleue' from line 351. It amends it to: 'Bewar therfore y rede the the more'. The London-based autobiographical particulars of Hoccleve's poem are also shorn from the Canterbury version, perhaps to allow for more general application of the moral lesson of moderation. (See Brown 2014)

42 LA MALE REGLE

As thy profyt may hyndre°, or thy renoun,   *hinder*
If it were execut in any wyse,
360 With manly resoun thriste° thow it doun.   *thrust*

Thy rentes annuel, as thow wel woost°,   *know well*
To° scarse been greet costes to susteene,   *too*
And in thy cofre° pardee is cold roost°,   *larder, cold roast (leftovers)*
And of thy manuel labour, as I weene°,   *know*
365 Thy lucre° is swich° þat it vnnethe° is seene   *reward, such, hardly*
Ne° felt. Of yiftes° seye I eek° the same.   *nor, gifts, also*
And stele°, for the guerdoun° is so keene°,   *steal, punishment, sharp*
Ne darst thow nat°, ne° begge also for shame.   *you don't dare, nor*

Than° wolde it seeme þat thow borwid haast°   *then, you have borrowed*
370 Mochil° of þat þat° thow haast thus despent°   *much, that which, you have already spent*
In outrage° and excesse, and verray waast°.   *extravagance, true waste*
Auyse thee, for what thyng° þat is lent   *anything*
Of verray right moot° hoom ageyn° be sent.   *must, home again*
Thow therin haast no perpetuitee°.   *permanent right*
375 Thy dettes paie°, lest þat thow be shent°,   *pay your debts, ruined*
And or° þat thow therto conpellid be°.   *before, you are compelled (to do so)*

Sum folk in this cas dreeden more offense
Of man, for wyly wrenches° of the lawe,   *cunning tricks*
Than he dooth eithir God or conscience,
380 For by hem° two he settith nat hawe°.   *those, not a trifle*
If thy conceit be swich°, thow it withdrawe°,   *thought be such, withdraw it*
I rede°, and voide it clene out of thyn herte,   *advise*
And first of God and syn° of man haue awe,   *then*
Lest þat they bothe make thee to smerte°.   *you suffer*

385 Now lat this smert° warnynge to thee be.   *hardship*
And if thow maist heereaftir be releeued
Of body and purs, so thow gye thee°   *conduct yourself*
By wit°, þat thow no more thus be greeued.   *wisely*
What riot is, thow taastid haast and preeued.
390 The fyr, men seyn, he dreedith þat is brent° –   *who is burned*
And if thow so do, thow art wel ymeeued°.   *guided*
Be now no lenger fool, by myn assent.

Ey, what is me, þat to myself thus longe
Clappid° haue I? I trowe° þat I raue°.   *chattered, think, rave*
395 A, nay – my poore purs and peynes° stronge   *pains*

---

360. Cf. line 174, 'manly cowardyse'.

367–8. Hoccleve refers here to the parable of the unjust steward: Luke 16:1–13 (see 16:3 especially). He also uses this in *Regiment*, lines 981–7.

372–3. 'Consider this: whatever is lent must, by right, be returned again.'

393–4. Another meta-moment, in which 'Hoccleve' calls attention to himself. (Cf. 351–2.) These lines give the impression of Hoccleve chattering away to himself.

LA MALE REGLE 43

Han artid° me speke as I spoken haue.	have compelled
Whoso him shapith° mercy for to craue°	intends, ask
His lesson moot° recorde in sundry wyse°,	must, various ways
And whil my breeth may in my body waue°,	stir
400 To recorde it vnnethe I may souffyse°.	I can barely suffice

O God, O Helthe! Vnto thyn ordenance,	
Weleful° lord, meekly submitte I me.	healthful
I am contryt and of ful repentance	
Þat euere I swymmed in swich nycetee°	such foolishness
405 As was displesaunt to thy deitee.	
Now kythe° on me thy mercy and thy grace.	show
It sit° a god been of his grace free°.	suits, generous
Foryeue°, and neuere wole I eft trespace°.	forgive, trespass any longer

My body and purs been at ones seeke°,	both sick
410 And for hem° bothe, I to thyn hy noblesse,	them
As humblely as þat I can, byseeke,	
With herte vnfeyned°, reewe° on our distresse.	earnest, have pity
Pitee haue of myn harmful heuynesse.	
Releeue the repentant in disese°.	in distress
415 Despende on me a drope of thy largesse°,	generosity
Right in this wyse°, if it thee lyke and plese.	way

Lo, lat my lord the Fourneval, I preye,		
My noble lord þat now is tresoreer°,	treasurer	
From thyn hynesse haue a tokne or tweye°	two	
420 To paie me þat due is for this yeer		
Of my yeerly .x. li.° in th'eschequeer°,	ten pounds, the Exchequer	
Nat but° for Michel terme° þat was last.	only, Michaelmas	
I dar nat speke a word of ferne yeer°,	previous years	**Annus ille fuit**
So is my spirit symple° and sore agast°.	humble, truly afraid	**annus restrictionis**
		annuitatum

425 I kepte nat° to be seen inportune°	I do not want, (as) importunate
In my pursuyte – I am therto ful looth° –	very reluctant
And yit° þat gyse ryf is° and commune°	yet, practice is rife, widespread
Among the peple now, withouten ooth°.	truly
As the shamelees crauour° wole°, it gooth,	beggar, wishes
430 For estaat real° can nat al day werne°,	royalty, refuse
But poore shamefast man ofte is wrooth°,	dismayed
Wherfore for to craue° moot° I lerne.	beg, must

423–4. gloss: 'That year was the year of the restriction of annuities.' This gloss allows us to date the poem more firmly. As Burrow notes, Furnival was head of the Exchequer from December 1404 to March 1407. The 'ferne yeer' (previous year) referenced in line 423 would have been the year spanning Easter 1404 to Easter 1405. Based on dates of payments, Burrow fixes the date of composition for the poem between Michaelmas (September 29) 1405 and March 26, 1406 (Burrow 1994: 15).

44 LA MALE REGLE

The prouerbe is: 'the doumb° man no lond getith°'.
Whoso nat spekith° and with neede is bete°,

435 And thurgh arghnesse° his owne self forgetith,
No wondir thogh anothir him forgete.
Neede hath no lawe, as þat the clerkes trete,
And thus to craue artith° me my neede,
And right wole eek° þat I me entremete°,

440 For þat I axe is due°, as God me speede.

And þat that due is, thy magnificence
Shameth to werne°, as þat I byleeue.
As I seide, reewe° on myn inpotence,
Þat likly am to sterue° yit or eeue°,

445 But if° thow in this wyse me releeue.
By coyn° I gete may swich° medecyne
As may myn hurtes alle, þat me greeue°,
Exyle cleene, and voide me of pyne°.

silent, gets no land
doesn't speak up, is overcome with need
through timidity

to beg compels
justice also demands, involve myself
because that for which I ask is owed

would be ashamed to refuse
have pity
starve, before evening
unless
with money, such
that pain me
pain

434–6. If you forget yourself (i.e., don't speak up for yourself, although you have a clear need), of course others will forget you too.

FOR HENRY V AT KENNINGTON

Date: c. March 1413

❧

The event to which Hoccleve's heading refers occurred on March 21, 1413. (Burrow 1994: 20; see gloss to line 6) This event celebrated the 'homage accorded by the English peers to Henry V on his accession' (Seymour 1981: 128). Henry IV died on March 20, 1413. Hoccleve is pledging allegiance to the new king while continuing his project of shaping the king's moral sensibilities – an effort begun in earnest with the *Regiment of Princes*. Chief among Hoccleve's priorities in the poem is to encourage the new king to rule justly and morally, and to strengthen the Church in the fight against heresy.

Jenni Nuttall cautions against labelling this an 'occasional' poem. This poem – and other similar 'political' poems in HM 111 – do not hope to 'reproduce or commemorate elements of the public display that defined the ceremonies by which Hoccleve dates their moment of composition and the status of their addressees.' Nuttall notes the unprecedented nature of this particular ceremony: it 'took place before the coronation because the lords spiritual and temporal were already gathered at Westminster awaiting the resumption of the parliament that had been suspended during Henry IV's final illness.' While the first stanza indicates that Hoccleve's relationship to Henry V has changed, the subsequent stanzas comprise 'plain imperatives, directing Henry toward self-governance and virtue.' (Nuttall 2015: 5) As such, the poem serves as an extension of the spirit sparked in the *Regiment*, in which Hoccleve seizes the occasion to instruct the prince (now king).

David Watt notes that 'the textual apparatus that situates this poem in the manuscript suggests that Hoccleve wants his audience to judge this poem by imagining the king as its initial reader, just as they might imagine Lady Hereford reading the "Complaint Paramont" or Duke Humphrey reading "Learn to Die."' (Watt 2013: 45)

FOR HENRY V AT KENNINGTON

Ceste balade ensuante feust faite au tresnoble Roy H le Vᵗ, que dieu pardoint, le iour que les seigneurs de son Roialme lui firent lour homages a Kenyngtoun

The kyng of kynges°, regnyng ouer al,   *i.e., Christ*
Which stablisshid° hath in eternitee   *established*
His hy might°, þat nat varie he may ne shal,   *great power*
So constant is his blisful deitee,
5 My lige lord°, this yow graunte he°,   *i.e., Henry V, (may) he grant you this*
That your estaat rial°, which þat this day   *royal*   **videlicet xxjº die**
Haath maad me lige to your souereyntee,   **Marcij. anno regr**
In reule vertuous continue may.   **vostri primo**

God dreede°, and ficche° in him your trust verray.   *fear/respect God, fix*
10 Be cleene in herte and loue chastitee.
Be sobre°, sad°, iust; trouthe obserue alway.   *serious, dignified*
Good conseil take and aftir it do yee.
Be humble in goost°, of your tonge attempree°,   *spirit, temperate*
Pitous and merciable° in special°,   *merciful, especially*
15 Prudent, debonaire°, in mesure free°,   *courteous, adequately generous*
Nat ouerlarge°, ne vnto gold thral°.   *too extravagant, nor covetous*

Be to your liges° also sheeld and wal.   *subjects*
Keepe and deffende hem° from aduersitee.   *them*
Hir wele° and wo in your grace lyth al.   *their well-being*
20 Gouerneth hem° in lawe and equitee°;   *them, fairness*
Conquere hir° loue, and haue hem° in cheertee.   *their, them*
Be holy chirches champioun eek ay°.   *also always*

Heading: This following balade was made for the most noble King Henry V, may God pardon him, on the day that the lords of his realm paid homage to him at Kennington

1–4. Cf. 1 Timothy 6:14–16. It is notable that the first lines sent to the new king, in the earliest hours of his accession, commend not the new king, but the 'king of kings', Christ. It sets the tone for Henry remembering to turn his sights to that mightier king above all – and for the moral emphasis of the poem as a whole. Cf. *Regiment*, lines 4967–70.

6. gloss: That is to say, the 21st day of March, in the first year of your reign [March 21, 1413]

9. Here begins a series of moral advice delivered by Hoccleve to the new king, a litany that extends through line 34. In style, it resembles some of Chaucer's more advisory/moral poetry such as 'Gentilesse' and 'Truth'.

9–16. Cf. Titus 1:8, 2:1–2. Cf. also 'Gentilesse', lines 9–11, where Chaucer encourages the reader to be 'trewe of his word, sobre, pitous [compassionate], and free [generous], / clene of his gost [pure in spirit], and [to] love bisinesse [activity] / Against the vice of slouthe'. Hoccleve's virtues correlate closely: 'sobre', committed to truth, compassionate, generous, 'cleene in herte' and 'humble in goost'. Scogan included Chaucer's 'Gentilesse' in a 'Moral Balade' read to Prince Henry (and his brothers), circa 1406–7. Hoccleve's poem might have echoed Scogan's (and hence, Chaucer's), and brought to mind similar guidance, six or seven years later.

22. Hoccleve makes explicit his defense of the Church here. The object of the prince's protection shifts from a more general 'your liges' (17) to the Church.

Susteene hir right. Souffre no thyng doon be
In preiudice of° hire, by no way.   against

scilicet, ecclesiam sanctam
25 Strengthe your modir° in chacyng away   i.e., Holy Church
Th'errour°, which sones of iniquitee   i.e., heresy
Han sowe ageyn° the feith, it is no nay°.   have sown against, truly
Yee therto bownde been of duetee°.   you are duty-bound
Your office° is it now, for your suertee,   duty
30 Souffreth nat Crystes feith to take a fal.
Vnto his° peple and youres, cheerly° see   Christ's, lovingly
In conseruyng of your estat real.

Syn° God hath sent yow wit° substancial   since, intellect
And kynges might, vertu putte in assay°.   to the test
35 And lige lord, thogh my conceit° be smal,   intellect
And nat my wordes peynte fressh and gay°,   my words are unadorned
But clappe and iangle° foorth as dooth a iay°,   chatter, bird
Good wil to yow shal ther noon faille in me°,   my good will shall be unfailing
Byseechyng vnto God þat, to his pay°,   liking
40 Yee may gouerne your hy dignitee.

Amen.

---

25. superscript: That is, Holy Church. This clarifies 'your modir': Henry is to strengthen the Mother Church.

26. Cf. 2 Kings 7:10. Hoccleve uses 'errour' repeatedly throughout the shorter poems to describe heresy.

41. 'Amen'. It is notable that the poem ends with this word, offering itself as prayer. So too with 'Knights of the Garter', 'Mother of God', and 'The Bones of Richard II'. The three datable poems among these four are dated to the period 1413–16 (or, indeed, 1413–14 if the earlier date is taken for 'Garter').

KNIGHTS OF THE GARTER
Date: c. April 1414 or May 1416

☙

The heading to this poem indicates two separate balades, centered on the same occasion. The occasion in question was a gathering of the Order of the Garter (Order of St George), the most prestigious of medieval chivalric orders, although there is the question of whether the meeting was that on April 23, 1414, or that on May 24, 1416. Vincent Gillespie identifies textual evidence pointing towards the latter date, a grander occasion in which Emperor Sigismund (the Holy Roman Emperor) was invested with the regalia of the Order of the Garter. Gillespie notes that the poem seems to indicate that Henry has been on the throne for a while (lines 15, 17–18), and he reads a reference to the Council of Constance (1414–18) into the phrase 'on your constance we awayten alle' (line 24). If the poem is dually addressed, then the phrase 'our worthy kyng and Cristen emperour' (line 26) would seem to encapsulate Henry V and Sigismund both, as Gillespie notes. (Burrow 1994: 21–2; Gillespie 2011: 38–9; Martin (2019) also argues strongly in favor of the 1416 date.)

Hoccleve marks the beginning of the second balade with a large initial in HM 111 (line 33), but the two flow into (and out of) one another; they are twinned, they mirror. Each poem is comprised of four eight-line stanzas. Each stanza rhymes ababbcbc. Furthermore, within each poem, the same rhymes are retained between stanzas: so the 'a' rhyme for the first balade remains '-esse' throughout the entire poem, and the 'b' rhyme remains '-our', etc.

The 'twin' nature of these balades would take on added significance when considering the context of the 1416 meeting: style might mimic content between the two: two engines of Christian might, appareled equally, placed side by side.

KNIGHTS OF THE GARTER

Cestes balades ensuyantes feurent faites au tresnoble Roy H. le quint que dieu pardoint & au treshonurable conpaignie du Iarter

To yow, welle° of honur and worthynesse,	source
Our right Cristen kyng°, heir and successour	i.e., Henry V
Vnto Iustinians° deuout tendrenesse	Justinian's
In the feith of Ihesu°, our redemptour° –	Jesus, redeemer
5 And to yow, lordes of the Garter°, flour°	knights of the Garter, flower
Of chiualrie, as men yow clepe° and calle –	name
The lord of vertu, and of grace auctour,	
Graunte the fruyt of your loos° nat appalle°.	reputation, wither
O lige lord þat han eek° the liknesse	has also
10 Of Constantyn°, th'ensaumple° and the mirour	Constantine, model
To princes alle, in loue and buxumnesse°	obedience
To holy chirche, O verray sustenour	
And piler° of our feith, and werreyour°	pillar, warrior
Ageyn° the heresies bittir galle°,	against, poison
15 Do foorth, do foorth: continue your socour°,	support
Holde vp Crystes baner° – lat it nat falle.	Christ's banner
This yle°, or° this, had been° but hethenesse°,	island, before, would have been, heathendom
Nad been° of your feith the force and vigour.	had it not been
And yit this day the feendes fikilnesse°	devil's treachery
20 Weeneth° fully to cacche° a tyme and hour	hopes, catch
To haue° on vs, your liges, a sharp shour°,	wage, attack
And to his seruitute° vs knytte and thralle°.	bondage, enslave
But ay° we truste in yow, our protectour;	always
On your constance° we awayten alle.	fortitude
25 Commandith þat no wight° haue hardynesse°,	person, daring
Our worthy kyng and Cristen emperour,	

Heading: These following balades were made for the most noble King Henry V, may God pardon him, and for the most honorable Order of the Garter

3. Justinian, sixth-century Byzantine emperor, known for fiercely suppressing heresy in order to protect the Christian church.

10. Constantine was a fourth-century Roman emperor (d. 337), the first Roman emperor to convert to Christianity, held up in Hoccleve's poetry as an exemplar of Christian masculinity. Cf. 'To Sir John Oldcastle', 217–40.

11–16. Whereas Hoccleve's approach in 'For Henry V at Kennington' is to exhort the new king to support Holy Church, in this poem Hoccleve praises Henry as the very orthodox supporter that he had imagined in that prior poem.

17. 'yle'. Cf. 'Mother of Grace', line 136; 'Epistle of Cupid', lines 15–17.

19–22. Cf. 1 Peter 5.8.

24. Gillespie reads a reference to the Council of Constance (1414–18) into the phrase 'on your constance we awayten alle'. See introductory note to this poem.

26. If this poem is addressed to Henry V and Sigismund both, then this line would seem to encapsulate both figures. (Burrow 1994: 21–2; Gillespie 2011: 38–9)

50 KNIGHTS OF THE GARTER

Of the feith to despute more or lesse
Openly among peple, where errour
Spryngith al day and engendrith° rumour. — begets
30 Makith swich° lawe, and for aght may befalle°, — such, whatever happens
Obserue it wel – therto been yee dettour°. — obliged
Dooth so, and God in glorie shal yow stalle°. — install

YEE lordes eek° shynynge in noble fame, — also
To which° appropred° is the maintenance — whom, assigned
35 Of Crystes cause, in honour of his name,
Shoue on and putte his foos to the outraunce°. — defeat his foes
God wolde so; so wolde eek° your ligeance°. — also, king · quia Rex illam iustissimam partem tenet
To tho° two prikkith° yow your duetee°. — those, hasten, duty
Whoso nat keepith this double obseruance
40 Of meryt and honour, nakid is he.

Your style° seith þat yee been foos to shame. — formal designation
Now kythe° of your feith the perseuerance — demonstrate
In which an heep° of vs arn halt° and lame. — bunch, are limping
Our Cristen kyng of Engeland and France,
45 And yee, my lordes, with your alliance,
And othir feithful peple þat ther be,
Truste I to God shul qwenche° al this nusance, — eradicate
And this land sette in hy prosperitee.

Conqueste of hy prowesse° is for to tame — the outcome of great power
50 The wylde woodnesse° of this mescreance° — lunacy, treachery (heresy)
Right to the roote. Rype° yee þat same. — seek out
Sleepe nat this, but for Goddes plesance,
And his modres, and in signifiance° — to signify/prove
Þat yee been of Seint Georges liueree°, — guild

27–9. Note the emphasis on disputation of the faith here, and its link to error and rumor. Hoccleve uses the word 'errour' repeatedly in connection with Lollardy.

32. Nuttall notes that this installation (God installing Henry in glory, if he holds up Christ's banner (16)) supersedes 'his physical installation in his individual stall as Sovereign of the Garter'. (Nuttall 2015: 6)

37–8. gloss: Because the king holds that to be most just.

38. 'tho two'. That is, God and your 'ligeance' [king]. This doubling, and the mention of 'double obseruance / Of meryt and honour' in the following lines, is interesting in these twinned balades. 'Ligeance' can mean 'allegiance of a feudal vassal to a lord or of a subject to a sovereign', or the authority of such a lord/sovereign (*MED*). The Latin gloss points to the latter meaning.

43. 'an heep of vs arn halt and lame'. That is, Lollards.

44–8. Eradicating the error of heresy, both at home and abroad, was a main focus of the Council of Constance. The late Wyclif was a focus of the deliberations – and Jan Hus was tried (and ultimately executed) for his beliefs at Constance.

50. 'wylde woodnesse'. Cf. the language of madness used in Hoccleve's 'Complaint' (*Series*). One critical reading of that poem aligns Hoccleve's stated 'recovery date' with the opening of the Council of Constance – the moment at which the collective body of the English church began healing from heresy. See Langdell 2018: Chapter 1.

54. The Order of the Garter was formed in honor of St George, patron saint of England.

KNIGHTS OF THE GARTER   51

55   Dooth him seruice and knyghtly obeissance°.   obedience
      For Crystes cause is his, wel knowen yee.

      Stif° stande in þat, and yee shuln greeue and grame°   steadfast, injure and enrage
      The fo to pees°, and norice of distaunce°.   enemy of peace, nursemaid of discord
      That now is ernest, torne it into game.
60   Dampnable° fro feith were variance°.   reprehensible, discord
      Lord lige, and lordes, haue in remembrance
      Lord of al is the blissid Trinitee,
      Of whos vertu, the mighty habundaunce°,   abundance
      Yow herte and strengthe° in feithful vnitee.   hearten and strengthen you

65   Amen.

      C'est tout.

61–4. ' … remember that the Lord of all is the blessed Trinity, whose virtue – that mighty abundance – shall hearten and strengthen you in unity.' Cf. 'For Henry V at Kennington', lines 1–3; *Regiment*, lines 4969–70. In each case, Hoccleve positions God (here as the Trinity) as 'lord' or 'king' of all – thereby reminding Henry of his place in a greater hierarchy.

65–6. The double sign-off here – Amen, and C'est tout – seems both to tie the two poems together as one, and to offer the poems as prayer. The idea of ending in 'feithful vnitee' also helps with the theme of binding together, making whole.

MOTHER OF LIFE

Date: unknown (before 1426)

❧

This is one of four Marian pieces in HM 111 (the others being item 1, 'Complaint Paramount', item 10, 'Mother of God', and item 18, 'Balade for Robert Chichele'); it is complemented by the three Marian pieces (items 4–6) in HM 744. Mary's role as 'mediatrice' [mediator] / 'mene' [intermediary] is on display here – a role reprised throughout Hoccleve's shorter poems (see note to lines 14–16).

The speaker of this poem is burdened with guilt, and the presence of sin is sensory – it stinks, soils, and shrinks from sight. Reference to the 'stynk of synne' (line 17) aligns the poem with 'Balade for Robert Chichele', written for the brother of archbishop Henry Chichele: the speaker's request there that God 'Graunte pardoun of our stynkyng errour' has been read as a reference to heresy, which is described as an 'errour' in poems such as 'Oldcastle' (see introduction to 'Balade for Robert Chichele'). The 'I' of the poem is surely generalized – it speaks on behalf of sinful mankind and illuminates Mary's power as intercessor – and yet the stench of sin that pervades the poem suggests more local transgressions and heresies, as well. The presiding spirit of guilt – such strong guilt that the speaker is ashamed, and forced to hide – speaks to the collective wounds of the English church at Hoccleve's time.

MOTHER OF LIFE   53

MOTHER OF LIFE

Ad beatam virginem

Modir of lyf, O cause of al our welthe,
Fyndere of grace and of our medecyne,
Whereas an appil° refte° our lyf and helthe,   *apple (of Eden), bereft us of*
And marie[d]° vs vnto ay lastyng pyne°,   *wed, everlasting pain*
5 As sones of perdicion and ruyne°,   *wickedness and ruin*
That matrymoyne° thy virginitee   *matrimony (between mankind and devil)*
Dissolued and vnbownden° hath, Virgyne,   *unbound*
And at our large maad vs walke free°.   *enabled us to walk free*

O blessid be thow, vessel of clennesse°,   *purity*
10 In whom our soules salue° list habyte°.   *salve, wishes to reside*
O tree of lyf, swettest of al swetnesse,
In thy fruyt yeue° vs grace to delyte.   *give*
And thogh thy sone cause haue° vs to smyte°   *has cause, to strike us down*
For our giltes, yit our mediatrice°,   *mediator*
15 As thow hast euere doon, thow him excite°   *encourage*
Vnto mercy, for þat is thyn office°.   *duty*

My soule is stuffid so with stynk of synne,
Þat ay it dreedith° beforn thee appeere,   *it always fears*

Heading: To the blessed Virgin

2. 'our medecyne'. Cf. lines 10, 50; 'Mother of Grace', lines 15–19; 'Balade for Robert Chichele', line 154.

3–4. See Genesis 3. The collective 'vs' is mankind. The speaker is not personalized so much as emblematic of all people.

5. Cf. John 17:12; 2 Thessalonians 2:3–4. Cf. 'For Henry V at Kennington', line 26: 'sones of iniquitee' (describing heretics in that instance).

6. 'That matrymoyne'. That is, the marriage between (sinful) mankind and damnation.

6–8. Cf. Luke 1:26–38. Here, the Virgin is responsible for saving mankind from eternal damnation. She earns an agency usually attributed to Christ – and redolent of Christ's descending to hell to save worthy pre-Christians in the Harrowing of Hell. We see in the following stanza the reason for this: Mary served as the 'vessel' through which Christ came into the world, making our salvation possible.

8. Cf. *Regiment*, lines 274–7.

9–10. The 'salue' [healing medicine] that abides in Mary is Christ.

11–16. See Genesis 2:9; 3:22, 24. Cf. Proverbs 3:18; Revelation 2:7, 22:2.

13–14a. 'and although your son has cause to strike us down for our sins … '

14–16. Mary is seen here as the peace-making intermediary, capable of calming Christ's potential anger, and moving him to mercy. Hoccleve often uses 'mediatrice' and 'mene' to emphasize Mary's capacity as intermediary/mediator: see lines 89–96; 'Oldcastle', line 256, 'Mother of God', lines 44, 83; 'Mother of Grace', line 59, 'Balade for Robert Chichele', line 125, 'Monk Who Clad the Virgin', line 8.

17. 'stynk of synne'. Cf. lines 33, 66; 'Balade for Robert Chichele', line 152: 'Graunte pardoun of our stynkyng errour'.

54 MOTHER OF LIFE

Lest for the filthe, which þat it is ynne,
20 Thow torne away thy merciable cheere°,   merciful face
And deyne° nat accepte my preyeere.   deign
And if my trespas heere I nat confesse,
How shal I doon, O Crystes modir deere,
Whan God shal iuge° vs alle, more and lesse?   judge

25 O why, my synnes – why, my wikkidnesses –
With your venym my soule slayn han yee°,   have you
And put in it so° desperat gastnesses°   such, terrors
Þat mercy may ne list° beholde me?   may wish not to
Why oppressith your heuy aduersitee
30 The hope of myn exaudicioun°,   prayer being granted
And shame in yow maad hath so large entree°   such a great incursion
Þat yee the vois° me reue° of orisoun°?   voice, rob, prayer

Allas thy shame, O thow filthy offense,
In the presence of shynynge holynesse!
35 O shenshipe° of vnclene conscience   shame
In the beholdynge of pured clennesse!
O caitif° soule inuolued in dirknesse,   miserable
What wilt thow do? Where is thy remedie?
Who may thy mescheef and thy greef redresse°,   repair
40 Syn° of thy gilt thow darst nat mercy crie?   since

Lo, blessid womman among wommen alle,
Syn° my spirit nat dar° putte vp his bille   since, dare not
Thy grace ne° thy mercy for to calle,   nor
But in his mazidnesse° abydith stille,   confusion
45 My thristy soule drynke may hir fille
Of sorwe, and bathe in sorwe and heuynesse°.   grief
Hir ferdful° shame hir shende° wole and spille°,   fearful, ruin, slay
For to hire helthe nat shee dar° hir dresse°.   she dares not, apply herself

My synnes yernen° þat thyn hy pitee   desire
50 Fully hem kneew° for hir curacioun°,   knew them, their healing
But they lothen appeere° beforn thee,   loathe to appear

19–21. Cf. 2 Chronicles 6:42, 30:9; Psalms 50:11; Ecclesiasticus 18:24.

24. The reference is to the Last Judgment; the speaker worries that he will not be able to answer for his sins then, as he is unable to now. See Job 31:14.

26. Cf. Deuteronomy 32:33; Genesis 3:14–15.

29–32. 'Why do you (my sins) trouble the hope of my prayers being granted, and why has shame (for my sins) revealed itself so much that you rob me of the voice of prayer?'

30. 'exaudicioun'. An apparent neologism, meaning the granting of a prayer.

33. 'filthy offense'. Cf. lines 17, 66. The sensory detail is potent throughout, deepening the sense of abject sinning in the face of purity.

41. See Luke 1:28.

45–6. Cf. Psalms 59:5, 79:6.

MOTHER OF LIFE   55

For hir° cursid abhominacion°.   *their, abomination*
O spryng and welle of our sauuacioun°,   *salvation*
My dirke soule of thy grace enlumyne°,   *illuminate*
55 And keepe it fro the castigacioun°   *punishment*
That it disserued hath° in helle pyne°.   *has deserved, the pain of hell*

If I confesse myn iniquitee°,   *wickedness*
Lady, þat I wroght haue° in thy presence,   *have pursued*
Wilt thow me werne° thy benignitee°?   *deny me, mercy*
60 If þat my gilt and my dampnable offense
Of giltes alle haue an excellence°,   *i.e., if they be especially prominent*
Shal thy mercy be lesse than it oghte?
May nat thy mercy with my gilt dispense,
And pardoun gete of þat þat it miswroghte°?   *did amiss*

65 The more þat my gilt passith° mesure,   *surpasses*
And stynkith in thy sones sighte and thyn,
The gretter neede hath it of his cure°   *attention*
And of thyn help. Wherfore, lady myn,
My soule fro the net and fro th'engyn°   *snare*
70 Of him þat waytith it to slee°, thow keepe.   *waits to slay it*
His sotil° snares and cacchynge twyn°   *sly, catching trap*
In my memorie ficchid° been ful deepe.   *fixed*

Lady, thyn help nat wole I me despeire°.   *despair*
For in myn herte fully I conceyue
75 Þat thow to heuene art the laddre and steire°   *stair*
By which men clymben, blisse to receyue°.   *receive*
Despeir heereaftir shal me nat deceyue°   *shall not deceive me*
Þat I ne shal ay° thee byseeche of grace.   *should not always*
Thy might°, I woot° wel, is my gilt to weyue°,   *power, know, remove*
80 And of my trespas pardoun me purchace.

Thow Crystes modir sholdest neuere han be
Ne had° our synnes causid it certayn°.   *had not, certainly*
Forwhy? It had be no necessitee°   *it would not have been necessary*
But for thow qwikne shuldest° vs agayn,   *save that you should revive*
85 Þat for our gilt original° wern slayn.   *original sin*
Thow art his modir, wherfore I thee preye°   *I pray to you*

---

53. Cf. John 4:13–14. See also 'Mother of God', line 88.

66. Hoccleve continues the sensory escalation here, but delves into sensory mixing – sight and smell. Cf. lines 17, 33.

68–72. See notes to line 26. Cf. also 2 Kings 22:6; 2 Timothy 2:26.

74–6. This phrase recalls the story of Jacob's ladder: see Genesis 28.

77–8. 'Despair shall no longer deceive me (in making me believe) that I shouldn't always appeal to you for grace.' That is, the speaker will ignore despair, and continue to petition Mary for grace henceforth.

81–2. 'You would never have needed to become Christ's mother, were it not for our sins having caused it, certainly.'

56 MOTHER OF LIFE

To saue me. Haue thow no desdayn,
Þat of bountee° and mercy art the keye. — goodness

Euene as the moone a mene° is verraily — an intermediary
90 Betwixt vs and the sonne°, of whom hir light — sun
Shee takith, and it vniuerselly
Yeueth° vnto the world whan it is nyght, — gives
In swich a wyse° God, thy sone right°, — such a way, true
The light of grace betook° vnto thee, — bestowed
95 For to mynistre it vnto euery wight° — person
Þat thereof list enlumyned to be°. — who wished to be illumined thereby

Thyn humble goost° and maydens chastitee, — spirit
For our behoue° han so mochil wroght° — benefit, have done so much
In sundry wyse°, as þat wel knowen we, — various ways
100 Þat thee to thanke we souffyse noght°. — i.e., we can't thank you sufficiently
Thow hast vs vnto swich a plyt° ibroght, — such a (good) state
Þat he, þat lord was sumtyme of vengeance°, — who was once a lord of vengeance
With his blood hath our synful soules boght°, — i.e., Christ bought our sins with his death
And is now lord of mercy and souffrance°. — patience

105 Where is a streighter way vnto° mankynde — for
To God, thy sone, our soules for to lede,
Than where as þat we may thy sone fynde
Beforn his fadir, with his wowndes rede°, — red (bloody) wounds
And the before hem°, mercy for to grede°? — you before them, request
110 Thy sone his body shewith al bybled°; — shows all bloody
And to thy sone also, thy maydenhede° — your maidenhood (Mary)
Shewith the pappes° wherwith he was fed. — shows the breasts

O blessid Ihesu, for thy modres loue,
And modir, for the hy dileccion° — divine love
115 Þat thow hast to thy sone in heuene aboue,
Haueth me, bothe, in your proteccion.
Plante in myn herte swich correccion° — such correction
Þat I your grace and your mercy may haue,
And fully stande in youre affeccion,
120 Or° my body be clothid in his graue°. — before, grave

C'est tout.

---

89. The metaphor used here is reminiscent of 'To Sir John Oldcastle', lines 313–20. See also note to lines 14–16, above.

102–4. When incarnated as man, through Mary, God becomes 'lord of mercy', and eases his vengeance towards mankind.

110–12. This juxtaposition of the infant Jesus with an adult, crucified Jesus recurs in Hoccleve's devotional verse: cf. 'Inuocacio ad Patrem', lines 85–91; 'Ad filium', lines 1–7; 'Monk Who Clad the Virgin', lines 6–7.

THE BONES OF RICHARD II

Date: 1413

☙

This poem boasts one of the most intriguing relationships between heading and content. The heading prepares one to read about an occasional poem focused on the re-interment of Richard II's bones by Henry V, an event that took place in 1413, most likely in mid-December: Henry V paid for Richard II's remains to be moved from Langley to Westminster Abbey. (Strohm 1996: 102) The moment is fragile and freighted with meaning: Henry's father, Henry IV, had deposed and imprisoned Richard in 1399, leading to Richard's death in jail. Henry V's choice to have Richard reburied at Westminster Abbey could be read as an acknowledgment of his father's misdeed, and an attempt to exercise more virtuous behavior. But the poem itself makes only glancing mention of that event, and focuses instead mostly on the threat of heresy to the realm. The poem uses the occasion of the reburial to raise the issue of heresy's constant threat, to position Henry V as an upholder of Holy Church and defender of the realm against heretics (15–16), to raise the question of what a heretical king might portend (25–9), to use Richard's reburial as evidence of Henry's virtuous kindness (30–4), and to position Henry to champion the church against heresy (41–8).

The heading also serves the function of calling attention to the date of the poem – late 1413 – placing it just a couple years before Hoccleve's most extended rebuke of heresy in 'To Sir John Oldcastle' (summer 1415). It is worth noting that the immediate audience for the poem appears to be senior ecclesiastical officials, as suggested in line 17 – 'O reuerent goostly fadres yee.'

THE BONES OF RICHARD II

Ceste balade ensuyante feust faite tost apres que les osses du Roy Richard feurent apportez a Westmouster

	Whereas þat this land wont was° for to be	was accustomed
	Of sad byleeue° and constant vnioun,	unyielding belief
	And as þat holy chirche vs taghte, we	
	With herte buxum° lerned our lessoun,	obedient
5	Now han we changid our condicioun.	
	Allas, an heep° of vs the feith werreye°;	a group, challenge the faith (the church)
	We waden so deepe in presumpcioun	
	Þat vs nat deyneth° vnto God obeye.	we deign not
	We rekken nat thogh° Crystes lore° deye°.	don't care if, teachings, die
10	The feend hath maad vs dronke of the poisoun	
	Of heresie, and lad vs° a wrong weye	led us (along)
	Þat torne shal to our confusioun°	destruction
	But if þat left be this abusioun°.	unless we abandon this deception
	And yit, seur confort° haue I, thynkith me:	sure comfort
15	Our lige lord, the kyng°, is champioun	Henry V
	For holy chirche. Crystes knyght is he,	
	Forwhy°, O reuerent goostly° fadres yee,	which is why, spiritual
	And we your sones eek°, han enchesoun°	also, have reason
	Right greet° to thanke God in Trinitee,	truly great
20	Þat° of his grace hath sent this regioun	who
	So noble an heed°. Looke vp, thow Albioun°:	a head (leader), England
	God thanke, and for thy Cristen prince preye,	
	Syn° he fo° is to this rebellioun.	since, foe
	He of thy soules helthe is lok and keye.	

Heading: The following balade was made just after the bones of King Richard were transported to Westminster

1–8. The first stanza aligns this poem with 'For Henry V at Kennington' and 'Knights of the Garter', both of which concern Henry V (shortly after his accession to the throne), and both of which take the fight against heresy as a key focus. The focus on the prior unity and glory of 'this land' (line 1) chimes with appeals to emulate past figures such as Justinian in 'Oldcastle' and 'Knights of the Garter'. Line 6 recalls 'Knights of the Garter', line 43: 'an heep of vs arn halt and lame'. That line, as with lines 6–8, uses the plural first person, both drawing attention to heretics and including them in the address, in the collective 'vs' of the English believer.

15–16. Cf. 'Knights of the Garter', lines 9–16.

17. 'reuerent goostly fadres'. This line positions Hoccleve's initial listeners/readers as senior ecclesiastics. (Cf. Nuttall 2015: 5)

19. For this conflation of God and Trinity, cf. line 30, and 'Knights of the Garter', line 62.

23. That is, the Lollard rebellion.

24. Cf. 'Mother of Life' (previous poem), line 88.

THE BONES OF RICHARD II   59

25   What mighten folk of good byleeue° seye   *good belief*
        If bent were our kynges affeccion
        To the wrong part? Who sholde hem help purueye°?   *help them provide for themselves*
        A kyng set in þat wrong opinioun
        Mighte of our feith be the subuersioun°.   *upending*
30   But eterne God, in persones three°,   *i.e., the Trinity*
        Hath reyned° dropes of conpassioun,   *rained*
        And sent vs our good kyng, for our cheertee°.   *for the sake of charity*

        See eek° how our kynges benignitee°   *also, kindness*
        And louyng herte his vertu can bywreye°.   *reveal*
35   Our kyng Richard þat was, yee may wel see,
        Is nat fled from his remembrance aweye.
        My wit souffysith nat to peyse and weye°   *measure and weigh*
        With what honour he broght is to this toun°,   *town*
        And with his queene at Westmynstre in th'abbeye
40   Solempnely in toumbe° leid adoun.   *in a tomb*

        Now God, byseeche I, in conclusioun,
        Henri the .V.ᵉ in ioie° and hy nobleye°   *joy, great nobility*
        Regne on vs yeeres many a milioun.
        And whereas þat men erren and forueye°,   *stray and lose their way*
45   Walkynge blyndly in the dirk aleye
        Of heresie – O lord God, preye I thee,
        Enspire hem, þat no lenger they foleie°.   *go astray*
        To feithes path hem lede thy pitee°.   *(may) your pity lead them to faith's path*

        Amen.

25–32. This stanza rather startlingly raises the possibility of the king's own allegiances being with the 'wrong part' – i.e., the Lollards. This suggestion is quickly dismissed, but it is telling that Hoccleve would even introduce the thought. See 'To Sir John Oldcastle' (written two years later) for Henry's connection to that famous Lollard knight. The link between heresy and Richard's reburial here is somewhat tenuous, but seems to rest on Henry's benevolence: his kindness is made evident in the reburying of his predecessor; God has graced us with a king who is both not-Lollard and benevolent.

33–40. The heading to this poem would seem to suggest that the focus would be the reburial of Richard II. In fact, the poem mainly focuses on the threat of heresy; only in this stanza do we touch on Richard's re-interment, offered as an example of Henry's kindness.

41–3. For this exaggeration, cf. 'Balade to Edward, Duke of York', lines 68–9.

BALADE TO EDWARD, DUKE OF YORK

Date: before October 1415

☙

The dating of this dedicatory piece is based on Edward's death at Agincourt in October 1415. Edward was first cousin to Henry IV, and translator/writer of the hunting treatise, the *Master of Game* (Burrow 1994: 23). In the second stanza, Hoccleve remembers that Edward once 'at Londoun' asked him for a selection (or perhaps all) of his 'balades'. It is not clear which poems were included with the dedication, but one imagines an early attempt at the type of collections that Hoccleve ventured almost a decade later with the Huntington holographs. (Nuttall and Watt draw a comparison between this encounter between Hoccleve and Edward and the similar encounter between Gower and Richard II on the Thames, mentioned in *Confessio amantis*; see 2022: 4.)

Seymour notes the similarity in meter, purpose, and ideas between this poem and 'Balade to John, Duke of Bedford' (Seymour 1981: 127). 'Balade to Edward' joins that poem, and the *Regiment of Princes* envoi, as items in HM 111 that are written to accompany other texts/collections. They point beyond the borders of HM 111, and signal other manuscripts.

HM 111, fol. 32v (detail), The Huntington Library, San Marino, CA.

BALADE TO EDWARD, DUKE OF YORK

Go, litil pamfilet, and streight thee dresse° — go straight
Vnto the noble-rootid gentillesse° — nobility
Of the myghty prince of famous honour,
My gracious lord of York, to whos noblesse
5 Me recommande with hertes humblesse°, — humility
As he þat haue his grace and his fauour
Fownden alway, for which I am dettour° — debtor
For him to preye, and so shal my symplesse° — innocence/lowliness
Hertily do, vnto my dethes hour.

10 Remembre his worthynesse, I charge thee –
How ones° at Londoun desired he — once
Of me, þat am his seruant and shal ay°, — shall always be
To haue of my balades swich plentee° — as many
As ther weren remeynynge° vnto me. — remaining
15 And for nat wole I to his wil seyn nay°, — as I would not deny his will
But fulfille it as ferfoorth° as I may, — far
Be thow an owtere° of my nycetee°, — publisher, foolishness
For my good lordes lust and game and play.

My lord byseeke eek° in humble maneere — also beseech
20 That he nat souffre thee for to appeere
In th'onurable° sighte or the presence — the honorable
Of the noble princesse and lady deere,
My gracious lady, my good lordes feere°, — wife
The mirour of wommanly excellence.
25 Thy cheere° is naght°, ne haast noon eloquence — manner, nothing
To moustre° thee before hire yen cleere°. — show, her clear eyes

---

1. 'Go, litil pamfilet'. Cf. *Troilus and Criseyde*, 5.1786 ('Go litel book, go litel myn tragedye'); *Regiment* envoi (HM 111, no. 14), line 1 ('O litil book … '); and the beginning to Chaucer's 'Retraction', where he references either the 'Parson's Tale' or the *Tales* as a whole as 'litel tretis' (line 1). Note Hoccleve later refers to this 'pamfilet' as a 'book' (a foul one at that), line 55.

2. 'noble-rootid gentilesse'. Cf Chaucer, 'Gentilesse', lines 1, 8.

5. 'hertes humblesse'. Cf. *Regiment* envoi, line 19; 'Balade to John, Duke of Bedford', line 2.

10–14. Hoccleve's account of this meeting in London is striking, and evokes the type of encounter that would lead to such a commission. For 'seruant', cf. 'Dialogue' (*Series*), line 560. The notion of copying whichever of his 'balades' are 'remeynynge' to him is also intriguing – it indicates that the book in question is a collection, like HM 111 and HM 744, full of shorter pieces. Is 'remeynynge' being used loosely, to suggest anything he has to hand? Or might it mean remaining after Hoccleve had already given Edward a sample of other poems, or after a batch of poems was lost or otherwise taken?

18. The idea of offering these poems for Edward's 'lust and game and play' resonates with the Friend in the 'Dialogue' (*Series*), who proposes that Hoccleve write tales in honor of women, for Duke Humphrey's 'desport and mirthe' while in 'daliance' with women. Both posit the aristocratic recipient using poetry for fun.

23. 'My gracious lady'. Edward's wife was Philippa de Mohun (d. 1431).

For myn honour were holsum thyn absence.

Yit ful fayn wolde I haue° a messageer — *I would gladly have*
To recommande me with herte enteer° — *full heart*
30   To hir benigne° and humble wommanhede. — *gracious*
And at this tyme haue I noon othir heer
But thee, and smal am I, for thee, the neer°. — *I'm not much closer (even with you)*
And if thow do it nat, than shal þat dede° — *act*
Be left°, and þat nat kepte I out of drede°. — *left (undone), I wouldn't wish that*
35   My lord – nat I – shal haue of thee poweer.
Axe him° licence; vpon him crie and grede°. — *ask him for, implore*

Whan þat thow hast thus doon, than aftirward
Byseeche thow þat worthy Prince Edward
Þat he thee leye apart°, for what may tyde, — *put you aside*
40   Lest thee beholde my maistir Picard.
I warne thee þat it shal be ful hard
For thee and me to halte° on any syde, — *advance*
But he espie vs°. Yit no force°. Abyde. — *without him seeing us, not to worry*
Let him looke on; his herte is to me ward° — *towards me*
45   So freendly þat our shame wole he hyde.

If þat I in my wrytynge foleye°, — *err*
As I do ofte – I can it nat withseye° – — *deny*
Meetrynge amis or speke vnsittyngly°, — *inappropriately*
Or nat by iust peys° my sentences weye°, — *fitting weight, balance*
50   And nat to the ordre of endytyng obeye,
And my colours sette oftesythe° awry, — *often*
With al myn herte wole I buxumly° — *humbly*

---

27. 'Your absence (from her sight) would be more beneficial to my honor.'

28–36. The object of address is still the 'litil pamfilet' that Hoccleve is sending to Edward. Hoccleve is asking, in an especially circuitous way, that Philippa also see the poems in question. He commands the 'pamfilet' to ask Edward for license to be seen by Philippa, but leaves this entirely in Edward's hands.

40. 'my maistir Picard': as with 'Balade to John, Duke of Bedford' (and its embedded address to Massy), here Hoccleve pivots to Picard. Picard is thought to be a clerk of the chapel who was given power of attorney by Edward in 1394. As with the dedicatory verse for Bedford, Hoccleve notes his ability to 'speke vnsittyngly' [inappropriately] and asks Picard to 'amende' and 'correcte' where he goes amiss (48, 53). (Peterson and Wilson 1977: 52; Watt 2013: 50–1; Langdell 2018: 131–2)

45. The notion that Picard, a friendly if ruthless reader, would 'hyde' the shame of both book and writer (should it fail to pass muster), aligns with Massy in 'Balade to John, Duke of Bedford', capable of 'secreetly' correcting whatever he finds amiss in Hoccleve's writing (line 18). (Cf. lines 52–4 of the present poem.) These are stealthy confidants.

46–51. Cf. 'Balade to John, Duke of Bedford', lines 12–14, where Hoccleve also draws attention to the potential for mismetering, and misuse of rhetorical colors. Hoccleve is more exhaustive in his listing of possible defects here, and he introduces the idea of an 'ordre of endytyng [writing]' – like a monastic order – which recalls the *Regiment* and the old man's side by side placement of the 'orders' of 'wedlok' (active life) and 'preesthode' (line 1478).

It to amende and to correcte him preye°,   ask him
For vndir his correccioun stande Y.

55 Thow foul book, vnto my lord seye also
    Þat pryde is vnto me so greet a fo
    Þat the spectacle° forbedith he me,   eyeglass
    And hath ydoon of tyme yore ago°;   has done for some time
    And for my sighte blyue° hastith me fro,   quickly
60 And lakkith þat þat sholde his confort be°,   lacks that which should comfort him
    No wondir thogh thow haue no beautee.
    Out vpon pryde, causere of my wo.
    My sighte is hurt thurgh hir aduersitee°.   (pride's) injury

    Now ende I thus: the holy Trinitee,
65 And our lady, the blissid mayden free°,   generous/gracious
    My lord and lady haue in gouernance,
    And grante hem ioie° and hy prosperitee,   grant them joy
    Nat to endure oonly two yeer or three,
    But a .m.l° – and if any plesance   thousand (years)
70 Happe mighte, on my poore souffissance°,   ability
    To his prowesse and hir benignitee°,   good will
    My lyues ioie° it were, and sustenance.   life's joy

    C'est tout.

55–63. Cf. 'Balade to John, Duke of Bedford', lines 8–9, where Hoccleve also bemoans his failing eyesight. What makes the present book especially 'foul' is precisely this issue. Pride forbids him to wear spectacles. See also 'To Sir John Oldcastle' (1415), lines 417–24, in which Hoccleve uses the metaphor of sight passing through a spectacle to describe the use of icons in focusing devotion and prayer.

65. The Virgin Mary.

69–72. Hoccleve is conveying that, should Edward and Philippa derive any pleasure at all out of these poems, it would be his (Hoccleve's) life's joy. Hedged as it is in a prayerful stanza, invoking the Trinity and the Virgin Mary, the note brings to mind whether the couple might derive spiritual benefit from the poems, too. The collection could have been one similar to HM 744 (the first seven items of which could well have been included by this time), which opens with a series of poems to the Trinity and Mary. Hoccleve's use of 'sustenance' in the final line, to describe what he derives from their benefit, also blends secular and spiritual connotations: see 'Mother of God', line 91; and 'Balade and Roundel to Henry Somer', line 33.

MOTHER OF GOD

Date: unknown (before 1426)

❧

This poem is attributed to Chaucer in two manuscripts – Edinburgh, National Library of Scotland MS Advocates 18.2.8, and Oxford, Bodleian Library MS Arch. Selden B.24 – and was printed in some early Chaucer anthologies as his 'Mother of God'. In this respect, it shares common ground with 'The Monk Who Clad the Virgin' (HM 744, no. 6), which was integrated into the *Canterbury Tales* in one manuscript as the 'Ploughman's Tale'.

'Mother of God' is formally aligned with 'Inuocacio ad Patrem' and 'Mother of Grace' (HM 744, nos. 1 and 5): all three poems consist of twenty seven-line rhyme royal stanzas, totaling 140 lines.

The latter part of 'Mother of God' (lines 99–140) is translated from the second and third sections of the Latin prayer 'O intemerata et in aeternum benedicta, specialis et incomparabilis virgo', as shown in Stokes 1995. Stokes prints the relevant section of the Latin prayer alongside Hoccleve's text, pp. 78–9. The prayer in question was a popular one, found commonly from the twelfth century onwards. The original has a tripartite structure: the first part directed to Mary, the second to St John, and the third part to both. Hoccleve borrows from the second and third parts in his translation.

Mother of God

Ad beatam virginem

Modir of God, and virgyne vndeffouled°,   undefiled
O blisful queene, of queenes emperice°,   empress of (all) queens
Preye for me þat am in synne mowled°,   rotten
To God thy sone, punysshere of vice,
5   Þat of his mercy, thogh þat I be nyce°,   foolish
And negligent in keepyng of his lawe,
His hy mercy my soule vnto him drawe.

Modir of mercy, wey of indulgence,
Þat of al vertu art superlatyf°,   supreme
10   Sauere of vs by thy beneuolence,
Humble lady, mayde, modir, and wyf,
Causere of pees°, styntere° of wo and stryf,   peace, eliminator
My preyere vnto thy sone presente,
Syn° for my gilt I fully me repente.   since

15   Benigne confort of vs wrecches alle,
Be at myn endyng°, whan þat I shal deye.   death
O welle of pitee, vnto thee I calle.
Ful of swetnesse, helpe me to weye
Ageyn the feend°, þat with his handes tweye°   against the devil, two hands
20   And his might° plukke° wole at the balance   power, pull
To weye vs doun. Keepe vs from his nusance.

And, for thow art ensaumple° of chastitee,   the paragon
And of virgynes worsship and honour –
Among alle wommen blessid thow be –
25   Now speke and preye to our sauueour
Þat he me sende swich° grace and fauour,   such
Þat al the hete of brennyng leccherie°   burning lechery
He qwenche in me, blessid maiden Marie.

Heading: To the blessed Virgin

1–2. The preceding poem ('Balade to Edward, Duke of York') pivots to Marian devotion in its final stanza, forming an implicit link between that poem's end and the present poem's focus. Note also the link between 'blisful queene' here, and the (worldly) princess in the previous poem (line 22).

8. 'Modir of mercy'. Cf. line 63.

13–14. For Mary's intercessory role, cf. lines 25–6, below; 'Oldcastle', line 256; 'Mother of Life', lines 14–16, 89–96; 'Mother of God', lines 44, 83; 'Mother of Grace', line 59; 'Balade for Robert Chichele', line 125; 'Monk Who Clad the Virgin', line 8.

16. This topic – the desire for divine solace at one's 'endyng' – becomes the focus of 'Learn to Die', the final item in HM 744.

20–1. Cf. Daniel 5:27.

22–3. Cf. 'Epistle of Cupid', lines 398–9, 421–9; 'Mother of Grace', lines 67–70.

66 MOTHER OF GOD

O blessid lady, the cleer light of day,
30   Temple of our lord and roote of al goodnesse,
Þat by prayere wypest cleene away
The filthes of our synful wikkidnesse,
Thyn hand foorth putte° and helpe my distresse,   *put forth*
And fro temptacioun deliure me
35   Of wikkid thoght, thurgh thy benignitee°.   *kindness*

So þat the wil fulfild be of thy sone,
And þat of the holy goost he m'enlumyne,
Preye for vs, as ay° hath be thy wone°.   *always, custom*
Lady, alle swiche emprises° been thyne.   *such undertakings*
40   Swich an aduocatrice°, who can dyuyne   *such an advocate*
As thow – right noon – our greeues° to redresse°?   *troubles, put right*
In thy refuyt° is al our sikirnesse°.   *refuge, security*

Thow shapen art by Goddes ordenance,
Mene° for vs, flour° of humilitee.   *mediator, flower*
45   Ficche° þat, lady, in thy remembrance,   *fix*
Lest our fo, the feend, thurgh his sotiltee°,   *treachery*
Þat in awayt lyth for to cacche° me,   *catch*
Me ouercome with his treccherie.
Vnto my soules helthe thow me gye°.   *guide*

50   Thow art the way of our redempcioun,
For Cryst of thee hath deyned for to take
Flessh and eek° blood, for this entencioun°,   *also, intention*
Vpon a crois to die for our sake.
His precious deeth made the feendes° qwake,   *devils*
55   And Cristen folk for to reioisen euere°.   *rejoice always*
From his mercy helpe vs we nat disseuere°.   *depart*

Tendrely remembre on the wo and peyne
Þat thow souffridist in his passioun
Whan watir and blood out of thyn yen tweyne°,   *two eyes*
60   For sorwe of him, ran by this° cheekes doun.   *these (Mary's)*
And syn° thow knowest þat the enchesoun°   *since, reason*
Of his deeth was for to saue al mankynde,
Modir of mercy, þat haue in thy mynde.

---

30. 'roote of al goodnesse'. Cf. 'The Monk Who Clad the Virgin', line 5: 'roote of humblesse' (also describing Mary).

35. 'benignitee'. Hoccleve uses this word – in connection with Mary – to close the previous poem, 'Balade to Edward, Duke of York': see line 71.

50–3. Cf. Luke 1:26–38; Acts 5:30–31.

54–5. Cf. James 2:19, 4:7.

57–8. This is the focus of the first poem in HM III, 'Complaint Paramount'.

63. 'Modir of mercy'. Cf. line 8.

MOTHER OF GOD 67

Wel oghten we thee worsshipe and honure,
65 Paleys° of Cryst, flour° of virginitee, palace, flower
Syn° vpon thee was leid the charge and cure° since, care
The lord to bere° of heuene and eerthe and see° bear, sea
And alle thynges þat therynne be.
Of heuenes kyng thow art predestinat° predestined
70 To hele our soules of hir seek estat°. their sick state

Thy maidens wombe, in which our lord lay,
Thy tetes°, whiche him yaf to sowke° also breasts, gave to suck
To our sauynge, be they blessid ay°. always
The birthe of Cryst our thraldom° putte vs fro. bondage
75 Ioie° and honour be now and eueremo joy
To him and thee, þat vnto libertee
Fro thraldam han vs qwit°. Blessid be yee. delivered

By thee, lady, ymakid is the pees° peace is made
Betwixt angels and men, it is no doute.
80 Blessid be God, þat swich° a modir chees°. such, chose
Thy gracious bountee spredith al aboute.
Thogh þat oure hertes steerne been and stoute°, obdurate
Thow to thy sone canst be swich a mene° such an intermediary
That alle our giltes he foryeueth clene.

85 Paradys yates° opned been by thee, paradise's gates
And broken been the yates eek° of helle. gates also
By thee the world restored is, pardee.
Of al vertu thow art the spryng and welle.
By thee al bountee°, shortly for to telle, goodness
90 In heuene and eerthe by thyn ordenance
Parforned° is, our soules sustenance. carried out

Now, syn° thow art of swich° auctoritee, since, such
Lady pitous, virgyne wemmelees°, flawless
Þat our lord God nat list° to werne° thee wishes not, deny
95 Of thy requeste – I wot° wel, doutelees – know
Than spare nat, foorth thee to putte in prees° endeavor
To preye for vs, Crystes modir deere.
Benygnely° wole he thyn axyng° heere. graciously, asking

---

65. 'Paleys of Cryst'. This builds on the metaphor employed in line 30, where Mary is 'Temple of our lord'. See also lines 113–16. On 'flour of virginitee': cf. line 44, 'flour of humilitee'.

72–3. Cf. 'The Monk Who Clad the Virgin', lines 6–7.

86. The image of the broken gates of hell reflects the 'Harrowing of Hell', in which Christ is thought to have descended to hell after his death to grant salvation to virtuous pre-Christian figures such as Adam and Moses.

88. Cf. John 4:13–14. See also 'Mother of Life', line 53.

99–105. John, the beloved disciple, is offered as a surrogate son for Mary, upon Jesus's death. See John 13:23, 19:25–7. Here begins the portion of Hoccleve's poem derived from the Latin prayer 'O intemerata … '

68 MOTHER OF GOD

Apostle, and freend familier of Cryst,
100 And his ychosen virgyne, Seint Ion°,   Saint John
Shynynge apostle and euangelyst,
And best beloued among hem echon°,   each of them (the disciples)
With our lady, preye I thee to been oon
Þat vnto Cryst shal for vs alle preye.
105 Do this for vs, Crystes derlyng°, I seye.   Christ's darling

Marie and Ion, heuenely gemmes tweyne° –   two heavenly gems
O lightes two, shynyng in the presence
Of our lord God, now do your bysy peyne°   i.e., take pains
To wasshe away our cloudeful offense,
110 So þat we mowen° make resistence   can
Ageyn° the feend°, and make him to bewaille°   against, devil, regret
Þat your preyere may so moche auaille.

Yee been tho° two, I knowe verraily,   those
In which the fadir God gan edifie° –   began building
115 By his sone oonly-geten° specially –   only begotten
To him an hows°. Wherfore I to yow crye,   house
Beeth leches° of our synful maladie°.   be healers, disease
Preyeth to God, lord of misericorde°,   mercy
Oure olde giltes þat he nat recorde.

120 Be yee oure help and our proteccioun,
Syn°, for meryt of your virginitee,   since
The priuilege of his dileccioun°   love
In yow conformed God vpon a tree°   i.e., on the cross
Hangyng, and vnto oon of yow seide he,
125 Right in this wyse, as I reherce can:
'Beholde heere, lo: Thy sone, womman.'

---

106. Seymour suggests a conscious echo of the zodiac's Gemini in 'heuenely gemmes tweyne' – heavenly twins. (Latin source: 'o duae gemmae caelestes'.) Cf. also 'Epistle of Cupid', line 421, where St. Margaret is described as a 'precious gemme'.

109. 'cloudeful'. A neologism, reflecting how the 'offense' in question has dimmed our divinely bestowed virtue, as a cloud dims light. Hoccleve adapts this from his Latin source: 'uestris radiis scelerum meorum effugate nubila' (cf. lines 108–9). Note that Mary and Jesus are described as shining lights in line 107. Cf. also 'To Sir John Oldcastle', lines 313–16.

113–16. Latin source: 'Vos estis illi duo in quibus Deus pater per filium suum specialiter aedificauit sibi domum'. Cf. lines 30, 65; John 14:2.

117. Cf. line 70.

122. 'dileccioun'. Cf. Hoccleve's use in *Regiment*, line 851; 'Complaint Paramount', line 235. The only previous record of this word in the *MED* is from the Wycliffite Bible, describing Jesus's love for John in the prologue to the Apocalypse. (See note to lines 99–105 of this poem.) Latin source: 'meritum dilectionis suae'.

126. See note to lines 99–105, above.

MOTHER OF GOD 69

And to þat othir: 'Heer thy modir, lo.'
Than preye I thee þat for the greet swetnesse
Of the hy loue þat God, twixt yow two,
130 With his mowth made, and of his noblesse
Conioyned° hath yow, thurgh his blisfulnesse, conjoined
As modir and sone, helpe vs in our neede.
And for our giltes, make our hertes bleede.

Vnto yow tweyne° I my soule commende, two
135 Marie and Iohn, for my sauuacioun°. salvation
Helpith me þat I may my lyf amende.
Helpith now þat the habitacioun° dwelling place
Of the holy goost, our recreacioun°, (spiritual) renewal
Be in myn herte now and eueremore,
140 And of my soule wasshe away the sore.

Amen.

137–40. Cf. 2 Corinthians 13:13; Hebrews 9:14. The invitation for the Holy Ghost to make its dwelling place in the speaker's heart resonates with the building analogies used throughout the poem: see lines 30, 65, 113–16. For lines 137–40, cf. the Latin source: 'Agite queso, agite uestris gloriosis precibus ut cor meum inuisere et inhabitare dignetur Spiritus almus, qui me a cuntis uitiorum sordibus expurget'.

BALADE TO JOHN, DUKE OF BEDFORD
Date: before May 1414

ତ୨

The date for this poem – before May 1414 – rests on the fact that, after that date, John of Lancaster became duke of Bedford. John of Lancaster was the younger brother of Henry V. The dedication is thought to be for Bedford's own copy of the *Regiment of Princes*, although Hoccleve doesn't mention the *Regiment* by name. Copies of the balade are found in two *Regiment* manuscripts: London, British Library, MS Royal 17 D xviii, and Oxford, Bodleian Library, MS Dugdale 45. (Burrow 1994: 23, 53)

Seymour notes that this poem is written 'in the same metre, for the same purpose, at the same time, and with the same expression of ideas' as 'Balade to Edward, Duke of York' (Seymour 1981: 127). Both poems also imagine sub-readers of the given book – Picard in Edward's balade, and Massy in this poem.

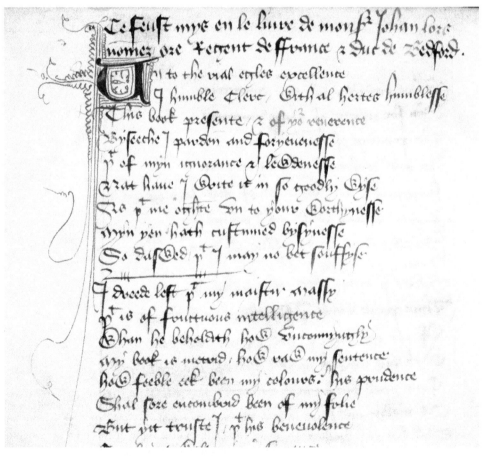

HM 111, fol. 37v (detail), The Huntington Library, San Marino, CA.

BALADE TO JOHN, DUKE OF BEDFORD

Ce feust mys en le liure de monseigneur Iohan, lors nommez, ore Regent de France & Duc de Bedford

Vnto the rial egles° excellence,	royal eagle's
I, humble clerc, with al hertes humblesse°,	humility
This book presente, and of your reuerence	
Byseeche I pardoun and foryeuenesse°	forgiveness
5 Þat, of myn ignorance and lewdenesse°,	lack of skill
Nat haue I write it in so goodly wyse°	such a good manner
As þat me oghte vnto your worthynesse.	
Myn yen° hath custumed bysynesse°	my eyes, habitual overactivity
So daswed° þat I may no bet° souffyse.	dazed, better
10 I dreede lest þat my maistir Massy,	
Þat is of fructuous° intelligence,	fruitful

Heading: This was placed in the book of Lord John, then so called, now Regent of France and Duke of Bedford

2. 'humble clerc'. Cf. 'Dialogue' (*Series*), line 560, where 'Hoccleve' declares himself Duke Humphrey's 'humble seruant and his man'. On the phrase 'hertes humblesse', cf. *Regiment* envoi, line 19; 'Balade to Edward, Duke of York', line 5.

3. 'This book'. Possibly referring to Bedford's own copy of the *Regiment*, although that work is not named explicitly.

4–7. 'myn ignorance and lewdenesse … ' Cf. line 27. On these professions of ignorance in fifteenth-century literature (and their use in navigating a politically volatile period), see Lawton, 'Dullness and the Fifteenth Century'. Hoccleve uses similarly self-deprecatory language in the *Regiment* envoi, lines 4 ('nakid … of eloquence'), 18–20 ('innocence / of endytynge … negligence'); and 'Balade to Edward, Duke of York', lines 46–55 (including directions to his 'foul book'). But the present poem is the only dedicatory verse in which Hoccleve uses 'lewdnesse' [a state of ignorance/being uneducated/not smart] to describe himself. In 'To Sir John Oldcastle', 'lewde' is used polemically to describe women who attempt theological inquiry (line 147) and as an insult for presumptuous Lollards more generally (line 352). Cf. also 'Worshipful Maiden', line 34; 'Epistle of Cupid', line 282; and 'Three Roundels', line 28.

8–9. Hoccleve also complains of poor eyesight (and a reluctance to wear spectacles) in 'Balade to Edward, Duke of York', lines 55–63.

10. 'maistir Massy': the identity of this 'Massy' has been the matter of some debate. For an overview, see Watt 2013: 45–8. It is possible, as suggested by Turville-Petre and Wilson, that the individual is William Massy, who served as Receiver-General and General Attorney to John of Lancaster (1975: 130). Watt points out that Hoccleve may well have encountered Massy in London and Westminster, perhaps in the Inns of Court. The 'dual' address in this balade – ostensibly for Bedford, but also directed to Massy – is seen also in 'Balade to Edward, Duke of York', where a figure named Picard becomes the subsidiary subject of Hoccleve's address. (On this dynamic, see Langdell 2018: 129–32.)

11. 'fructuous intelligence': the phrase recalls the *Regiment*'s 'fructuous entendement' (line 1963), used to describe Chaucer.

72 BALADE TO JOHN, DUKE OF BEDFORD

Whan he beholdith how vnconnyngly° — unskillfully
My book is metrid, how raw my sentence°, — understanding/knowledge
How feeble eek° been my colours°, his prudence — also, (rhetorical) colors
15 Shal sore encombrid been° of my folie. — be sorely burdened
But yit truste I þat his beneuolence
Conpleyne wole myn insipience° — foolishness
Secreetly, and what is mis°, rectifie°. — amiss, amend

Thow, book, by licence of my lordes grace,
20 To thee speke I, and this I to thee seye:
I charge thee, go shewe° thow thy face — show
Beforn my seid maistir, and to him preye
On my behalue þat he peise and weye° — measure and weigh (consider)
What myn entente° is – þat I speke in thee – — intention
25 For rethorik hath hid fro me the keye
Of his tresor°, nat deyneth hir nobleye° — treasure, nobility
Dele with noon° so ignorant as me. — deal with anyone

C'est tout.

12–14. In drawing attention to the potential for mismetering here, and misuse of rhetorical colors, Hoccleve parallels 'Balade to Edward, Duke of York', lines 46–51. In both cases, it is the subsidiary reader (Massy here, Picard there) who would be cognizant of these formal aspects of Hoccleve's verse. In 'Balade to Edward,' Hoccleve describes a lack of attention to these formal qualities as a disobedience to the 'ordre of endytyng'.

16–18. The idea of Massy 'secreetly' conveying what he finds lacking or foolish is intriguing. The tone is jesting, but it also recalls *Richard the Redeless* – a poem that announces its 'secrette' status, and invites the reader to engage in amending it (lines 57–63). (Langdell 2018: 130–1) It is also notable that Hoccleve invites Massy to correct 'what is mis'. Line 17: 'insipience' is an apparent neologism; see also Hoccleve's use at *Series* 5.228.

24. 'What myn entente is … ' These final lines are rather enigmatic: Hoccleve's 'entente' [intention] here comes across as hidden, something that he invites Massy to seek out. He blames this on his own ignorance and lack of facility in rhetoric, but the treasure-and-key metaphor would seem to expand to encompass the very question of intention in the book – a treasure hidden, needed to be sought out. If the book in question is indeed the *Regiment*, then there would be relevance to Hoccleve's own envoi to that poem, in which he describes himself as 'privy' to its 'sentence' (line 10).

26. Seymour changes 'his' to 'hir' in this line, presumably to agree with the pronoun at the end of line. Furnivall leaves 'his' and 'hir' as is, as they appear in the manuscript. I follow that practice, to preserve the original ambiguity: one possibility is that 'hir' is 'their', referring to Bedford and Massy both.

BALADE TO THE CHANCELLOR

Date: c. August 1406–January 1407 (probable)

☙

John Burrow posits Thomas Langley as the most likely recipient of this poem. Langley served as Chancellor from March 2, 1405 to January 30, 1407, having served as Keeper of the Privy Seal immediately before (from 1401 to 1405). Langley became bishop of Durham in August 1406. If the poem is indeed addressed to him, it would have been written between then and January 1407, when Langley departed the Chancery (Burrow 1994: 15).

This poem begins a four-poem run of experiments with the interlocking double croisée: Hoccleve also uses this form in 'Balade and Roundel to Henry Somer', the '*Regiment of Princes* envoi', and 'Victorious King'. The fact that these poems arrive consecutively in HM 111 (items 12–15) suggests that Hoccleve is grouping them by form. (On Hoccleve's experiments with the double croisée, see General Introduction: 'Sequencing, Form, & the Question of Design'.)

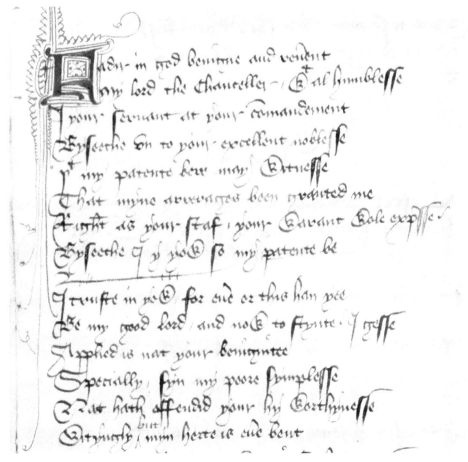

HM 111, fol. 38r (detail), The Huntington Library, San Marino, CA.

BALADE TO THE CHANCELLOR

Fadir in God, benigne° and reuerent,   *kind*
My lord the Chanceller, with al humblesse,
I, your seruant at your commandement,
Byseeche vnto your excellent noblesse,
5 Þat my patente° bere may witnesse   *official document*
That myne arrerages° been granted me –   *unpaid sums*
Right° as your staf, your warant° wole expresse –   *straight/true, authorizing document*
Byseeche I yow, so my patente be.

I truste in yow, for euere or this han yee°   *always before this have you*
10 Be my good lord; and now to stynte°, I gesse,   *stop*
Applied is nat your benignitee°,   *kindness/generosity*
Specially syn° my poore symplesse°   *especially since, innocence/lowliness*
Nat hath° offendid your hy worthynesse   *has not*
Wityngly°. But° myn herte is euere bent   *purposely, rather*
15 To sheete° at yow good wil, in soothfastnesse° –   *shoot (as an arrow), truly*
Therein am I ful hoot° and ful feruent.   *truly ardent*

O my lord gracious, wys, and prudent,
To me, your clerc, beeth of your grace free°.   *generous*
Let see now: cacche a lust° and a talent°   *catch a desire, will*
20 Me to haue in your fauour and cheertee°.   *charity*
Thereon wayte I. I wayte on your bountee,
That to so manye han shewid gentillesse°.   *generosity*
Let me be no stepchyld been, for I am he
That hope haue in yow, confort, and gladnesse.

25 C'est tout.

---

1. 'Fadir in God': this phrase indicates that the poem is addressed to a bishop. Burrow posits Thomas Langley as the most likely candidate here. See note above.

4–8. Hoccleve is requesting that the recipient help facilitate payment of Hoccleve's arrears (unpaid sums due to him).

7. 'staf'. Likely a bishop's staff, given Langley's position. There's a potential joke here – Langley's 'warant' would be true/straight as his staff, which is of course curved at the top, like a shepherd's crook.

8. In HM 111, Hoccleve writes 'Byseeche I y yow'. I take the extra 'y' as an instance of dittography, and omit it in the text.

9–10. These lines may refer to the time under which Hoccleve worked for Langley at the Privy Seal.

15–16. The arrow metaphor is striking here: Hoccleve's good will is propulsive.

18. 'your clerc': Langley had served as Keeper of the Privy Seal before his elevation to Chancellor; Hoccleve seems to be drawing on their previous working relationship here.

21. 'wayte I. I wayte'. Note the chiasmic structure; cf. 'Learn to Die', line 134.

23. 'stepchyld'. Uses of this term are rare before this instance. Hoccleve's meaning is somewhat opaque. It is possible Hoccleve only means that he would feel neglected without Langley's support. It is also possible that Hoccleve means that Langley had served a father-like role (while at the helm of the Privy Seal), professionally speaking; and now that he is remarried – to the Chancery, to the Church – Hoccleve has become something of a stepchild.

BALADE AND ROUNDEL TO HENRY SOMER

Date: late 1408–1409

❦

Henry Somer served as Under-Treasurer ('Souztresorer') – the title that Hoccleve specifies for him in the heading to this piece – from summer 1408 to autumn 1410. This poem most likely dates to the period between Michaelmas (September 29) and Christmas in 1408 or 1409, given the information in Hoccleve's heading, and within the poem itself (see note to lines 14–19; Burrow favors the 1408 date – see Burrow 1994: 16). This is the first of two poems addressed to Somer in HM 111; the second is 'The Court of Good Company' (item 17). In both cases, the spirit is both petitionary and jovial. In the present poem, Hoccleve puns on Somer's surname, developing seasonal, fruitful metaphors that lead to a harvest-time request for payment. It is notable that – as with 'Good Company' – Hoccleve drives a collective address on behalf of colleagues. Hoccleve's Privy Seal colleagues John Bailey, John Hethe, and John Offord are mentioned in lines 25–6, where Hoccleve also names himself (see note to those lines, on those colleagues). The poem is also notable for its ending roundel, one of two pieces in the holographs that employ this form. (For the other, see 'Three Roundels', HM 744 no. 9.)

This is the second poem in a four-poem run of experiments with the double croisée stanza. (On Hoccleve's use of this form, see General Introduction: 'Sequencing, Form, & the Question of Design'.)

HM 111, fol. 38v (detail), The Huntington Library, San Marino, CA.

BALADE AND ROUNDEL TO HENRY SOMER

Cestes balade & chanceon ensuyantz feurent faites a mon Meistre .H. Somer quant il estoit Souztresorer

The sonne°, with his bemes of brightnesse, — sun
To man so kyndly is and norisshynge,
Þat lakkyng it, day nere° but dirknesse. — would be nothing
To day he yeueth° his enlumynynge°, — gives, light
5 And causith al fruyt for to wexe° and sprynge. — grow
Now, syn° þat sonne may so moche auaille, — since
And moost with Somer° is his soiournynge, — summer (with pun on Somer)
That sesoun bonteuous° we wole assaille°. — bountiful, address

Glad cheerid Somer, to your gouernaille° — guidance
10 And grace we submitte al our willynge.
To whom yee freendly been, he may nat faille,
But he shal haue his resonable axynge°. — request
Aftir your good lust, be the sesonynge° — by the ripening
Of our fruytes°, this laste Mighelmesse°, — crops, Michaelmas
15 The tyme of yeer was of our seed ynnynge°, — harvest
The lak of which is our greet heuynesse°. — sadness

We truste vpon your freendly gentillesse°, — generosity
Yee wole vs helpe and been our suppoaille°. — support
Now yeue° vs cause ageyn this Cristemesse° — give, Christmas
20 For to be glad, O lord – whethir° our taille° — perhaps, tally (amount owed)
Shal soone make vs with our shippes saille
To port salut°? If yow list°, we may synge; — safe harbor, wish
And elles° moot vs° bothe mourne and waille — otherwise, we must
Til your fauour vs sende releeuynge°. — (financial) relief

Heading: This following balade and song were made for my master H. Somer, when he was under-treasurer

1–8. Cf. 'Complaint' lines 1–7 as an intriguing point of contrast. Whereas those lines open the *Series* seasonally, setting an autumnal tone, this poem for Somer sets a suitably summery tone, with its attendant signifiers: fruitfulness, warmth, light.

9–18. Cf. 1 John 5:12,14–15; John 15:16.

14–19. Hoccleve's reference to payments due 'laste Mighelmesse', and the hope of enjoyment 'this Cristemesse' help to date the poem. He would be referring to Michaelmas (September 29) 1408 or 1409. Michaelmas also carries the connotation of harvest time – the period when one reaps crops.

21. 'shippes'. As Seymour notes, this is a pun on 'the great noble [coin], valued at one half-mark, issued by Edward III in 1344 to commemorate the naval victory off Sluys in 1340, and stamped with a large ship'. (1981: 111) They hope to 'sail' to safe harbor with/on replenished coin. Cf. 'The Court of Good Company', line 29; 'Three Roundels', line 11.

BALADE AND ROUNDEL TO HENRY SOMER 77

25 We, your seruantes Hoccleue and Baillay,
Hethe and Offorde, yow byseeche and preye:
Haastith° our heruest as soone as yee may!   hasten
For fere of stormes, our wit is aweye°.   we're anxious
Were our seed inned°, wel we mighten pleye,   if we had our harvest
30 And vs desporte° and synge, and make game;   amuse ourselves
And yit this rowndel° shul we synge and seye,   roundel
In trust of yow, and honour of your name:

SOMER, þat rypest° mannes sustenance   ripens
With holsum hete of the sonnes warmnesse,
35 Al kynde of man thee holden is° to blesse.   you are bound

Ay° thankid be thy freendly gouernance   forever
And thy fressh look of mirthe and of gladnesse,
        Somer, etc.

To heuy folk of thee the remembrance°   the memory of you
40 Is salue and oynement° to hir seeknesse°,   ointment, their illness
Forwhy° we thus shul synge in Cristemesse,   which is why
        Somer, etc.

───────────────

25–6. Hoccleve names himself and his Privy Seal colleagues John Bailey ('Baillay'), John Hethe, and
John Offord ('Offorde'). These four clerks, including Hoccleve, 'formed the nucleus of the active
scribes at the Privy Seal from the second half of Henry IV's reign until the death of Henry V'
(Sobecki 2019: 66). Both Hethe and Offord also worked for the France-based Privy Seal Office, c.
1417–22 (Sobecki 2021: 257, 260). Bailey died in 1420 and mentions Hoccleve (and Hoccleve's wife)
in his will (see Sobecki 2019: Chapter 2). See further: Sobecki 2021: 257–63 (on Hethe and Offord,
and their handwriting); Watt 2013: 58–61; Kern 1916; Brown 1971.

28. 'our wit is aweye'. Cf. 'Complaint Paramount', line 217: 'Poore Marie, thy wit is aweye'. Cf. also
'Complaint', lines 59 and 64, in which Hoccleve's wit is personified and goes away, only to return
'hoom … aȝein'.

29. Note the linguistic resonance with the opening to Hoccleve's *Series*: 'seed inned' recalls the *Series*'
'Aftir þat heruest inned had hise sheues' (1.1). (Cf. Watt 2013: 30)

30. On the intersection between collective speech (on behalf of associates), anxiety, and a contrasting
'game' and play, see *Regiment*, lines 1009–15.

33–42. This roundel is both a poem in its own right, and part of the greater piece. It has much in
common with the 'Three Roundels' found as the penultimate element of HM 744. (This roundel
rhymes, however, abb ab abb; whereas the 'Three Roundels' each rhyme abba ab ba abba, with
the first quatrain serving as the recurring chorus.) Note the focus on naming there and here: the
second of the 'Three Roundels' in HM 744 gives Hoccleve an opportunity to self-name, and here
the name 'Somer' is part and parcel of the roundel – as Hoccleve notes, the roundel is performed
'In trust of yow, and honour of your *name*' (32; italics mine). The text also suggests that it would
have been sung aloud (line 31). It is intriguing that the roundel-oriented poems in HM 111 and 744
both include Hoccleve's name.

39. 'heuy'. Cf. 'Three Roundels', lines 46–7, the song, 'mirthe', and 'gladnesse' giving way to a 'lessoun
of heuynesse' [that is, Learn to Die].

REGIMENT OF PRINCES ENVOI
Date: c. 1410–11

❧

This envoi is appended to the end of Hoccleve's most popular long poem, the *Regiment of Princes* (c. 1410–11). The *Regiment* was written for Prince Henry, the future Henry V. The main text of the poem delivers a series of exempla on the habits and virtues of a good ruler. The opening 2,000 lines, by contrast, feature a conversation between a 'Hoccleve' narrator and an unnamed old man. The poem survives more or less complete in over 40 manuscripts, making it one of the most widely read Middle English poems.

The version of the envoi found in HM 111 is remarkable in that it differs from other existing versions of the envoi in three instances, all of which occur in the final stanza: 'humblesse' in line 19 (changed from 'meeknesse'); 'wil' in line 22 (from 'herte'); and 'God' in the final line (changed from 'he'). (For further analysis, see Langdell 2018: 180–1.)

The inclusion of an envoi – offered on its own – lends support to the 'collection of forms' view of the Huntington holographs. A reader hoping to find a good example of the envoi (alongside petitionary verse, roundels, rhyme royal, etc.) has that particular form to hand. The presence of the envoi also, of course, ties this collection (and its author) quite firmly to that very popular poem.

Hoccleve employs the double croisée stanza here (on which, see General Introduction: 'Sequencing, Form, & the Question of Design'.) Only three rhymes are used in the entire poem (-o, -ence, -esse), and the form allows for catch-rhymes between stanzas. Hoccleve's use of such a virtuosic and unique form, while feigning humility and deference, sets the tone for this envoi and its internal power plays.

It is notable that Hoccleve names himself in the previous poem in HM 111, and then includes this portion of his most famous poem directly afterwards – perhaps aiming to link name and work.

REGIMENT OF PRINCES ENVOI

Ceste balade ensuyante feust mise en le fin du liure del Regiment des Princes

O litil book, who yaf° thee hardynesse°	gave, daring
Thy wordes to pronounce in the presence	
Of kynges ympe° and princes worthynesse,	king's offspring
Syn° thow al nakid art of eloquence?	since
5 And why approchist thow his excellence	
Vnclothid, sauf° thy kirtil° bare also?	save, cloak
I am right seur his humble pacience	
Thee yeueth° hardynesse° to do so.	gives you, courage
But o° thyng woot° I wel: go wher thow go,	one, know
10 I am so pryuee° vnto thy sentence°,	privy, meaning/doctrine
Thow haast and art, and wilt been eueremo,	
To his hynesse of swich beneuolence°.	such good will
Thogh thow nat do him due reuerence	
In wordes, thy cheertee° nat is the lesse.	charity/respect
15 And if lust° be to his magnificence	desire
Do by thy reed°, his welthe it shal witnesse.	counsel
Byseeche him, of his gracious noblesse,	
Thee holde excusid° of thyn innocence	to excuse you
Of endytynge°, and with hertes humblesse°,	writing, humility
20 If any thyng thee passe of negligence,	
Byseeche him of mercy and indulgence,	
And þat for thy good wil he be nat fo	
To thee, þat al seist° of loues feruence°.	who says everything, ardor
Þat knowith God, whom no thyng is hid fro.	
25 C'est tout.	

Heading: The following balade was placed at the end of the book of the Regiment of Princes

3. The parallel phrases 'kynges ympe' and 'princes worthynesse' both refer, of course, to Prince Henry. The first phrase helps to tie Henry's identity that much more to Henry IV.

4–6. Hoccleve employs the 'unclothed' metaphor here to indicate a 'naked' text, bare of eloquence. Cf. 'Balade to Edward, Duke of York', lines 8, 46–63; 'Balade to John, Duke of Bedford', lines 5, 10–27.

10. 'pryuee'. It is intriguing that Hoccleve uses this word here in the envoi to his masterwork; it raises the question of Hoccleve tying authorship of the *Regiment* to his position in the Privy Seal (or 'Privee Seel', which he mentions in the *Regiment*; see lines 802, 1464). On the idea of Hoccleve being privy to a work's 'sentence' (and hence capable of vouching for its good will), cf. 'Balade to John, Duke of Bedford', lines 22–4.

11. For syntax, cf. Revelation 1:8.

15–16a. 'If his highness desires to follow your advice … '

19. 'hertes humblesse'. This phrase is also used in 'Balade to Edward, Duke of York', line 5; 'Balade to John, Duke of Bedford', line 2.

24. Cf. 'Epistle of Cupid', line 400: 'And God, fro whom ther may no thyng hid be'.

VICTORIOUS KING

Date: perhaps c. 1415–16

❧

Given the reference to Henry V as 'victorious kyng', Seymour (following Furnivall) dates this poem to 1415–16, shortly after Henry's return from Agincourt on November 23, 1415. Henry had been crowned relatively recently (April 9, 1413), and so references to Hoccleve and his colleagues as 'seruantz of the olde date' (line 20) would make sense: they would be working to bridge their service (and allegiance) from the old regime to the new. And, of course, Henry's military success at Agincourt would have earned him the title 'victorious kyng'.

Hoccleve uses the double croisée form here (on which, see General Introduction: 'Sequencing, Form, & the Question of Design'). This poem ends a four-poem run of items experimenting with that form.

Continuity in subject matter from the previous poem should also be noted: we transition here from the envoi to the *Regiment of Princes*, Hoccleve's advice-to-princes text for Prince Henry, to his salute to Henry, potentially following the king's victory at Agincourt, about four years later.

The present poem also shares much in common with the fourth item in HM 111, 'For Henry V at Kennington', likely written two or three years earlier. That poem is also an early dispatch to Henry in the first years of his reign (in that case, the first days). Both are written in the same form – using double croisée stanzas – and both show respect to the king, without ladling too much praise. Both greet him respectfully, and then give ample space to Hoccleve's own objective or need: in 'Kennington', the ongoing moral education of the prince, and the need to respect the church in its fight against heresy; and in 'Victorious King', the need for financial support for Hoccleve and his fellows.

Line 8 of the poem references Newgate prison. Helen Hickey has discussed Hoccleve's decision to feature this prison rather than Ludgate, the debtors' prison. Among the possible reasons for the choice is that the 'prisoner's parade' to Newgate would have brought the subjects down 'the same streets where Henry's glorious and lavish pageant took place after his victory at Agincourt', albeit in reverse – with the prisoners processing in the opposite direction. This raises the question of whether Hoccleve meant to bring that victory procession to mind. (Hickey, in Nuttall–Watt 2022: 209–10)

VICTORIOUS KING

Item au Roy, que dieu pardoint

Victorious kyng, our lord ful gracious,
We, humble lige° men to your hynesse, — loyal
Meekly byseechen yow, O kyng pitous,
Tendre pitee haue on our sharp distresse.
5 For, but° the flood of your rial largesse° — except that, royal generosity
Flowe vpon vs, gold hath vs in swich° hate — such
Þat of his loue and cheertee° the scantnesse — charity
Wole arte° vs three to trotte° vnto Newgate. — compel, trot (march)

Benigne° lige lord, O hauene and yate° — kind, haven and gate
10 Of our confort, let your hy worthynesse
Oure indigences° softne and abate. — poverty
In yow lyth al; yee may our greef redresse°. — alleviate
The somme° þat we in our bille expresse — sum
Is nat excessif, ne outrageous°. — nor extravagant
15 Our long seruice also berith witnesse;
We han for it be ful laborious°. — truly hard-working

O lige lord, þat han be plenteuous° — who has been generous
Vnto your liges of your grace algate°, — in every way
Styntith nat° now for to be bonteuous° — don't stop, generous
20 To vs, your seruantz of the olde date.
God woot° we han been ay°, eerly and late, — knows, always
Louynge lige men to your noblesse.
Lat nat the strook of indigence° vs mate°, — poverty, defeat

Heading: Piece for the king, may God pardon him

1. Cf. the opening to 'Henry V's Last Return' (HM 744, no. 8): 'Victorious Cristen prince', and 'Dialogue' (*Series*), line 554: 'our lord lige, our kyng victorious'.

8. Newgate: a prison in London. The threat is surely only for dramatic effect, not actual. It is not clear who is included in 'vs three' here, beyond Hoccleve. On Newgate, cf. 'Cook's Tale', line 4402. On Hoccleve's decision to refer to Newgate rather than Ludgate, the debtors' prison, see Hickey in Nuttall–Watt 2022: 207–10.

9. 'hauene'. Cf. 'Mother of Grace', line 97.

13. 'bille'. Reference to their bill aligns the poem with 'Balade to the Chancellor', in which Hoccleve's 'patente' (line 5) serves a similar function.

15. 'long seruice'. This phrase helps situate Hoccleve (and his two fellow supplicants) as Privy Seal employees, and longstanding ones at that.

20. 'seruantz of the olde date'. See introductory note to this poem. This phrase helps give the impression that Hoccleve is writing on behalf of himself and two colleagues to the new king, hoping to show their support and ensure seamless transition between regimes.

O worthy prince, mirour of prowesse.

25 C'est tout.

---

24. 'mirour of prowesse'. Hoccleve uses the word 'mirour' frequently to mean 'exemplar'. It is used in both secular and sacred contexts. Especially relevant here is its use in *Regiment*, line 5328, where Hoccleve addresses Prince Henry in tandem with all French princes and all (other) English princes, asking them to serve as 'miroures' for their subjects by choosing peace over warfare (and therefore truly embodying Christ). If the present poem is indeed written in the wake of Agincourt, this presents a dissonant echo. (In *Regiment*, that line also reverberates with Hoccleve's early description of Chaucer as 'mirour of fructuous entendement' (line 1963).)

BALADE TO JOHN CARPENTER
Date: unknown (before 1426)

❧

John Carpenter (1370–1441) served as town clerk of London from 1417 to 1438. Burrow posits that the poem was likely originally addressed to someone else, given the name Carpenter is written over an erasure (and the three syllables in Carpenter interrupt the meter) (Burrow 1994: 16). Burrow and Doyle have suggested that Carpenter may have been the recipient of HM 111, given Hoccleve's willingness to interpolate his name here (2002: xxvii). Watt notes that, while that claim is necessarily tentative, Carpenter 'probably was the *kind* of reader' that Hoccleve had in mind: he may well have been aware of many individuals named therein, such as Massy and Picard. (Watt 2013: 61) Lee Patterson has argued for Carpenter's role in preserving another of Hoccleve's works, the *Series*. (2001: 90–2) While we do not know the extent of Carpenter's role in preserving that work, we do know that he played an active role with regard to Lydgate's *Dance of Death*, which is collected with the *Series* in all non-autograph manuscripts. (See Appleford 2008)

Note that this poem and the next – 'The Court of Good Company' – are both 'begging' poems (or poems with financial requests) written in rhyme royal; whereas, the other three such poems – the earlier balade to Somer, 'Victorious King', and the 'Balade to the Chancellor' – are written in the eight-line double croisée form.

BALADE TO JOHN CARPENTER

See heer, my maister Carpenter, I yow preye,
How many chalenges ageyn° me be, — *charges against*
And I may nat deliure hem° by no weye, — *them*
So me werreyeth° coynes scarsetee°, — *I wrestle so with, poverty*
5 That ny° cousin is to necessitee. — *close*
Forwhy° vnto yow seeke I for refut°, — *wherefore, refuge*
Which þat of confort am ny° destitut. — *nearly*

gloss: A de B et C de D etc. Ceste balade **feust tendrement consideree et bonement execute**

Tho° men, whos names I aboue expresse, — *those*
Fayn wolden° þat they and I euene were; — *eagerly wish*
10 And so wolde I, God take I to witnesse.
I woot° wel I moot° heere or elleswhere — *know, must*
Rekne of my dettes°, and of hem answere°. — *account for my debts, settle them*
Myn herte, for the dreede of God and awe,
Fayn wolde it qwyte°, and for constreynt of lawe. — *pay*

15 But, by my trouthe°, nat wole it betyde°. — *vow, it won't happen*
And, therfore, as faire° as I can and may, — *courteously/gently*
With aspen herte° I preye hem° abyde, — *trembling heart, them*
And me respyte° to sum lenger° day. — *give me an extension, later*
Some of hem grante°, and some of hem seyn nay. — *grant (such an extension)*
20 And I so sore ay° dreede an aftirclap° — *always sorely, fear a reprisal*
That it me reueth° many a sleep and nap. — *robs me of*

If þat it lykid vnto your goodnesse° — *i.e., if you would be willing*
To be betwixt [hem] and me swich a mene° — *such an intermediary*
As þat I mighte kept be fro duresse°, — *hardship*
25 Myn heuy thoghtes wolde it voide° clene. — *wipe*
As your good plesance is, this thyng demene°. — *take control of this*
How wel þat yee doon, and how soone also,
I suffre may in qwenchynge° of my wo. — *quenching (voiding)*

C'est tout.

---

1. gloss: A of B and C of D etc. This balade was tenderly considered and executed generously/kindly. ['A de B et C de D etc.' is presumably a representation of the names of people requesting payment: e.g., John of Norwich and Simon of Wits' End. The actual names would have accompanied the initial version of this poem.]

4–5. Cf. 'Knight's Tale', lines 3041–2.

8. See gloss above, note to line 1.

17. 'aspen herte'. Cf. *Regiment*, line 1954.

23. 'mene'. Hoccleve asks Carpenter to serve as a 'mene' [intermediary] between his creditors and him. Hoccleve often uses this word – or 'mediatrice' – in a devotional context to describe the role of the Virgin Mary. See, e.g., 'Mother of God', lines 44 and 83; 'Mother of Grace', line 59; and 'The Monk Who Clad the Virgin', line 8.

28. Cf. final line of 'Male Regle' (line 448).

THE COURT OF GOOD COMPANY
Date: April 1421

ᆭ

This convivial poem is written to Henry Somer, reminding him of his duties in hosting an upcoming meeting of a Temple dining club, the Court of Good Company. The most likely date for the meeting in question would have been May 1, 1421, and as the poem refers to the dinner occurring 'thorsday next' (56, 70), we can assume the poem itself was written in late April 1421. In writing the poem, Hoccleve is responding to a letter sent by Somer to the Court, which Hoccleve references (line 3). Given the date for the dinner in question is both May 1 and a Thursday (see lines 39, 56, 70), the eligible years would have been 1410 or 1421. Furnivall and Seymour both opted for the earlier option. However, Henry Somer had only held the title by which Hoccleve refers to him here – Chancellor of the Exchequer – since June 1410. Hence, May 1, 1421 is the most likely date. (See Burrow 1994: 29)

As a petitionary poem written on behalf of (or perhaps *with*) his associates, this poem aligns with 'Balade and Roundel to Henry Somer' – written for the same recipient over a decade prior. As Nuttall notes, this poem was written a few months after the completion of the 'Complaint' and 'Dialogue' (in the *Series*), but the works are not really consonant: 'The *Series* depicts a melancholic, socially isolated poet, deeply conscious of his own mortality and undertaking his final poetic work (*Dialogue*, 239–94), while the *balade* to Somer presents a persona full of wit, joie de vivre, and sociability.' Nuttall notes that this is a reminder that 'Hoccleve's self-presentation is inevitably partial and purposeful, temporary rather than defining'. (Nuttall 2015: 2)

The Court of Good Company

Ceste balade ensuyante feust par la Court de bone conpaignie, enuoiee a lonure sire Henri Somer, Chaunceller de Leschequer & vn de la dicte Court

Worsshiful sire, and our freend special,
And felawe° in this cas, we calle yow. *(dining) companion*
Your letre sent vnto vs, cleerly, al
We haue red, and vndirstanden how
5 It is no wit° to your conceit°, as now, *not wise, to your mind*
Vse the rule foorth as we been inne°, *to live as we have been*
But al anothir rule to begynne.

Rehercynge how, in the place of honour,
The Temple, for solace and for gladnesse,
10 Wheras nat oghte vsid been errour
Of ouer mochil waast or of excesse,
First wern we fowndid to vse largesse° *generosity*
In our despenses°; but for to exceede *expenses*
Reson, we han espyed°, yee nat beede°. *have seen, you ask us not to*

15 Yee allegge eek° how a rule° hath be kept *also mention, standard*
Or° this, which was good, as yee haue herd seyn, *before*
But it now late cessid° hath, and slept – *ceased*
Which good yow thynkith were vp take ageyn;
And, but if it so be°, our court certeyn *i.e., unless we return to that standard*
20 Nat likly any whyle is to endure,
As hath in mowthe many a creature°. *i.e., as many people have said*

Yee wolden, þat in conseruacioun° *preservation*
Of oure honour, and eek° for our profyt, *also*
Þat th'entente° of oure old fundacioun° *intention, organization*
25 Obserued mighte been, and to þat plyt° *condition*
Be broght as it was first, and passe al qwyt° *deliver all*
Out of the daunger of outrageous° waast, *excessive*
Lest with scorn and repreef feede vs swich taast.

Heading: The following balade, made by the Court of Good Company, was sent to the honorable Sir Henry Somer, Chancellor of the Exchequer and one [member] of the said Court

1–2. Hoccleve balances the registers of address here: Somer is Chancellor of the Exchequer – 'worsshiful sire' – but also a 'freend' and 'felawe', a colleague in the Court of Good Company.

3. 'letre'. This situates Hoccleve's poem as a verse response to (what appears to be) an actual letter, sent by Somer. Cf. the playful epistolary debate in 'Epistle of Cupid' (HM 744, no. 7). Lines 3–4: 'we have all thoroughly read the letter you sent us … '

9. 'The Temple'. Seymour suggests the 'Middle Temple, to which Chester's Inn belonged' (see *Regiment*, line 5). (Seymour 1981: 112)

10–14. 'where there ought not to have been overmuch waste or excessive spending, first we spent freely and generously; but we now see that you bid us not to be unreasonable [in our spending].'

17. That is, while the Court previously practiced restraint, it now tends towards extravagance.

18. 'which you think would be good to take up again'

THE COURT OF GOOD COMPANY 87

Vnto þat ende, .vjᶜ.º shippes grete | six
30 To yeueº vs han yee grauntid and behightº, | give, pledged
To byeº ageyn our dyner, flour or whete, | buy
And besyde itº, as reson woleº and rightº, | along with that, as is reasonable
Paie your laghº, as dooth anothir wight | pay your share
Þat by mesure rulith him and gyethº, | by moderation is ruled and guided
35 And nat as he whom outrage maistriethº. | who is ruled by excess

In your letre, contened is also
Þat if vs listº to chaunge in no maneere | we wish
Our neewe gyseº, ne twynneº therfro, | approach, nor depart
The firste day of May yee wole appeere –
40 Þat day yee sette be with vs in feereº – | in companionship
And to keepe itº, yee wole be reedy. | i.e., enforce the old (moderate) rule
This is th'effect of your letre, soothly.

To the whiche, in this wyseº we answere: | way
Excesseº for to do be yee nat bownde, | extravagance
45 Ne noonº of vs, but do as we may bereº. | nor any, as we can
Vpon swich rule, we nat vs ne grownde.
Yee been discreetº, thogh yee in good habowndeº. | prudent, although you are wealthy
Dooth as yow thynkith for your honestee.
Yee – and we alle – arn at our libertee.

50 At our laste dyner, wel knowen yee,
By our stywardes limitaciounº | order
(As custume of our court axith to be,
And ayº at oure congregacion | always
Obserued, left al excusacionº) | without exception
55 Warned yee wern for the dyner arrayeº | to provide for the dinner
Ageyn Thorsday next, and nat it delaye.

---

29. Somer has sent six 'shippes grete'. A 'shippe' is a 'great noble [coin], valued at one half-mark'. (Seymour 1981: 111) See also 'Balade and Roundel to Henry Somer', line 21; 'Three Roundels', line 11.

33. 'lagh'. An apparent neologism, possibly taken from spoken English.

39. This helps date the poem more precisely. Hoccleve notes twice that May 1, when the Court next meets, will be a Thursday (lines 56, 70), helping to situate the planned-upon date as Thursday, May 1, 1421. By extrapolation, Hoccleve is writing (or delivering) this poem in the week before, the final week of April. The May 1st date also has significance for Somer's name: as the weather warms, there is the promise that Somer 'wole appeere'. Hoccleve puns extensively on Somer (as summer, resplendent with sunlight) in 'Balade and Roundel to Henry Somer'.

40. 'That day you set to join us (dine with us)'

48. That is, do what you think best.

52–4. 'As is the custom of our court, and is always observed at our gathering, without exception'

56. See note to line 39.

88 THE COURT OF GOOD COMPANY

We yow nat holde auysid° in swich wyse   *we don't advise you*
As for to make vs destitut þat day
Of our dyner. Take on yow þat empryse°.   *enterprise*
60 If your lust be, dryueth excesse away.
Of wyse men mochil folk lerne may:
Discrecion mesurith euery thyng;
Despende aftir your plesance and lykyng.

Ensaumpleth vs, let seen, and vs miroure°.   *be an example and mirror for us*
65 As þat it seemeth good to your prudence,
Reule þat day, for the thank shal be youre.
Dooth as yow list be drawe in consequence°.   *draw as much (wine) as you like*
We trusten in your wys experience –
But keepith wel your tourn°, how so befalle,   *i.e., do as you've promised*
70 On Thorsday next, on which we awayte alle°.   *which we all await*

C'est tout.

57–60. That is, you do not have to be extravagant, but don't make us go hungry.

62. This line neatly sums up the moral of 'Male Regle', as well – and it chimes with the ends towards which it was used in the Canterbury registers (for which, see the introductory note to that poem).

69–70. See note to line 39. This ending rings the smallest note of warning: whatever you do, keep your promise and do your duty.

BALADE FOR ROBERT CHICHELE

Date: unknown (before 1426)

☙

The heading to this poem states that it was translated for Robert Chichele, brother of Archbishop Henry Chichele. Robert was 'a prosperous member of the London Grocers Company and twice Lord Mayor who died in 1439' (Burrow 1994: 25). This *chanson d'aventure* poem is translated from an Anglo-Norman original (beginning, 'En mon deduit a moys de may'), which was identified in 1923 by H.E. Sandison, copied 'by a fifteenth-century English hand into a manuscript of the *Roman de la Rose*' (Burrow 1994: 25) – Cambridge, St. John's College, MS G. 5 (James 173). The text from that manuscript is printed in Sandison 1923. Charity Scott Stokes identified the text in two British Library manuscripts: MS Add. 44949 (the 'Tywardreath Psalter') and MS Royal 20 B.iii. The full text is found only in the Royal manuscript. Stokes prints the last 40 lines of the poem, not found in Sandison. (See Stokes 1995)

There is a mirroring between the end of HM 111 and that of HM 744, in that both collections' final texts concern preparation for death. Here, the speaker prays to Jesus and Mary to help intercede in saving his soul from the devil when his soul departs his body. He reminds Mary (and Jesus, through her) that his soul has been bought at a great price (the price being Jesus's death), and that such a dearly bought item should not be easily lost to another.

BALADE FOR ROBERT CHICHELE

Ceste balade ensuyante feust translatee au commandement de mon meistre Robert Chichele

As þat I walkid in the monthe of May
Besyde a groue in an heuy° musynge,   *somber*
Floures dyuerse I sy°, right fressh and gay,   *I saw different flowers*
And briddes° herde I eek° lustyly synge,   *birds, also*
5 Þat to myn herte yaf a confortynge°.   *gave comfort*
But euere o° thoght me stang vnto the herte: *one*
Þat dye I sholde, and hadde no knowynge
Whanne ne whidir° I sholde hennes sterte°.   *when nor where, depart*

Thynkynge thus, byfore me I say°   *saw*
10 A crois depeynted° with a fair ymage.   *cross painted*
I thoghte I nas but asshes and foul clay;
Lyf passith as a shadwe in euery age,
And my body yeueth° no bettre wage°   *gives, reward*
Than synne, which the soule annoyeth° sore.   *disturbs the soul*
15 I preyde God mercy of myn outrage°,   *wrongdoing*
And shoop° me him for t'offende no more.   *resolved*

On God to thynke it yeueth a delyt°,   *gives pleasure*
Wel for to doon° and fro synne withdrawe –   *to do well*
But for to putte a good deede in respyt°   *to put off a good deed*
20 Harmeth. Swich° delay is nat worth an hawe°.   *such, not worth anything*
Wolde God, by my speeche and by my sawe°,   *by what I say*
I mighte him and his modir do plesance,
And, to my meryt, folwe Goddes lawe,
And of mercy housbonde a purueance°.   *make an arrangement*

Heading: This following balade was translated at the request of my master Robert Chichele

1–8. Cf. 'Complaint' (*Series*), lines 1–7, where the seasonal setting (autumn there) feeds directly into the narrator's state of mind (and heart). Where the two are in synchrony there, here they are at odds: the lively May flowers and birds giving way to a reminder of death. The opening is also somewhat reminiscent of Chaucer's *Canterbury Tales* opening: there, the springtime (April) sights and sounds summon the narrator to religious pilgrimage. Here, in Hoccleve, May sights and sounds are the springboard for religious meditation. The May setting also links this poem to the previous poem (in which the date for the dinner is set at May 1). 'Epistle of Cupid' also purports to have been written in May – specifically May 1402.

9–16. Sandison notes that Hoccleve retains the same rhymes in this stanza from the second stanza of the original Anglo-Norman poem: -ay and -age. (The end-words in the original are regarday, ymage, tay, vmbrage, nay, damage, delitay, outrage.) (Sandison and Fiske 1923: 236) This might suggest that Hoccleve knew Chichele would be familiar with the original, and might delight in this feat.

11. Cf. Genesis 3:19.

15. 'God'. Anglo-Norman: 'ihesu crist'.

21–4. Cf. Psalms 1:2; Psalms 118:14–15.

BALADE FOR ROBERT CHICHELE   91

25 Modir of Ihesu, verray° God and man,	true
Þat by his deeth victorie of the feend° gat°,	over the devil, claimed
Haue it in mynde, thow blessid womman –	
For the wo, which vnto thyn herte sat	
In° thy sones torment, forgete it nat.	during
30 Grante me grace to vertu me take,	
Synne despyse, and for to hate al that	
That may thy sone and thee displesid° make.	displeased
Mercyful lord Ihesu me heere, I preye,	
Þat right vnkynde and fals am vnto thee.	
35 I am right swich°; I may it nat withseye°.	such, deny
With salte teeres craue I thy pitee,	
And° herte contryt. Mercy haue on me	and with
Þat am thy recreant caytyf° traitour.	cowardly miserable
By my dissertes° oghte I dampned be,	by what I deserve
40 But ay° thy mercy heetith me socour°.	always, warms me with comfort
Lady benigne, our souereyn refuyt°,	refuge
Seur trust haue I to han, by thy prayeere,	
Of strengthe and confort so vertuous fruyt	
That I shal sauf° be, Crystes modir deere.	saved
45 My soules ship gouerne thow, and steere.	
Let me nat slippe out of thy remembrance,	
Lest, whan þat I am rype vnto my beere°,	i.e., when I die
The feend° me assaille, and haue at the outrance°.	devil, conclusion (of my life)
To thanke thee, lord, hyly holde I am,	
50 For my gilt, nat for thyn, þat° woldest die –	who
Who souffrid euere swich a martirdam°?	such a martyrdom
Yit thy deeth gat of the feend the maistrie°,	achieved victory over the devil
And þat al kynde of man° may testifie.	all mankind
O, blessid be thy loue charitable,	
55 Þat list° so deere° our synful soules bie°,	wished, dearly (expensively), buy
To make vs sauf° wher we weren dampnable°.	safe, worthy to be damned
Now thy socour°, O Heuenes Emperice°.	comfort, Heaven's Empress
Fro me, wrecche, torne thow nat thy face.	
Theras I deepe wrappid am in vice,	
60 Gretter neede haue I thyn help to purchace°.	obtain
Vnto the souerain leche° preye of grace	highest healer

27–9. For the reader experiencing HM III cover to cover, these lines would evoke the first item, 'Complaint Paramount'; the collection is bookended with poems of Marian devotion.

38. Anglo-Norman: 'Tray*tour* truant chetif recru'.

45. 'soules ship'. Cf. 'Complaint Paramount', lines 222–4; 'Ad spiritum sanctum', line 57; 'Learn to Die', lines 199–203, 911–17.

49–56. Cf. Romans 6:23; 1 Corinthians 15:26; 2 Timothy 1:9–10.

61. 'souerain leche', cf. lines 110, 154.

92 BALADE FOR ROBERT CHICHELE

Þat he my wowndes vouchesauf° to cure, — see fit
So þat the feend my soule nat embrace°, — i.e., obtain
Althogh I haue agilt ouer mesure°. — beyond measure

65 Wel oghten we thee thanke, gracious lord,
Þat thee haast humbled for to been allied
To vs. Auctour of pees° and of concord, — author of peace
On the crois was thy skyn into blood died°. — dyed with blood
Allas, why haue I me to synne applied?
70 Why is my soule encombrid° so with synne? — laden
Lord, in al þat I haue me misgyed°, — in every way I have misled myself
Foryeue°; and of my trespas wole I blynne°. — forgive, cease

Lady, wardeyn° of peple fro ruyne, — protector
Þat sauedest Theofle and many mo,
75 Of thy grace myn herte enlumyne°. — illumine
For, as I trowe°, and woot° it wel also, — trust, know
Thy might is me to warisshe° of my wo. — cure
Of thy benigne° sone mercy craue°, — kind, ask
Of þat forueyed° haue I, and misgo°. — strayed, gone amiss
80 His wil is thyn. My soule keepe and saue.

Lord Ihesu Cryst, I axe of thee pardoun.
I yilde me to thee, lord souereyn.
My gilt confesse I, lord. Make vnioun
Betwixt thee and my soule, for in veyn
85 My tyme haue I despendid° in certeyn. — spent
Some of the dropes of thy precious blood,
Þat the crois made as weet° as is the reyn°, — wet, rain
Despende° on me, lord merciable and good. — lavish

Lady, þat clept° art modir of mercy, — called
90 Noble saphir°, to me þat am ful lame — sapphire
Of vertu, and am therto enemy,
Thy welle of pitee, in thy sones name,
Lete on me flowe to pourge my blame,
Lest into despeir þat I slippe and falle.
95 For my seurtee° to keepe me fro blame, — security
Of pitee mirour°, I vnto thee calle. — paragon

65–72. The focus here on the narrator's sinfulness, juxtaposed with Christ's sacrifice, is also a main focus of 'Ad filium'.

74. 'Theofle'. Theophilus of Adana, a sixth-century cleric who, having sold his soul to the devil, begged forgiveness from the Virgin Mary.

86–8. Cf. 1 Peter 1:18–19.

89–90. Cf. Anglo-Norman: 'Miere de mercy roigne saphire / Vaillant de noble engrain'.

90. Cf. 'Knights of the Garter', line 43.

92. Cf. 'Mother of God', line 17.

96. 'Of pitee mirour'. The syntax is confusing here: Mary is being heralded as 'mirour' [exemplar] of 'pitee' [pity/compassion].

BALADE FOR ROBERT CHICHELE   93

Synne, þat is to euery vertu fo°,   a foe to every virtue
Betwixt God and me maad hath swich debat°   has made such discord
Þat my soule is dampned for eueremo,
100   But if þat mercy, which hath maad th'acat°   the purchase
Of mannes soule – þat was violat°   defiled
By likerous° lust and disobedience,   lascivious
For which our lord Ihesu was incarnat –
Me helpe make the feend resistence°.   (divine mercy) help me resist the devil

105   Lady, þat art of grace spryng and sours°,   source
Port in peril, solas in heuynesse°,   comfort in sadness
Of thy wont bontee° keepe alway the cours.   accustomed goodness
Lat nat the feend at my deeth me oppresse.
Torne the crois to me, noble princesse,
110   Which vnto euery soor is the triacle°.   wound is the medicine
Thogh my dissert be naght° of thy goodnesse,   though I'm undeserving
Ageyn° the feendes wrenches° make obstacle.   against, wiles

Lord, on thy grace and pitee myn herte ay°   always
Awaitith to purchace thy mercy.
115   Allas – I, caytif, wel I mourne may,
Syn° the feend serued oftensythe° haue Y.   since, often
It reewith me°. Do with me graciously,   I regret it
For I purpose to stynte of° my synnes.   I intend to cease
What ageyn° thee mistake° hath my body,   against, transgressed
120   My soule keepe fro the feendes gynnes°.   wiles

Blessid virgyne, ensample° of al vertu,   exemplar
Þat peere° hast noon, of wommanhode flour°,   peer (equal), flower
For the loue of thy sone, our lord Ihesu,
Strengthe vs to doon him seruice and honour.
125   Lady, be mene° vnto our sauueour,   mediator
Þat our soules þat the feend waytith ayᵛ   always
To hente°, and wolde of hem° be possessour,   steal, them
Ne sese° hem nat in the vengeable° day.   seize, vengeful

The flessh, the world, and eek° the feend, my fo,   also
130   My wittes alle han at hir retenance°.   at their service
They to my soule doon annoy and wo.
Forwhy°, lord, dreede I me of° thy vengeance.   therefore, I fear
With mercy my soule into blisse enhance°.   raise

---

106. Cf. line 45; 'Ad spiritum sanctum', line 57. Anglo-Norman: 'En tristour solas en perile port'.
110. Cf. lines 61, 154.
121–2. Anglo-Norman: 'Plaine de grace virgine pure / Sule sanz pere de femes flour'.
122. Cf. 'Henry V's Last Return', line 35.

94 BALADE FOR ROBERT CHICHELE

Worthy marchant, saue thy marchandie°,   *merchandise*
135 Which þat thow boghtest with dethes penance.
Lat nat the feend haue of vs the maistrie°.   *take control of us*

Excellent lady, in thy thoght impresse
How and why thy chyld souffrid his torment.
Preye him to haue on vs swich° tendrenesse   *such*
140 Þat in the feendes net we be nat hent°.   *trapped*
At the day of his steerne iugement,
Lat nat° him leese þat° he by deeth boghte.   *don't let, lose what*
I woot° wel, therto hath he no talent°.   *know, desire*
Mynge° him theron, for thee so to doon oghte.   *encourage*

145 Whan in a man synne growith and rypith°,   *grows and ripens*
The fruyt of it is ful of bittirnesse;
But penitence cleene away it wypith,
And to the soule yeueth° greet swetnesse.   *gives*
O steerne iuge°, with thy rightwisnesse°,   *judge, righteousness*
150 Medle° thy mercy and shewe° vs fauour.   *excite, show*
Vnto our soules, maad to° thy liknesse,   *in*
Graunte pardoun of our stynkyng errour.

O glorious qweene, to the repentaunt
Þat art refuyt°, socour°, and medecyne,   *refuge, comfort*
155 Lat nat the foule feend make his auaunt°   *boast*
Þat he hath thee byreft° any of thyne.   *taken from you*
Thurgh thy preyere, thow thy sone enclyne°   *incline your son*
His merciable° grace on vs to reyne°.   *merciful, rain*
Be tendre of vs, O thow blissid virgyne,
160 For if thee list°, we shuln to blisse atteyne°.   *wish, shall attain bliss (salvation)*

C'est tout.

134–6. Cf. Matthew 13:44–6; 1 Corinthians 6:20; 'Learn to Die', lines 911–17. Cf. lines 134–5 to the Anglo-Norman: 'Sauuez le mercez trecher marchaunt / Qe rechatastes a gref penaunce'.

137–40. This call to remembrance (Mary remembering Jesus's death) both reflects back on 'Complaint Paramount' (at the beginning of HM 111) and looks forward to the first poem in HM 744, 'Inuocacio ad Patrem', in which the speaker exhorts God to remember Jesus, his suffering, and his humanity.

145–6. Cf. Romans 7:5

147–52. Cf. James 3:9; Genesis 1:27. Cf. lines 151–2 to the Anglo-Norman: 'A l'alme qi feistez a ta figure / & pardoun grauntez a moi pechour'. Hoccleve adds 'stynkyng', and substitutes 'our' for 'moi'. Gillespie reads this 'stynkyng errour' as suggestive of heresy, the error examined by Chichele's brother (Archbishop Henry Chichele) at the Council of Constance. (Gillespie 2011: 40) Line 152: cf. 'Mother of Life', lines 17, 66.

HUNTINGTON LIBRARY, MS HM 744

ↄ

INUOCACIO AD PATREM

Date: unknown (before 1426)

❧

With this poem, Hoccleve begins a sequence of three invocations to the three persons of the Trinity. The first is by far the longest of the three invocations. While addressed to God, the Father, the focus quickly shifts to the role of the Son (Christ) in interceding, serving as a mediator between mankind and God, and exciting mercy from the Father.

With rare exceptions (noted below) these three poems depart from much of the more topical verse in the holographs, in that they offer little evidence of composition dates or political/ecclesiastical occurrences. The Marian verse contained in HM 744 is similarly hard to date.

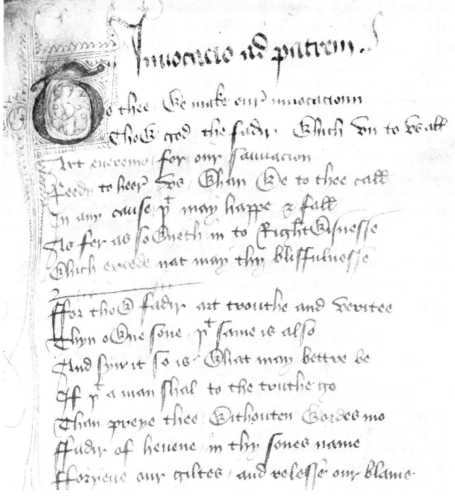

HM 744, fol. 25r (detail), The Huntington Library, San Marino, CA.

INUOCACIO AD PATREM

To thee we make oure inuocacioun,
Thow God, the fadir, which vnto vs alle
Art eueremo, for our sauuacion°,   salvation
Reedy to heere vs whan we to thee calle,
5 In any cause þat may happe and falle°,   happen and befall
As fer as sowneth into rightwisnesse°,   concerns righteousness
Which excede nat may thy blisfulnesse.

For thow, fadir, art trouthe and veritee°.   righteousness and truth
Thyn owne sone þat same is also;
10 And syn° it so is, what may bettre be,   since
If þat a man shal to the truthe go,
Than preye thee°, withouten wordes mo°, pray (that) you, more
Fadir of heuene, in thy sones name,
Foryeue° our giltes and relesse° our blame. forgive, alleviate

15 Fadre and sone, yee been knyt° foreuere   bound
So sadly° þat nothyng þat man may thynke completely
Or speke yow may vnbynde or disseuere.
Than°, fadir, lat our preyere in thee synke,   then
And of thy pitous mercy yeue vs drynke°, give us a taste
20 In tokne° þat ther is no variance   as a sign
Betwixt yow two° þat been but o substance°. i.e., God and Christ, one entity

O fadir, God, kyng of eterne° glorie,   eternal
With herte repentaunt we thee byseeche
That thow haue of thy sone swich memorie° remember your son so well
25 That thy pitee be nothyng for to seeche°, unnecessary to seek out
Our sorwes for to augmente° or to eeche°, intensify, ache
But þat by him thyn ire asswagid be°, your anger be assuaged
Bycause þat thyn owne sone is he.

Heading: Invocation to the Father

8. Cf. John 14:6.

15–21. In this stanza, Hoccleve shifts from the focus only on God – and, with him, truth and righteousness – to God and Christ together, and manifestations of mercy.

21. Cf. John 1:1–4; 10:30. 'Substance' denotes the divine essence that God and Christ share.

27–8. As Cré notes, Hoccleve 'interweaves the absolute and the relative' here: God is at once the 'origin of both the Son and the Holy Ghost', one with both, and also a relatable father figure who needs to be reminded of his son's deeds, so that he might have mercy on other human beings. (Cré 2018: 420)

INUOCACIO AD PATREM 99

	For often by the intercessioun	
30	Of sones is the fadres wratthe appesid°,	appeased
	And they þat for hir° gilt were in prisoun,	their
	In yren° bondes greuously disesid°,	iron, oppressively troubled
	Deliured been and of hir bondes esid°,	released from their bonds
	Þat sholde han ronne into dethes sentence°,	should have been executed
35	Hadde nat be° the sones reuerence°.	were it not for, courtesy
	And nat oonly yit grauntid was hir lyf°,	i.e., he not only saved their life
	But, ouer þat°, han had encrees° of grace.	beyond that, increase
	Tho° sones eek° weren so ententyf°	those, also, devoted
	Þat of hir° fadres kowden they purchace°	their, obtain
40	So greet loue withynne a litil space°,	short time
	Vnto° the gilty folk of which I spak,	for
	Þat of good lordshipe hadde they no lak.	
	Thus fro seruantz voidith malencolie°	eradicates anger
	Of lordes at hir° sones good instaunce°.	their, urging
45	Almighty fadir of the heuenes hye°,	high
	We thee byseeche þat of our greuance°	offense
	Thow vouchesauf to graunte vs allegeance°,	relief
	At instance° of thy blessid sone and deere –	at the urging
	And in thy loue make vs shyne cleere.	
50	The way of grace grante vs for to take,	
	Þat we may maken our confessioun	
	Vnto thy name, and of our bondes blake°	black
	Vnbownden be, thurgh our contricioun,	
	And aftir be of swich° condicioun	such
55	As þat may lyke vnto thy deitee°.	as may please your godhead
	And othir° nat, we preyen moot° it be.	otherwise, may
	And vs, whom þat our dissertes° manace°	desserts (deserved consequences), threaten
	The mortel sentence, to lyf restore	
	By preyere of thy sone, and sende vs grace	

29–35. Cré suggests that this stanza, and its mention of a son's intercession in his father's – the king's – affairs, might amount to an 'endorsement' of Prince Henry, if this poem is dated to the period before Henry V ascended the throne. Cré notes that God is referred to as 'kyng' in line 22, deepening the resonance. (Cré 2018: 418–19) 'Intercessioun' (line 29) is an apparent neologism.

43–4. 'Thus, a lord's anger at servants can be eradicated at the urging of a son.'

49. Cf. Judges 5:31.

51, 53. Hoccleve references the acts of confession and contrition as formal steps in the process of penance. As such, he underscores the role that people can play in the service of their own forgiveness.

57–9. 'And restore us to life through the prayer of your son – we whose just desserts invite the death sentence … ' That is, we deserve death given our actions, but are restored to eternal life through the intercession of Christ. Cf. line 58 to line 34, where the son is capable of intervening in the case of one otherwise facing 'dethes sentence'.

100 INUOCACIO AD PATREM

60 Thy lawes keepe and wirke aftir thy lore°, — teaching
And oure offenses þat stike in vs sore
With herte careful° bewaille and weepe, — sorrowful heart
Er° our careyne° into the eerthe creepe. — before, corpse

Whom shul we preye our mene° for to be, — mediator
65 But° thy sone on the crois þat starf and dyde° — except, who perished and died
For our trespas and oure iniquitee,
Þat sit preyyng° for vs on thy right syde? — who sits praying
He is the lamb þat with his wowndes wyde
Before his tormentoures heeld his pees° — held his peace (i.e., did not complain)
70 For al his grief, al were he° giltelees. — although

For whan his body scourgid was and bete°, — beaten
And al byspet° was his blessid visage°, — spat upon, face
For aght° they kowde rebuke him or threte°, — for all, threaten
He kepte him coy°; he owtid° no langage. — quiet, uttered
75 Ther mighte no thyng° chaungen his corage, — nothing could
But° his torment he took in pacience, — but (instead)
And dyde for our trespas and offense.

Fadir, beholde, of thy benignitee° — kindness
And of iustice, we requeren° this: — ask
80 Þat syn° thy sone, by the wil of thee, — since
Dyde° to wynne þat° was thyn and his, — died, that which
For to redresse° þat þat° was amis, — repair, that which
Considere it, and reewe° on vs tendrely, — have pity
Syn° thow art callid fadir of mercy. — since

85 He is þat meek and spotlees innocent,
Þat for our gilt to dye nothyng dradde°, — was unafraid
Which to his deeth was maad obedient,
And in his torment ful greet delyt° hadde, — delight
Remembrynge how we synful folkes badde° — bad
90 Redempt° sholde be, thurgh his passioun, — redeemed
Out of the daunger of the feend° adoun°. — devil, below

---

64. Reference to Christ as a 'mene' [mediator] here links him in representation to the Virgin Mary, who is repeatedly positioned as 'mene' and mediator throughout Hoccleve's Marian verse.
64–70. Cf. Luke 23:33–4; Isaiah 53:5–9.
84. Cf. Luke 6:36.
85–91. This description is reminiscent of the Old Testament description of the Passover lamb: cf. Exodus 12:5. Line 87: cf. Philippians 2:8.

INUOCACIO AD PATREM   101

Thy godhede him made our nature take°,   i.e., made him become human
And wexe° a man of flessh and blood and boon°,   become, bone
And on the crois he dyde for our sake,
95   Þat tendre louyng lord to vs echoon°;   each one
Swich° a louere was ther neuere noon.   such
Forgete our giltes and remembre hem noght°;   them not
Mercyful lord, putte al° out of thy thoght.   all (our sins)

Lat thy loue ay° to vs endure and laste.   always
100   The gracious yen° of thy magestee°,   eyes, majesty
We thee byseeche on thy sone thow caste.
Shewe° thy mercy and thyn hy° pitee,   show, great
Which þat may thoght, spoken, ne° writen be,   nor
And on thy sone preeue° hit heere in deede.   prove
105   Beholde his sydes, and see how they bleede.

His giltlees° handes, how they stremen°, see,   innocent, flow
With blody stremes. And þat we han wroght°   that which we have done
Ageyn° thy wil, fadir, we preyen thee   against
Foryeue° it vs, and reuolue in thy thoght   forgive
110   How deere° þat thy sone hath vs boght.   expensively
At gretter prys° ne mighte vs no man bye°   price, buy
Than for our giltes and our synnes dye.

His feet and handes with nayles been perced.
See whiche annoyes° hath our redemptour°.   afflictions, redeemer
115   Alle his tormentes may nat be reherced
By noon enditour°, ne° by translatour,   writer, nor
Ne no wight elles°, for so many a stour°,   nor any other person, an attack
And so greuous, souffrid he for our synne,
Þat to telle al mannes wit is to thynne°.   too thin (insufficient)

120   With sharpe thornes, fadir, wel thow woost°,   you know well
Coroned° was thy sone, and sore pyned°,   crowned, painfully tormented

---

96. The Christ as lover motif is common in medieval religious writing, found in works ranging from *Ancrene Wisse* to the *Wooing Group* texts, Julian of Norwich's *Revelations of Divine Love*, and *The Book of Margery Kempe*.

103. Cf. 1 Corinthians 2:9.

104–5. The idea of proof, anchored in the wounded body of Christ, recalls the story of Doubting Thomas – although of course here it is God that is being asked to examine Christ's wounds, and the proof sought is proof of God's own mercy. See John 20:19–29.

109–12. Cf. 1 Corinthians 6:20. Lines 111–12: 'There is no higher price to pay, in absolving us of our sins, than to pay the price of one's life.'

113. Cf. John 20:25.

115–19. The terms 'enditour' [writer] and 'translatour' stand out, because they echo Hoccleve's own role throughout the holograph poems: at times as translator, at times as a writer of original verse. On the claim of insufficient wit, cf. 'Worshipful Maiden', lines 33–4; and David Lawton's notion of the 'ultimate' or 'transcendent' dullness: Lawton 1987: 769.

120–1. See Matthew 27:29.

INUOCACIO AD PATREM

And wowndid to the herte, and yald the goost°. (he) yielded his spirit
An harder deeth may nat been ymagyned.
His fressh colour, þat whilom was beshyned°, once was luminous
125 With swich° beautee þat it wolde al thyng glade°, such, gladden anything
Wax wan and dusk° and pale, and gan° to fade. turned gray and dim, began

Beholde thy sones humanitee,
And mercy haue on our seek feeblenesse°. ailing weakness
Beholde his toren membres°, fadir free°, torn limbs, generous father
130 And lat our substance° in thyn herte impresse. let our humanity
Thynke on thy sones peyne and heuynesse°, pain and sadness
As I before spoken haue and seid,
And vnbynde vs þat been° in synnes teid°. who have been, tied (up) in sins

Fadir and lord of mercy, on vs reewe°, pity us
135 Þat for° our synnes stynken in thy sighte. who because of
Thow grante vs grace vices to escheewe°, avoid
And of our synful birdoun° thow vs lighte°. burden, relieve us
Ageyn° the feend° encorage vs to fighte, against, devil
And stifly° graunte vs in thy cause stonde, steadfastly
140 And flitte° nat when we take it on honde. deviate

---

122. Cf. John 19:30.

127–30. These lines intertwine God's love for his son with compassion for all mankind. Evocation of Christ's Passion ('toren membres') infuses a prayer for God's mercy. The common denominator is humanity, 'our substance'. Of these lines, Cré writes: 'In a metaphor related to all people's names being written in the palm of God's hand (Isaiah 49:16), this line inverts deification of the soul (which receives an imprint of the divine in contemplation) to the rendering human of the person of the father, who receives an imprint of the humanity not just of his son, but of all sinners who call on his mercy.' (Cré 2018: 423) Line 130. 'substance': cf. line 21.

133. Cf. Luke 13:16.

134–40. Cf. Psalms 37:5; Matthew 11:30.

AD FILIUM

Date: unknown (before 1426)

☙

This poem – an invocation to Christ, the Son of God – is the second in a sequence of three poems addressing, respectively, the three persons of the Trinity. While Christ already featured in the first poem, 'Inuocacio ad Patrem', and served there as an intermediary, capable of bridging the gap between mankind and God, here an outpouring of apology – amidst meditation on the Passion – excites guilt and the need for penitence. The 'I' of the narrator expands to include all (sinful) mankind, and it positions the reader as both saved by Christ and complicit in his torture and death (in that Christ had to be born and suffer, in order to save wayward humanity).

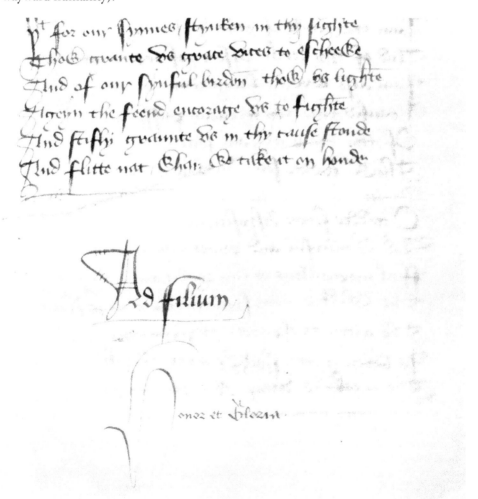

HM 744, fol. 28r (detail), The Huntington Library, San Marino, CA.

AD FILIUM

Honor et Gloria

O blessid chyld Ihesu, what haast thow do°	what have you done
Þat for vs shuldist souffre swich Iewyse°?	such persecution
Louynge chyld, what stired° thee therto,	motivated
That thow woldest be treted in swich wyse°?	such a way
5 What causid thee to take þat empryse°?	enterprise
What was thy gilt and thyn offense, I preye,	
And cause of deeth, and dampnyng° eek°, I seye?	legal sentence, also
I am the wownde of al thy greuance°.	injury
I am the cause of thyn occisioun°	slaughter
10 And of thy deeth, dessert° of thy vengeance.	deserving
I am also verray flagicioun°.	true incitement
I causid thee thy greuous passioun.	
Of thy torment I am solicitour° –	instigator
Thow, Goddes sone, our lord and sauueour.	
15 O Goddes secree disposicioun°,	secret arranging
And wondirful and priuee° iugement,	hidden
Ful merueillous° is thy condicioun.	marvelous
The wikkid man synneth; the good is shent°.	destroyed
The gilty trespaceth; the innocent	
20 Is beten. And the shrewe° dooth offense;	wretch
The meek is dampned° in his innocence.	damned
The peyne° þat the wikkid man disserueth°	pain, deserves
The giltelees° receiueth paciently;	innocent

Heading: To the Son, honor and glory

1–7. In this stanza the young Jesus is juxtaposed with the dying Jesus: the Son of God is seen in his earliest and latest days, simultaneously. As such, purity and innocence clash with the shock of torture and death, deepening the sense of wrongdoing and blame. Cf. 'Ad Patrem', lines 85–91.

2. 'Iewyse'. The word refers not only to Jewishness, but also to Jewish aggression and deception. It reflects the anti-Semitic prejudice of Hoccleve and his contemporaries. The same anti-Semitism is on display, for instance, in Chaucer's 'Prioress's Tale'.

8–14. As Cré notes, the similarity between Christ and the rest of humanity established at the end of the previous poem, as a means of moving God to compassion for mankind, transitions in this poem to a division between the speaker (sinful/guilty mankind) and the object (Christ). The opposition is maintained throughout the poem. (Cré 2018: 420–1) Hoccleve's evocation of the Passion also continues throughout. The image of a thin, bloody, crucified Christ resurfaces especially in lines 36–56, when Hoccleve draws upon the seven deadly sins. It continues an imagistic thread begun in the previous poem. Cf. Isaiah 53:5.

9. 'occisioun'. Among the earliest recorded instances of this word, borrowed from French, meaning slaughter. The word 'occisions' (meaning murders) is found in Christine de Pizan's 'Epistre au dieu d'amours' (the source for Hoccleve's 'Epistle of Cupid'), line 682.

11. 'flagicioun'. An apparent neologism, from Latin, meaning (it would seem) incitement.

AD FILIUM 105

The lord his seruant in his gilt preserueth° — protects
25 Fro punysshyng°, and bieth° it deerly — punishment, buys
Himself – and þat the man dooth wikkidly,
God keepith him fro punisshyng and teene°, — harm
And al þat charge° him list° for him susteene°. — load, he wishes, carry

Fro whenne°, blessid sone of God, fro whenne — from whence
30 Descendid is thy greet humilitee?
Whens comth the loue we feele in thee brenne°? — burn
Fro whens eek° is procedid thy pitee? — also
And fro whens growith thy benignitee°? — kindness
Whens strecchith thy loue and affeccioun?
35 Fro whens is sprongen° thy conpassioun? — springs

I am he þat wroght haue° synfully, — have done
And thow, giltlees, took vpon thee the peyne°. — pain (punishment)
I dide amis; I synned greuously,
For which thow greeued° were in euery veyne. — pained
40 Thy louyng charitee nat list desdeyne° — does not hesitate
To bye° our gilt, thogh thow were innocent, — pay for
But on the crois° souffriddist thy torment. — cross

I woxe am° prowd; thow keepist thy meeknesse. — have grown
My flessh is bolned°; thyn is woxen° thynne. — swollen, has grown
45 Myn herte is wrappid in vnbuxumnesse°; — disobedience
And thow buxum°, our soules for to wynne, — obedient
Boghtest deere° our corrupt and roten synne. — expensively
My lust obeied vnto glotonye°, — gluttony
But thee list nat° thee to þat lust applie°. — desire not, succumb

50 I was rauysshid° by concupiscence, — seized
For to eten of the vnleefful° tree; — unlawful (forbidden)
And for my lust and inobedience,
Thy feruent loue and parfyt° charitee, — perfect
O blisful chyld, to the crois ladden thee°; — led you to the cross
55 Whereas þat I took the deffendid° thyng, — forbidden
Thow deidest for me, Ihesu, heuene kyng.

24–8. 'The lord protects his servant from punishment, and pays for it dearly himself – and whatever man does wickedly, God keeps him from punishment and harm, and bears that load [of guilt] himself.'

43–63. Hoccleve references four of the seven deadly sins here – pride, lust, gluttony, and greed. He omits sloth, wrath, and envy.

47. Cf. 1 Corinthians 6:20.

50–6. Hoccleve references the Garden of Eden, and Adam and Eve's trespass in eating of the tree. See Genesis 3. The 'I' of the narrator is clearly a broad, collective first person, including all of mankind.

106 AD FILIUM

In mete° and drynke, I delyte me;   food
And on the gibet° took thow greet duresse°;   gallows (cross), suffering
Betwixt tho° two is greet dyuersitee°.   those, difference
60 Taastid haue I the fair apples swetnesse;
Of galle° thow taastist the bittirnesse;   bitter drink
Eeue° me gladith° with a lawwhyng ye°, Eve, delighted me, laughing eye
And, weepynge vpon thee, reewith° Marie.   fretted

   O kyng of glorie, thow beholde and see
65 What peynes thow suffridist for our sake.
And syn° þat we so deere costed thee°,   since, cost you so much
Thow keepe vs fro the might of feendes blake°.   black devils
Lat nat thy charitable loue asslake°,   subside
And graunte vs grace thee to loue and drede°,   fear/revere
70 And yeue° vs heuene whan þat we be dede.   give

57–63. Hoccleve juxtaposes the relative comforts of the 'I' with the pains of Christ. Here too Adam stands in for mankind: the laughing eye of Eve contrasts with Mary's weeping eye.

63. Cf. John 19:25.

64. Christ ends the poem as 'kyng of glorie', marking a shift from his wounded, compromised condition in the earlier stanzas of the poem to his regal position, after death and resurrection. See also line 56, 'heuene kyng'. These phrases link back to the beginning of 'Ad Patrem', where God is presented as 'kyng of eterne glorie' (line 22).

64–7. Cf. Psalms 23:8.

AD SPIRITUM SANCTUM

Date: unknown (before 1426)

❧

This poem ends a three-poem run of invocations in turn to each person of the Trinity. The Holy Spirit is lauded as alternately vivifying, illuminating, and salvific. The final line of the poem pivots from a focus only on the Holy Spirit to an address to the 'Trinity' as a whole, marking the end of the triad of poems.

While these opening three poems on the Trinity are a unit in and of themselves, they flow well into the next three pieces, which all feature the Virgin Mary. In serving as a mini-collection within the larger collection, the Trinity poems correlate with the 'twin' balades (HM 111, nos. 5–6); the series of four poems in the double croisée form in HM 111 (items 12–15); and the 'Three Roundels' (HM 744; no. 9). The series of three Marian poems in HM 744 that follow (nos. 4–6) form another implicit mini-collection.

HM 744, fol. 30r (detail), The Huntington Library, San Marino, CA.

AD SPIRITUM SANCTUM

Now holy goost of the hy deitee°,	high deity (God)
Loue and holy communicacioun	
Of fadir and sone, blessid thow be.	
O thow benigne° consolacioun	gracious/good-willed
5 Of heuy° folk, O our sauuacioun°,	troubled, salvation
O tendre hertid, cause of al quieete°,	peace
Our bittirnesse torne° al into sweete.	turn
And by thy mighty vertu, we thee preye	
Þat oure hertes filthy priuetee°	chamber
10 Thow vouchesauf° to clense and wasshe aweye.	see fit
Thurgh thy mercy, ther make thyn entree°,	entrance
O holy goost – there enhabyte thee,	
And the dirk halkes° of our soules lighte	dark corners
And glade° with thy firy lemes° brighte.	gladden, flames
15 And oure hertes – whiche by long roghnesse,	
Welkid° been, and forgoon° han hir° vigour,	withered, gone, has their
By enchesoun° of excessyf drynesse –	cause
Dewe habundantly° with thyn holsum shour°.	rinse abundantly, shower
Our soules lurkyng sores and langour,	
20 With thy brennyng° dart and thy loues broond°,	burning, fire
Visite and helpe. Our helthe is in thyn hoond°.	hand
Kyndle eek° and qwikne° with thy lyfly lemes°	also, animate, life-giving flames
Our slouthy° hertes, of vertu° bareyne°.	slow, virtue/power, barren
Our soules perce with thy shynyng bemes.	
25 To thy godhede thow vs knytte and cheyne.	
The ryuer of thy lust lat on vs reyne.	
Of worldly sweet venym souffre vs nat taaste,	
Ne° our tyme in this world misspende and waaste.	nor

Heading: To the Holy Spirit

1–3. Cf. 1 John 5:7.

10. Cf. Hebrews 9:14.

14. 'firy lemes': The fire/heat imagery associated with the Holy Spirit mixes with water imagery in the following stanzas. The Spirit's role is both to enflame/invigorate and to flood/quench. See lines 18, 20, 22, 26, 57, etc. The fire imagery also recalls the imagery of the Pentecost: see Acts 2:3–4.

22. 'lyfly'. Cf. Hoccleve's use in *Regiment* line 1972, where 'lyfly' is used as an adverb, assisting in the description of the transcendent power that Chaucer's books carry, even after the writer's death. On this use, and the comparative use in Thomas Usk and the Digby 102 poems see Langdell 2018: 165–70. Hoccleve also uses 'lyflynesse' (noun) in the *Regiment* to describe the animating nature of a soul (2724–26) and the vivid quality of Chaucer's 'resemblance' (4992–3).

23. 'slouthy'. An apparent neologism, meaning slow, slothful, lazy. Cf. Luke 24:25.

22–8. As Cré notes, the Holy Spirit acts here (and throughout this poem) less as a mere intercessor, and more as 'the very force of life itself'. (Cré 2018: 422)

AD SPIRITUM SANCTUM 109

O God, we thee byseeche thow vs deeme°,   *(that) you judge us*
30   And our cause fro wikkid folk discerne.
Thow graunte vs grace thee to plese and qweeme°,   *gratify*
And to thy wil and plesaunce vs gouerne.
Our seekly freeltee° beholde and concerne,   *sickly frailty*
And reewe° on our brotil° condicioun,   *have pity, brittle*
35   And for our gilt sende vs contricioun.

Wher thow makist thyn habitacioun,
We knowen weel, and fully leeuen we°   *we believe (that)*
Thow, for fadir and sone, a mansioun
Makist, in whom thee list herberwe thee°.   *you like to house yourself*
40   Ful happy and ful blissid man is he,
For his spirit may reste sikirly°,   *securely*
Vnabassht° of the feend°, oure enemy.   *unafraid, devil*

Come on, confort of our soules seeknesse°,   *sickness*
And ay° reedy in our necessitee°.   *always, (time of) need*
45   Of wowndes leche°, helpere in distresse,   *doctor*
O come now foorth, strengthe of our freeltee°,   *frailty*
Clensere of our gilt and iniquitee,
Releeuere of hem° þat doun° slippe and slyde,   *those, down*
Ground of meeknesse and destroyour of pryde.

50   Of fadrelees children, O fadir free°;   *kind*
Of widwes, esy iuge°, and hope and trust;   *comforting guide*
Of poore folk and° in aduersitee,   *and (those)*
Refuyt° and help. Helpe vs, for so thow must;   *refuge*
Of oure soules, rubbe away the rust.
55   Thy grace to receyue make vs able,
And kythe° in vs þat thow art merciable°.   *show, merciful*

O lodesterre of shipbreche°, seur° port,   *lodestar of shipwreck, sure*
O oonly helthe of our mortalitee,
O holy goost, cause of al our confort,
60   Singuler honur of alle þat be,
Telle vs to whom recours haue may we,

---

30. 'wikkid folk'. Given the anti-Lollard context of other devotional poems in the holographs, it is possible that this refers to Lollards.
36–9. Cf. John 14:2.
45. 'wowndes leche'. Cf. *Series* 2.92–8.
50–3. Cf. Psalms 9:10, 67:6.
55–6. Cf. 2 Corinthians 9:8.
57. 'lodesterre of shipbreche'. Cf. 'Complaint Paramount', lines 222–4; 'Balade for Robert Chichele', line 45; 'Learn to Die', lines 199–203, 911–17.

AD SPIRITUM SANCTUM

But° vnto thee, þat with thyn holsum breeth   *except*
Maist saue vs alle fro th'eternel deeth.

O holy goost, lyke it to thy goodnesse,
65   To oure axynge° meekly condescende°.   *requests, deign (to answer)*
Mercy haue on our synne and wikkidnesse,
And fro the feendes malice vs deffende.
To fadir, sone, and to thee, we commende
Our soules, hem° to haue in gouernance.   *them*
70   O Trinitee, haue vs in remembrance.

61–3. Cf. John 6:69; Acts 17:25; Job 27:3–4.
66. Cf. Psalms 50:3.
70. This line seals the first three poems in HM 744, and binds them together.

WORSHIPFUL MAIDEN

Date: unknown (before 1426)

☙

With this poem, the figure of the Virgin Mary enters into HM 744, a collection thus far only populated by the persons of the Trinity. This poem begins a three-poem run of Marian poems, culminating with Hoccleve's Marian miracle, 'The Monk Who Clad the Virgin'. While the first three stanzas of this poem address Mary directly, with stanza four the address pivots to Jesus (as God/Son of God), and Hoccleve highlights the cooperative mercy of mother and Son. A superscript disambiguation delineates powers, with Christ sparing the sinner, and Mary serving as an active intercessor, praying on mankind's behalf.

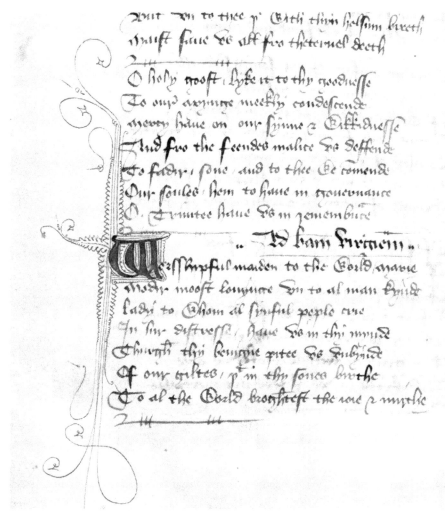

HM 744, fol. 31v (detail), The Huntington Library, San Marino, CA.

WORSHIPFUL MAIDEN

Ad beatam virginem

Worsshipful maiden to the world, Marie,
Modir° moost louynge vnto al mankynde, — mother
Lady to whom al synful peple crie
In hir° distresse, haue vs in thy mynde. — their
5 Thurgh thy benigne° pitee vs vnbynde — gracious
Of our giltes, þat in thy sones birthe
To al the world broghtest the ioie and mirthe°. — joy and happiness

To whom shal I truste so sikirly° — confidently
To axen help in my necessitee° — (time of) need
10 As vnto thee, thow modir of mercy,
For to the world mercy cam in by thee°. — mercy came into the world through you
Thow baar° the lord of mercy, lady free°. — you bore, gracious lady
Who may so lightly° mercy vs purchace — easily
Of God, thy sone, as thow, modir of grace?

15 Lady, right as it is an impossible° — just as it is impossible
Þat thow sholdest nat haue in remembrance
Why thow baar° God, so it is incredible° — bore (were pregnant with), unbelievable
To any wight° of catholyk creaunce° — person, (orthodox) Christian belief
Thee nat to reewe on° our synful greuaunce. — pity
20 Forthy°, lady benigne and merciable°, — therefore, kind and merciful
Vnto thy sone make vs acceptable.

O God, þat maad art sone vnto womman
For mercy, and thow, womman, which also
By grace art maad modir to God and man,
25 Outhir° reewe on vs° wrecches ful of wo – — Either, pity us
Thow sparyng and thow preyynge – dooth so, — scilicet deus / scilicet domina
Or elles wisse° vs whidir° for to flee — instruct, where
To hem þat° been mercyfuller° than yee. — those who, more merciful

---

Heading: To the blessed Virgin

4. The emphasis on memory and mercy continues on from the previous poems in HM 744. Cf. 'Ad Patrem', lines 83, 109–10, 130 (and for forgetting, lines 97–8); 'Ad spiritum sanctum', line 70.

5–6. As Cré notes, the binary opposition of sinful speaker and virtuous recipient (in Mary) recalls a similar dynamic in 'Ad filium', two poems prior. (2018: 422)

7. Cf. Luke 2:10–11.

26. Above 'Thow sparyng', Hoccleve writes in superscript, 'scilicet deus' [that is God], and above 'thow preyynge', 'scilicet domina' [that is the lady]. Mary is being beseeched to act as an intercessor. Hoccleve is clarifying that the first 'thow' in the phrase refers to Christ (capable of sparing us), and the second to Mary (who prays on our behalf). Cf. the dual address in 'Knights of the Garter', line 26.

WORSHIPFUL MAIDEN   113

If it so be, as wel I woot° it is,   I know well
30   That so greuous is myn iniquitee
And þat I haue wrogt so moche° amis,   done so much
So smal my feith, so slow my charitee,
And lord, so vnkonnynge° is vnto thee   unskilled
And thy modir my lewde orisoun°,   simple prayer
35   So inparfyt° my satisfaccioun°   flawed, penance

Þat neithir of my giltes° indulgence°   sins, mercy
Ne° grace of helthe in no maner wyse°   nor, in any manner
Disserued° haue I for my greet offense.   deserved
Lo, þat meene I, þat is my couetyse°:   strong desire
40   That whereas my dissert° may nat souffyse°,   what I deserve, suffice
The grace and mercy of yow bothe tweye°   two
Ne faille nat – þat is it þat I preye.

Mercyful lord, haue vpon me mercy.
And lady, thy sone vnto mercy meeue°.   stir
45   With herte contryt preye I thee meekly,
Lady, thy pitee on me, wrecche, preeue°.   prove
Bisyly preye°, for I fully leeue°   busily pray, believe
For whom thow preyest God nat list denye°   would not wish to deny
Thyn axynge, blessid maiden Marie.

---

32. Cf. Luke 24:25.

33–4. 'unkonnyng … lewde orisoun'. 'lewde', like 'unkonnyng', carries the resonance of unlearned/
uneducated/unlettered. Cf. David Lawton's notion of the 'ultimate' or 'transcendent' dullness
(1987: 769). Also cf. 'Ad Patrem', lines 115–19. For Hoccleve's own apparent training as a priest, see
Regiment, lines 1447–56. On 'lewde', cf. 'To Sir John Oldcastle', lines 147, 352, where the word is
used to describe Lollards.

35. 'satisfaccioun'. The speaker here worries over the imperfect state of the expiatory prayers delivered
after the act of confession.

36–42. Cf. Ephesians 2:8–9; Matthew 19:25–6. Lines 36–8: ' … that I deserve neither mercy for my sins,
nor grace of health in any manner, so great is my offense.'

40–2. 'Even though I am unworthy and do not deserve it, I pray that your (joint) grace and mercy will
not abate.'

MOTHER OF GRACE
Date: unknown (before 1426)

◆

With its 140 lines (twenty seven-line stanzas), this poem recalls 'Inuocacio ad Patrem' – the invocation to God with which HM 744 begins, a poem of identical length and form.

The focus in 'Mother of Grace' is on the intercessory power of the Virgin – her ability to help effect comfort and change for the prayerful Christian. The poem is especially rich with metaphor: from the 'oil' of Mary's mercy, to images of rain, stars, fruitful trees, the sun and moon, and the soft fabric of Mary's womb (stained purple with Christ's death).

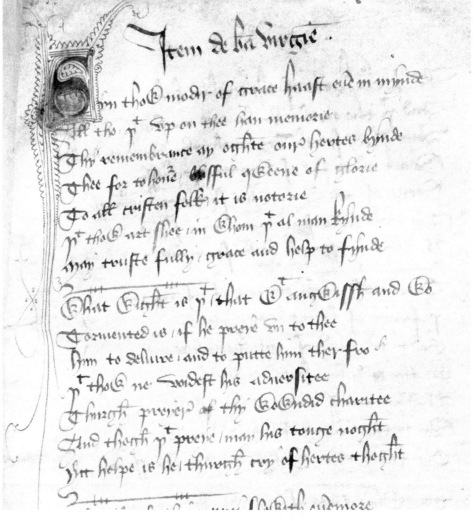

HM 744, fol. 33r (detail), The Huntington Library, San Marino, CA.

MOTHER OF GRACE

Item de beata virgine

Syn° thow, modir° of grace, haast euere in mynde   *since, mother*
Alle tho þat vpon thee han memorie°,   *those that hold you in mind*
Thy remembrance ay° oghte oure hertes bynde   *always*
Thee for to honure, blisful qweene of glorie.
5   To alle Cristen folk it is notorie°   *well known*
Þat thow art shee in whom þat al mankynde
May truste fully grace and help to fynde.

What wight is þat that° with angwissh and wo   *what person exists who*
Tormented is, if he preye vnto thee
10 Him to deliure, and to putte° him therfro,   *push*
Þat thow ne voidest° his aduersitee   *not relieve*
Thurgh preyere of thy wowndid charitee°?   *love*
And thogh þat preye may his tonge noght°,   *though his tongue may not pray*
Yit helpe° is he thurgh cry of hertes thoght°.   *helped, through his heart's lament/prayer*

15 The oyle° of thy mercy flowith eueremore   *oil*
Therein, noon ebbe° hath dominacion°.   *no ebb (receding), has sway*
That licour° our wowndes greuous and sore   *liquid*
Serchith°, and is our ful curacion° –   *searches/fills, entire cure*
That is the way of our sauuacion°.   *salvation*
20 And syn° þat therof is so greet plentee,   *since*
And thow so liberal°, glad may we be.   *you (are) so generous*

Al þat the heuene of the eerthe takith,
And þat the eerthe by heuenes moistnesse
Doun° shed, foorth bryngith thy vertu it makith,   *down*
25 So art thow ful of vertuous richesse.
Sterre of the see°, whos shynynge brightnesse   *star of the sea*
The dirke soule of man makith to shyne,
And him preserueth hoolly fro ruyne°,   *preserves wholly from ruin*

Heading: Piece about the blessed Virgin

1–3. On the role of memory in these openings to poems in HM 744, see note to 'Worshipful Maiden', line 4. The play with mind and memory is especially visible here: note the movement between 'in mynde', 'memorie', and 'remembrance' in the first three lines.

8–14. 'What person is there, tormented by anguish and woe, who would pray to you for deliverance, and who you would not relieve through your own tender, wounded prayer? And even though he may not pray with his tongue, still he might be helped through the prayer of his heart.'

15–18. 'oyle'. Cf. the oil and wine that the Good Samaritan uses to heal the stranger's wounds: Luke 10:34.

22–5. 'All that the heaven takes from earth, and all that the earth sheds of heaven's moisture, your virtue comes forth in such a way – you are so full of virtue.' Cf. Isaiah 45:8; and the language of dew and cleansing in 'Ad spiritum sanctum', lines 10, 18, 26.

26–8. Cf. 'Ad spiritum sanctum' line 57, where the Holy Spirit is 'lodesterre of shipbreche, seur port'.

116 MOTHER OF GRACE

Thow cause of al our ioie°, of lyf the tree — joy
30 Þat fruyt of helthe baar perpetuel°, — perpetually bears
God, in the rynde of our mortalitee,
In thy body him lappid euerydel°, — he was wrapped entirely
And his hynesse enclyned°, woot° I wel, — descended, know
Vnto the valeye of our lowlynesse,
35 Our firste gilt°, with his blood to redresse°. — trespass, put right

The whyt flees° of thy wombe virginal, — soft fabric (i.e., lamb's wool)
Of which the gowne of perpetuel pees° — eternal peace
Was maad withouten mannes werk° at al, — without male intervention (virginally)
Honur and thank be to it endelees.
40 For thy sone in his passioun doutelees
It into purpre° hath for mankynde died, — purple (bloody), dyed (with pun on died)
For þat him list° with vs to been allied. — he desired

Thow worthy art vnto the sonnes° light — sun's (with pun on son's)
Be likned, and proferred for to be
45 The cleernesse of the moone shynyng bright.
For as° an heuenely morwen°, thy bountee — like, morning
Eternel day hath gote° vs, lady free° – — has given, generous lady
That dirknesse of our soule away hath chaced°, — chased
And, out of thraldam°, freedam vs purchaced. — slavery

50 Thow art shee which° þat strengthest hertes chaaste — who
With a sad° and constant perseuerance. — fixed
What þat we iustly preye is sped° in haaste – — fulfilled
Swich° is thy grace and helply purueance° — such, helpful purveyance
To keepe vs fro the feendes destourbance.
55 Thow mennes hertes fyrest° with the hete — enflame
Of feith and charitee, as clerkes trete.

29–30. 'of lyf the tree'. See Genesis 2:9, 3:22–3; Proverbs 3:18, 11:30; Revelation 22:2, 22:14.

31. Cf. John 1:14; *Regiment* lines 3575–7, which depict God 'wrappid in our mortel rynde'.

35. 'Our firste gilt'. Mankind's first trespass against God, in the Garden of Eden. Christ's birth was seen to counteract this initial defiance.

36. See Luke 1:34–5.

36–42. This stanza imagines Mary's womb as material – a soft white fabric – from which is made the 'gowne' of eternal peace (i.e., Christ). This gown is dyed purple with the Passion, and the spilling of Christ's blood therein. The circumstance allows Hoccleve to pun on 'dyed' and 'died' – much as he puns on 'son' and 'sun' in the beginning of the next stanza. The moment also serves as an apt foreshadowing of the next poem in HM 744, in which a monk's prayers clothe the Virgin Mary.

43–5. Cf. 'Oldcastle' lines 313–14, where papal and regal power are posited in terms of sun and moon.

46–7. Cf. 1 Peter 2:9; Revelation 22:5, 22:16.

49. Cf. Galatians 4:31; Romans 6:22; John 8:36.

55–6. Cf. Luke 24:32.

And sooth it is°, O heuenes emperice,	it is true
Þat thow for vs – beforn the rightwisnesse°	before the righteousness
Of God thy sone, as our mediatrice° –	mediator
60 Preyest of custumable bisynesse°.	pray with habitual diligence
Cesse° thow nat, syn° for our wrecchidnesse	cease, since
Our redemptour thee hath in þat office°	(official) position
Ordeyned°, for to pourge vs of our vice.	appointed
Right as°, among the membres° of a man	just as, organs
65 Oonly his ye° is perceptible of° light,	eye, capable of perceiving
In swich° maneere, O thow blessid womman,	such
Among virgynes alle haast the might	
Oonly to shitte° in thee, as it is right,	enclose
Th'eternel glorie of Goddes magestee,	
70 For° thy clennesse and thyn humilitee.	because of
If þat the feend° wynd of temptacioun	devil
Putte in oure hertes, or floodes of pryde,	
Or othir vicious excitacioun°,	incitement
Our soules fro thy sone to dyuyde,	
75 Swich aduocatrice° art thow for our syde	such an advocate
That our tempestes may no whyle laste°.	may not last long
At thy preyere al styntid is° as faste,	all is stopped
And to wedir° of grace is torned al.	weather
To God so acceptable is thy preyere,	
80 The feendes malice hurte vs may but smal	
Syn° thow with vs art. Crystes modir deere,	since
Wel may the feend abassht been° in his cheere	the devil should be afraid
Thy° seruantz þat so oftensythe° assaillith,	(of) your, frequently
And, thurgh thyn help, his labour naght auaillith.	
85 By thee thy sone grantith foryeuenesseᵛ	forgiveness
To synful men; to laboreres, reste;	
To hem° þat been in peril, sikirnesse°;	those, safety
To seek° men, helthe – swich right as hem leste°.	sick, just as they desire
Of creatures alle, O thow the beste,	

57–63. Hoccleve gives Mary's appointment to the 'office' of 'mediatrice' an official, almost bureaucratic, bent. In purging us of our sins, she is fulfilling the duties of her post, and pleasing the individual (Christ) who appointed her to that position. Lines 61–3: cf. 1 Corinthians: 5:7; Isaiah 1:25.

65. 'perceptible'. An apparent neologism, meaning capable of receiving/perceiving.

71–8. Hoccleve employs an extended meteorological metaphor – passing from the wind of temptation (71) to floods of pride (72) and tempests (76), before resolving, on the other side of Mary's prayerful intercession (and the other side of a stanza break), in the calm weather of grace (78).

79–80. Cf. Romans 8:31.

85–98. The series of afflictions and comforts that Hoccleve lists in these two stanzas echo the structure of certain Beatitudes (Matthew 5:3–12), in which a seeming deficiency is turned into a strength. See especially the first four Beatitudes, and the final two.

118 MOTHER OF GRACE

90   Feith among freendes grantid is by thee,
     And betwixt foos, pees° and tranquillitee.   *peace*

     To hem° þat in disese and angwissh be,   *those*
     Grauntid is also consolacioun;
     In thynges þat been doutous°, certaintee;   *uncertain*
95   Solace and ioie° in tribulacioun;   *joy*
     In exyl, reconsiliacioun;
     In perisshynge, sikir hauene° and port.   *safe haven*
     Thus artow euerywhere al our confort.

     Syn swich° power to thee committid is,   *since such*
100 Þat soule of man is, as thee list it haue°,   *as you wish to have it*
     Amende, at oure axynge, that is mis°.   *what is amiss*
     Of duetee° we wole it axe° and craue.   *out of (moral) obligation, we will ask for it*
     In thee, next God, is al þat vs may saue.
     Thow, as thee list°, his herte mayst enclyne,   *as you wish*
105 And he consentith wel, þat thow it myne°.   *influence*

     Thy sone hath boght our soules at swich prys°   *at such price*
     Þat derrer° mighte no thyng han be boght.   *dearer (of greater price)*
     And he a chapman° is nat so vnwys;   *merchant*
     Thogh þat we synful been in deede and thoght,
110 Our soules lightly leese° he thoghte it noght°.   *easily lose, he would not think (to do)*
     He mercy werneth neuere° at thyn instance°,   *never denies mercy, urging*
     Forwhy° we thee preye of continuance.   *which is why*

     Our redemptour° by thee, modir of grace,   *redeemer*
     Grauntith honour, ioie°, and eternitee.   *joy*
115 Let see, the mercy of thy sone embrace,
     Preeue thee swich° as thow art wont° to be,   *prove yourself such, given*
     And thanne of grace seur ynow been we°.   *then we will be made sure of grace*
     For euere or° this hath been thy bysynesse°   *before, task*
     To purchace of our gilt foryeuenesse°.   *forgiveness*

---

86. Cf. Matthew 11:28.
87. Cf. Psalms 9:10, 45:2.
88. Cf. Mark 2:17; Ecclesiasticus 34:19–20.
90–1. Cf. Proverbs 16:7; Romans 5:10.
93. Cf. 2 Thessalonians 2:15–16.
95. Cf. 1 Thessalonians 1:6.
97–8. Cf. Psalms 106:28–30; 2 Corinthians 1:3. Cf. also 'Ad spiritum sanctum', lines 57–9.
99–101. 'Since such power is given to you, whatever the state of man's soul, amend what is amiss, at our asking, if you wish to.'
106–7. Cf. 1 Corinthians 6:20.

120	And now to stynte° of þat helply custume°,	cease, helpful custom
	Þat vnto mankynde is so profitable,	
	No wight° on him can taken or presume:	person
	Thy kynde° is nat for to be changeable,	nature
	But in vertu to be constant and stable.	
125	And so thow art, lady, withouten faille –	
	We doute it naght, no[w] do foorth thy trauaille°.	work

	Lady, in whom al vertu hath his reste,	
	Modir of mercy, modir of pitee,	
	Of al bountee thow verray cofre° and cheste,	case
130	Deffende vs fro the feendes sotiltee°,	devil's trickery
	Þat vs nat greeue° his greet iniquitee.	that we may not suffer
	Thy tendre loue vpon vs wrecches preeue°,	prove
	Þat been the sones exylid of Eeue°.	exiled sons of Eve

	Vnto thy blissid sone vs reconsyle.	
135	For to þat ende, and vnto þat entente°,	purpose
	As thow wel woost°, into this wrecchid yle° –	know well, island
	For our behoue° – his fadir him doun° sente.	benefit, down
	In mannes loue, how feruently he brente°,	burned
	His passion witnesse bere may° –	may bear witness (suffice as evidence)
140	Remembre on þat, and preye for vs ay°.	always

---

126. Again, Mary is reminded that her intercessory role is her God-given 'trauaille', her work. See note to lines 57–63, above.

130–3. The reference here is to mankind more generally, exiled from Eden as a result of Adam and Eve's trespass – but the phrase 'sones exylid of Eeue' is also evocative of Cain more specifically, who is exiled for killing his brother Abel. See Genesis 3:23–4, 4:11–15.

136. 'wrecchid yle'. Hoccleve seems to be using 'yle' [island] figuratively for the world – the place to which Christ was 'doun sente'. The phrase does take on intriguing significance, however, positioned as it is two poems before the 'Epistle of Cupid' in HM 744, a poem which opens on 'this yle / That clept is Albioun', where there is 'croppe and roote of gyle' (15–17).

140. This ending recalls the ending of 'Ad spiritum sanctum' (line 70).

THE MONK WHO CLAD THE VIRGIN

Date: unknown (before 1426)

❧

This 'miracle of the Virgin' was integrated into the *Canterbury Tales* in one manuscript – Oxford, Christ Church MS 152 – as the 'Ploughman's Tale', positioned between the 'Squire's Tale' and the 'Second Nun's Tale'. It includes a prologue with praise for the Virgin, much like Chaucer's 'Prioress's Tale'. It shares ground in this respect with 'Mother of God' from HM 111, which was attributed to Chaucer in two manuscripts (and in subsequent Chaucer anthologies).

According to the gloss, 'Monk' was written at the request of Thomas Marleburgh, who was a stationer and 'warden of the guild of Limners and Textwriters in 1423'. He had two shops on Paternoster Row. He died shortly after Hoccleve, in 1429. (Burrow 1994: 25)

Blurton and Johnson note that Hoccleve's poem joins Lydgate's own Marian miracle poem, *Dan Joos*, in reflecting a specific way in which Chaucerian legacy was imagined in the early fifteenth century: through a Marian lens that reflected back on the popularity of the 'Prioress's Tale'. Both Hoccleve's 'Monk' and Lydgate's *Dan Joos* are written in rhyme royal, the same form as 'Prioress's Tale'. 'Monk' is collected with *Dan Joos* in Cambridge, Trinity College, MS R.3.21; and *Dan Joos* is collected with 'Prioress' (and other poems of Marian devotion) in London, British Library MS Harley 2251. Blurton and Johnson also note that both *Dan Joos* and 'Monk' reflect not the antisemitism of 'Prioress', but rather its theme of song – 'the orthodox recitation of liturgical and paraliturgical materials'. (Blurton and Johnson 2015: 150)

THE MONK WHO CLAD THE VIRGIN

Item de beata virgine

Whoso desirith to gete and conquere
The blisse of heuene, needful is a guyde
Him to condue°, and for to brynge him there. — *lead*
And so good knowe I noon° for mannes syde, — *none*
5 As the roote of humblesse°, and fo° to pryde, — *humility, foe*
That lady of whos tetes° virginal — *breasts*
Sook° our redemptour°, the makere of al. — *nursed, redeemer*

Betwixt God and man is shee mediatrice° — *mediator*
For oure offenses, mercy to purchace.
10 Shee is our seur° sheeld ageyn° the malice — *sure, against*
Of the feend°, þat° our soules wolde embrace° — *devil, who, seize*
And carie hem vnto þat horrible place°, — *i.e., hell*
Whereas eternel peyne is, and torment
More than may be spoke of, thoght, or ment.

15 Now syn° þat lady, noble and glorious, — *since*
To al mankynde hath so greet cheertee –
That in this slipir° lyf and perillous, — *slippery/unpredictable*
Staf of confort and help to man is shee –
Conuenient is°, þat to þat lady free° — *(it) is suitable, generous*
20 We do seruice, honour, and plesance.
And to þat ende, heere is a remembrance.

Ce feust faite a l'instance de T. Marleburgh

Heading: Piece about the blessed Virgin

1. gloss: This was made at the request of T. Marleburgh
6–7. Cf. the first stanza of 'Ad filium', where the infant Jesus is immediately juxtaposed with the adult, dying Jesus. So too in these lines, the infant, nursing Jesus is immediately signaled as our redeemer, and as God, 'makere of al'.
8. 'mediatrice'. Cf. the previous poem, 'Mother of Grace', line 59, where Hoccleve also uses this word, and where Hoccleve also meditates on Mary's mediatory role.
10–14. Cf. 2 Thessalonians 1:7–9; Matthew 13:42. Line 14 recalls, in an inverted sense, 1 Corinthians 2:9.
17–18. Cf. Tobit 10:4; Psalms 22:4.
19–21. The prologue to this tale shares features in common with Chaucer's prologue to the 'Prioress's Tale': both position their respective tales as miracles of the Virgin, and both introduce the tales as having been written in honor of the Virgin.
21. The transition from prologue to tale recalls the rubrics and transitions used in the 'Complaint', the first section of the *Series*. The *Series* itself is Hoccleve's most *Canterbury Tales*-like production, in that it plays with the transition between dialogue, prologue, and tale. 'Monk' might be seen as a precursor in style to the *Series*. It was, after all, interpolated into one collection of the *Tales*; and it is the only shorter poem that follows this prologue-tale format.

Explicit prologus et incipit fabula

Ther was whilom°, as þat seith the scripture°,
— once, story

In France a ryche man and a worthy,

That God and holy chirche to honure

25 And plese enforced he him° bisily;
— he applied himself

And vnto Crystes modir° specially,
— mother

Þat noble lady, þat blissid virgyne,

For to worsshipe he dide his might and pyne°.
— pain (through righteous work)

It shoop° so þat this man had a yong sone
— happened

30 Vnto which he yaf informacion°
— gave instruction

Euery day to haue in custume and wone°
— as a regular practice

For to seye, at his excitacion°,
— urging

The angelike salutacion°
— Ave Maria (Hail Mary)

.L. sythes° in worsship and honour
— fifty times

35 Of Goddes modir, of vertu the flour°.
— flower

By his fadres wil, a monk – aftirward,

In th'abbeye of Seint Gyle – maad was he,

Whereas° he in penance sharp and hard
— where

Obserued wel his ordres duetee°,
— the duties of his order

40 Lyuynge in vertuous religioustee°.
— virtuous reverence

And on a tyme, him to pleye and solace°,
— amuse and comfort

His fadir made him come hoom to his place.

Now was ther, at our ladyes reuerence,

A chapel in it maad and edified°,
— built

45 Into which the monk, whan conuenience°
— appropriateness

Of tyme he had awayted and espied,

His fadres lore° to fulfille him hied°,
— instruction, hastened

And .L. sythes° with deuout corage
— fifty times

Seide Aue Marie°, as was his vsage°.
— Ave Maria (Hail Mary), custom

50 And whan þat he had endid his preyeere,

Our lady, clothid in a garnement°
— garment

Sleeuelees, byfore him he sy° appeere,
— saw

Whereof the monk took good auisament°,
— looked closely

Merueillynge him what þat this mighte han ment°,
— might mean

55 And seide, 'O goode lady, by your leeue,

What garnament is this, and hath no sleeue?'

---

49. For the biblical text of the Ave Maria, see Luke 1:28.

51. The theme of clothing the Virgin resonates with the previous poem in HM 744, 'Mother of Grace', in which the Virginal womb is discussed in material terms (lines 36–42). Cf. also the language of tearing one's coat, vis-à-vis the Virgin and Christ, at the end of 'Complaint Paramount', lines 239–45.

And she answerde and seide, 'This clothynge
Thow hast me youen°, for thow euery day — given
.L. sythe° Aue Maria seyynge, — fifty times
60 Honured hast me. Hensfoorth, I the pray,
Vse to treble° þat by any way, — regularly triple
And to euery x^the ° Aue ioyne° also — tenth, join
A Pater Noster°. Do thow euene so. — Our Father (prayer)

'The firste .L.^ti ° wole° I þat seid be — fifty, wish
65 In the memorie of the ioie° and honour — joy
That I had whan the angel° grette° me, — i.e., Gabriel, greeted
Which was right a wondirful confortour° — comforter
To me, whan he seide the redemptour° — redeemer
Of al mankynde I receyue sholde.
70 Greet was my ioie whan he so me tolde.

'Thow shalt eek° seyn the seconde .L.^ty.° — also, fifty
In honur and in mynde of the gladnesse
That I had whan I baar of° my body — carried in
God and man°, withouten wo or duresse. — i.e., Jesus
75 The .iii.^de L.^ty° in thyn herte impresse, — third fifty
And seye it eek° with good deuocioun — also
In the memorie of myn assumpcioun°, — Assumption (ascent into heaven)

'Whan þat I was coroned° queene of heuene, — crowned
In which my sone regneth, and shal ay°.' — always
80 Al this was doon þat I speke of and meene,
As the book seith, vpon an halyday°. — holy day
And than seide our lady, the glorious may°, — maid
'The nexte halyday wole I resorte° — return
To this place, thee to glade and conforte.'

85 And therwithal fro thens° departed shee, — from thence
The monk in his deuocion dwellynge,
And euery day Aue Maria he
Seide aftir hir doctryne and enformynge°. — instruction
And the nexte haliday aftir suynge°, — the next holy day to occur
90 Our lady fresshly arraied° and wel — dressed
To the monk cam, beynge in þat chapel,

---

63. For the biblical text of the Paternoster, see Matthew 6:9–13 and Luke 11:2–4.
64–70. Cf. Luke 1:46–55.
71–4. Cf. Luke 2:19, and Mary's comparative reticence there.
77. The Assumption of Mary is the moment in which she is translated to heaven at the end of her
earthly life. Since the Virgin in the tale is greeting the monk from heaven, she is remembering this
defining moment in her earthly existence.

124 THE MONK WHO CLAD THE VIRGIN

And vnto him seide, 'Beholde now
How good clothyng and how fressh apparaille
That this wyke° to me youen° hast thow.   *week, given*
95 Sleeues to my clothynge now nat faille.
Thee thanke I, and ful wel for thy trauaille
Shalt thow be qwit° heere in this lyf present,   *rewarded*
And in þat othir° whan thow hens art went.   *i.e., in heaven*

'Walke now and go hoom vnto th'abbeye.
100 Whan thow comst, abbot shalt thow chosen be°,   *you will be elected abbot*
And the couent° teche thow for to seye   *convent*
My psalter, as byforn taght haue I thee.
The peple also thow shalt in generaltee
The same lessoun to myn honur teche,
105 And in hire hurtes° wole I been hir leche°.   *their (spiritual) wounds, their healer*

'Vii^e yeer° lyue shalt thow for to do   *seven years*
This charge, and whan tho° yeeres been agoon,   *those*
Thow passe shalt hens° and me come vnto,   *i.e., will die*
And, of this, doute haue thow right noon°.   *do not doubt this*
110 By my psalter shal ther be many oon
Saued, and had vp° to eternel blisse   *sent up*
Þat, if þat nere°, sholden thereof misse°.'   *were not, miss out*

Whan shee had seid what lykid hire to seye°,   *what she wished to say*
Shee vp to heuene ascendid vp and sty°.   *rose*
115 And soone aftir, abbot of þat abbeye
He maad was, as þat tolde him our lady°.   *as our lady had told him*
The couent and the peple deuoutly
This monk enformed and taghte hir psalteer,
For to be seid aftir þat vii^e yeer°.   *those seven years*

120 Tho° yeeres past; his soule was betaght°   *those, given*
To God. He heuene had vnto his meede°.   *as his reward*
Who serueth our lady, leesith° right naght.   *loses*
Shee souffissantly qwytith° euery deede.   *rewards*
And now heeraftir the bettre to speede°,   *succeed*

---

102. 'psalter'. The 'set of prayers recited upon a rosary, so called because the fifteen decades of Aves [150 Ave Marias] correspond to the hundred and fifty psalms of the psalter'. (*MED*: 'sauter n.', sense 1f)

105. Cf. 'Ad spiritum sanctum', line 45; 'Mother of Grace', lines 15–21; *Series* 2.92–8.

119. That is, he taught the others so that they might continue the practice after those seven years had ended.

125 And in hir grace cheerly for to stonde,
Hir psalteer for to seye let vs fonde°.   try

Explicit.

---

126. Cf. line 102. The tale ends not only with a focus on the virtues and rewards of doing work in the service of the Virgin (which Hoccleve himself does in presenting this tale – and which he has done with the two Marian pieces preceding this one), but also with a reminder to recite 'hir psalteer' – i.e., the prayers of the rosary.

THE EPISTLE OF CUPID
Date: May 1402

❧

This is Hoccleve's translation of Christine de Pizan's 'Epistre au dieu d'amours' (1399). Hoccleve's rendition is a feat of compression: it sees Christine's 822-line poem re-envisioned and cut down to 476 lines. Christine's poem uses the conceit of Cupid (God of Love) issuing a royal missive, in which he responds to allegations of misogyny and male willfulness. It is a poetic contribution to Christine's role in the *Querelle de la Rose* (1399–1402) in which she and Jean Gerson debated the morality of the *Roman de la Rose* (and similarly misogynistic literature) against the Col brothers, in Paris.

Hoccleve's English response takes on some bold new political resonances when one considers the events that transpired in England between the writing of Christine's poem and Hoccleve's translation (1399–1402): in 1399, Richard II was deposed, and Henry IV claimed the English throne. This political rupture had personal implications for Christine: she had sent her son, Jean de Castel, to England in 1398–9 to serve as a companion for a son of John Montague, Earl of Salisbury. Montague had been loyal to Richard II, and was beheaded for his loyalty. Henry IV took Jean into his own court thereafter (where Jean would have had Henry's own sons, including the future Henry V, for company). By the time Hoccleve set out to write his translation, Christine had entered into an epistolary exchange with Henry, in which she sent over copies of her poems to ingratiate him, and feigned interest in coming to join Jean in the English court. Jean would eventually be returned to France, but at the time of Hoccleve's drafting, it would seem the situation was still very much uncertain, and Christine was still awaiting her son's return. (Laidlaw 1982; Langdell 2018: Chapter 2)

The placement of the 'Epistle' in HM 744 is intriguing. It joins 'Three Roundels' and 'Henry V's Last Return' in being the only non-religious verse in a collection otherwise dominated by *ars moriendi*, poems of Marian devotion, and the collection's opening triad to the Trinity. The religious focus of the broader collection does draw attention (through context) to the poem's closing focus on biblical female exemplars of virtue. It is worth noting too that Hoccleve constellates the 'Epistle' with 'Learn to Die' both in HM 744 and in the *Series*. In the latter, the mention of Hoccleve's 'Epistle' in the 'Dialogue' spurs Hoccleve's eventual translation of the first *Gesta Romanorum* tale (pitched as penance for his supposed misstep in writing the 'Epistle'). 'Learn to Die' then follows on the heels of the first *Gesta* tale. The 'Dialogue' raises the question of whether Hoccleve's 'Epistle' is supportive of women, or whether it is subtly derisive – a question that remains open in scholarship today.

THE EPISTLE OF CUPID

L'Epistre de Cupide

	Cupido, vnto whos commandement	
	The gentil kynrede° of goddes on hy	noble stock
	And peple infernal° been obedient,	damned people
	And the mortel folk seruen bisyly,	
5	Of goddesse Sitheree° sone oonly,	Cytherea (Venus)
	To alle tho° þat to our deitee	those
	Been sogettes°, greetynges senden we.	subjects
	In general we wole° þat yee knowe	would like
	Þat ladyes of honur and reuerence,	
10	And othir gentil wommen, han isowe°	have sown
	Swich° seed of conpleynte° in our audience,	such, complaint
	Of men þat doon hem outrage and offense°,	who affront or attack them
	Þat it oure eres greeueth° for to heere,	hurts our ears
	So pitous is th'effect of hir mateere°.	their objection
15	And, passyng alle londes, on this yle°	island
	That clept° is Albioun° they moost conpleyne.	called, Albion (England)
	They seyn þat there is croppe and roote of gyle°,	all manner of treachery
	So can tho° men dissimulen and feyne°,	those, dissemble and deceive
	With standyng dropes° in hire yen tweyne°,	tears, their two eyes
20	Whan þat hire° herte feelith no distresse,	their
	To blynde wommen with hir doublenesse°.	their duplicity
	Hir° wordes spoken been so sighyngly°,	their, sorrowfully
	And with so pitous cheere and contenance°,	such piteous looks on their faces
	That euery wight þat meeneth° trewely	every person who observes it
25	Deemeth þat they in herte han swich° greuance.	have such
	They seyn so importable° is hir° penance	unbearable, their
	Þat, but hir lady list° to shewe hem° grace,	unless their lady desires, them
	They right anoon moot steruen° in the place.	very soon must die

---

1. Cupid is classical mythology's god of love, often presented as son of Venus (goddess of love) and Mars (god of war). Hoccleve follows Christine in fashioning a royal letter of response from Cupid, god of love. Hoccleve's training in writing Privy Seal documents uniquely positioned him to write such an official document. See Fenster and Erler 1990: 10, 167–8.

3. The addition of 'pele infernal' into Cupid's followers is original to Hoccleve.

5. Cytherea is the place Venus was believed to have been born; as such it became one of the names by which she was known. Venus is the Roman name for the Greek goddess Aphrodite. Christine does not present Cupid as being the only son of Venus; for the relevance of Hoccleve's addition to Christine, and her son Jean, see Langdell 2018: Chapter 2.

15–21. While Hoccleve is adapting from his source here (Christine has 'sur tous pays se complaignent de France' (23)), the singling out of 'Albioun' as the central site where one finds deceptive and duplicitous men seems, in 1402, stunningly relevant. Henry IV has just seized the throne from Richard II (the king to whom Christine herself was loyal); and Henry now holds Christine's own son, against her will, in his court. Line 17: 'croppe and roote', cf. *Troilus and Criseyde* 2.348, 5.1245.

128 THE EPISTLE OF CUPID

'A, lady myn,' they seyn, 'I yow ensure,
30 Shewe° me grace, and I shal euere be,   show
Whyles my lyf may lasten and endure,
To yow as humble in euery degree°   way
As possible is, and keepe al thyng secree°,   private
As þat yourseluen lykith þat I do,
35 And elles moot° myn herte breste on two°.' otherwise may, burst in two

Ful° hard is it to knowe a mannes herte,   very
For outward may no man the truthe deeme°,   judge
Whan word out of his mowth may ther noon sterte°, none appear
But it sholde any wight° by reson qweeme°.   person, please
40 So is it seid of herte, it wolde seeme.
O feithful womman, ful of innocence,
Thow art betrayed by fals apparence.

By procees°, wommen meeued of° pitee,   In turn, stirred by
Weenyng° al thyng were as þat tho° men seye, thinking, all things are as those
45 Graunten hem° grace of hir benignitee°, grant them, their kindness
For they nat sholden for hir° sake deye°,   their, die
And with good herte sette hem° in the weye   them
Of blisful loue, keepe it if they konne°.   can
Thus othir whyle° been the wommen wonne°. sometimes, the women are taken

50 And whan the man the pot hath by the stele°, pot has by the handle
And fully of hire° hath possessioun,   her
With þat womman he keepith nat to dele° desires not to deal with (or have sex with)
Aftir, if he may fynden in the toun°   town
Any womman his blynd affeccion
55 On to bestowe. Foule moot° he preeue°.   may, prove (to be)
A man, for al his ooth°, is hard to leeue°.   oaths, believe

And for° þat euery fals° man hath a make°, as, deceitful, friend
As vnto euery wight is light to knowe°, as every person easily knows
Whan this traitour the womman hath forsake,
60 He faste him speedith vnto his felowe.
Til he be there his herte is on a lowe°.   on fire
His fals deceit ne may him nat souffyse°, won't suffice for him
But of his treson tellith al the wyse°.   in every way

Is this a fair auant°? Is this honour?   boast
65 A man himself to accuse and diffame°?   disgrace
Now, is it good confesse him° a traitour,   to confess himself
And brynge a womman to a sclaundrous° name, slanderous
And telle how he hir body hath doon shame?
No worsship° may he thus to him conquere°, honor, acquire for himself
70 But ful greet repreef° vnto him and here°. dishonor, her

---

61. 'on a lowe'. Cf. 'Learn to Die', line 703.

THE EPISTLE OF CUPID 129

To here°, nay, yit was it no repreef°, — her, reproof
For al for pitee was it þat shee wroghte°, — acted
But he þat breewid hath al this mescheef,
Þat spak so faire and falsly° inward thoghte, — pleasingly and deceptively
75 His be the shame, as it by reson oghte°, — ought (to be)
And vnto here° thank perpetuel°, — her, endless thanks
Þat in a neede helpe can so wel.

Althogh þat men by sleighte and sotiltee° — cunning and cleverness
A cely°, symple°, and ignorant° womman — guileless, innocent, unaware
80 Betraye, is no wondir, syn° the citee — since
Of Troie, as þat the storie telle can,
Betrayed was thurgh the deceit of man,
And set afyre° and al doun ouerthrowe, — on fire
And finally destroyed, as men knowe.

85 Betrayen men nat remes grete° and kynges? — great realms
What wight is° þat can shape° a remedie — what kind of person is there, make
Ageynes° false and hid° purposid° thynges? — against, hidden, scheming
Who can the craft° tho castes° to espye°, — has the skill, those plots, see
But° man whos wil ay° reedy is t'applie — except (a), always
90 To thyng þat sovneth into° hy falshede°? — concerns, great falsehood
Wommen, bewaar of mennes sleighte, I rede°. — advise

And, ferthermore, han° the men in vsage° — have, as a custom
Þat whereas they nat likly been to speede°, — succeed
Swiche° as they been with a double visage° — such, double face
95 They procuren° for to pursue hir° neede. — enlist help, their
He preyeth him in his cause proceede,
And largely° him qwytith his trauaille°. — generously, he rewards his work
Smal witen wommen° how men hem° assaille. — little do women know, them

---

78–85. Cf. 'Epistre', lines 536–48. Christine's poem includes both the reference to the fall of Troy, and the line regarding the betrayal of realms and kings, but they occur much later in her poem. Hoccleve's choice to move this material up considerably underscores its relevance to contemporary politics. Hoccleve's descriptors (cely, symple, ignorant) are also drawn from the original: 'une chose simplete, / Une ignorant petite femmellette' (547–8; cf. 101). According to Greek legend, the impetus for the Trojan War was Paris of Troy's theft of Helen, wife of Menelaus (King of Sparta). The Greeks waged a long war against Troy, which eventually led to the city's fall. Chaucer's *Troilus and Criseyde* is set in the midst of the Siege of Troy.

85–91. While the 'Epistre' has an equivalent to the question in line 85 (see lines 541–2), the rest of the material in this stanza is original. This stanza would have been particularly resonant in London circa 1402 – the betrayal of 'remes grete and kynges' was certainly a palpable and recent event, after Henry IV's very recent deposition (and the eventual death) of Richard II in 1399. The rest of this stanza raises the question of who might be situated to counter such scheming. The answer seems to be people – like Hoccleve himself, perhaps – who are attuned to the misdeeds of such willful men.

92–5: That is, when men feel they're unlikely to succeed, they'll enlist the help of others – other two-faced men – who will spur them on in their endeavors.

130   THE EPISTLE OF CUPID

     To his felawe° anothir wrecche seith,   *friend*
100 'Thow fisshist faire°. Shee þat hath thee fyrid°   *you're wasting your time, inflamed you (with love)*
     Is fals and inconstant and hath no feith.
     Shee for the rode° of folk is so desyrid,   *ride*
     And as an hors fro day to day is hyrid°,   *hired*
     That whan thow twynnest° from hir conpaignie°,   *depart, company*
105 Anothir comth, and blerid° is thyn ye°.   *bleary, eye*

     'Now prike° on faste and ryde thy iourneye   *spur/ride*
     Whyl thow art ther. Shee behynde thy bak
     So liberal is shee can no wight withseye°,   *no person refuse*
     But qwikly of anothir take a snak°,   *bite*
110 For so the wommen faren, al the pak°.   *i.e., every one*
     Whoso hem° trustith, hangid moot° he be.   *them, may*
     Ay° they desiren chaunge and noueltee°.'   *always, newness (e.g., new lovers)*

     Whereof procedith this but of enuye°?   *envy*
     For° he himself here ne wynne may°,   *because, cannot win her*
115 Repreef° of here° he spekth, and villenye,   *reproof, her*
     As mannes labbyng° tonge is wont alway.   *babbling*
     Thus sundry° men ful often make assay°   *various, attempts*
     For to destourbe folk in sundry wyse°,   *various ways*
     For° they may nat accheuen hire empryse°.   *because, achieve their goal*

120 Ful many a man eek° wolde for no good°,   *also, good (reason)*
     Þat° hath in loue spent his tyme and vsid,   *who*
     Men wiste° his lady his axyng withstood°,   *knew, refused his requests*
     And þat he were° of his lady refusid,   *had been*
     Or waast and veyn° were al þat he had musid°, *wasted and vain, planned*
125 Wherfore he can° no bettre remedie   *knows*
     But on his lady shapith him° to lie.   *he prepares*

     'Euery womman,' he seith, 'is light° to gete.   *easy*
     Can noon seyn nay° if shee be wel isoght°. *none can say no, solicited well*
     Whoso may leiser han° with hire° to trete°,   *has free time, her, deal*
130 Of his purpos ne shal he faille noght°,   *he won't fail*
     But° on maddyng° he be so deepe broght   *unless, to madness*
     Þat he shende° al with open hoomlynesse°. *destroys, shamelessness*
     Þat louen wommen nat°, as þat I gesse.'   *women don't love that*

---

100. Fenster and Erler note a resonance with *Troilus and Criseyde*, 2.327–8 (1990: 207). The phrase
    'fisshist faire' translates to 'fish well' / 'made a good catch', but here it is being used ironically.
102–3. There is strong sexual connotation here, which is continued through the following stanza.
120–6. That is, men prevaricate for no visible benefit – other than that, if they don't lie about the
    woman in question, the focus will be on the fact that they (the men) have been rejected, and that
    all their work has been in vain.

THE EPISTLE OF CUPID   131

To sclaundre° wommen thus, what may profyte, — slander
135 To gentils° namly° þat hem armen sholde, — noblemen, especially
And in deffense of wommen hem delyte°, — delight themselves
As þat the ordre of gentillesse° wolde? — nobility
If þat a man list° gentil to be holde°, — wishes, to be known as noble
Al moot he flee° þat is to it contrarie. — he must avoid everything
140 A sclaundryng° tonge is therto aduersarie. — slandering/lying

A foul vice is of tonge to be light°, — to be too free with your tongue
For whoso mochil clappith°, gabbith° ofte. — talks much, lies
The tonge of man so swift is and so wight° — fast
Þat wan° it is areisid° vp on lofte°, — when, raised, high (loud)
145 Reson it sueth° so slowly and softe — follows it
Þat it him neuere ouertake may.
Lord, so the men been trusty° at assay°. — presumptuous, when put to the test

Albeit° þat men fynde o° womman nyce°, — although, one, foolish
Inconstant, rechelees°, or variable, — reckless
150 Deynous° or prowd, fulfillid of malice, — haughty
Withoute feith or loue, and deceyuable,
Sly, qweynte° and fals, in al vnthrift coupable°, — wily, guilty of wicked deeds
Wikkid and feers° and ful of crueltee, — fierce
It folwith° nat swiche° alle wommen be. — follows, such

155 Whan þat the hy God angels fourmed hadde,
Among hem° alle whethir ther was noon — them
Þat fownden was malicious and badde?
Yis, men wel knowen ther was many oon
Þat for hir° pryde fil° from heuene anoon°. — their, fell, at once
160 Shal man therfore alle angels prowde name°? — call all angels proud
Nay, he þat that susteneth° is to blame. — maintains this

Of xiiᵉ ° apostles, oon° a traitour was. — twelve, one
The remanaunt° yit goode were and treewe. — remaining (apostles)
Thanne, if it happe men fynden par cas° — perhaps

-----

137. 'ordre of gentillesse'. Cf. Chaucer's 'Gentilesse', which was reframed in Scogan's 'Moral Balade' (c. 1406–7), a few years after Hoccleve's 'Epistle of Cupid'. Also cf. 'For Henry V at Kennington', which echoes much of Chaucer's moral advice in 'Gentilesse' (itself drawn from Boethius and Dante). For phrasing, cf. 'Oldcastle', line 198 ('ordre of knyght'); 'Balade to Edward', line 50 ('ordre of endytyng'); *Regiment*, line 1478 ('ordres of preesthode and of wedlok').
143–6. 'A tongue is so fast that when it is held up on high (in a loud voice), reason follows so slowly that it will never catch up.'
155–61. The obvious example of a fallen angel is Satan. See Luke 10:18; 2 Peter 2:4. Cf. 'Epistre', lines 193–6. Soon after in 'Epistre', Christine offers Hutin de Vermeilles (knight) and Othe de Grandson (knight and poet) as positive examples of manhood (see lines 223–44). Hoccleve omits this material.
162–3. Among Jesus's twelve disciples, the one traitor was of course Judas (see Luke 22:2–4). This example regarding Jesus's disciples does not have a direct equivalent in Christine's 'Epistre'.

THE EPISTLE OF CUPID

165 O womman fals°, swich° is good for t'escheewe,
And deeme nat þat they been alle vntreewe.
I see wel mennes owne falsenesse
Hem causith° wommen for to truste lesse.

one false woman, such (a view)

causes them

O, euery man oghte han° an herte tendre
170 Vnto woman, and deeme hire° honurable,
Whethir his shap be eithir thikke or sclendre°,
Or he be badde or good, this is no fable.
Euery man woot°, þat wit hath resonable,
Þat of a womman he descendid is.
175 Than° is it shame° speke of hire° amis.

ought to have

her

whether he's thick or thin

knows

then, shameful, her

A wikkid tree good fruyt may noon foorth brynge,
For swich° the fruyt is as þat is the tree.
Take heede of whom thow took thy begynnynge°.
Lat thy modir° be mirour vnto thee.
180 Honure hire°, if thow wilt honurid be.
Despyse thow nat hire° in no maneere°,
Lest þat therthurgh thy wikkidnesse appeere.

such

i.e., who gave birth to you

mother

her

her, way

An old prouerbe seid is in Englissh:
Men seyn þat brid or foul° is deshonest,
185 Whatso it be, and holden ful cherlissh°,
Þat wont is° to deffoule his owne nest.
Men to seye of wommen wel it is best,
And nat for to despise hem° ne° depraue,
If þat hem list° hire° honur keepe and saue.

bird or fowl

truly uncouth

which is given

them, nor

they wish, their

190 Ladyes eek° conpleynen hem on clerkis,
Þat they han maad bookes of hir deffame°,
In whiche they lakken° wommennes werkis°,
And speken of hem° greet repreef° and shame,
And causelees hem yeue° a wikkid name°.
195 Thus they despysid been on euery syde,
And sclaundred° and belowen° on ful wyde°.

also

defaming them

disparage, actions

them, reproof

causelessly give them, reputation

slandered, reviled, widely

176–82. This stanza is particularly evocative of the situation unfolding between Christine, her son Jean, and Henry IV in the early years of the fifteenth century (see introduction to poem). Note the shift to 'thow' in the address here. There is the suggestion in Christine's autobiographical *Vision* that her son grew accustomed to the fine lifestyle of Henry's court, and that he was reluctant to return to France, where he would live in less lavish fashion. The admonition here to 'take heede of whom thow took thy begynnynge' carries special resonance. (See Langdell 2018: Chapter 2; cf. 'Epistre', lines 168–9, 750–4.) Lines 176–7: cf. Ecclesiasticus 27:7; Matthew 7:17–18, 12:33; and Fenster and Erler note a parallel with Chaucer's *Legend of Good Women*, 2394–5 (1990: 208). Lines 179–80: cf. Exodus 20:12.

183–9. The proverb says not to foul your own nest. By extrapolation – since every man comes of a woman, and you are asked to honor your mother – you should honor she who made you, and women in general.

THE EPISTLE OF CUPID   133

Tho° wikkid bookes maken mencion — those
How they betrayeden, in special,
Adam, Dauid, Sampson°, and Salomon°, — Samson, Solomon
200 And many oon mo°. Who may rehercen al — more
The tresoun þat they haue doon and shal?
Who may hire° hy° malice conprehende°? — their, great, grasp
Nat the world°, clerkes seyn; it° hath noon ende. — not anyone, i.e., their malice

Ouyde°, in his book callid *Remedie* — Ovid
205 *Of Loue*, greet repreef° of wommen writith, — reproof
Wherein I trowe° he dide greet folie, — believe
And euery wight° þat in swich cas° delitith. — man, in a similar situation
A clerkes custume° is whan he endytith° — scholar's custom, writes
Of wommen, be it prose, rym, or vers°, — rhyme or verse
210 Seyn they be wikke, al knowe he° the reuers°. — although he knows, reverse

And þat book scolers lerne in hir° childhede, — their
For° they of wommen bewaar sholde in age°, — so, over time
And for to loue hem° euere° been in drede°, — them, always, afraid
Syn° to deceyue is set al hir corage°. — since, their will
215 They seyn peril to caste° is auantage°, — expelling danger, advantageous
          scilicet libri
Namely swich° as men han in be trappid°, — especially such, have been ensnared
For many a man by wommen han mishappid°. — have met misfortune

No charge° what so þat the clerkes seyn. — No matter
Of al hir° wrong wrytyng do we no cure°. — their, not care
220 Al hir° labour and trauaille° is in veyn°, — their, work, in vain
For betwixt vs and my lady Nature
Shal nat be souffred, whyl the world may dure°, — last
Clerkes, by hire outrageous° tirannye, — their excessive
Thus vpon wommen kythen° hire maistrye°. — to show, their mastery (dominance)

197–9. See Genesis 3:1–20 (Adam), 2 Samuel 11:1–27 (David), Judges 16 (Samson), and 3 Kings 11:1–11 (Solomon). Cf. 'Epistre', lines 267–72. The phrase 'wikkid bookes' here is evocative of Jankyn's 'book of wikked wives' (Chaucer's 'The Wife of Bath's Prologue', line 685). In the *Series*, discussion of female complaint includes both Hoccleve's 'Epistle of Cupid' and a reference to the Wife of Bath as an 'auctrice' (see 2.694, 754), a word apparently coined by Hoccleve. Fenster and Erler note that these four Old Testament figures (also in Christine) were regularly used as exemplars of men 'beguiled by women'; Christine's use paraphrases a Latin proverb. See Fenster and Erler 1990: 84.

204–5. Ovid's *Remedia Amoris* (c. 2 AD). Cf. 'Epistre', lines 281–5; Christine continues discussing Ovid in lines 365–88.

209. Cf. 'Epistre', line 261: 'Dictiez en font, rimes, proses et vers'. On Hoccleve drawing attention to the form of writing (prose versus verse, etc.), cf. the end of 'Tale of Jereslaus's Wife' (third item of the *Series*), in which the moralization is copied into the manuscript, 'in prose … hoomly and pleyn' (3.977).

215. Hoccleve includes a superscript 'scilicet libri' over 'They seyn', clarifying 'That is, the books'.

221–4. Cf. 'Epistre', lines 297–300.

134 THE EPISTLE OF CUPID

225 Whilom° ful many of hem° were in our cheyne   at one time, them
    Tyd°, and lo now, what for vnweeldy° age,   tied, feeble (old)
    And for vnlust°, may nat to loue atteyne°,   sloth, attain
    And seyn þat loue is but verray dotage°.   foolishness
    Thus, for þat° they hemself° lakken corage,   because, themselves
230 They folk excyten by hir wikked sawes°,   their wicked sayings
    For to rebelle ageyn° vs and our lawes.   against

    But maugree° hem þat° blamen wommen moost,   in spite of, those who
    Swich° is the force of oure impressioun°   such, influence
    Þat sodeynly° we felle can° hir boost°   suddenly, can overcome, their boast
235 And al hir wrong ymaginacioun°.   their misguided thinking
    It shal nat been in hire elleccioun°   their choice
    The foulest slutte in al a town refuse,
    If þat vs list°, for al þat they can muse,   we wish

    But hire° in herte as brennyngly° desyre   her, burningly
240 As thogh° shee were a duchesse or a qweene.   as if
    So can we mennes hertes sette on fyre,
    And, as vs list°, hem° sende ioie and teene°.   we wish, them, joy and harm
    They that to° wommen been iwhet so keene°,   against, honed so sharp
    Our sharpe strokes, how sore they smyte,
245 Shul feele and knowe, and how they kerue° and byte.   cut

    Pardee°, this greet clerk, this sotil° Ouyde,   By God, cunning
    And many anothir, han deceyued be°   have been deceived
    Of° wommen, as it knowen is ful wyde,   by
    What°, no men more, and þat is greet deyntee°.   truly, a great pleasure
250 So excellent a clerk as þat was he –
    And othir mo°, þat kowde° so wel preche,   more, who could
    Betrappid wern° for aght° they kowde teche.   were ensnared, despite all

    And trustith wel þat it is no meruaille°,   marvel
    For wommen kneewen pleynly hire entente°.   their intention
255 They wiste° how sotilly° they kowde assaille   knew, slyly
    Hem°, and what falshode in herte they mente°,   them, intended
    And tho° clerkes they in hir daunger hente°.   those, in their power seized
    With o° venym anothir° was destroyed,   one, another (venom)
    And thus the clerkes often were anoyed.

260 This° ladyes ne gentils° nathelees°   these, noble, nevertheless
    Weren nat, they þat wroghten° in this wyse°,   acted, in this way
    But swiche° filthes þat wern vertulees: such

---

229. In this context, 'corage' can mean sexual desire, courage, or inclination.
237. 'slutte'. The first recorded use of this word, which has uncertain etymology, likely drawn from spoken English. Cf. 'Epistre', lines 333–5; Christine uses 'fillettes' and 'pietaille'. See also *Regiment*, line 3769.
246–52. Referring still to Ovid's *Remedia Amoris* (see lines 204–5).
260–1. 'These ladies were not noble, nevertheless, those who acted in this way ... '

THE EPISTLE OF CUPID   135

They qwitten° thus thise° olde clerkes wyse.   take revenge on, these
To clerkes forthy° lesse may souffyse°   therefore, suffice
265 Than to depraue° wommen generally,   disparage
For honur shuln° they gete noon° therby.   shall, none

If þat tho° men þat louers hem pretende°,   those, who pretend to be lovers
To wommen weren feithful, goode, and treewe,
And dredden° hem° to deceyue and offende,   feared, them
270 Wommen to loue hem wolde nat escheewe°,   refuse
But euery day hath man an herte neewe –
It vpon oon° abyde° can no whyle.   one (person), remain
What force is it° swich° oon for to begyle?   what does it matter, such

Men beren eek the wommen vpon honde°   also accuse the women
275 Þat lightly°, and withouten any peyne,   easily
They wonne been°. They can no wight withstonde°   are won, no man withstand
Þat his disese list to hem conpleyne°.   who wishes to complain of his discomfort
They been so freel°, they mowe hem nat restreyne°,   frail, cannot restrain themselves
But whoso lykith° may hem° lightly haue,   desires, them
280 So been hire° hertes esy in to graue°.   their, easy to impress (upon)

To maistir Iohn de Meun°, as I suppose,   Jean de Meun
Than° it was a lewde occupacioun°   then, foolish act
In makynge of the *Romance of the Rose*:
So many a sly ymaginacioun°   scheme
285 And perils for to rollen vp and doun,
So long procees°, so many a sly cautele°,   such a long discourse, trick
For to deceyue a cely° damoisele.   innocent

Nat can we seen, ne° in our wit conprehende,   nor
Þat art° and peyne and sotiltee° may faille   trickery, deceit
290 For to conquere, and soone make an ende,
Whan man a feeble place shal assaille,
And soone also to venquisshe a bataille°,   win a battle
Of which no wight° dar° make resistence,   person, dare
Ne herte hath noon to stonden at deffense.

272–3. '[Man's heart] does not stay on one person for long. What does it matter to deceive such a person?'

281–3. Jean de Meun (c. 1240–1305) is one of two writers of the *Roman de la Rose* – the writer of the second, and significantly longer, part of the text (c. 1275). The *Rose* is at the center of the epistolary debate that Christine took part in from 1399 to 1402, on which see *Debating the Roman de la Rose* (ed. McWebb). Cf. 'Epistre', lines 389–406.

288. Possibly a slight echo of 1 Corinthians 2:9.

136 THE EPISTLE OF CUPID

295	Than moot° it folwen of necessitee,	must
	Syn° art askith° so° greet engyn° and peyne,	since, requires, such, skill
	A womman to deceyue, what° shee be,	whatever
	Of constance they been nat so bareyne°	barren
	As þat some of tho sotil° clerkes feyne°,	those clever, feign
300	But° they been as þat wommen oghten be:	but instead
	Sad°, constaunt, and fulfillid of pitee°.	serious, full of pity
	How freendly° was Medea to Iasoun°	friendly, Jason
	In the conqueryng of the flees of gold°?	golden fleece
	How falsly quitte° he hire° affeccion,	repaid, her
305	By whom victorie he gat°, as he hath wold°?	got, as he desired
	How may this man, for shame, be so bold	
	To falsen hire° þat from deeth and shame	her
	Him kepte, and gat him so greet prys° and name°?	reward, reputation
	Of Troie also the traitour Eneas°,	Aeneas
310	The feithlees man, how hath he him° forswore	himself
	To Dydo, þat queene of Cartage° was,	Carthage
	Þat him releeued of his greeues° sore.	suffering
	What gentillesse° mighte shee do more	kindness
	Than shee, with herte vnfeyned°, to him kidde°,	earnest heart, showed
315	And what mescheef° to hire° of it betidde°.	misfortune, her, befell
	In our legende of martirs° may men fynde,	martyrs
	Whoso þat lykith° therin for to rede,	wishes
	That ooth° noon, ne byheeste°, may men bynde.	oath, nor promise
	Of repreef ne° of shame han they no drede°.	nor, fear
320	In herte of man conceites treewe° arn dede°.	honest thoughts, dead
	The soile is naght°; ther may no trouthe growe.	nothing
	To womman is hir° vice nat vnknowe°.	their, unknown

302–8. Referring here to the Greek myth of Jason and the Golden Fleece. Medea uses her magic to assist Jason in retrieving the golden fleece, on the condition that he marry her. According to Euripides, they get married but the union does not end happily: after ten years together, Jason leaves Medea for King Creon's daughter, Creusa. In retaliation, Medea murders Creusa, Creon, and the sons she had raised with Jason, before fleeing to marry King Aegeus. Cf. 'Epistre', lines 437–44.

309–15. Cf. 'Epistre', lines 445–60. Another example drawn from Greco-Roman myth: Aeneas, who surfaces in the *Iliad* and whose exploits are chronicled at length in Virgil's *Aeneid*. During the Fall of Troy, the Trojan Aeneas flees, and eventually lands in Carthage, where he is received by Queen Dido. Dido falls in love with Aeneas, but – reminded of the aims of his broader mission – the hero departs, breaking Dido's heart. The queen commits suicide upon Aeneas's departure. Aeneas is relevant to the 'Epistle' also because he is a son of Venus, half-brother to Cupid. Troy also has a direct connection to Britain for medieval writers, through the figure of Brutus: Brutus, a descendant of Aeneas (who would go on to found Rome), was thought to have been the founder and first king of Britain – and is the person from whom 'Britain' gets its name. (After the example of Dido and Aeneas in 'Epistre', Christine also gives Penelope and Ulysses as an example, but Hoccleve omits this.)

316. 'legende of martirs'. Fenster and Erler, Ellis, and Skeat equate this with Chaucer's *Legend of Good Women*; there might be a nod here, but this should not be read as an indisputable reference to Chaucer.

THE EPISTLE OF CUPID 137

Clerkes seyn also ther is no malice
Vnto° wommannes crabbid° wikkidnesse.   like, spiteful
325 O womman, how shalt thow thyself cheuyce°,   defend yourself
Syn° men of thee so mochil harm witnesse?   since
Yee, strah°! Do foorth° – take noon heuynesse°.   straw, carry on, cast off sadness
Keepe thyn owne, what° men clappe or crake°,   whatever, say or gossip
And some of hem° shuln smerte°, I vndirtake°.   them, shall suffer, promise

330 Malice of wommen, what is it to drede°?   fear
They slee° no men, destroien no citees.   slay
They nat oppressen folk, ne ouerlede°,   nor overpower (them)
Betraye empyres, remes°, ne duchees°,   realms, nor duchies
Ne men byreue° hir landes, ne hir mees°,   nor rob men of, nor their houses
335 Folk enpoysone°, or howses sette on fyre,   poison
Ne° fals contractes maken for noon hyre°.   nor, no payment

Trust, parfyt° loue, and enteer° charitee,   perfect, complete
Feruent wil and entalentid° corage   rousing
To thewes° goode, as it sit wel to be°,   behaviors, as it is fitting
340 Han wommen ay° of custume° and vsage,   always, habit
And wel they can a mannes ire° asswage°   anger, assuage
With softe wordes, discreet and benigne.
What they been inward shewith owtward signe.

Wommannes herte to no creweltee
345 Enclyned is, but° they been charitable,   but rather
Pitous°, deuout, ful of humilitee,   compassionate
Shamefast°, debonaire° and amiable,   modest, kind
Dreedful° and of hir° wordes mesurable°.   respectful, their, discreet
What womman thise hath nat, par auenture°,   perhaps
350 Folwyth nothyng° the way of hir° nature.   not at all, her

---

330–6. These lines are drawn from 'Epistre', lines 641–7, where they are positioned later, following the biblical material on Eve and Mary. Hoccleve moves them up in his adaptation, before the biblical material. As with lines 85–91, these lines carry a potent political relevance, given the date (1402) at which the poem purports to have been written. The things that women are said *not* to do in the present stanza – slaying men, oppressing people, over-exerting their power, betraying realms and empires, etc. – are pertinent both to Richard II (who was accused of being tyrannical in his over-exertion of regal power) and Henry IV (who violently seized the throne from Richard).

337–43. The ability of women to encapsulate all virtues that men lack begins to crystallize in this stanza. Here, women are said not to be duplicitous, contrary to the men we have entertained thus far: what you see on the outside reflects accurately what is inside (cf. lines 36–9). The good qualities attributed to women in lines 337–8 reflect the type of virtue usually attributed to the Virgin Mary, prefiguring the focus on biblical women in the latter stanzas of the poem. Indeed, the qualities listed in lines 337–8 are attributed to biblical women who served Jesus in Christine's 'Epistre', lines 563–6, including 'parfaicte amour', 'grant charité', 'fervante voulenté', and 'courage entalenté'. Hoccleve moves these descriptors up in his version, out of their biblical context (while keeping the biblical material itself, below), perhaps to create a dissonance which is later resolved when we consider the Virgin Mary as worthy of such attributes.

344–50. The notion that women are not naturally inclined to cruelty – and the adjectives charitable, debonaire, amiable, etc. – are drawn from Christine: lines 657–80.

138 THE EPISTLE OF CUPID

Men seyn oure firste modir°, nathelees°, → mother (i.e., Eve), nevertheless
Made al mankynde leese° his libertee, → lose
And nakid° it of ioie°, doutelees, → deprived, joy
For Goddes heeste° disobeied shee → commandment
355 Whan shee presumed to ete° of the tree → eat
Which God forbad þat shee nat ete of sholde,
And nad° the feend° been, no more she wolde. → had not, devil

Th'enuyous swellyng° þat the feend, our fo°, → puffing with pride, foe
Had vnto man in herte for his welthe° → good fortune/happy state
360 Sente a serpent and made hire° to go → her
To deceyue Eeue, and thus was mannes welthe
Byreft him by the feend, right in a stelthe°, → sneakily
The womman nat knowyng of the deceit.
God woot°, ful fer° was it from hir conceit°. → knows, very far, her intention

365 Wherfore we seyn, this good womman Eeue
Our fadir Adam ne deceyued noght.
Ther may no man for a deceit it preeue° → prove
Proprely, but° if þat shee in hir thoght → unless
Had it conpassid° first, or it was wroght°, → planned it, before it was done
370 And for swich° was nat hire impressioun°, → such, her intention
Men calle it may no deceit, by resoun.

No wight° deceyueth but he it purpose°. → person, unless he intends it
The feend this deceit caste°, and nothyng shee°. → plotted, i.e., and not Eve
Than is it wrong for to deeme or suppose
375 Þat shee sholde of þat gilt° the cause be. → guilt/sin
Wytith° the feend, and his be the maugree°, → blame, offense
And for excusid haue hire innocence°, → excuse her innocence
Sauf° oonly þat shee brak° obedience. → save, broke (her)

Touchynge which, ful fewe men ther been –
380 Vnnethes° any, dar° we saufly° seye, → hardly, dare, safely
Fro day to day, as men mowe° wel seen – → may
But þat the heeste° of God they disobeye. → laws
This haue in mynde, sires, we yow preye.
If þat yee be discreet° and resonable, → wise
385 Yee wole hire° holde the more excusable. → her

351–7. See Genesis 3:1–20. The material involving Eve is repositioned by Hoccleve, allowing a direct trajectory from Eve to Mary (and then St Margaret), and deepening the trajectory from literary/mythical examples to biblical/Christian examples. This is a pivot point in the poem, away from secular and/or classical examples of reprehensible men, and towards biblical examples of virtuous women. Line 357: ' … and if the devil had not existed, she (Eve) would not have (eaten of the tree).'

363–73. Cupid's defense of Eve here rests on intention: Eve wasn't aware that she was being tempted; the devil is thus really to blame. We cannot argue that she attempted to deceive Adam because it was not premeditated nor wholly intentional. Christine makes the same argument: 'Epistre', lines 604–16.

THE EPISTLE OF CUPID · 139

And wher men seyn in man is stidfastnesse°,	steadfastness
And womman is of hir corage° vnstable°,	her heart, changeable
Who may of Adam bere swich° witnesse?	bear such
Tellith on this: Was he nat changeable?	
390 They bothe weren in a cas semblable°,	a similar situation
Sauf° willyngly the feend deceyued Eeue.	except that
So dide shee nat Adam°, by your leeue.	she didn't (deceive) Adam

Yit was þat synne happy° to mankynde.	fortunate (i.e., felix culpa)
The feend deceyued was, for al his sleighte°,	cunning
395 For aght° he kowde him° in his sleightes wynde°.	all that, man, ensnare
God, to descharge° mankynde of the weighte	discharge
Of his trespas, cam doun from heuenes heighte,	
And flessh and blood he took of a virgyne°,	i.e., the Virgin Mary
And souffred deeth, man to deliure of pyne°.	to deliver man from pain

400 And God, fro whom ther may no thyng hid be,	
If he in womman knowe° had swich° malice,	known, such
As men of hem° recorde in generaltee,	them
Of our lady°, of lyf reparatrice°,	Mary, restorer
Nolde han be° born. But for þat shee of vice	(he) would not have been
405 Was voide°, and of al vertu wel, he wiste°,	clear, knew
Endowid, of hire° be born him liste°.	her, he desired

Hire hepid° vertu hath swich° excellence	her full/gathered, has such
Þat al to weyk° is mannes facultee	too weak
To declare it, and therfore in suspense	

393–9. Cf. John 3:16; Luke 1:26–38; Acts 5:30–1. The idea of *felix culpa* (meaning 'happy fall') holds that the fall of Adam and Eve, in Eden, was ultimately beneficial because it paved the way for Christ's redemption of mankind. The final four lines of the stanza indicate this: God becomes incarnate, as Jesus, through the Virgin Mary, in order to lighten the collective weight of sin from mankind.

400. This line is very similar to the final line of Hoccleve's *Regiment* (line 5463), written some eight years later. More specifically, it is similar to the final line of the *Regiment* envoi found in HM 111 (where the word 'God' is used, instead of the more ambiguous 'he' found in all non-autograph copies of the *Regiment* envoi).

401–6. The poem takes a devotional turn here; commendation of Eve leads to praise for the Christian woman *par excellence*, Mary, Mother of God (first mentioned in line 398). The type of superlative praise heaped upon Mary reflects back on the virtue attributed to women more generally above, lines 337–50. Whereas the earlier commendation comes across as idealized, this commendation of Mary is in line with orthodox thought: if she were not void of vice, God would not have chosen her to be Jesus's mother. The turn to Mary here also reminds the reader of HM 744 of the series of three Marian pieces (nos. 4–6) immediately preceding this poem. By the end of this poem, the 'Epistle' seems not like an aberration, but rather – at least on one level – as a different approach to Marian devotion. Line 403, 'reparatrice': An apparent neologism, borrowed from Latin. The word aligns with Hoccleve's treatment of Mary as 'mediatrice' in 'Mother of Grace' (line 59) and 'The Monk Who Clad the Virgin' (line 8).

407–9. Ellis notes a possible echo of the 'Prioress's Tale', 475–6, 481–2 (Ellis 2001: 111). Cf. 'Inuocacio ad Patrem', lines 115–19.

140 THE EPISTLE OF CUPID

410	Hir° due laude° put moot° needes be.	her, praise, must
	But this we witen° verraily°: þat shee,	know, truly
	Next God, the best freend is þat to man longith°.	belongs
	The keye of mercy by hir girdil hongith°,	hangs
	And of mercy hath euery wight° swich° neede,	person, such
415	Þat, cessyng° it, farwel the ioie° of man!	lacking, joy
	Of hir° power it is to taken heede°.	her, note should be taken
	Shee mercy may, wole°, and purchace can°.	will, can obtain
	Displese hir nat. Honureth þat womman,	
	And othir wommen alle, for hir sake;	
420	And, but° yee do, your sorwe shal awake.	unless
	Thow precious gemme°, martir Margarete,	gem
	Of thy blood dreddist noon effusioun°.	feared no spilling
	Thy martirdom ne may we nat foryete°.	forget
	O constant womman, in thy passioun	
425	Ouercam the feendes temptacioun,	
	And many a wight° conuerted thy doctryne	person
	Vnto the feith of God, holy virgyne.	
	But vndirstondith, we commende hir noght	
	By encheson° of hir virginitee.	reason
430	Trustith right wel, it cam nat in our thoght,	
	For ay° we werreie° ageyn° chastitee,	always, fight, against
	And euere shal. But this leeueth° wel yee:	believe
	Hir louyng herte, and constant to hir lay°,	faith
	Dryue out of remembrance we nat may.	

---

413. Mention of Mary's 'girdil' here, in tandem with her mercy, casts the mind back to the previous item in HM 744: 'The Monk Who Clad the Virgin'.

418–20. These lines would seem to encapsulate the moral of Hoccleve's poem, or as close as we get: Mary serves (within an orthodox medieval perspective) as the exemplar of supreme virtue; as such, you should honor her – and honor all women, for her sake. Cf. 'Epistre', lines 572–6.

421. St Margaret of Antioch's legend includes escaping the sexual advances of Olybrius, governor of Antioch, while proclaiming herself a Christian; being swallowed by a dragon but escaping; and converting multitudes to Christianity (Farmer 2011). Fenster and Erler note that Hoccleve draws on the opening passage of the *Legenda Aurea*'s Margaret story, wherein Margaret is described as a 'pretiosa gemma' (cf. line 421). The figure of the 'marguerite' (as pearl) also plays a central role in Usk's *Testament of Love*. See Fenster and Erler 1990: 210–11 for further information. The material on St Margaret is original to Hoccleve. In Christine's 'Epistre', St Nicholas of Myra is instead put forward as an exemplary saint (lines 704–5).

422. 'effusioun'. Among the earliest recorded instances of this word in English, borrowed from Latin and French.

428–34. The playful fiction of Cupid as narrator, speaking on behalf of Love, comes back into focus here – another Hocclevian addition. Cf. *Roman de la Rose*, lines 16587–91.

THE EPISTLE OF CUPID 141

435	In any book also wher can yee fynde	
	Þat of the wirkes, or the deeth or lyf	
	Of Ihesu, spekth or makith any mynde°	speaks or makes mention
	Þat wommen him forsook, for wo or stryf?	
	Wher was ther any wight so ententyf°	devoted
440	Abouten him as wommen? Pardee, noon.	
	Th'apostles him forsooken euerichoon°.	every one

Wommen forsook him noght°, for al the feith   not
Of holy chirche in womman lefte° oonly.   remained
This is no lees°, for thus holy writ seith.   no lie
445 Looke, and yee shuln so fynde it, hardily°.   truly
And therfore it may preeued° be therby   proved
That in womman regneth° al the constaunce,   reigns
And in man is al chaunge and variaunce.

Now holdith this for ferme° and for no lye°   as sound, lie
450 Þat this treewe and iust° commendacioun   just
Of wommen is nat told for flaterie,
Ne° to cause hem° pryde or elacioun°,   nor, them, vainglory
But oonly, lo, for this entencioun°:   intention
To yeue° hem° corage of perseuerance   give, them
455 In vertu, and hir° honur to enhaunce.   their

The more vertu°, the lasse° is the pryde.   (the) virtue (is), less
Vertu so noble is and worthy in kynde,
Þat vice and shee may nat in feere° abyde.   woman
Shee puttith vice cleene out of mynde.
460 Shee fleeth from him; shee leueth him behynde.
O womman, þat of vertu art hostesse,
Greet is thyn honur and thy worthynesse.

435–44. Matthew's account comes closest to confirming this point of view: see Matthew 26:56 (cf. Mark 14:50), 27:55–6. See also Mark 15:40–1; John 19:25–7; Luke 23:49. Cf. 'Epistre', lines 569–90. Christine is more explicit about the entire faith being left in the hands of only *one* woman: 'Toute la foy remaint en une femme' (571) – i.e., Mary.

445. Cf. Hoccleve's exhortation to the Friend in the 'Dialogue' (*Series*) to 'looke in the same book' and see what is truly written (2.775). In that instance, the book in question is in fact the 'Epistle of Cupid'. Hoccleve argues that – contrary to the Friend's understanding – the 'Epistle' ends virtuously for women, which the Friend would have seen if he had 'red it fully to the ende' (i.e., read these final lines).

449. Here, Cupid pivots towards the concluding four stanzas. This first of the final stanzas states Cupid's intention in writing the poem. Christine's explication is much longer in 'Epistre', and more focused on defense and excoriation, but for the notion of offering 'corage of perseuerance / In vertu', see lines 767–8.

142   THE EPISTLE OF CUPID

Than° thus we wolen° conclude and deffyne°:   *then, will, come to an end*
We yow commaunde, our ministres echoon°,   *each one*
465   Þat reedy been to oure heestes° enclyne°,   *commands, follow*
Þat of tho° men vntreewe, our rebel foon°,   *against those, foes*
Yee do punisshement, and þat anoon°.   *soon*
Voide hem° our court, and banisshe hem foreuere,   *Expel them from*
So þat therynne they ne come neuere.

470   Fulfillid be it, cessyng al° delay –   *without any*
Looke ther be noon excusacion°.   *no leniency*
Writen in th'eir°, the lusty monthe of May,   *in the air*
In our paleys°, wher many a milion   *palace*
Of louers treewe han habitacion,
475   The yeer of grace, ioieful and iocounde°,   *joyful and pleasant*
MCCCC and secounde°.   *1402*

Explicit epistola Cupidinis

463–76. Cupid returns to the fiction of the 'air court' of love, where he addresses his 'ministres'.
    Lines 472 and 476 together give the precise date – one of the most specific dates given within Hoccleve's shorter poems. Christine ends her poem by listing several of the classical gods assembled in Cupid's court (lines 801–20); Hoccleve omits this.

HENRY V'S LAST RETURN

Date: c. 1421

❧

This poem centers on Henry V's last return from France in February 1421. The prayer for Henry's soul included in the heading indicates that it was entered into the manuscript after Henry's death on August 31, 1422. This is the latest of Hoccleve's poems for Henry V, all the rest of which are included in HM 111 (nos. 4, 5–6, 8, 14, 15).

As shown in the notes, the terminology used to describe and praise Henry has much in common with that used to praise Duke Humphrey and Henry in the 'Dialogue' section of the *Series* – which was being written at roughly the same time.

HM 744, fol. 50v (detail), The Huntington Library, San Marino, CA.

HENRY V'S LAST RETURN

Ceste balade ensuante feust faite pur la bien venue du tresnoble Roy H le Vᵗ, que dieu pardoint, hors du Roialme de France, cestassauoir sa dareine venue

> Victorious Cristen prince, our lord souereyn°,   sovereign
> Our lige lord, ful dred and douted°, we,   respectful and in awe
> Youre humble and buxum liges° treewe, seyn   obedient subjects
> Right thus vnto your rial° dignitee: royal
> 5 Henri the .v.ᵗʰᵉ welcome be yee.
> Welcome be your famous excellence,
> Swerd of knyghthode and flour of sapience°.   flower of wisdom
>
> Yee been welcome, heir and regent of France,
> Our gracious kyng, the ensaumple° of honour.   exemplar
> 10 Right feithfully, with hertes obeissance°,   obedience
> Welcome be yee, worthy conquerour,
> Which – no peril eschuyng°, ne° labour –   avoiding no danger, nor
> In armes knyghtly han yow put in prees°,   thrown yourself into combat
> And twixt° two remes° knyt han vp the pees°.   between, realms, peace
>
> 15 Your worthynesse excedith and surmountith
> The prowesse of kynges and pryncees alle.
> Fame so seith° – thus al the world acountith°.   says as much, regards (it)
> What may we seyn°, or what may we yow calle.   say
> We can, for noon aart° þat may happe or falle°,   no learning, happen or occur
> 20 Your worthy deedes, as vs oghte°, preise°.   as we ought (to), praise
> They been so manye and so mochil peyse°.   so consequential

---

Heading: This following balade was made for the return of the most honorable King Henry V, may God pardon him, from the realm of France, that is to say, his last return

1–2. Henry is named as 'roy' [king] in the heading to the poem, and 'prince' in this first line. 'Victorious Cristen prince … Our lige lord … ': cf. opening to HM III no. 15 (also written for Henry V): 'Victorious kyng … '; and 'Dialogue' (*Series*) line 2.554: 'our lord lige, our kyng victorious'. Line 2: 'ful dred and douted' can also mean 'very worried and uncertain'.

5. The first lines of this poem follow a particularly Hocclevian mode, the 'delayed signified'. (Cf. 'Male Regle', lines 1–8; *Regiment*, lines 4978–84.) The present poem offers a paler version, in which the signifiers 'prince', 'lord', and 'rial dignitee' give way at last to a firm and unequivocal signified: 'Henri the v'.

7. 'flour of sapience'. Cf. *Regiment*, line 1962, where Chaucer is heralded as 'flour of eloquence'.

8. 'heir and regent of France': Henry's new title, acquired in the Treaty of Troyes (May 21, 1420).

9. 'the ensaumple of honour'. Cf. 'Dialogue', lines 603–9, where Duke Humphrey is put forward as a 'mirour, / Therin to see the path vnto honour.'

14. Henry's ability to 'knyt … vp the pees' also likely refers to the Treaty of Troyes (see note to line 8).

HENRY V'S LAST RETURN   145

Ignorance is vnto vs swich a fo°,   such a foe
If we dilate° sholde and drawe along   tarry
Your prys and thank°, we kowden nat do so.   reputation and regard
25   To litil° seyn we sholde, and do yow wrong,   too little
Nat on our willes but wittes along°.   not by choice but by fault of intelligence
And syn° þat therto oure intelligence   since
Souffysith nat, we keepe moot° silence.   must keep

But, souerein lord lige, as we seide aboue,
30   Welcome be your excellent hynesse° –   highness
With al our spirites and hertes loue –
More welcome than we can expresse.
Your hy presence is tresor° and richesse   treasure
To vs ful greet, forwhy° to vs echone°   therefore, to each of us
35   Welcome be your peereles° persone.   peerless

C'est tout.

22–8. A striking stanza, in which Hoccleve pivots from modesty to silence: because no amount of
thanks or praise would be sufficient, he will offer nothing at all. Line 28: cf. *Regiment*, lines 1014–15.

29. The pivot here, signaled with 'but', serves to underscore the tonal shift, and therefore highlights the
ambiguous tone of the previous two stanzas. In its abruptness, it shares much with the phrase 'passe
over', which Hoccleve learned from Chaucer: see e.g., *Regiment*, lines 113, 1618, etc. The message
seems to be: we have no words with which to praise you; nevertheless, you are welcome.

33. 'tresor'. Cf. 'Male Regle', line 1. The word is mostly otherwise used, in the shorter poems, in
Hoccleve's 'Learn to Die'.

35. 'peereles persone'. Note proximity in pronunciation to 'perillous' [perilous], which Hoccleve uses
earlier in HM 744: 'Monk Who Clad the Virgin', line 17. Hoccleve also uses the noun 'peril'
frequently in his shorter poems (cf. line 12).

THREE ROUNDELS

Date: unknown (before 1426)

❧

These 'chaunceons' are in company with the roundel that completes Hoccleve's 'Balade and Roundel to Henry Somer' (HM 111, no. 13). There, the roundel is presented as something 'we' will 'synge and seye' (line 31) – the 'we' likely referring to Hoccleve and his associates Bailey, Offord, and Hethe, named in the poem. Similarly, the link with which 'Three Roundels' ends describes 'our song', giving the impression that this might have been sung aloud.

The ending link, knitting these roundels to Hoccleve's *ars moriendi* treatise, 'Learn to Die', is a unique occurrence in the holographs. 'Ad spiritum sanctum' ends with lines that tie together the first three poems of HM 744, as a Trinitarian triptych. And the first six items of HM 744 are all devotional poems (and hence implicitly held together); but never elsewhere does Hoccleve make such an overt statement linking the pieces. The playfulness of the roundels stands in stark contrast to the 'heuynesse' of 'Learn to Die', and this couplet makes the tonal pivot all the more conspicuous.

It should be noted that such tonal juxtaposition seems to have been something Hoccleve was interested in, stylistically, in these final years of his career. 'Learn to Die' is similarly sandwiched starkly between two lively *Gesta Romanorum* tales in the *Series*. Whereas the interlinking dialogues with the Friend in that work set up both *Gesta* tales, there is no prologue directly before 'Learn to Die'; and the dialogue after the treatise just serves to set up the second *Gesta* tale. This gives the impression of the treatise being wedged into the *Series* by Hoccleve – it makes the tonal shift all the more remarkable.

All three roundels follow the same rhyme scheme: abba ab ba abba, with the first quatrain serving as the recurring chorus.

Hoccleve's most obvious inspiration for these roundels would have been Chaucer's 'Complaint to His Purse', in which the speaker also mixes love poetry with pecuniary petition: the purse is personified there, and becomes 'my lady dere' (line 2), 'quene of comfort' (13), and 'saveour' (16). Hoccleve's 'Lady Money' is similarly a secular 'goddesse' (18). Hoccleve's poem, however, grants Lady Money her own voice, whereas Chaucer's poem is one-sided. (Note that Hoccleve also refers to 'lady Moneye' in his *Series*: 2.184.)

THREE ROUNDELS   147

Three Roundels

Cy ensuent trois chaunceons: l'une conpleynante a la dame monoie; et l'autre la response d'ele a cellui qui se conpleynt; et la tierce la commendacion de ma dame

Wel may I pleyne° on yow, Lady Moneye,	complain
Þat in the prison of your sharp scantnesse	
Souffren° me bathe in wo and heuynesse,	allow
And deynen° nat of socour° me purueye°.	deign, comfort, provide

5 Whan þat I baar° of your prison the keye,   bore
    Kepte I yow streite°? Nay, God to witnesse!   stingily
        Wel may I, etc.

    I leet yow out. O now, of your noblesse,
    Seeth vnto me. In your deffaute°, I deye°.   absence, die
10   Wel may I, etc.

    Yee saillen al to fer°. Retourne, I preye!   too far
    Conforteth me ageyn this Cristemesse°.   Christmas
    Elles I moot° in right a feynt° gladnesse   must, weak
    Synge of yow thus, and yow accuse and seye:
15   Wel may I, etc.

    La response:

    Hoccleue, I wole° it to thee knowen be: wish

Heading: Here follow three songs: one a complaint to Lady Money; and the other the response from her to he who complained; and the third the commendation of my lady

5–6. The prison/key metaphor would seem to mean, 'when I was able to spend you freely … ' (not keep you locked up). It gestures to the metal latch on a purse (which must be opened in order for Lady Money to 'walk free'). 'Streite' can mean 'stingily' or 'confined'.

11–12. The mention of 'Cristemesse' as a time for restoration of financial security, and the sailing metaphor, both tie this roundel to the corresponding Somer poem, with its own closing roundel (HM 111 no. 13) – see lines 19–22. Whereas the Somer poem is datable to 1408–1409, and hence the Christmas flagged there would fall in one of those years, the Christmas in 'Three Roundels' is harder to date. If the 'shippes' metaphor in the Somer poem is a punning reference to the 'great noble' coin, as Seymour suggests, Hoccleve might be expanding that pun here – Lady Money 'sails' too far (via her 'shippes').

17. 'Hoccleue'. This is the only point at which Hoccleve's name appears in this manuscript. In HM 111, his name appears in 'Male Regle' (line 351; his name is also in the heading to that poem) and 'Balade and Roundel to Henry Somer' (line 25). Each of these instances is close enough to the middle of the given manuscript to avoid the page loss evident in early and late pages (and seen evidenced in both manuscripts – the first pages missing in HM 111, and the final pages in HM 744). The same is true of Hoccleve's self-namings in the *Series* and the *Regiment*. Interestingly, two out of three of Hoccleve's self-namings in the holographs occur in the roundel context: in 'Somer' when setting up the roundel, and here in the midst of a roundel. In both cases, the poet is talking about money, supplicating. In this case, the fact that his name is the first word of the first stanza means the name is repeated throughout.

148 THREE ROUNDELS

I, Lady Moneie, of the world goddesse,
Þat haue al thyng vndir my buxumnesse°, command
20 Nat sette by thy pleynte risshes three°. don't care about your complaint

Myn hy° might haddest thow° in no cheertee high, had you
Whyle I was in thy slipir sikirnesse°. slippery safekeeping
        Hoccleue, etc.

At instance° of thyn excessif largesse°, because, free-spending
25 Becam I of my body delauee°. unclean/immoderate
        Hoccleue, etc.

And syn° þat lordes grete obeien me, since
Sholde I me dreede of thy poore symplesse°? poverty/ignorance
My golden heed akith° for thy lewdnesse°. aches, foolishness
30 Go, poore wrecche. Who settith aght° by thee? sets anything
        Hoccleue, etc.

        C'est tout.

Of my lady wel me reioise I may:
Hir golden forheed is ful narw° and smal, very narrow
35 Hir browes been lyk° to dym reed° coral, are similar, red
And as the ieet° hire yen° glistren ay°. jet (black), her eyes, glisten always

Hir bowgy° cheekes been as softe as clay, baggy
With large iowes° and substancial. jowls
        Of my lady, etc.

40 Hir nose a pentice° is, þat it ne shal sloping roof
Reyne° in hir mowth, thogh shee vprightes lay. rain
        Of [my lady], etc.

---

18. Here, Lady Money is positioned (playfully) as a worldly 'goddesse'. Cf. 'Male Regle', where Health
is positioned as an 'Eerthely god' (line 8).

32. 'C'est tout'. This particular sign-off, a familiar sight throughout the holographs, divides the three
roundels into two segments. The first two roundels form the first piece: a call and response between
Hoccleve and Lady Money. The second piece (and third roundel) reads as a satirical paean to 'my
lady'.

33–47. The final roundel is a satirical portrait, pitched as the inversion of what was considered 'desirable
female beauty' in the period. Seymour offers Chaucer's description of the Prioress in the *Canterbury
Tales* as counterpoint, the idea of what was considered attractive (General Prologue, lines 152–6).
Indeed, all such portraits in the General Prologue might have given Hoccleve inspiration as he
embarked on this description.

34. 'golden forheed': cf. line 29.

THREE ROUNDELS   149

Hir mowth is nothyng scant°, with lippes gray.   not small
Hir chin vnnethe° may be seen at al.   hardly
45 Hir comly° body shape° as a footbal,   fair, is shaped
And shee syngith ful lyk° a papeiay°.   just like, parrot
            Of [my lady], etc.

C'est tout.

Aftir our song, our mirthe, and our gladnesse,
50 Heer folwith a lessoun of heuynesse.   **Salomon Extrema gaudij**
                                                     luctus occupat, etc.

---

45. 'footbal'. Her body is likened to the ball used in this early form of football (the antecedent to
  modern soccer/football/rugby). Hoccleve's is among the earliest literary references to the object in
  English literature. (The *OED* lists only one other contemporary use before 1425.)
49. gloss: Solomon: Sorrow takes hold at the end of joy. [Drawn from Proverbs 14:13.]

LEARN TO DIE

Date: unknown (before 1426)

❧

This is Hoccleve's translation of the *ars moriendi* chapter of Henry Suso's *Horologium sapientiae* (1334), the second most popular devotional work of the period, after *Imitation of Christ*. The translation also appears, in a slightly different form, in Hoccleve's *Series* (written c. 1419–26). It is unclear whether Hoccleve had translated 'Learn to Die' prior to writing the *Series* – and used the *Series* in part as a framework for collecting that treatise, alongside the two *Gesta Romanorum* tales – or whether he translated it after writing the two opening sections of the *Series*, the 'Complaint' and 'Dialogue'.

This is by far the longest of Hoccleve's 'shorter poems', almost doubling the respective lengths of 'La Male Regle', 'To Sir John Oldcastle', and 'The Epistle of Cupid' (its closest contenders for length). The fact that Hoccleve saw fit to copy it into both surviving late-career compilations (the Huntington holographs and the Durham *Series*) indicates a level of pride in its completion. Indeed, the work serves as a fitting culmination to his writing career: it blends a particularly Hocclevian investment in interiority and psychological intensity, an earnest desire to assist in the moral formation of his readers, and an exploration of the line between the metaphorical and the real.

The HM 744 version of the text lacks the final leaves, and so the Durham version is used as copy text from line 673 in this edition.

LEARN TO DIE

Hic incipit ars vtilissima sciendi mori, cum omnes homines, etc.

'Syn° alle men naturelly desyre   *since*
To konne°, O eterne Sapience°,   *know, eternal Wisdom*
O vniuersel prince, lord and syre,
Auctour° of nature, in whos excellence   *author*
5 Been hid° alle the tresors° of science°,   *hidden, treasures, knowledge*
Makere of al, and þat al seest and woost°,   *who sees and knows all*
This axe° I thee, thow lord of mightes moost,   *ask*

Thy tresor of wisdam and the konnynge°   *knowledge*
Of seintes, opne thow° to me, I preye,   *open yourself*
10 That I thereof may haue a knowlechynge°.   *an understanding*
Enforme eek° me and vnto me bywreye°,   *also, reveal*
Syn° thow of al science° berst° the keye,   *since, knowledge, bear*
Sotile° materes° profounde and grete   *profound/mysterious, matters*
Of whiche I feruently desire trete.'

15 'O sone myn, sauoure° nat to hie°   *reach, not too high*   **Sapientia**
But dreede°. Herkne°, and I shal teche thee   *fear (humble yourself), listen*
Thyng þat shal to thy soule fructifie°.   *enrich*
A chosen yifte° shalt thow haue of me.   *gift*
My lore° eternel lyf shal to thee be.   *lesson*
20 The dreede° of God, which the begynnyng is   *fear/awe*
Of wisdam, shalt thow leere°, and it is this.   *learn*   **inicium sapiencie etc.**

Heading: Here begins the very useful art of learning to die, since all men …

2. Sapience (Latin: Sapientia) is the embodiment of divine wisdom in the poem. She is gendered female in Suso (although the Image that takes center-stage is a 30-year-old male (lines 91, 378)). After the death of the Image, Sapience returns in her original form to further instruct the disciple. Sapience also traditionally aligns with Christ (see, e.g., lines 25–6). The terms used in the following line (prince, lord, syre), and the superlative address ('author of nature') reinforces the Christ-like nature of Sapience/Sapientia in the poem's opening stanza, while blending gender.

4–5. Cf. Colossians 2:1–3.

8–14. Cf. Ephesians 3:8; Proverbs 2:3–5; Romans 11:33.

21. gloss: The beginning of wisdom [is the fear of the Lord]. See Psalms 110:10: 'The fear of the Lord is the beginning of wisdom.' The phrase is also found at Proverbs 1:7; Proverbs 9:10.

152 LEARN TO DIE

Now herkne° a doctrine substancial.   *hear*
First, how lerne die telle wole Y.
The second, how þat a man lyue shal.
25 The iii^{de} °, how a man sacramentally°   *third, i.e., through Eucharist*
Receyue me shal, wel and worthyly.
The iiii^e °, how with an herte clene and pure   *fourth*
That a man loue me shal and honure.'

'Tho thynges iiii°, good lord, haue I euere   *four things*   **Discipulus**
30 Desired for to knowe, and hem to leere°.   *to learn them*
Vnto myn herte ther is nothyng leuere°.   *more precious*
A bettre thyng can I nat wisshen heere.
But tellith me this, this fayn wolde I heere:
What may profyte the lore of dyynge°   *lesson of dying*
35 Syn° deeth noon hauyng is, but a pryuynge°,   *since, depriving*

For shee man reueth° of lyf the swetnesse?'   *robs*
'Sone, the art to lerne for to die   **Sapientia**
Is to the soule an excellent swetnesse,
To which I rede° thow thyn herte applie.   *advise*
40 There is noon aart þat man can specifie
So profitable ne° worthy to be   *nor*
Preferred aartes alle° as þat is shee.   *(over) all arts*

To wite° and knowe þat man is mortel   *understand*
It is commune° vnto folkes alle.   *common*
45 Þat man shal nat lyue ay° heer, woot° he wel.   *always, knows*
No trust at al may in his herte falle
That he eschape° or flee may dethes galle°.   *escape, poison*
But fewe þat can die° shalt thow seen.   *i.e., die well*
It is the yifte° of God, best þat may been.   *gift*

50 To lerne for to die is to haue ay°   *always*
Bothe herte and soule redy hens° to go,   *hence*
Þat when deeth cometh for to cacche hir pray°,   *catch her prey*

23–8. Hoccleve translates directly from the Latin here (527: 2–4), including the contents of the present poem (line 23), as well as the subsequent three chapters of the *Horologium sapientiae* (lines 24–8) – the text takes the reader from learning to die, to learning to live, to receiving the Eucharist, and then to loving Wisdom with a pure heart. Hoccleve's decision to include the spectrum of contents is intriguing, not least because the heading indicates that only the *ars moriendi* section will appear. In the *Series*, the narrator's note directly after 'Learn to Die' suggests that he had thought about translating the other chapters, but ultimately decided against it; but that also conflicts with what Thomas says to the Friend in the 'Dialogue', where 'Learn to Die' is singled out as the text to translate (2.205–6). Including the full contents here shows the reader the material that Hoccleve perhaps felt uncomfortable translating – including material on the Eucharist, a deeply divisive and provocative subject at the time. The contents list also reinforces the Christ–Sapience alignment within the poem (25–6).

43–4. See Ecclesiastes 9:4; cf. Job 30:23.

48. That is, few know how to die *well* – few know the Christian art of preparing sufficiently for death.

LEARN TO DIE 153

Man rype° be the lyf to twynne° fro,   *ready, depart*
And hire° to take and receyue also,   *her*
55 As he þat the comyng of his felawe°   *friend*
Desirith and therof is glad and fawe°.   *joyful*

But more harm is: ful many oon shalt thow fynde
Þat ageyn° deeth maken no purueance°.   *against, preparation*
Hem lothen° deeth for to haue in hir° mynde.   *they hate, their*
60 That thoght they holden thoght of encombrance.
Worldly swetnesse sleeth° swich° remembrance.   *slays, such*
And syn° to die nat lerned han they,   *since*
Fro the world twynne° they wolde in no wey.   *depart*

They mochil of hir° tyme han despendid°   *their, have spent*
65 In synne, and forthy° whan vnwaarly° deeth   *therefore, unexpectedly*
Vpon hem fallith, and they nat amendid°,   *not prepared (unrepented)*
And shal from hem° byreue° wynd and breeth,   *them, take*
For shee vnreedy fynt hem° whan shee sleeth°,   *finds them, slays*
To helle goon the soules miserable
70 There to dwelle in peyne perdurable°.   *everlasting pain*

Deeth wolde han ofte a brydil° put on thee,   *horse's bridle (restraint)*
And thee with hire° led away she wolde,   *her*
Nadde° the hand of Goddes mercy be.   *had not*
Thow art right mochil° vnto þat lord holde°   *very much, beholden*
75 Þat, for° thow wrappid were in synnes olde,   *even though*
He sparid thee. Thy synnes now forsake
And vnto my doctrine thow thee take.

More to thee profyte shal my lore°   *my lesson will profit you more*
Than chosen° gold, or the bookes echone°   *choice, every book*
80 Of philosophres. And, for that° the more   *so that*
Feruently sholde it stire thy persone
Vndir sensible° ensaumple°, thee to one°   *perceptible (apparent to the senses), example, to unite you*
To God, and thee the bettre for to thewe°,   *teach*
The misterie° of my lore° I shal thee shewe°.   *mystical truth, teaching, show you*

---

59. 'They hate to bear death in mind.'
63. ' … they don't want to leave the world at all.'
64–70. Cf. Revelation 21:8; Ecclesiastes 9:11–12. 'Miserable' (line 69): this is among the very earliest instances of the word in English.
68. Death is gendered female here. Cf. lines 36, 155–62, 685–6, 910.
71–7. Cf. Job 30:11; Isaiah 30:27–8, 48:9. Line 73: 'were it not for God's merciful hand'.
78–9. Cf. Ecclesiasticus 29:14; Proverbs 8:11, 16:16; Baruch 3:30.
81. 'stiren' is also used in 'Dialogue' (*Series*), when talking about his inspiration in translating this treatise: 'Not hath me stirid my deuocioun / To do this labour, ȝe shullen vnderstonde, / But at the excitinge and mocioun / Of a deuoute man' (2.232–5).

154 LEARN TO DIE

85 Beholde inward° the liknesse and figure   *inwardly*
Of a man dyyng and talkyng with thee.'
The disciple of þat speeche took good cure°   *heed*
And in his conceit° bisyly soghte he°,   *mind, he searched*
And therwithal° considere he gan° and see   *then, he began to consider*
90 In himself put° the figure and liknesse   *placed*
Of a yong man of excellent fairnesse°,   *beauty*

Whom deeth so ny° ransakid hadde and soght°   *closely, searched*
That he withynne a whyle° sholde die.   *a (short) while*
And for his soules helthe had he right noght
95 Disposid°. Al vnreedy° hens to hie°   *made provision, unready, to go hence*
Was he, and therfore he bygan to crie
With lamentable vois, in this maneere,
That sorwe and pitee greet was it to heere:

'Enuyrond° han me dethes waymentynges°.   *surrounded, griefs*   **Circumdederunt m**
100 Sorwes of helle han compaced° me.   *have encompassed*   **gemitus mortis**
Allas, eterne° God, O kyng of kynges,   *eternal*
Wherto was I born in this world to be?
O allas, why in my natiuitee°   *infancy*
Nad I° perisshid? O, the begynnynge   *had I not*
105 Of my lyf was with sorwe and with wepynge,

And now myn ende comth. Hens° moot° I go   *hence, must*
With sorwe, waylynge, and greet heuynesse°.   *sadness*
O deeth, thy mynde° is ful of bittir wo   *i.e., the memory of you*
Vnto an herte wont vnto° gladnesse,   *accustomed to*
110 And norisshid in delicat swetnesse.

85–93. The disciple begins his interaction with the 'liknesse and figure' (inverted at line 90) of a dying man (Suso: 'similitudinem hominis morientis' (528:3–4)). Hoccleve later repeatedly uses the term 'ymage' (e.g., line 169) to describe the figure. For a discussion of this terminology, in relationship to Suso and biblical precedent, see Rozenski 2008. Hoccleve also uses 'liknesse' to describe his image of Chaucer in the *Regiment of Princes* (line 4995), whereas 'ymage' is used for religious images (icons) in *Regiment* (lines 4999–5007) and 'Oldcastle' (lines 409–24). Hoccleve's insistence on using 'ymage' in 'Learn to Die' may underscore the dying man's role as a religious image – with all the sacred functions available therein. The stanza break after line 91 is noteworthy: before the break, the image conjured is of a fair young man; after the break, we realize he is dying and we adjust our imaginations accordingly. The effect of this abrupt transition is furthered in Bodleian Library, Selden supra 53, where a vivid miniature of the disciple standing next the bedbound dying man is placed between these stanzas. Line 92: 'ransaken' can mean ransack, rob, steal, and mistreat, as in modern usage; it can also mean investigate, examine, scrutinize, search. On Hoccleve's use of the term, see Stephanie Trigg in Nuttall–Watt 2022: especially pp. 153–8.

99–100. gloss: The sorrows of death surrounded me. [See Psalms 17:5–6: 'The sorrows of death surrounded me: and the torrents of iniquity troubled me. The sorrows of hell encompassed me: and the snares of death prevented me.']

103–4. See Job 3:11: 'Why did I not die in the womb, why did I not perish when I came out of the belly?'

108–10. See Ecclesiasticus 41:1; cf. Luke 6:25. For 'thy mynde', cf. Suso: 'memoria tua' (528:14).

LEARN TO DIE   155

Horrible is thy presence and ful greuable° | very offensive
To him° þat yong is, strong, and prosperable°. | he, prosperous

Litil wende° I so soone to han deid°. | thought/expected, have died
O cruel deeth, thy comynge is sodeyn°. | sudden
115 Ful vnwaar° was I of thy theefly breid°. | unsuspecting, thiefly blow
Thow haast as in awayt vpon me leyn°. | i.e., ambushed
Thyn hour was vnto me ful vncerteyn.
Thow haast vpon me stolen and me bownde.
Eschape° I may nat now my mortel wownde. | escape

120 Thow me with thee drawest in yren cheynes°, | iron chains
As a man dampned° wont is to be drawe° | damned/condemned, be drawn
To his torment. Outrageous° been my peynes°. | excessive, pains
O now for sorwe and fere of thee, and awe,
With handes clight° I crie and wolde fawe° | clutched, gladly
125 Wite° the place whidir° for to flee. | know, where
But swich oon° fynde can I noon°, ne° see. | such one (a place), none, nor

I looke on euery syde bisyly,
But help is noon. Help and confort been dede.
A vois horrible of deeth sownyng° heere Y, | speaking
130 Þat seith me° thus, which encreceth° my drede: | (to) me, increases
"Thow die shalt. Resoun noon, ne kynrede°, | nor family
Frendshipe, gold, ne noon othir richesse° | nor any other riches
May thee deliure out of dethes duresse°. | restraint

Thyn eende is come; comen is thyn eende.
135 It is decreed. There is no resistence."
Lord God, shal I now die and hennes weende°? | depart hence
Whethir nat chaunged may be this sentence?
O Lord, may it nat be put in suspense°? | i.e., paused
Shal I out of the world so soone go?
140 Allas, wole° it noon othir be° than so? | will, be no other (way)

O deeth, O deeth, greet is thy crueltee.
Thyn office° al to sodeynly° doost thow. | duty, too suddenly
Is ther no grace? Lakkist thow pitee?
Spare my youthe. Of age rype ynow° | old enough
145 To die am I nat yit°. Spare me now. | not yet
How cruel þat thow art, on me nat kythe°. | do not demonstrate on me
Take me nat out of the world so swythe°.' | quickly

120–22a. 'You drag me with you in iron chains, as a condemned man would be dragged to his torment.'
123–6. Cf. Psalms 138:7–10.
131–3. Cf. Psalms 88:49. In Suso, the voice of death initially says 'Filius mortis es tu' [you are the son of death; cf. 1 Kings 20:31] – a striking phrase, which Hoccleve omits. (528:24)
134–40. Cf. Ezekiel 7:2–3, 6–9. Line 134: The chiastic structure in this line is enhanced in Durham, when 'come' reads 'comen'.
146. 'Do not demonstrate your cruelty on me (i.e., by taking me).'

156 LEARN TO DIE

Whan the disciple this conpleynte had herd,
He thoghte al þat he spak nas but folie°, — was but folly
150 And in this wyse° hath vnto him answerd: — way
'Thy wordes, freend, withouten any lie,
Þat thow haast but smal lerned testifie°. — show that you have learned little
Euene° to alle is dethes iugement. — equal
Thurghout the world strecchith hir paiement.

155 Deeth fauorable is to [no] maner wight°. — no kind of person
To alle hirself shee delith equally.
Shee dreedith° hem° nat þat been of greeth° might, — fears, them, great
Ne° of the olde and yonge hath no mercy. — nor
The ryche and poore folk eek° certeynly — also
160 Shee sesith°. Shee sparith right noon estaat°. — seizes, no social class
Al þat lyf berith with hir chek is maat°. — anyone who bears life is checkmated by her

Ful many a wight° in youthe takith shee — person
And many oon also in middil age
And some nat til they right olde be°. — are very old
165 Wendist° thow han been at swich auantage° — believed, such an advantage
Þat shee nat durste° han paied thee thy wage, — dared not
But oonly han thee spared and forborn°, — refrained from killing
And the prophetes deid han heerbeforn?'

Than spak th'ymage, answeryng in this wyse°: — way
170 'Soothly° thow art an heuy° confortour. — truly, grave
Thow vndirstandist me nat as the wyse.
They þat continued han° in hire errour°, — have, their error
Lyuynge in synne vnto hir° dethes hour, — their
Worthy be dampned° for þat they han wroght°, — (to) be damned, have done
175 And how ny° deeth is they ne dreede noght°. — near, fear not

Tho° men ful blynde been and bestial°. — those, ignorant
Of þat shal folwe aftir this lyf present
Forsighte swiche° folk han noon° at al. — such, have none
I nat bewaille dethes iugement.
180 But° this is al the cause of my torment: — rather

153–4. Cf. Ecclesiastes 3:19.
161. This phrase is original to Hoccleve (not in Suso). Cf. Chaucer's *Book of the Duchess*, line 659. On medieval literary use of chess (and its implications for political power plays), see Adams 2006.
165–8. Cf. Zechariah 1:5; John 8:53. The meaning here is: did you think Death would spare you alone, when she has taken even the prophets (i.e., even the most holy among us)? Line 166: 'paied thee thy wage' = paid you what you were owed – i.e., death.
169. Here, as elsewhere, Suso describes the Image as 'similitudo mortis' [similitude/likeness of death] – but Hoccleve uses 'th'ymage' throughout to denote this similitude.
176. Cf. Psalms 48:13.
177–8. 'Such people have no foresight of what will happen after this life.'

LEARN TO DIE 157

The harm of vndisposid° deeth I weepe. — unprepared-for
I am nat reedy in the ground to creepe.

I weepe nat þat I shal hennes twynne°, — depart hence
But° of my dayes I the harm bewaille, — but rather
185 Fruytlees past sauf with° bittir fruyt of synne. — except for
I wroghte° in hem° nothyng þat mighte auaille — did, in them (i.e., in those days)
To soules helthe. I dide no trauaille° — labor
To lyue wel, but lened to the staf
Of worldly lustes. To hem° I me yaf°. — them, gave myself

190 The way of trouthe I lefte, and drow° to wrong. — drew (directed myself)
On me nat shoon° the light of rightwisnesse°. — shone not, righteousness
The sonne° of intellect nat in me sprong. — sun
I weery am of my wroght° wikkidnesse. — evil
I walkid haue weyes of hardnesse
195 And of perdicion. Nat kowde I knowe
The way of God. Wikkid seed haue I sowe°. — sown

Allas, what hath pryde profyted me,
Or what am I bet° for richesse hepynge°? — how am I better, hoarding riches
Alle they as a shadwe passid be°, — all are like a shadow passing
200 And as a messager faste rennynge°, — running
And also as a ship þat is sailynge
In the wawes° and floodes of the see°, — waves, sea
Whos kerf° nat fownde is° whan passid is shee. — whose wake, is not found (disappears)

Or as a brid°, which in the eir° þat fleeth°, — bird, air, flies
205 No way fownde is of the cours of his flight.
No man espie can it°, ne it seeth°, — can spot it, nor see it
Sauf° with his wynges the wynd softe and light — save
He betith, and kuttith° th'eir with the myght — cuts
Of swich stirynge°, and foorth he fleeth° his way, — such movement, flies
210 And tokne°, aftir þat, no man see ther may. — (a) trace

Or as an arwe° shot out of a bowe — arrow
Twynneth° the eir°, which foorthwith° redily° — divides, air, immediately, entirely
Agayn is closed, þat man may nat knowe
Wher þat it paste, no wight° the way sy° – — person, saw

---

181. 'I lament the harm incurred by not preparing (suitably) for death.' The Image is clarifying that he is not upset that he has to die – only that he did not better prepare for death when he had the chance.
183–5. Cf. Proverbs 10:16. The fruit the Image has yielded is the fruit of sin.
190–224. See Wisdom 5:6–15. (For the 'wikkid seed' of line 196, see Isaiah 1:4, 14:20; cf. Psalms 36:28; Matthew 13:38.) After a series of vivid comparisons, in lines 215–17 the Image indicates his condition – he has left nothing good behind, no trace of virtue. The focus is on the lack of a trace. Line 220: Here I use the Durham reading – 'which' for 'with'; likely Hoccleve miscopied in HM 744, seeing 'with' at the head of the line, two lines below.

158 LEARN TO DIE

215 Right so°, syn° þat I born was, fare haue Y°.   just like this, since, I have fared (thus)
    Anoonrightes°, I styntid° for to be,   instantly, ceased
    And tokne° of vertu shewid° noon in me.   trace, showed

    I am consumed in my wikkidnesse.
    Myn hope is as it were a wolle loke°,   lock of wool
220 [Which] the wynd blowe° away for his lightnesse,   blows
    Or smal foom° þat disparpled° is, and broke   foam, scattered
    With tempest, or as with wynd waastith° smoke,   dispelling
    Or as mynde° of an hoost° þat but a day   the memory, a guest
    Abit°, and aftir passith foorth his way.   stays

225 Forwhy°, my speeche is now in bittirnesse,   wherefore
    And my wordes been ful of sorwe and wo.
    Myn herte is ploungid° deepe in heuynesse.   plunged
    Myn yen° been al dymme and dirke also.   eyes
    Who may me graunte þat I may be so°   i.e., the same
230 As I was whan I beautee hadde and strengthe,
    And had beforn me many a yeeres lengthe

    In whiche I the harm mighte han° seen beforn,   have
    Þat now is on me falle? I yaf no charge°   I gave no care
    Of the good precious tyme. I haue it lorn°.   lost
235 But as the worldly wynd bleew in my barge
    Foorth droof° I therwith, and leet goon° at large°   drove, let go, freely
    Al loos° the bridil of concupiscence,   entirely loose
    And ageyn° vertu made I resistence.   against

    My dayes I despente° in vanitee.   spent
240 Noon heede I took of hem°, but leet hem° passe,   them, them
    Nothyng° consideryng hir precioustee°,   in no way, their preciousness
    But heeld myself freeborn as a wylde asse.
    Of the aftirclap° insighte had no man lasse°.   later misfortune, less
    I ouerblynd was; I nat sy ne dredde°   I didn't see nor dread
245 With what wo deeth wolde haaste° me to bedde.   hasten

223–4. Although seemingly paradoxical, 'hoost' can mean an invited guest, which makes more sense in
    this context. See *MED* 'hoste n. (2)', sense 2. Cf. Suso: 'et tamquam memoria hospitis unius diei
    praetereuntis' (530:8–9).
225–6. See Job 23:2, 6:3; cf. 10:1.
227–8. See Lamentations 5:17.
235. As Ellis notes, Hoccleve deepens the nautical metaphor used by Suso, drawn from Acts 27:15 – an
    account of Paul and his followers succumbing to a storm *en route* to Rome. Suso has: 'sed datis
    flatibus navi' (230:15), which Hoccleve expands.
235–7. 'But wherever the worldly wind blew my barge, there I drove – and let go freely, entirely slack,
    the bridle of lust.'
236–8. Cf. James 1:14.
239–42. Cf. Psalms 77:33, 143:4; Ecclesiastes 7:16. For the 'wylde asse' in line 242, cf. Job 11:12 (also
    noted by Ellis).

LEARN TO DIE 159

And now, as fisshes been with hookes caght,
And as þat briddes° been take° in a snare, · birds, are taken
Deeth hath me hent°. Eschape° may I naght. · seized, escape
This vnwaar° woful hour me makith bare · unexpected
250 Of my custumed ioie° and my welfare. · usual joy
The tyme is past. The tyme is goon for ay°. · forever
No man reuoke or calle ageyn it may.

So short was nat þat tyme þat is goon
But I of goostly lucres° and wynnynges · spiritual riches
255 Mighte haue in it purchaced many oon°, · i.e., many a spiritual reward
Excedyng in value alle eerthely thynges
Inconparablely, but to his wynges
The tyme hath take him, and no purueance
Therein made I my soule to auance°. · advance

260 Allas I, caytif°, for angwissh and sorwe · wretch
My teeres trikelen by my cheekes doun.
No salt watir me needith begge or borwe°. · borrow
Myn yen° flowen now in greet foysoun°. · eyes, streams
Allas this is a sharp conclusioun –
265 Thogh I the tyme past conpleyne° and mourne, · complain
For al my care wole it nat retourne°. · will it not return

O my lord God, how laach° and negligent · lax
Haue I been. Why haue I put in delay
And taryynge myn amendement°? · moral correction
270 Wherto haue I dissimuled°, weleaway? · been dishonest/evasive
Allas so many a fair and gracious day
Haue I lost, and be fro me goon and ronne° · left
That mighte in hem° my soules helthe han wonne. · them (those days)

Myn hertes woful waymentacions°, · lamentations
275 Who can hem° telle? Or who can hem° expresse? · them, them
Now fallen on me accusacions
Wondirly thikke° of my wroght° wikkidnesse. · extremely forceful/rapid, evil
In flesshly lust and ydil° bysynesse · idle
I leet my dayes dryue foorth and slippe°, · slip (away)
280 And nat was scourgid° with penaunces whippe°. · beaten, the whip of penance

Why sette I so myn herte in vanitee?

––––––––––––––

246–50. See Ecclesiastes 9:12 (also noted by Ellis).
253–9. Cf. 1 Corinthians 9:24, 14:1. The Image laments that he did not spend his time earning spiritual
(rather than earthly) riches.
260–3. Cf. Jeremiah 9:18, 9:1.
281. Cf. Psalms 4:3.

160 LEARN TO DIE

O why ne had I lerned for to die?
Why was I nat ferd° of Goddes maugree°?   *afraid, God's rebuke*
What eiled me° to bathe in swich° folie?   *what caused me, such*
285 Why nadde° reson goten the maistrie°   *hadn't, control*
Of me? Why? For my spirit was rebel,
And list° nat vndirstande to do wel.   *desired*

O, alle yee þat heere been present,
Yee þat floure° in youthes lusty grennesse,   *bloom*
290 And seen how deeth his bowe hath for me bent,
And tyme couenable° han to redresse°   *sufficient, have to put right*
Þat° youre vnruly youthes wantonnesse   *what*
Offendid hath, considereth my miserie.
The stormy seson folwith dayes merie.

295 Let me be youre ensaumple° and your mirour,   *example*
Lest yee slippe into my plyt° miserable.   *plight*
With God despende° of your dayes the flour°.   *spend, flower*
If yee me folwe, into peril semblable°   *similar*
Yee entre shuln°. To God yee yow enable°.   *you shall enter, make yourself fit*
300 In holy wirkes your tyme occupie,
And, whil tyme is, your vices mortifie°.   *cease*

Allas, O youthe, how art thow fro me slipt.
O God eterne°, I vnto thee conpleyne°   *eternal, complain*
The wrecchidnesse in which þat I am clipt°.   *bound*
305 Lost is my youthe. I smerte° in euery veyne   *ache*
The gilt that wroght hath° my synful careyne°.   *(for) the guilt that has distressed, body*
O youthe, thy fresshnesse and iolitee
Hatith thy soothes° to be told to thee.   *truths*

No lust° had I to doon as I was taght.   *desire*
310 Thereof had I ful greet desdeyn and hokir°.   *scorn*
Whan men conseillid weel, I herde it naght.
Nat so moche as by an old boote or cokir°   *shoe*
Sette I therby. Into myn hertes lokir°   *locker*
Entre mighte noon hoolsum° disciplyne.   *no wholesome*
315 No wil had I to good conseil enclyne°.   *submit (myself)*

288–94. Cf. Ecclesiastes 11:9–10. The Image all of a sudden suggests a wider audience, rather than just the disciple. Hoccleve follows his source in this regard: Suso has 'Eya vos omnes, qui adestis' (530: 28–9).

295–6. Original to Hoccleve (not found in Suso). Cf. 'mirour' language in 'Epistle of Cupid' (line 179), the *Regiment* (e.g., lines 1963, 3577, 5328), the *Series* (1.157–61), and 'To Sir John Oldcastle' (line 160).

297. 'Spend your youth [the flower of your days] with God.'

298–9. That is: if you do as I did, you will enter into the same suffering that I now endure.

309–15. Cf. Proverbs 5:12–13 (noted by Ellis). Line 310: 'desdeyn and hokir', cf. *Series* 2.741–2: 'My wyf mighte haue *hokir and greet desdeyn* / If I sholde in swich cas pleye a soleyn.'

Lord God, now in a deep dych° am I falle.   ditch
Into the snare of deeth entred am Y.
Bet° had it been than it had thus befalle   better
Neuere han be born° of my modres body,   to have been born
320 But therein han perisshid vttirly,
For I despente° in pryde and in bobance°   spent, vanity
The tyme lent to me to do penance.'

To which answerde the disciple tho°,   then   Discipulus
'Lo, we die alle, and as watir we slyde   Ecce morimur et quasi
325 Into the eerthe, which þat neueremo°   nevermore   etc
Retorne shal, but on a sikir° syde   safe
We standen alle, for God nat wole hyde°   will not hide
His mercy fro man. Whoso list it craue°,   i.e., whoever desires it
Be repentaunt, and mercy axe° and haue.   ask

330 God haastith° nat the gilt° of man to wreke°,   hastens, sins, punish
But curteisly abydith° repentaunce.   awaits
Heere° me now, what I shal seye and speke: hear
For þat thow haast offendid, do penaunce.   penitenciam age de
Torne vnto God with hertes obeysaunce°.   obedience   transactis, et conuertere ad
335 Axe° him mercy, which° is al merciable°,   ask, who, merciful   dominum
And saued shalt thow been. This is no fable.'

Th'ymage of deeth answerde anon to that: Ymago: quis est hic
'How spekist thow, man? Shal I me repente?   sermo quem tu loqueris,
Shal I me torne? O man, ne seest thow nat°,   you don't see   debeo penitere, debeo me
340 Ne° takist thow noon heede ne entente°   nor, nor attention   conuertere etc.
Of dethes angwisshes þat me tormente,
And oppressen so greuously and sharpe
That I not° what to do or thynke or carpe°?   I don't know, say

As a partrich° þat with the hawk is hent°   partridge, seized
345 And streyned° with his clees° so is agast°   constrained, claws, is so afraid
That his lyf ny° from him is goon and went,   nearly
Right° so my wit is cleene fro me past   just
And in my mynde is ther no thoght ne cast°   nor scheme
Othir than serche a way how deeth eschape°,   how to escape death
350 But I in veyn theraftir looke and gape.

318–19. Cf. Jeremiah 20:14.
324. gloss: Lo, we [all] die, and like … [Cf. Durham: Ecce omnes morimur et quasi aque dilabimur in terram etc. (Lo, we all die and like water flow into the earth, etc.) See 2 Kings 14:14.]
327–9. Cf. Joel 2:13.
333–5. gloss: Do penance for those deeds, and return to the Lord.
337–41. gloss: Image: What are these words that you speak? I should repent? I should turn?
347. On the Image's 'wit' sundering, cf. 'Complaint Paramount' line 217, and 'Complaint' (*Series*), lines 59, 64.

162 LEARN TO DIE

Nat wole it be°, for deeth me doun oppressith.   *it won't be (thus)*
The twynnynge° of my lyf ful bittir is,   *surrendering*
Þat hurtith me greuously and distressith.
Ful holsum had it been to me or° this   *before*
355 Penance han doon° for þat° I wroghte° amis   *to have done, what, did*
Whyles my tyme was in his rypnesse°,   *i.e., when I had time and wits*
For þat had been° the way of sikirnesse°.   *would have been, security*

But he þat late to penance him takith°   *but he who takes to penance late*   Qui autem tarde
Whethir he verraily or feynyngly°   *authentically or falsely*   penitencie se
360 Repente, he not°. Vncertain it him makith.   *he doesn't know*   committit, dubius
Wo is me þat my lyf so sinfully   erit quia nescit
I ledde, and to correcte it lachid Y°.   *I delayed*   vtrum vere vel
Ageyn° my soules helthe haue I werreied°,   *against, struggled*   ficte peniteat
That for it haue no bettre purueied°.   *provided*

365 Allas to° longe hath been the taryynge°   *too, procrastination*
And the delay of my correccioun.
A good purpos withoute begynnynge°,   *a good plan without starting it*
Good wil withouten operacioun°,   *work*
Good promesse° and noon execucioun,   *promise*
370 Foorth dryue° amendes fro morwe to morwe°   *chase away, from one day to the next*
And neuere doon – þat causith now my sorwe.

O morwe°, morwe, thow haast me begilt°.   *tomorrow, made me sin*
O whethir this miserie nat exceede
Al worldly wrecchidnesse? Allas, my gilt.
375 Wel worthy is it þat myn herte bleede,
And with angwissh and wo him fostre and feede.
See how my dayes ny arn° slipt me fro°.   *are nearly, from me*
Xxxᵗⁱ ° yeer of myn age away been go°.   *thirty, has gone*

Ful wrecchidly, God woot°, haue I hem° lost,   *knows, them*
380 And al myn owne self is it to wyte°.   *blame*
So good a piler° was I neuere, or post,   *pillar (support)*
Vnto my soule. As o° day me delyte   *one*
In vertu, or aght wel° to God me qwyte°,   *anything good, offer*
As þat I mighte haue doon or oghte,
385 By aght I woot°, I neuere aftir þat soghte°.   *by anything I know, sought*

358–62. gloss: If a man partakes in penance late, it will be doubtful, for he will not know whether he truly or feigningly repents … [The Image notes that if you wait until the last minute to repent, you cannot be sure you are truly repenting – your mind is too distraught to know the difference.]

372. 'begilten' may mean 'cause to sin' or 'make guilty' (*MED*); but only one use is listed prior to Hoccleve. It is also possible Hoccleve is translating Suso's 'O cras, cras … decepisti me, et deceptus sum' (532:7–9; 'O tomorrow, tomorrow … you deceived me, and I am deceived' (Judges 11:35)), in which case: O tomorrow, tomorrow, you have deceived me.

378. Hoccleve retains the age given in Suso: 'triginta anni' (532:11).

381–5. The Image regrets not better supporting his soul – e.g., spending even one day delighting in virtue or anything God might wish to reward (in heaven).

LEARN TO DIE   163

Lord God, how shamefully stande I shal
At the doom° beforn thee and seintes alle,   Judgment Day
Wher I shal arted be° to rekne of al°   be compelled, to account for all
Þat I doon haue and left. Whom shal I calle
390 To helpe me? O how shal it befalle?
My torment and my wo me haaste and hie°   hasten me
Hens for to twynne°. As blyue° shal I die.   to depart hence, quickly

O now this day more ioie° and gladnesse   joy
I wolde haue of a litil orisoun°   prayer
395 By me seid with hertes deuout sadnesse°,   firm devotion
As the angelyk salutacioun,
Thanne I wolde haue of many a millioun
Of gold and siluer. Foule° haue I me born°,   foully, conducted myself
And folyly°, þat sy° nat this beforn.   foolishly, saw

400 Whan I mighte haue it seen, than° wolde I noght.   then
How manye houres haue I lost þat neuere
Retorne shuln? How mochil haue I wroght°   done (amiss)
Ageyn° myself? My lust° was to perseuere   against, desire
In vicious lyf°, and from it nat disseuere°.   immoral living, depart
405 I lefte þat° good was, and necessarie   what
Vnto my soule, and dide the contrarie°.   opposite

More than was neede or expedient°   necessary or suitable
Vnto the help of many anothir wight°   person
Entended° I. I was ful inprudent.   attended
410 I took noon heede° to myself aright.   no attention
By soules profyt sette I nat but light°.   I hardly valued it at all
Whan tyme was, fynde cowde I no tyme
Me to correcte of myn offense and cryme.

But now feele I þat vnto the gretnesse
415 Of merites celestial° had been bet°   heavenly rewards, it would have been better   Vere nunc cognoui quod ad magnitudinem premiorum celestium etc.
My wittes han kept with soules clennesse
Than, þat left, with herte corruptly set
And ageyn deedes vertuous ywhet°,   and fortified against virtuous deeds
Helpe me mighte any mannes prayeere,
420 Thogh xxx^ti ° yeer he preyd had for me heere.   thirty

394–8. Cf. the angelic salutation (Ave Maria/Hail Mary) at Luke 1:28. For the comparison with gold and silver, see Psalms 118:72; cf. Tobit 12:8.
407–9. When he could have been focusing on his own spiritual well-being, he instead spent his time attending to others.
414–16. gloss: Truly I now know that to the great rewards of heaven …
414–20. 'Now I feel it would have been better, in order to reap heavenly rewards, to have preserved my wits with a clean soul than (lacking that), with a heart corruptly set and fortified against good deeds, to rely on the prayers of another, even if he had prayed for me for a full thirty years.'

164   LEARN TO DIE

O herkneth° now, herkneth now alle yee   listen
Þat heere been and seen my wrecchidnesse.
The tyme, as þat yee seen, now faillith me.
My freendes preide I° þat they sum almesse°,   I begged my friends, some alms
425   Of th'abundance of hir goostly richesse°   their spiritual riches
And wirkes goode, wolden to me dele°   give
In my greet neede for my soules hele°,   health

And eek° in releef and amendement   also
Of my giltes, but hire° answer was nay.   their
430   They seiden, "Therto yeuen° oure assent   give
Wole we nat in no manere of way°,   will we not at all
Lest it vs and yow nat souffyse may°."   lest it be insufficient for us both
On euery paart° thus am I destitut°.   side, deserted
Fynde can I no socour ne refut°.   no help nor refuge

435   O God benigne°, O fadir merciable°,   kind, merciful
Beholde and reewe° vpon thy pacient.   take pity
To me, thyn handwerk°, be thow socourable°.   handiwork (creation), helpful
That I greetly haue erred and miswent°,   gone astray
Me wel remembrith this tyme present.
440   Allas, why stood I in myn owne light
So foule? O lord, now me helpe of° thy might.   with

How grete richesses spirituel
And heuenely tresors°, had I been wys°,   treasures, wise
Mighte I han gadrid°, and nat dide a del°.   have gathered, and didn't (gather) any
445   O good lord God, O lord of paradys,
Ful leef° to me now were, and of greet prys°,   truly desirable, great value
Of satisfaccion the leeste deede°.   the least deed performed as penance
Right dereworthe° were it in this neede.   precious

---

421. Again, this gives the impression of a wider audience. Also found in Suso: 533:8–9. Cf. lines 288–94, 456.

424–32. That is, he asked his friends to give him alms, for his soul's health, but they said no, lest there not be enough for both him and them. Cf. Matthew 25:9.

435–7. On God as 'father of mercies', see 2 Corinthians 1:3 (noted in Ellis). On man as God's handiwork, see e.g., Isaiah 45:9; 11–12; Job 14:15; Psalms 137:8.

440–1. 'Allas … foule': question original to Hoccleve (not found in Suso).

442–4. Cf. Matthew 6:19–21.

446–7. 'How desirable, and how valuable, it would be to do even the least work of satisfaction now.'

LEARN TO DIE 165

	O now the leeste crommes° þat ther falle	smallest crumbs
450	Fro the lordes bordes° and tables doun	tables
	Refresshe wolden me right wel withalle°,	completely
	But noon fynde I of swich° condicioun	such
	Þat yeue° me wole° any porcioun.	give, will
	I haue espyd° the frendshipe is ful streit°	discovered, very difficult
455	Of this world. It is mirour of deceit.	

	Reewe° eek° on me, yee alle, and pitee haue,	have pity, also
	And whiles your force and vigour may laste,	
	And han eek tyme°, or° yee be ny° your graue,	also have time, before, near
	Into bernes° of heuene gadereth° faste	barns, gather
460	Tresor celestial°, þat atte laste	heavenly treasure
	Yee may receyue, whan þat yee shuln twynne°	shall depart
	From hens, the blisse þat shal neuere blynne°.	cease

	And beeth nat voide of vertu, ne° empty,	nor
	Whan þat the deeth anothir day to yow	
465	Approche shal, as yee may see þat Y	
	Am voide of deedes vertuous right now.'	
	'Freend,' quod the disciple, 'I see wel ynow°	enough
	Thy torment and thy greuous passioun°,	suffering
	Of which myn herte hath greet conpassioun,	

Discipulus

	And by almighty God, I thee coniure°	implore you
	Þat thow me yeue reed° how me to gye°,	give me advice, guide myself
	Lest þat I heeraftir, par auenture°,	by chance
	Into lyk° peril haaste may and hye°	similar, hasten
	Of vndisposid sodein deeth°, and drye°	unprepared sudden death, suffer
475	The wo which I considere þat thee vexith,	
	Wherthurgh myn herte sore agrysed wexith°.'	my heart grows frightened

	Than spak th'ymage, 'The best purueance°	provision
	And wit is haan verray contricioun°	to have true contrition (remorse)
	In strengthe and hele° of the misgouernance°	when strong and healthy, misconduct

Ymago

449–55. See Luke 16:19–25: the story of the beggar who wished to be satiated on the crumbs that fell from the rich man's table. The beggar is comforted in the afterlife; whereas, the rich man (who denied the beggar) is tormented. In the story, the worldly food (crumbs) is contrasted with the spiritual nourishment that the rich man is denied in the afterlife. In the poem, however, the Image would seem to hunger for spiritual 'crumbs' – even the smallest holy sustenance. Lines 454–5 are original to Hoccleve (not found in Suso).

459–62. Cf. Matthew 13:30; Luke 16:9; Proverbs 3:9–10.

468 'greuous passioun'. Suso does not use 'passionem' here, but rather 'dolorem tuum' [your sorrow, 533.27]. Hoccleve's use of the word allows him to rhyme 'conpassioun' in the following line (adapting 'et idio ex corde tibi compatior' (533.27)), and it arguably deepens the parallel between Christ and Image. Cf. biblical references to Christ's passion: Acts 1:3 [passionem suam]; Hebrews 2:10 [passionem]; and cf. lines 2, 745–9 of the poem. Suso uses 'passionem meam' to describe the Image's passion towards the end of the poem, at 539:8 (cf. line 832).

166   LEARN TO DIE

480 Of thy lyf, and plener° confessioun	total
Make of thy gilt, and satisfaccioun	
And asseeth° do, and alle vices leue°	atonement, abandon all vices
That heuenes blisse mighten thee byreue°.	that might deprive you of heaven

And so with al thyn herte is it the beste
485 Keepe thee foorth as þat thow this day right°,   *this very day*
Or tomorwe, or this wike at the fertheste°,   *this week at the most*
Sholdest departe fro this worldes light,
And therwithal enforce° thow thy might,   *strive*
As I shal seyn, in thyn herte to thynke,
490 And thow shalt it nat reewe ne forthynke°.   *not regret nor resent it*

Caste° in thyn herte as now° thy soule were   *place (imagine), as if now*
In purgatorie and hadde pyned be°   *had been tormented*
.X. yeer° in a fourneys brennynge° there,   *ten years, burning furnace*
And this oonly yeer were grauntid thee
495 For thyn help. So beholde often and see
Thy soule in the flaumbes of fyr brennynge°,   *flames of burning fire*
With a wrecchid vois thus to thee cryynge:

"Of alle freendes, thow, the derwortheste°,   *most precious*
Do to thy wrecchid soule help and socour°,   *comfort*
500 Þat is al desolat. Purchace it reste.
See how I brenne°. O reewe on my langour°.   *burn, have pity on my affliction*
Be for me so freendly a purueiour°   *provider (of relief)*
That in this hoot° prisoun I no lengere°   *hot, longer*
Tormentid be. Lat it nat thus me dere°.   *hurt me so*

505 The worldes fauour cleene is fro me went.
Forsake am I. Frendshipe I can noon fynde.
There is no wight° þat to the indigent°   *person, needy*
Puttith his helply hand. Slipt out of mynde
I am. In peynes sharpe I walwe and wynde°,   *writhe and rave*
510 And of my wo ther is no wight þat recchith°.   *no person who cares*
Nat knowe I frendshipe or to whom it strecchith°.   *to whom to extend (friendship)*

Men seeken thynges þat to hemself longe°,   *i.e., men think only of themselves*

Right margin gloss (at lines 498–500): O amicorum omnium dulcissime succurre etc.

495–7. The Image asks the disciple to imagine his own soul in purgatory, having been tortured for ten years. In Suso, it is clearer that the voice calling out is the voice of his soul: 'attende vocem ipsius miserabilem … ' (534:7–8).

498–500. gloss: O sweetest of all friends, help, etc.

505–11. The language here is remarkably close to Thomas's own language of regret and exclusion in the 'Complaint'. 'Slipt out of mynde / I am' (508–9) is original to Hoccleve, and especially reminiscent of the 'Complaint' (1.80–1; quoting Psalms 30:12–13). For lines 507–8, cf. also Proverbs 31:20; Deuteronomy 15:11.

512. Cf. Philippians 2:21.

And leuen me in the flaumbes vengeable°. — vengeful flames
O good freend, lat me nat thus pyne° longe.'" — suffer
515 To which the disciple, with cheere stable°, — an even expression   Discipulus
Seide, 'Thy lore° were profitable — your lesson
Whoso it hadde by experience°, — i.e., to he who has experienced it
As thow haast. Therto yeue° I may credence. — give

But thogh thy wordes sharpe and stiryng seeme,
520 To many a man auaille they but lyte°. — they would help but little
They looke apaart and list° take no yeeme° — wish to, heed
Vnto the ende which mighte hem° profyte. — them
Yen° they haan°, and seen nat worth a myte° – — eyes, have, see (spiritually) hardly at all
Eres° also, and may nat with hem° heere°. — ears, them, hear
525 They weene longe for to lyuen heere°. — they think they'll live a long time

And, for they vndisposid° deeth nat dreede°, — unprepared-for, fear
Forsighte at al han tho° wrecches right noon — those
Of the harm þat therof moot folwe neede°. — that must needs follow
They deemen° stande as sikir as a stoon°. — think (they), as secure as a stone
530 But wel I see by thee, so moot I goon°, — so might I go
They shul han cause it for to dreede and doute,
Or° þat hir° lyues light be fully oute. — before, their

Whan dethes messager comth, sharp seeknesse°, — severe illness
Freendes and felawes hem haaste and hie°, — hasten themselves over
535 The seek° man to conforte in his feeblesse°, — sick, frailty
And al thyng þat good is they prophecie.
They seyn, "Thogh thow seek° in thy bed now lie, — sick
Be nat agast°. No dethes euel haast thow°, — afraid, you won't have a miserable death
For this thow shalt eschape wel ynow°." — you will indeed recover from this

540 Thus bodyes freendes been maad enemys
To the soule, for, whil seeknesse greeueth° — illness oppresses
The man continuelly, yit so vnwys
Is he þat his enformours° he wel leeueth°. — advisers, believes
He hopith to been hool°, and he mescheueth° — to be healed, deteriorates
545 Whereas he wende° haan recouered be. — anticipated
Vndisposid° to die, sterueth he°. — unprepared, he dies

---

515. 'with cheere stable': Hoccleve's addition (cf. Suso 534:15).
521–2. Cf. Psalms 10:11.
523–4. Cf. Jeremiah 5.21; Psalms 113:14; Ezekiel 12:2; Mark 8:18.
540–3. That is, his friends are unhelpful in this case, because they give the sick man false security that
he will recover (rather than helping him repent and prepare for death).

168 LEARN TO DIE

Right so thyn herkneres and thyn auditours°,   just so your listeners
Tho° þat greet trust haan° in mannes prudence,   those, have
Nat list hire peynes putte, or hir labours,°   don't like to make the effort
550 To execute thyn holsum sentence°.   to act on your advice
Thow mightest as weel keepe thy silence.
They by thy wordes yeuen nat a leek°.'   don't care at all
To which th'ymage thus answerde and speek: **Ymago**

'Forthy°, whan they in dethes net been hent°,   therefore, seized
555 Whan sodeyn wrecchidnesse hem° shal assaille,   them
Whan deeth, as tempest sharp and violent,
With woful trouble hem° shal vexe and trauaille°,   them, burden
They shuln crie aftir help and thereof faille,
For they in hate sapience hadde°,   they detested wisdom
560 And despisid my reed°, and heeld it badde.   advice

And right as now ther been but fewe fownde,
Þat, of my wordes conpunct°, wole hir° lyf   conscience-struck by my words, will their
Correcte, ne amende in no stownde°,   nor ever change
Nat may to hem auaille my motyf°,   my counsel won't help them
565 But they hir synnes vsen ay foorth ryf°,   they continue sinning frequently
And haan no lust° fro synnes hem° withdrawe,   have no desire, themselves
No more than they neuere had herd my sawe°.   account

Right so, for the malice° of tyme°, and lak   wickedness, the age
Of goostly° loue, and for th'iniquitee°   spiritual, because of the wickedness
570 Of the world, vertu is so dryue abak°,   is chased into retreat
Þat fewe to the deeth disposid be°   few are prepared for death
So weel þat° list° this worldes vanitee   such that, (they) desire
Leue°, and for desir of lyf þat shal euere   abandon
Endure°, coueiten hens to disseuere°.   i.e., eternal life, wish hence to depart

575 But whan deeth on hem stelith with hir darte°,   stealthily attacks them
They vnredy, wownded in conscience,
Nat oonly goon hens° whan they hens departe°,   go hence (to the afterlife), depart (from this life)
But they with a manere of violence
Been hent° away, so þat ful greet prudence   are carried
580 They wolde han holde it° han deid as a man°,   have held it, to have died as a man
And nat as a beest þat no reson can°.   as a beast without reason

---

547–52. The disciple now appears more swayed by the Image's lesson; he has shifted, however, to being
doubtful that others will hear it and amend their lives as a result.
554. Cf. 2 Kings 22:6; Psalms 17:6.
555–60. See Proverbs 1:27–30.
568–74. Cf. Job 11:11–20.
575–81. Cf. Ecclesiastes 3:19.

LEARN TO DIE   169

If of this commun peril th'enchesoun°   the cause
Thee list° to knowe, I wole it now expresse.   you desire
The desyr of honours out of resoun°,   crazed desire for honor/fame
585   The body bathynge in worldly swetnesse,
Eerthely loue, and to greet° greedynesse   overmuch
In mukhepynge°, blynden many an herte,   wealth-hoarding
And causen folk into tho perils sterte°.   rush into those perils

If thow desire the perils to flee
590   Of vndisposid deeth, my conseil heere°.   listen to my advice
This heuy plyt° in which thow seest now me,   plight
Reuolue ofte in thy mynde, and by me leere°   learn
For to be waar°. If thow in this maneere   be mindful
Wilt do, it shal be thy greet auantage°   advantage
595   And ese thee° at thy laste passage°.   comfort you, i.e., at your death

It shal vnto thee profyte in þat hour
That oonly die° shal it nat the gaste°,   dying alone, not frighten you
But deeth eek°, as ende of worldly labour   also
And begynnynge of blisse ay þat shal laste°,   bliss everlasting
600   Abyde thow shalt, and desire faste
With al thyn herte it to take and receyue,
And al worldly lust° leye apaart and weyue°.   desire, leave behind

Euery day haue of me deep remembrance.
Into thyn herte let my wordes synke.
605   The sorwe and angwissh and greuous penance
Which thow haast seen in me, considere and thynke
That of peril thow art ful ny the brynke°.   near the edge
Remembre on my doom°, for swich° shal thyn be: suffering (punishment), such
Myn yistirday, and this day vnto thee.

610   Looke vpon me and thynke on this nyght ay°   always
Whiles thow lyuest. O how good and blessid
Art thow, Arcenius, which þat alway

591–3. These lines underscore why it has been so useful to think of the dying man as 'th'ymage' throughout: the disciple is asked to return to this poignant image often, as a spur to penitence and virtuous living. (Cf. lines 603–9, below.)

595. The idea of a 'laste passage' prefigures the image in the final stanza of the poem: lines 911–17.

596–602. Cf. John 12:24–5; 1 Peter 5:10. Line 597: ' … that dying alone will not frighten you … '

603. The Image fashions itself into a memorial icon of sorts – an image to be recalled regularly, to spur penance and virtuous living. Cf. the prescribed use of the Chaucer image in the *Regiment*, vis à vis memory: *Regiment* lines 4992–8.

604. Cf. 'Complaint' (*Series*), line 7.

608–9. See Ecclesiasticus 38:23 (also noted in Ellis).

612. The Image commends Arsenius for having always kept the hour of his own passing in his heart, and on his mind. Arsenius (c.350–445) was one of the Desert Fathers, praised for always keeping the hour of his death in mind. Note that the disciple is not being addressed here as Arsenius.

170 LEARN TO DIE

This ilke° hour haddist in thyn herte impressid.
That man, as in holy writ is witnessid,
615 Which whan God comth and knokkith atte yate°,
Wakyng him fynt°, he blessid is algate°.

same
knocks at the gate
finds, in all ways

Blessid is he þat thanne fownden is
Redy to passe, for he blisfully
Departe shal, and truste right weel this:
620 Thogh deeth assaille and vexe greuously
The good lyuere° – or slee him sodeynly° –
Howso he die he gooth vnto þat place
Whereas° confort is, refresshynge and grace.

one who lives morally, slay him suddenly
where

He shal be purged cleene and purified
625 And disposid the glorie of God to see.
Angels shuln keepe him, and he shal be gyed°
And led by citeins of the hy contree°,
And of the court of heuene vp taken be,
And of his spirit shal been the issynge°
630 Into eternel blisse the entrynge°.

guided
citizens of heaven
sending forth
entering

But allas, where shal my wrecchid goost°
This nyght become°? Whidir shal it go?
What herbergh° shal it haue, or in what coost°
Shal it arryue? Who shal receyue it, who?
635 O, what frendshipe shal it haue tho°?
O soule abiect, desolat, and forsake°,
Greet cause haast thow for fere and wo° to qwake.

spirit
arrive
dwelling, coast
then
forsaken
fear and woe

Wherfore I, hauyng of myself pitee,
Amonges heuy wordes I out shede°
640 Teeres in greet habundance° and plentee.
But nat auaillith me°, it is no drede°,
Hensfoorth weepe and conpleyne, and crie and grede°,
For in no wyse chaungid it be may.
Al mankyndes fo° stoppid hath my way.

pour out
abundance
it doesn't help me, there is no doubt
lament
mankind's foe (the devil)

645 In hidles in awayt as a leoun°
He hath leyn, and my soule led hath he
Into the pit of deeth al deepe adoun°.

hiding in wait like a lion
down

615–16. Cf. Luke 12:36.
617–23. Cf. Wisdom 4:7.
624–630. Cf. Acts 7:55; Revelation 21:23–4, 22:3–4.
636. Hoccleve draws two of these adjectives directly from Suso: 'desolata', 'abiecta'; and for 'forsake': 'derelicta' (536:9).
639–40. Cf. Lamentations 2:18.
645–7. For the lion, cf. 1 Peter 5:8; Lamentations 3:10 (noted in Ellis); 'Friar's Tale', lines 1657–8. For the pit of death, cf. Psalms 27:1, 29:4, 87:7.

LEARN TO DIE 171

O my lord God, this sharp aduersitee° misfortune
To stynte of speeche° now conpellith me. to cease speaking
650 I may no more hensfoorth speke and bewaille°. moan/lament
My tonge and eek° my wit so now me faille. also

Ther is noon othir, I see weel ynow°. enough
The tyme is come. As blyue° I shal be deed. soon
See how my face wexith° pale now, grows
655 And dim my look and as heuy as leed°. heavy as lead
Myn yen° synke eek° deepe into myn heed, eyes, also
And torne vp-so-doun°, and myn handes two upside-down
Wexen° al stif and stark° and may nat do°. turn, rigid, no longer work

Prikkynges of deeth me, wrecche, conpace°. surround
660 Stirtemeel gooth my pous° and elles naght. my pulse throbs frenetically
Mortel° pressures sharply me manace. deadly
My breeth begynneth faille, and eek° the draght° also, drawing
Of it fro fer° is fet° and deepe kaght°. far-off, fetched, deeply arrested
No lengere I now see this worldes light.
665 Myn yen° lost han° hire office° and might. eyes, have, their purpose

But now I see with myn yen mental° mind's eyes
Th'estat° al of anothir world than this. state/condition
I am ny goon°. As faste° passe I shal. nearly gone, quickly
O my lord God, a gastful° sighte it is. terrifying
670 Now of confort haue I greet lak and mis.
Horrible f[]eendes and innumerable
Awayten on my soule miserable.

The blakefaced Ethiopiens
Me enuyrone°, and aftir it abyde surround me
675 To hente it° whan þat it shal passen hens°, to snatch (the soul), hence
If þat parauenture° it so betyde perchance
Þat the lot therof falle vpon hir° syde. their
Hir viserly° faces grim and hydous° their mask-like, hideous
Me putte in thoghtful dreedes encombrous.

Ha me miserum
puncture mortis
amarissime me
circumdant etc.

---

659. gloss: O wretched me. Death's sharpest jabs surround me …
662–3. 'My breath starts to fail; it feels far-off, arrested.'
664–5. Hoccleve expands on Suso's 'Lucem huius mundi amplius non video' (536: 23–4), allowing in his rendition for the failure of the ocular faculty.
666–8. Here, the Image achieves a kind of foresight, a taste of the afterlife – specifically, purgatory (see line 692). Line 666: among the very first recorded instances of the word 'mental'. (Also found in Hoccleve's *Series*: see 2.640.)
671. Hoccleve writes 'freendes' for 'feendes' in HM 744. It is 'feendes' (devils) in Durham, which makes more sense in the context.
673. The remaining stanzas of the poem (beginning here) are missing from HM 744. I use Durham as the base text for the missing section.

172 LEARN TO DIE

680 O streit° and steerne iuge and domesman°,   strict, judge and arbiter
Thow weyest moche°, in deemynge° me, wrecche,   weigh (consider) much, judging
Tho° thynges whiche fewe folkes can   those
But smal by sette, or of hem charge or recche°.   consider and take heed of them
Lo, deethes strook haastith me hens to fecche°.   to go hence
685 My membres° shee so thirlith° and distressith   limbs, pierce
That nature ouercome is, shee witnessith.

O gastful° is the iust iuges° lookynge   terrifying, just judge's   o terribilis aspec[
Vnto me, now present thurgh fere and dreede,   iusti iudicis mih[
Which sodeynly° shal come, himself sheewynge°.   suddenly, revealing himself   iam presenti per[
690 Farwel freendes and felawes, for neede   timorem subito
Moot Y vnclothe me of lyues weede°.   I must shed life's gown   venturus etc; nu[
To purgatorie Y shal as streight as lyne°,   shall go directly (straight as a line)   valete socii etc.
For myn offenses ther to suffre pyne°,   to suffer pain (punishment)

And thens twynne Y nat til maad haue Y gree°   I won't depart until I have done penance
695 Of the leeste ferthyng° þat Y men shal,   for the least farthing (for each small thing)
In whiche place Y beholde and see
Affliccioun and sorwe ynow at al°,   more than enough
There Y no ioie° see, but wo oueral°.   joy, suffering everywhere
The fyry flaumbes vpon heighte ryse,
700 In which the soules brenne° in woodly wyse°.   burn, fiercely

They vp now possid been° and now doun throwe,   brought up now
Right as° sparcles of fyr aboute sprede   just as
Whan þat a greet toun° set is on a lowe°   town, on fire
And al is fyred bothe in lengthe and brede°.   width (all aflame far and wide)
705 Wo been tho° soules in tho brondes rede°   those, those red blazes
For peyne of which torment ful lowde and hye
They in this wyse° ful pitously crye: way

681–3. Referring to the process of judgment undertaken after death. See Revelation 20:11–15.
685–6. Death is gendered female here. Cf. lines 36, 68, 155–62, 910.
687. gloss: O terrible appearance of the just judge, now present in my fears, suddenly coming …
Goodbye now friends …
687–9. Cf. 1 Samuel 2:10; Isaiah 11:3–4.
692–3. Cf. Suso: 'oculum mentis ad purgatorium, quo iam deducendus sum' (537: 4–5). Hoccleve omits
the reference to the 'oculum mentis' (mind's eye).
694–5. See Matthew 5:26 (although note the different context).

LEARN TO DIE 173

"Now mercy haue on our captiuitee°. — captivity

To yow, our freendes, namely we preye.

710 Wher is your help now? Wher is your chiertee°? — charity

Whidir been the promesses goon to pleye° — disappearing promises

Of yow, our cousins eek°? Can yee portreye — our kinsmen too

Your wordes so gayly°, and effect noon° — cheerfully, no effect

Folwith°, but al as deed is as a stoon? — follows

715 By youre desires inordinat°, — unruly

And eek° of othir mo°, ourself han we — also, more

Broght into this plyt° and wrecchid estat°. — plight, state

Ioie han we noon°, but of wo greet plentee°. — we have no joy, plenty

Allas, why nat vpon vs reewen yee°? — why don't you pity us

720 We dide al our might to do yow° plesance, — i.e., friends and kinsmen

And yee no routhe° han on our sharp greuance°. — compassion, intense suffering

Ful euele° we rewarded been of yow. — very badly

We brenne°, and yee the fyr nat qwenche a deel°. — burn, don't quench at all

Allas, we nadden for ourself or° now — we hadn't for ourselves before

725 Ydoon°. We were auysid nothyng weel°. — done (better), counseled poorly

Worldly trust is as slipir as an eel°. — as slippery as an eel (unreliable)

Al is nat treewe þat the world promettith°. — promises

Ful wys is he þat therby litil settith.

The leeste torment of this purgatorie

730 Þat we souffren excedith in sharpnesse

Tormentes alle of the world transitorie°. — mortal world

Heere of torment more is the bittirnesse

In an hour than the worldes wikkidnesse

May hurte or greeue in an .C. yeer°. — a hundred years

735 Greet is th'affliccioun þat we han heer°. — we have here

But aboue alle kyndes of tormentis

Of Goddes blissid face the absence° — the absence of God's face

Greeueth° moost. Þat lak, our moost [woful sent is]." — hurts

---

gloss (right margin, lines 708–9):
pro dolore cruciatum clamant singule et dicunt, miseremini mei, miseremini mei saltem vos amici mei vbi est nunc amicorum meorum adiutorium vbi sunt promissiones bone consanguineorum meorum etc.

---

708. gloss: They wail and cry aloud, tormented with suffering, each saying: 'Have pity on me, have pity on me, at least you, my friends. Where is now the help of my friends? Where are the fair promises of my kinsmen?' (Translation from Colledge 1994: 254) Lines 708–9: see Job 19:21.

712–14. 'Can yee ... stoon?' original to Hoccleve; not found in Suso.

725. Herein lies a central, implicit rebuke: the Image is a victim, suffering from a lack of good advice and guidance earlier in life. Cf. Simpson: the image 'disappears, unaided by friends, unaided by any sacramental system.' (2010: 83)

726. Cf. *Regiment*, line 1985. Hoccleve adds this line; it is not found in Suso.

732–4. That is, an hour's torment in purgatory is worse than would be suffered in a century on earth.

736–8. Cf. Deuteronomy 31:17–18; 2 Thessalonians 1:7–9. The absence of God's face is in fact the greatest (and most painful) punishment of all. Line 738: In Durham, a phrase has been rubbed out at the end of this line. All other witnesses, save BL MS Harley 172 (Ha), have 'woful sent is' here. Ha offers instead: 'the cause ys oure offence'.

174 LEARN TO DIE

For a memorie° leue Y this sentence°   memorial, doctrine
740 To thee, and heere Y die in thy presence.'
Whan the disciple sy° þat he was past   saw
And deed, he tremblid and was sore agast°.   deeply frightened

Aboute he torned him, and thus seide he:
'Wher art thow now, O Sapience eterne°?   eternal Wisdom
745 O good lord, haast thow now forsaken me?
Wilt thow thy grace me denye and werne°?   refuse
Thow seidest sapience Y sholde lerne,
And now Y am broght to the deeth almoost,
So troublid is my spirit and my goost.

750 This sighte of deeth so sore me astoneth°   confounds me so deeply
Þat wite Y can vnnethe°, in soothfastnesse°,   I hardly know, truth
But am in doute wher the soothe woneth° –   where the truth lies
That is to meene, if this be in liknesse
Or in deede°, swich° is my mazidnesse°.   or in reality (versus similitude), such, confusion
755 But how it be, lord, Y byseeche thee
Be my confort in this perplexitee.

Neuere the perils of deeth vndisposid°   unprepared death
In my lyf kneew I, as Y do now right.
Withyn myn herte been they deepe enclosid°,   deeply enclosed
760 And so sadly° therin picchid and pight°   firmly, pitched and set
Þat hem foryete lyth nat in my might°.   that I can't forget them
That gastful° sighte Y hope shal profyte   terrifying
Vnto my soules helthe nat a lyte°.   greatly (not a little)

Dwellynge place Y haue espyd and see
765 Han we noon in this wrecchid world changeable.
Forwhy°, vnto þat blisful hy contree°,   therefore, i.e., Heaven
Which nat may varie but is permanable°,   unchanging
Shape Y me strecche°. O lord God merciable°,   I direct myself, merciful
Y mercy axe°. Vpon me, wrecche, reewe°.   ask, have pity
770 Hensforward wole Y lede a lyf al neewe.

---

740. The Image announces his death quite plainly here. James Simpson notes, 'The image is fully
equipped with eyes, ears, an imagination, and a soul, and it's dying. [...] In fact the image is most
fully alive as it's dying.' (Simpson 2010: 82)

745–9. The disciple's words to Sapience echo Psalms 21:2, the words spoken by Christ on the cross: 'O
God my God [...] why hast thou forsaken me?' See Mark 15:34; Matthew 27:46. The disciple's fear
echoes that of the tomb guards after Christ's death and disappearance, and the appearance of the
visiting angel: Matthew 28:4.

750–6. The disciple expresses confusion ('mazidnesse' (754)) as to what the death of the Image really
means: is it death in reality, or just figurative death? His use of 'liknesse' here is significant because
it is the first time the word is used in connection with the Image since the Image is first introduced
(lines 85–91). While the Image is 'alive', it is referred to as 'ymage' (a practice unique to Hoccleve,
not found in Suso).

763. That is, he hopes it will be very beneficial ('nat a lyte' meaning 'not just a little').

764–70. Cf. John 14:2; Hebrews 13:14.

LEARN TO DIE 175

Now lerne for to die Y me purpose.
Hensfoorth penance wole Y nat delaye.
My lyf to amende wole Y me dispose.
For syn° thoghtes of deeth so me esmaye°   since, frighten me so
775 Wel° more, Y am seur, deeth me shal affraye°   much, death (itself) shall frighten me
Whan þat eschue° Y shal nat hir presence.   escape
O ther thyn help, eterne Sapience.

Now wole Y voide° fethirbeddes° softe,   relinquish, feather-beds
The pilwes nesshe° and esy materas°   soft pillows, comfortable mattresses
780 On whiche me careyne° hath tymes ofte   my body
Walwid and leyn. Now stande I in swich cas°   such a situation
Þat me thynkith al greet folie it was.
Of clothynge eek° fy on the precioustee°,   also, richness
And slouthe of sleep also lettynge° me.   hindering

785 Syn° Y tormentid am so greuously   since
With thynges smale, how sorwes so grete
Souffre mighte Y, if now die sholde Y,
Þat° neuere or° this my synnes kowde lete°?   who, before, cease
O, what matire of helle fyr the hete
790 Mighte in me thanne fynde. Certes°, greet,   certainly
For which my body of cold swoot° is al weet°.   sweat, wet

Now woot° I weel what thyng þat may auaille°   know, help
My soule, and it keepe fro perisshynge.
By souffrance of greet labour and trauaille,
795 And excercyse of vertuous lyuyunge,
Wole Y it helpe, left al taryynge°,   without any delay
Þat in swich an houres extremitee°,   in the final hours
No peyne° but reste fynde may shee°.   pain, i.e., the soul

O holy and mercyful sauueour
800 Of so bittir deeth souffre me nat dye.   o sancte et misericors
Thogh Y be thikke° wrappid in errour,   thickly   saluator, tam amari
                                                               morti ne tradas me

---

771–2. The disciple has come full circle, shedding all skepticism and applying Sapience's lesson. The demonstration has been successful. He models the ideal response: conversion to a new way of life.

778–82. The bed details are original to Hoccleve. Cf. Suso: 'Tolle, tolle nunc a me lectisterniorum mollitiem vestium pretiositatem, torporem somni me impedientem'. (538: 14–15)

794–5. Cf. Thomas's motivations for translating this treatise in the 'Dialogue' (2.205–31): the act of translation might itself be seen as a 'excercyse of vertuous lyuyunge'.

798. The disciple's soul is gendered female here.

799. gloss: O holy and merciful Savior, do not deliver me to so bitter a death. (Translation from Colledge 1994: 256) Colledge notes this is taken 'from the Dominican Breviary for the office of the fourth week in Lent' (256).

176   LEARN TO DIE

See, befron thee plat° on the grownd Y lye,   flat
Weepynge for myn excessyf folye,
And, curteys° lord, of thy benignitee°   courteous, generosity
805 This grace vouchesauf° to grante me.   see fit

Aftir thy lust° be my punysshement   as you desire
Whyle Y am heere, and good lord nat reserue
To othir place the chastisement
Which þat Y, wrecche, heere in this world disserue.
810 Let me abye it° heere or þat Y sterue°,   suffer for it, before I die
For in þat place horrible is swich° sharpnesse   such
Of peyne þat no wight° can it expresse.   person

O how vnwys or° this haue Y been ay°,   before, always
Syn° þat deeth vndisposid° and the peyne   since, unprepared
815 Of purgatorie Y kowde by no way
Considere, ne° how it kowde distreyne°.   nor, torment (me)
Set was myn herte in othir thoghtes veyne,
Þat yaf me lettynge and impediment°   that prevented me
To thynke vpon the perils consequent.

820 But now thurgh fadirly amonestynge°   fatherly admonishment   sed nunc paterne
My myndes yen° þat cloos were and shit°   eyes, that were closed and shut   admonitus oculo
I opne, and of tho° perils am dredynge.'   those   aperio etc.
And Sapience answerde anoon to it:
'My sone, to do so it is greet wit°,   very wise
825 Whyles thow yong art and haast strengthe and force
Thy lyf for to correcte, thee enforce°.   undertake it

Whan þat deeth cometh, which cruel and fel° is,   terrible
Whom thow nat maist withstonde ne withsitte°,   withstand nor resist
Help ne refuyt° is ther for thee noon ellis°   nor refuge, no other
830 But° to the mercy of God thee committe.   except
By no way þat nat leue ne ommitte°.   neither leave nor neglect
My passioun putte eek twixt° my doom° and thee,   also between, judgment
Lest more than neede is adrad thow be°.   lest you're needlessly afraid

---

802–3. Cf. Mark 14:35.
806–12. Cf. Ecclesiasticus 11:27–9. The disciple asks to be punished for his sins here (in this life) rather
    than in the afterlife, where the punishment will be far greater. Colledge notes this is taken 'from the
    Dominican Breviary for the office of the Wednesday of the third week after Trinity' (256).
820. gloss: But now through fatherly admonishment, I open my eyes …
821–2. The imagery of a mental eye closed then opened recalls the story of Saul/Paul, whose sight
    is restored by Christ, and who undergoes spiritual rebirth simultaneously. See Acts 9:17–19. Cf.
    Genesis 3:7.
832. See note to line 468.

LEARN TO DIE   177

	My rightwisnesse° nat so mochil dreede°	righteousness, fear not so much
835	Þat thow fro trust and hope of mercy twynne°.	depart
	Contrytly mercy axe° and thow shalt speede°.	ask, fare well
	Now restfullere° in thy goost° be withynne	more peaceful, spirit
	Þat ouer ferd art°. Thee pourge of thy synne.	who are too fearful
	Scourge thyself with repentances rod.	
840	Begynnynge of wisdam is dreede of God°.	the fear/awe of God

	Scriptures serche, and by hem° shalt thow leere°	them, you will learn
	Þat vnto man is it greet auantage	
	Deeth to haue ofte in mynde, in this lyf heere.	
	If yeeres manye and vnto good age	
845	Man lyue, and in alle hem° glad and sauage°	all of them, bold
	Be, good is the dirk hour and dayes wikke°	evil
	Remembre or° þat he come to the prikke°.	before, point (of no return)

Si annis, inquit sapiens, multis vixerit homo et in omnibus hiis letus fuerit, meminisse debet tenebrosi temporis etc.

	For whan þat tyme is comen, and þat hour,	
	Repreeued° shal be the past vanitee°.	reproved, one's misspent past
850	Remembre therfor on thy creatour°	creator (God)
	In thy fressh youthe and lusty iolitee°,	happy cheer
	Or° tyme come of sharp aduersitee,	before
	And or° þat yeeres approche of disese	before
	In whiche thow wilt seyn° they nat thee plese°,	you will say, they don't please you

	And or° asshen° into hir eerthe° also,	before, ashes, their earth
855	Whereof they were°, ageyn hem thidir dresse°,	came, again they return
	And thy spirit to God whens it cam fro	
	Retourne. God, with al thyn herte, blisse°.	thank/worship
	Thanke him. Shewe° vnto him thy kyndenesse,	show
860	For he to thee now opned hath the way	
	Wherthurgh thow maist be saued, is no nay°.	undoubtedly

	Ful fewe been° þat so with hertes ere°	there are very few, ear
	Konne apparceyue° th'instabilitee	can perceive
	Of the world, and konne° of the deeth han fere°	can, have (appropriate) fear
865	Which þat alway lyth in awayt pryuee°,	lies hidden in wait
	Ne° þat of the ioie and felicitee	nor
	Of heuene, which ay° shal laste and endure,	always
	Take any manere heede at al, or cure°.	attention

---

840. See lines 20–1, above.

844–7. gloss: Wisdom says, 'If a man live many years and rejoice in them all, he must remember the dark time … ' (Adapted from Colledge 1994: 256) See Ecclesiastes 11:8 (also noted in Ellis).

850–8. Drawn from Ecclesiastes 12:1,7 (noted in Ellis). Cf. Genesis 3:19.

178   LEARN TO DIE

Lifte vp thyn yen°. Looke aboute and see — eyes
870   Diligently how many folkes blynde
In hir conceites° nowadayes be. — their thoughts
They close and shitte° the yen° of hir° mynde. — shut, eyes, their
They nat keepe° in hir conceit° serche° and fynde — don't care, their mind, (to) search
Vnto what ende needes° they shuln drawe, — necessarily
875   And al for lak of dreede of God and awe.

They stoppe hire° eres, for they nat ne keepe° — their, they don't care
Heere° how conuerted be°, and receyue helthe. — (to) hear, (to) be converted
Correccion is noon; they let it sleepe.
They been so dronken of this worldes welthe
880   That deeth, or° they be waar°, right in a stelthe — before, aware
Fallith vpon hem, which condicioun
Hem cause shal hastyf perdicioun°. — shall cause them swift damnation

The peple now let seen innumerable
Þat for deeth vndisposid lost han be°. — who have been lost due to unprepared death
885   Considere and, if thy wit° be therto able, — intellect
Noumbre of hir multitude the plentee°. — count the entire multitude
Eeek° of hem° þat in thy tyme with thee — also, those
Dwelt han, looke how þat they been take° away. — taken
Thow seest wel, they from hens been past for ay°, — forever

890   And as they heere han do°, so shuln they haue°. — as they have done here, have (in the afterlife)
What multitude in yeeres fewe ago°, — recent years
Thee yit lyuynge°, han leid been° in hir° graue – — in your lifetime, have been laid, their
What brethren, cousins°, felawes° and mo° — kinsmen, friends, more
Of thy knowleche°. Beholde alle tho°. — that you knew, those
895   Thynke eek°, with hem° hire° olde synne goon° is. — also, them, their, gone
Touche vnto hem°, speke and axe hem° of this, — reach out to them, ask them

And they with wepynge and with waymentynge
Shuln to thee seye and thus ageyn answere,
Blessid is he þat can see the endynge,
900   And synnes þat the soule hurte and dere° — injure
Eschue° can, and hem° flee and forbere°, — avoid, them, abstain from
And þat in my conseil° hath good sauour°, — counsel, find fulfilment
Disposynge him alway vnto þat hour.

869–78. Cf. Isaiah 6:10 (noted in Ellis). 876–7: That is, they stop their ears because they do not care to be converted and healed.
883–4. 'Consider now the innumerable people who are already lost due to unprepared death.'
890. 'As they do here (on earth), accordingly shall they be rewarded (in the afterlife).'

LEARN TO DIE   179

And therfore, alle vicious° thynges left,   immoral   **prepara te ad**
905 Weel thee dispose° and reedy make thee   prepare yourself well   **viam vniuerse**
     To dye, lest the tyme be thee reft°   be taken from you   **carnis ad horam**
     Or° þat thow be waar°, for no certeintee   before, aware   **mortis quia pro**
     Haast thow therof. Thow art nothyng° pryuee   not at all   **certo nescis qua**
     Therto. Deeth is nat fer° – right atte yate°   not far, right at the gate   **hora veniet et**
910 Shee is. Be reedy for to dye algate°.   always   **quam prope est.**
                                                                                   Ecce in ianuis
                                                                                   est etc.

     Right° as a marchant° stondynge in a port,   just, merchant
     His ship þat charged° is with marchandyse°   loaded, merchandise (cargo)
     To go to fer parties°, for confort   far places
     Of himself lookeþ þat it in sauf wyse°   safely
915 Passe out°, right so, if thow wirke as the wyse°,   departs, proceed wisely
     See to thy soule so, or thow hens weende°,   before you go hence (to the beyond)
     Þat it may han the lyf þat haath noon eende°.'   i.e., that your soul may have eternal life

     Amen.

---

904. gloss: Prepare for the way of all flesh, for the hour of death, because you do not know for certain
  when it will come, nor how near it is. See, it is at the doors. Lines 909–10: cf. Matthew 24:33.
910. Death is gendered female here. Cf. lines 36, 68, 155–62, 685–6.
911–17. This closing image expands on Suso's original. In the original, a traveler stands at port looking
  for a fast ship headed to distant lands, so that he might not be left behind: 'Et ideo sicut viator in
  portu navem velociter pertranseuntem longinquas partes petentem stans prospectat, ne se neglegat
  … ' (540:7–9).

OCCURRENCES OF SHORTER POEMS BEYOND HM 111/744

಄

TABLE: Occurrences of shorter poems beyond HM 111/744

	Complaint Paramount (111–01)	Male Regle (111–03)	Mother of God (111–10)	Duke of Bedford (111–11)	Regiment envoi (111–14)	Victorious King (111–15)	Monk Who Clad (744–06)	Epistle of Cupid (744–07)	Learn to Die (744–10)	Regiment of Princes	Series
A					×					×	
Ad					×					×	
Ad2	×							×*			
Ad3	×										
Ar					×					×	
As					×					×	
B									×	×	×
B2								×			
B3	×							×			
Ba											
C					×				×	×	×
Ca		×									
Cc					×		×			×	
Ch											
Co	×										
D					×				×	×	×
D1					×					×	
D2					×			×		×	
D3					×			×		×	
Do					×					×	
Du				×	×					×	
Eg	×					×		×			
F					×	×				×	
Fi1					×					×	
Fi2					×					×	
G	×				×					×	
Ga					×					×	
Gg					×					×	
H	×									×	
H3					×					×	
Ha									×		
Ha1					×					×	
Ha2					×					×	

OCCURRENCES OF SHORTER POEMS BEYOND HM 111/744

	Complaint Paramount (111-01)	Male Regle (111-03)	Mother of God (111-10)	Duke of Bedford (111-11)	Regiment envoi (111-14)	Victorious King (111-15)	Monk Who Clad (744-06)	Epistle of Cupid (744-07)	Learn to Die (744-10)	Regiment of Princes	Series
Ha3					×					×	
Hh					×					×	
Kk					×					×	
L					×				×	×	×
M	×										
N	×										
Na					×					×	
Na2			×								
Ne										×	
Qu					×					×	
R					×				×	×	×**
R2					×					×	
R3				×	×					×	
R4					×					×	
Ra1					×					×	
Ra2					×					×	
Ro					×					×	
S					×				×	×	×
S2			×					×			
Sl1					×					×	
Sl2					×					×	
So					×					×	
T					×					×	
Tc								×			
Tr1								×			
Tr2							×	×			
U											
U2	×										
Un	×										
Y					×					×	×

* fragment (only four stanzas)

** *Series* without 'Complaint' and 'Dialogue'

Note: this table does not include *Regiment* manuscripts that lack the envoi

TEXTUAL VARIANTS

❧

See pp. ix–x for a full list of manuscripts and sigla.

COMPLAINT PARAMOUNT

Non-autograph witnesses are comprised of two subgroups: (Subgroup 1): Eg, G, M, N, U2; (Subgroup 2): Ad3, B3, Co, H, Un.

Note that lines 1–42 of the base text are transcribed from Eg, due to missing leaves in H1.

2 In] GU2 To; 3 wilt thow] B3CoGUn *trsp.*; ne] Ad3Co *om.*, wot] Co knowe; 4 Syn] B3 *adds* now; thow] B3 *om.*; hast to the deth] G to þe deþ hast; 6 him to thee] Un þe to him; 7 noon othir] Ad3 no man; or] GU2 ne; 8 also] *H eke; 12 hath] Ad3 *adds* the; with] B3CoGU2Un in; 14 eek] Ad3B3CoU2Un with, M *adds* with; 15 alle] B3CoGHUnU2 a, Ad3 *om.*; 16 woful] Ad3B3CoHUn heuy; hertes] B3CoU2 *add* which; 17 art hire] U2 þeir; counceyloure] U2 socour; 18 That] U2 *om.*; hy] Ad3B3CoHUn thy; vertu] U2 *adds* þou; 19 of] B3Un or; thy] *so also* M; *other MSS om.*; 21 Which] Ad3 *om.*; agasted] *so also* MN; *other MSS* abashed; Which that me sore agasted and affright] M And in my wombe thi palace dyghte; 22 thy] Ad3 *om.*; 24 O] Ad3CoU2Un *om.*; it] Co *adds* soo; 25 me as weel] B3 *om.*, Ad3CoUn me; 26 wo] B3 *om.*; 27 þat] Ad3 *om.*; may] Ad3B3CoGU2 *om.*; counfort] B3CoGU2 *add* may; I may no counfort] Un no comfort I may; 29 þat] Ad3 *om.*; aplace] Ad3 on place, Co apace, U2 in place; 31 thus] CoM *om.*, Co *adds* vn to me; 32 thow] *so also* M; *other MSS add* tho; me] B3CoUn *add* in; 33 þat] Ad3M þe ylke, B3GNU2Un þilke; 34 it] CoG *om.*; 35 rafte] Ad3B3CoU2Un berafte; lorne] Ad3 for lorne; 37 wordes] EgMN word; 38 al] Co yll; 41 sone] Ad3B3Un rathe; 42 now] Ad3 *om.*; evene] G heuen; 45 tetes] B3HUn brestes, Ad3Co breste, M pappes; 46 which on hy] *H the which that, *ex.* Ad3 þat, Un whiche þat; 47 What] N That; 49 That] M Thou; nat ne seest] Ad3 seste notte; wombe] Ad3B3CoHUn herte, EgGMNU2 body; 52 soule] *H *adds* eke; 53 ne] Ad3 *om.*; I] H *om.*; 54 me make] Ad3 *trsp.*; 55 martire] EgMNU2 martirdam; 56 þat myn … see] B3GHU2 þat my3t myn herte (U2 hurt *corr. from* hert) I se, EgMN þat myght myn hurte see; 57 O2] M *om.*, GNU2 a; 58 and] *H *adds* thou; modir deere] B3EgMN *trsp.*; 59 entente] Un *om.*; or1] H *om.*; to2] Ad3 *om.*; or2] EgGMNU2 of, Un and; 60 broghten … foorth] *H engendered ye me; 61 to me become] G bicome to me; a] Ad3 *om.*; 63 folk] Eg men; heuy] M any; 64 nat doon] *H *trsp.*; 65 syn] Ad3CoEgGNUn sith, B3H sich, MU2 swich; 66 yee] B3 *om.*; me make] *H (ex. EgMN) to make, EgMN to haue; 68 Me to doon ese] *H (ex. Eg) Me for to esen, Eg Me to ese; 70 oghten] Ad3EgMNU2 *add* to; 71 sone] U2 *adds* Ihesus; 72 oonly] *H singularly; on] Un in; 74 in] CoEgGHMNU2 on; 75 a] Ad3 *om.*; 76 Eek] Ad3EgM Also; on] Ad3CoEgGMNUn of; 78 withdrawith] Ad3 draweþ; bittir deeth] Co bitterly; 79 wrongful] EgMN wronge; 80 thynke] *H *add* thou (Ad3B3 þe); in me þat] Ad3

þat in me; 81 this] Co *om.*; 83 sterue moot] Ad3Co moste sterue, M dye must; syn] Ad3 if, B3GMNU2Un sith; 84 shamely] *H shamefully; a] B3EgGMNU2 this, Ad3CoH þe; 85 the] G *om.*; 86 Thyn] Ad3 I; wyde] Ad3 depe and wide; 87 folk] Eg men, Ad3B3HUn þe world, Co þe worde, see] Un *om.*, it] Ad3Un þat, Co *om.*; 88 largeliche] Ad3CoHUn *add* now, EgGMN *add* lo; 89 syn] EgGMNU2 þat sith, B3CoUn þat; I] B3H it, B3CoU2Un I it; nat may] *H *trsp.*; it] Ad3CoEgMNU2Un *om.*; 90 And] H *om.*; 91 put art also] *H art also now put (EgGMN U2 also *after* put, Ad3 now *before* also); sone] *H *om.*; 92 wer … and] *H my son had been (Ad3 *om.* ben) a; 93 folk] Eg men, *H *adds* eke (Eg also, Ad3B3 *om.*); 94 knowleche] G *adds* of; thy] Ad3B3CoH his; hadde of thy persone] Ad3B3CoHUn of his persone had; 95 Thy name Pilat hath put] Ad3 Pilate putte vpe þi name, B3CoGHUn Pilate hath put þi name vp, EgMNU2 Pilate hath put up thi name; 96 it] Ad3B3CoGU2Un *om.*; 97 For] *H *add* þat; 98 al this see] Ad3B3CoEgGMNU2 see alle this; 99 þat] Ad3EgMN *om.*; 100 for] Eg *om.*; shewe] N hewe; 101 hertes greef] U2 hert greueth it; 102 Sone] U2 But sone; haddist] Eg *adds* here; a] EgMN *om.*; fadir] *H *adds* here (*ex* Eg); 104 þat] *H cause; he] Un *om.*; of] *H in; 105 That] Ad3B3CoHUn þis; a] EgMN *om.*; abreggynge] Co brekeynge; 106 in] Ad3 one, Co on; haddist] Co *adds* þowe; 107 for] B3CoHUn *om.*; pleyne] *H weep; 108 As] B3CoUn no; þat] *H now; thow] G *adds* now; 109 Þat] Ad3 þou; 110 Han] M *om.*; leid] Co browghte; to] Ad3 one, B3Un on, Co a; 111 with me in thee] Ad3 withe þe in me, B3CoUn in þe wiþ me; 112 hoolly] *H all wholly (N all holy, U2 al hol); deere] Ad3 *om.*; 113 al] B3 at; my2] Ad3CoUn *om.*; 114 it] B3 *om.*; 115 þat] Ad3 þou; 116 sone the] *H þis raunsom or; 119 what] B3 *om.*; thow wilt] Ad3 þou wilte itte, EgN þat it, G þu wylt þat, U2 þou wilt þat it; me] Ad3 I itte, EgN the, M *adds* it, Un þu; 120 so thow] Ad3B3CoGU2Un þat, EgMN þat so; kythist] Ad3B3CoGU2Un *add* so, Un lightest; 121 aftirward] Ad3 after; 123 That] *H *adds* þus; thurgh thy] *H with; 124 nat wole I] *H I wil not; 125 come of²] Ad3Un *om.*, Eg come; and] Un *om.*; as] Ad3 *om.*, Co all; 126 Departe from him] Ad3CoEgHMNU2Un Fro him departen; 127 thow] *H þe; 128 yee] *H *adds* now; 131 despitous] U2 spytous; 132 as1] U2 a; as2] *H *adds* euer; 133 Our] Ad3 3oure; 136 thow] Eg *om.*; 137 Of] *H Here of; the] H* þis; folk] Eg men; heere] *H *om.*; vnkeuered] Ad3B3CoEgGHU2Un *add* to, MN *add* for to; 138 moche] M mykil; holde him] Ad3 *trsp.*; 139 Than] Ad3CoHUn As; 140 nakid] *H (*exc.* Ad3) *adds* so; 141 do] B3 to; 142 Come of] *H Lat se; 143 if] B3CoGNU2Un *add* þat; so do] B3CoU2Un *trsp.*; 145 sparcle] *H droppe; 146 Remembre] Ad3 *adds* þe; 148 what] M that; thow] B3CoEgHNUn *add* so, M so; 149 þat] Ad3 has, Co haþe; and] Un *om.*; 150 and] B3CoUn þat; aourned] Ad3 ornede, EgM adorned, N adoned, U2 he orned; 151 þat] Ad3B3HU2 *om.*; werist] Ad3 wereste on, B3CoGHMU2Un on werest, EgN on weredist; 152 O] Un or; 153 Qwake] Ad3B3CoEgHU2Un Now qwake, G Now whake, MN Now quake þou; thow] Ad3 euen; 154 þat] Ad3 in; me vnto] *H þou me to; 155 It myn is] Ad3U2 myn it is, H myn is, M it is myn; 157 Tho] B3Un þe; dede] U2 *om.*; in thee þat] *H (*exc.* Co) þat in the, Co in þe; 158 of swich] B3 *om.*; 159 oghte] U2 *adds* to; clothe] Eg to calle hem, N to clepe hem; ageyn] U2 þeim; 160 thow art] *H art holden; 161 Holden for to do so] *H So for to do parde (M *om.* parde); 162 deeth] B3EgGHMNU2Un *add* now; neighith] Ad3 *adds* now; 164 my] M *om.*; 165 yeuest] Ad3B3EgNU2 *add* to; than] *H *adds* to; 166 Thogh he whom thow me yeuest] *H (*exc.* HU2) Thow so be that he a, H þo3 it be so þat he a, U2 Thou3 so þat he a; maiden] *H virgyne; 167 And thogh] *H If (Ad3 3itte) thu; iust] Ad3 justice; thow] Ad3 wolde, CoGM *om.*; weye] *H (*exc.* Ad3) woldest wey; 168 weighte] B3Un wight; him and thee] B3CoHUn þe and him; nat is] *H (*exc.* Ad3) *trsp.*; 169 and] EgMNU2Un *om.*; a2] EgMNU2 his, G is; 170 al away art] M art alwey, N alwey art; 171

186 TEXTUAL VARIANTS

Betwixt] B3CoGNU2Un By twene; ther] CoU2 *om.*; 175 Twixt] *H Of; for ay] Ad3Co *om.*; 176 me] *H (*exc.* B3) *add* but; 177 straunge were] *H *trsp.* (Ad3 were to þe strang); and] *H *adds* al; 178 thow my ioie] Ad3GU2 my joye þou, B3CoHMNUn my ioyes þu; 179 deeth his] HN dethis, Un deth in his; vengeable] Ad3 vnchaungeable; 180 Hath] H Is; 182 fro] EgMN *om.*; I] EgM *om.*, U2 *adds* am; away is] G alwey is, M *trsp.*, Un alwey am; now] G newe; 183 clepe and calle] *H (*exc.* EgM) clepen or name, EgM calle or name; Mara] CoGU2 Maria; 184 hennesforward] *H (*exc.* Ad3Eg) hennesforth, *H *add* and; may men] Co men, U2 *trsp.*; me] B3 *om.*; 185 clept be] B3CoNU2 be clepid, EgM be called; 186 I which is Ihesus] Ad3 I se þat is Ihesus, Eg he the which is called Ihesus, M he called Ihesus, N he which is cleped Ihesus; 187 al] Ad3 *om.*, B3CoGHU2Un O, EgMN and; is] Ad3 *adds* O, B3EgN *om.*; 188 þat I] B3U2Un *om.*, CoGH I, EgMN he; which] Ad3 *om.*, B3CoHUn *adds* þat; was] N *om.*; 189 Of] *H lo of; this day] B3 *om.*; bynome] *H beraft; 190 my] H *om.*; 191 and] M *adds* I; 192 I] Un *om.*; othir] Ad3 harte, M honour; 194 two] Ad3 H *om.*; 196 Ful] *H (*exc.* Un) O, Un *om.*; careful] *H (*exc.* M) *adds* now, M *adds* may; been wee] Ad3 we be; 197 Vnto] B3 vp into; 199 So] B3 no; in vs two] Ad3 in to, B3 into us, CoUn in two; 200 vs] *H (*exc.* G) *adds* to, G *adds* two to; restreyne] *H (*exc.* EgH) refreyne; 201 othir] EgMN *add* but; die] N drye; 202 steruen] M dy; par] Eg be, M in oon; 203 Sterue] M Dye; there] M here; and] *H (*exc.* G) *adds* right; heere] G *adds* ry3t; wole I] Eg N *trsp.*; wole I die] M dye wil I; 204 and1] B3CoEgGHMNUn *om.*; mourne and waile] U2 weyle morne; 205 wrong] EgMNU2 *add* for; 206 tho] GN þe; folk] Eg poepil; þat] B3CoUn whiche; weren] N *om.*; wont] B3 wonyd, Co *adds* for; 207 And1] *H to; to] *H *adds* the; 208 yee] Ad3 he; han] B3 *om.*; 209 is it] Ad3 *trsp.*; who] N how; 210 yit ful] Ad3 yitte moste in, EgN most, B3CoGHMU2Un 3it most; had] CoNUn *add* of; 211 loue] *H (*exc.* Ad3U2) *adds* which; me ioyned] Co *trsp.*; 212 sone] *H *adds* ful; 213 therin fynde I] U2 ffynde I therin; 214 the taast I feele and] *H I taste (B3 finde) and feele (B3 taste); 215 thy] Co *om.*; feele I deeth] *H (Ad3) deth fele I, B3 *adds* in; 216 poore] EgMN pure; 217 is] Ad3B3CoH *add* all, EgGMNU2 *add* now; 219 art] M *adds* so; 221 now2] Co *adds* þowe art; 222 And] Ad3 *om.*, Co a; þat] Ad3B3CoHUn doþ, M *om.*; or1] Ad3HU2 *om.*; or2] Ad3 *adds* a; ship or barge] G barge schyp; 224 woful] B3Un sory; 225 And] *H (*exc.* EgM) *adds* eke, EgM *add* also; haast thow eek lost] Co loste þu haste; eek] *H *om.*; 226 clept be by] Ad3B3CoHUn avaunte of, EgM be called by, GNU2 be clept by; thy] *H (*exc.* M) that; 228 hieth] *H hasteþ; hidir] G *om.*; 230 Hangith] *H lo hangith; al] *H *om.*; bybled] M bledynge; 231 and1] Ad3B3CoGHUn *om.*, EgMNU2 in; 232 see] B3 lo; 233 any] EgN *om.*; 234 Now] Ad3 Howe; your hertes] Ad3 3oure hartes 3oure hartes; oghten] Co *adds* be, U2 *adds* to; 235 loue] Eg kendnesse; dileccioun] Ad3 deuocione; 236 For] Ad3 *adds* of; he] G heye; 237 And] Ad3B3CoHUn *add* full; right] Ad3B3H *om.*; 238 on] Ad3B3CoHUn *om.*; myn] Ad3CoUn in; it] Co *adds* hym; 239 taar] M share; 240 sy men] *H saw 3e; neuere] Ad3 *om.*; 241 For] Ad3U2 *add* þe; þat shee] EgMN *om.*, U2 sche; of] U2 on; 242 tete] M pap; as] *H (*exc.* B3) and, B3 of; 243 hath torn] M is torne; gilt] Co *adds* and; 244 And hath] Ad3B3CoHUn And all, EgGN Hath of, M He hath, U2 He hath of; despent] Ad3 he blede, B3CoHUn isched, EgGMNU2 spilt; in] M ful; 245 it was] *H is lo (Eg his lo)

LA MALE REGLE

The sole other medieval witness to this poem is found in Register O of the Canterbury Cathedral Archives (Ca). Note that this copy is badly damaged, and as a result is missing the following lines: 1–32, 49–64, 81–8, 97–104, 409–48. The scribe also skips lines 113–345. One stanza (lines 345–52) arrives later in Ca, acting as the penultimate stanza to that version.

33 But] Ca *om.*; herd] Ca *adds* of; seye longe] Ca ful [ ]; 34 prosperitee] Ca that prosp[eritee is]; 35 can] Ca may; 36 put haue] Ca *trsp.*; 40 accusith] Ca *adds* me; 41 it] Ca he; 42 shee] Ca he; 43 hire] Ca his; hirself] Ca him self; 44 shee] Ca he; 45 it] Ca to; 65 As] Ca and 3yt; 66 hir] Ca his; 67 regnynge which] Ca And regneng that; 70 vnto] Ca to; 72 vnto] Ca yn to; 73 seen] Ca seyn; 74 likly for] Ca emynent; 75 þat moot] Ca he wol; 76 been execut] Ca [ ] alle hit; no] Ca and no; wole he] Ca to hym; 89 vnto] Ca to; 90 me cause wolde] Ca wolde me cause; 94 in] Ca into; 95 now] Ca *om.*; 96 it nat] Ca *trsp.*; 106 attemprely] Ca and temprely; 108 þat] Ca hys; 109 I take haue] Ca he; bothe] Ca *adds* hath take; 110 yeer] Ca *om.*; 111 wyntir] Ca 3eres; 112 hath leyd his knyf] Ca hys knyf hath leyd; 227 deceyuours] H1 deceyuous; 345 Despenses] Ca And al so despense3; 346 they be forbore] Ca ther is more; 350 with] Ca of; 351 Hoccleue] Ca ther fore; therfore] Ca the more; 352 thow thee dresse] Ca now dresse the; 353 Whoso] Ca *adds* that; 356 forthy] Ca therfore; 359 it] Ca they; 360 it] Ca hem a; 402 Weleful] Ca thow weleful; meekly] Ca lowly; 404 swymmed] Ca swam; 406 kythe] Ca scew; 407 sit] Ca syttyth; been] Ca to be; his] Ca *om.*; 408 Foryeue] Ca *adds* me lord; neuere wole I eft] Ca y no more wole

MOTHER OF GOD

2 of] Na2 our; 3 Preye] Na2S2 *add* thou; 4 sone] Na2S2 *add* the; 8 Modir] Na2S2 Thou moder; 9 vertu] S2 mercy; 10 vs] Na2S2 saulis; by] Na2 throu; 11 Humble] Na2S2 O humble; 13 vnto] Na2S2 to; sone] Na2S2 *add* þat thou; 14 for] Na2S2 of; I fully] Na2S2 hoolly I; 18 Full] Na2S2 Fulfillit; me] Na2 *adds* for; 20 And] Na2S2 *add* all; plukke wole] Na2S2 *trsp.*; 23 of] Na2S2 *add* all; 24 Among] Na2S2 Aboue; 25 and] Na2S2 now; 27 of] Na2S2 and; 28 qwenche] Na2S2 slake; 29 O] Na2S2 Most; the] Na2S2 *om.*; of] Na2 *adds* the; 31 by] Na2S2 *add* thi; 32 filthes] Na2S2 filth; synful] Na2S2 soulis; 33 Thyn hand foorth putte] Na2S2 Put forth thy hand; and] Na2 *om.*; helpe] Na2S2 *add* me in; 34 temptacioun] Na2S2 *add* lady; 35 thurgh] Na2S2 for; 38 Preye] Na2S2 *add* thou; ay] Na2 euir; 39 Lady] Na2S2 *om.*; emprises] Na2S2 *add* sekirly; 40 an] S2 *om.*; aduocatrice] Na2 aduocat; who can dyuyne] Na2S2 may no man deuyne; 41 right noon] Na2S2 lady; 44 Mene] Na2S2 To preye; 46 our fo] Na2S2 þat; 49 soules helthe] Na2S2 soule hele lady; 52 Flessh] Na2S2 Bothe flesche; eek] Na2S2 *om.*; for] Na2S2 to; 53 die] Na2S2 dryen; 56 From his mercy helpe vs] Na2S2 Help frome (S2 for) his mercy þat; 57 Tendrely] Na2S2 *om.*; on] Na2S2 eke vpon; wo] Na2S2 sorow; 58 in] Na2S2 into; 60 this] Na2S2 thy; 62 deeth] Na2S2 drynng; al] Na2S2 *om.*; 63 Modir] Na2S2 Thou modir; þat haue] Na2S2 *trsp.*; 66 charge and] S2 *om.*; 67 The lord to bere] Na2S2 To bere the lord; and1] Na2 of; 68 And] Na2S2 *add* of; 69 art] Na2S2 was; 71 which] Na2S2 *add* þat; 72 tetes] Na2S2 pappis; him yaf to] Na2S2 þat gave him; 73 To] S2 Vnto; be they blessid ay] Na2S2 blissit (S2 blissit blissit) be þou ay; 77 qwit] Na2S2 brot; 81 gracious] Na2S2 passing; 83 to thy sone canst] Na2S2 cast (S2 canst) to Crist; be] Na2S2 *add* for vs; 84 giltes] Na2 gilt; he] Na2S2 *om.*; 86 yates] Na2S2 *add* all; by] Na2S2 throu; 89 bountee] Na2S2 gudenes; 93 Lady pitous] Na2S2 Thou pitous lady and; 94 Þat our lord God nat list to werne thee] Na2S2 Preye thy dere sone my gilt forgeue it me; 95 wot] Na2S2 knowe; 96 foorth thee to putte] Na2S2 to put the forth; 97 modir] Na2S2 *add* so; 98 Benygnely wole he thyn axyng heere] Na2S2 For thy preyere he will benignely here; 100 his ychosen virgyne] Na2S2 virgyne ychois of him; 103 preye I] Na2S2 *trsp.*; to been oon] Na2 þou be one; 106 Ion] Na2S2 *add* o; 108 bysy] Na2S2 lusty; 109 cloudeful] Na2S2 *add* of;

110 mowen] Na2S2 myt; 112 may] Na2S2 *add* vs; 116 I to yow] Na2S2 to ȝow I; 121 meryt] Na2S2 mercy; 123 a] Na2S2 the; 124 vnto] Na2 to; 125 reherce] Na2 *adds* now; 127 heer] Na2 *add* is; 129 hy] Na2S2 holy; twixt] Na2S2 betwix; 130 his2] Na2S2 *add* hie; 131 Conioyned] Na2S2 Commaundit; 132 sone] Na2S2 *add* to; 133 giltes] Na2S2 synnes; bleede] Na2 blind; 134 tweyne] Na2S2 *add* now; 136 may my lyf amende] Na2S2 my lyf may mend; 141 Amen] Na2S2 *om.*; Na2S2 *add* Explicit oracio Galfridi Chaucer

BALADE TO JOHN, DUKE OF BEDFORD

2 al] DuR3 *om.*; humblesse] DuR3 lowlynesse; 7 worthynesse] DuR3 hy noblesse; 10 dreede] DuR3 *add* also; þat] DuR3 *om.*; 11 Þat is of fructuous] DuR3 That fructuous is of; 18 is mis] DuR3 *trsp.*; 20 this] DuR3 þus; 22 seid maistir] DuR3 maister Massy; to] DuR3 *om.*; 25 hid] Du him; 26 hir] Du *om.*, R3 his

REGIMENT OF PRINCES ENVOI

1 litil] QuR4Ra2 libel; yaf] CcQuR4 *add* to; thee] GgNa *add* that, Ra2 the the; 2 Thy] Qu This; wordes] Fi1Hh lordis; to] AdR2 *om.*; the] AsHh *om.*; 3 princes] Ar kynges; 4 Syn] AsKkLRa2SSl2SoTcY Sithen, Fi2 Sothe, GgH3Sl1 Sith, HhRo Sethe; al nakid art] Ra2R4 art al (Ra2 of) naked; 6 vnclothid] *H (exc. AAdCD2GgNaR) all nakyd; also] CD2R allone; 7 right] Cc wel, *H (exc. AAdCCcD2GgNaRRa1) full; humble] KkSl2So worþi; 8 Thee yeueth] Ad *trsp.*; hardynesse] CcDuGaH3KkR2Sl2SoTc *add* for; to do so] AdD2R so to doon, Ne do so; 9 woot I] AsFi2HhLRoS *trsp.*; wel] D2 *om.*; go1] ArHa2Ha3Ra2 *om.*; wher] ArHa2 *add* that, Ra2 *om.*; thow go] Ra2 *om.*; 10 so] Cc *om.*; 11 and1] GaKkSl2SoTc *om.*; been] CcDuGaH3Tc be; wilt been] Hh *trsp.*; 12 swich] DoNe whiche; 13 thow] H3 *adds* canst; nat do him] Cc do hym nouȝt, D2 vnto hym doo not, Fi1 doo not to hym, AsFi2LRRa1RoS not do to hym, Hh do to hym no; 14 cheertee] Ha3HhRo herte; nat is] AsDuFi1Fi2Ha3HhKkLRoSSl2Y *trsp.*; nat is the lesse] ArGaHa2 is neuerthelesse; 15 if] Ha3 *adds* it; his] C thi; 16 welthe] Ro helthe; it] CH3GgNa *om.*; 18 thee holde] AsFi1Fi2HhLRoS to holde þe, ArHa2 to hold; 19 humblesse] *H meeknesse; 20 thee] GaRa2 *om.*; 22 And] Sl1 *om.*; þat] GaHhKkSl2SoTc *om.*; wil] *H hert; nat] KkSl2 noo, Gg *adds* thi; 23 To thee] Gg *om.*; al] Ga *om.*; 24 Þat] HhR2 And that; God] CcRa2 *om.*, *H (exc. CcRa2) he; whom] ArD2DuHa2HhLRRoY þat

VICTORIOUS KING

1 ful] F moste; 4 on] F of; 6 Flowe] F Folowe; vs] F *om.*; 10 our confort] F your refute; 11 Oure] F Or; softne] F abreggen; 12 may] F nay; 14 ne] F nor; 16] F *adds* lenvoy (interlinear); 24 O worthy] F Excellent; Cest tout] F Explicit

THE MONK WHO CLAD THE VIRGIN

2 needful] ChTr2 holsom; 3 for to brynge him] Ch hym to brynge, Tr2 to bryng there; 4 And] Tr2 *om.*; 8 is shee] Tr2 *trsp.*; 10 is] ChTr2 *om.*; seur] ChTr2 *om.*; sheld] ChTr2 *add* ys; 13 eternel peyne] ChTr2 peyne ay duryng; 14 thoght] ChTr2 *om.*; 21 is] Tr2 *om.*; 22 Ther was whilom] Tr2 [W]hylom þer was; þat] Tr2 *om.*; 24 to] Tr2 dyd; 25 And] Tr2 *adds* to; he] Tr2 *om.*; 26 And vnto] Tr2 *om.*; modir] Tr2 *adds* most; 27 noble] Tr2 glorious; blissid] Tr2 blysfull; 29 þat] Tr2

om.; 30 Vnto] Tr2 *adds* the; 31 to haue] Tr2 *om.*; 35 goddes] ChTr2 cristys; the flour] ChTr2 myrroure; 45 Into] Ch in the, Tr2 into þe; 46 he had] Tr2 *om.*; 50 þat he] Ch he, Tr2 the monke; 54 him] Tr2 moche; þat] Tr2 *om.*; mighte han] Tr2 *om.*; 55 O] ChTr2 *om.*; 56 And1] Ch *om.*; 62 Aue] Ch *om.*; 63 thow] ChTr2 ryght; 64 wole I] Tr2 *trsp.*; 69 receyue] ChTr2 conceyue; 70 so me] Tr2 *trsp.*; 72 in2] Tr2 *om.*; 76 it eek] Tr2 them; with] Ch which; 78 þat] Ch *om.*; 81 seith] Tr2 telleth; 83 wole I] Tr2 *trsp.*; 87 Aue Maria he] ChTr2 suyng (Tr2 aftyr) her psalter he; 89 suynge] ChTr2 folwyng; 91 To the monk cam] Tr2 Came to the monke; 92 seide] ChTr2 *add* shee; 93 fressh] ChTr2 good; 99 and go] Tr2 *om.*; 100 shalt thow chosen be] ChTr2 chosyn shalt thow be; 101 for] Tr2 *om.*; 104 teche] ChTr2 preche; 105 in] ChTr2 of; hire] Tr2 *om.*; 108 passe shalt] Tr2 *trsp.*; 109 of this doute] ChTr2 her of dowte; thow] Ch *om.*; right] Tr2 *om.*; 110 shal ther be] Tr2 ther shalle; 113 lykid hire] ChTr2 *trsp.*; 114 vp1] Ch *om.*; vp2] ChTr2 *om.*; 116 þat] ChTr2 *om.*; tolde him] ChTr2 *trsp.*; 123 Shee souffissantly] Tr2 *trsp.*; 125 for] Tr2 *om.*; 126 Ch *adds* Amen.

THE EPISTLE OF CUPID

The main subgroup of non-autograph copies are: B2, D1, D3, F, T, U. Beyond this main subgroup there are four other copies: John Shirley's (Tr1), the fragment Ad2 (containing stanzas 50, 10, 11, 44), and two sixteenth-century copies, Ba and S2. The main subgroup copies rearrange Hoccleve's poem, likely due to an error in bifolia ordering in a common archetype: stanzas 1–19, 30–9, 50–9, 20–9, 40–9, 60–8 (D1 lacks stanzas 1–10, U lacks stanzas 29, 40–9, 60–8; F further complicates the order but appears to derive from the same archetype). Note further that, within stanzas 60–8, the main subgroup (except U, which lacks the ending) sequences the stanzas thus: 60, 63–4, 61–2, 65–8; the sequence is also thus in Ba, whereas S2 and Tr1 follow the same sequence as H2. For further comment, see Ellis 2001: 274–6.

2 of] BaD3 *add* the; 4 the] *H al; bisyly] D3 treuly; 5 Of] BaB2FTTr1U *add* the, D3 the; Sitheree sone] BaB2FTU *trsp.*, D3 Cithera; oonly] S2 sothly; 7 sogettes] *H *adds* hertely; greetynges] *H greteyng; senden] D3 se; 8 wole] U *adds* well; yee knowe] S2 *trsp.*; 9 and] Ba *adds* of; 12 men] F wymen; þat] Tr1 which; 13 for] S2 so; 14 hir] BaB2FTU this, D3 ther, Tr1 þe; 15 And] BaB2D3FTTr1U *om.*; passyng] S2 passid; alle] S2U *add* the; this] BaB2D3FTTr1U the litel, S2 the; 16 That clept is] Tr1 Ecleped; Albioun] S2 Britaine; 17 þat there] D3 that, S2 thare in; 21 his] B2D3FTU her, BaS2Tr1 thair; 22 spoken been] S2 *trsp.*; so sighyngly] S2 generaly; 23 And] BaB2S2TU *om.*; pitous] S2Tr1 *add* a; 25 þat they in herte] S2Tr1 in hert that thai; 28 right] Ba will; moot] BaB2FTU *om.*; the] BaS2 that; 30 Shewe] Ba As I haif, B2D3FTTr1U As doth, S2 3e do; me] Ba *om.*; 31 Whyles] *H *adds* that; and] Tr1 or; 32 humble] *H (*exc.* D3) *adds* and lowe; euery] *H (*exc.* Ba) eche, Ba ilk; 33 al] Tr1 yche; thyng] BaFTU *add* as; secree] B2 *om.*; 34 As þat] *H ryght as; lykith] B2 lust, BaS2TTr1U liste; 35 And] BaS2 Or; elles] S2 *adds* that; moot] *H *om.*; herte] Ba *adds* I wald it, B2D3FS2TU *add* mote, Tr1 *adds* I prey most; on] Ba in, B2FS2TTr1U a; 36 is it] BaB2D3FTTr1U *trsp.*; a] D3 *om.*; 37 no man] S2 noon; 38 out … noon] S2Tr1 may noon out of his mouth; ther] *H *om.*; 39 sholde … reson] BaB2D3FT by reson semed (D3: shulde) euery (Ba: ilk) wight to, S2Tr1U be resoun any wight schold l 40 is it] B2D3S2T *trsp.*; herte] B2D3FS2TTr1U *add* as; 42 betrayed] *H deceyved; 43 wommen meeued of] BaB2FT moveth oft woman; 44 weenyng] S2U *add* that; as] Ba *om.*; þat] BaB2D3FS2TU *om.*; 45 Graunten] BaB2D3FT They graunte; hem] D3 the; 46 For] S2 *om.*; they] BaB2D3FT that men, S2Tr1U that thei; nat sholden] *H *trsp.*; sake] S2

leue; 47 And with good herte] Tr1 Of goode entent þey; 49 Thus] BaB2D3F And thus; been the wommen] BaB2D3FS2TU women beth, Tr1 þeos wymmen beoþe; 50 the1] BaB2D3FS2TU this; man] Tr1 *adds* þus haþe, U *adds* hath; pot] BaB2D3FTU panne; hath] Tr1U *om.*; the2] Tr1 *om.*; 51 of hire hath] *H is in his; 52 he keepith] BaB2D3FS2TTr1U *trsp.*; nat] BaB2D3FTU no more, Tr1 more; 55 Foule] BaB2D3FTU Euel, Tr1 so yuel; 56 a man] Tr1 þeos men; his] D3 *om.*, Tr1 þeyre; leeue] BaB2D3FTU beleve; 59 traitour] Tr1 womman, U *adds* hath; the] *H this; womman] Tr1 traytour; 60 He faste] S2Tr1 He spedith; him speedith] BaB2D3FTU *trsp.*, S2Tr1 him fast; 61 on a lowe] Tr1 ouer throwe; 62 ne] BaD3TU *om.*; him nat] D3 S2 *trsp.*; 63 tellith] Tr1 *adds* him; 65 himself] Ba *om.*; to] *H *om.*; accuse] Ad2B2D3FT *add* thus, Ba *adds* himself; and] Ba *adds* so; 66 Now] Ad2BaBaB2D3FT *om.*; is it] Tr1 is þis; good] Ad2BaB2D3FT *add* to, Tr1 witte; him] Ad2BaB2FTTr1 him selfe; a] Tr1 *om.*; 67 to] B2 *om.*, S2 in, Tr1 til; a2] Ad2B2D3FT *om.*; 68 telle] S2 say; he] Tr1 *om.*; body] Tr1 *adds* he; 69 may he thus] S2 thus he may, U may he; to] S2 *om.*; him] S2U hym selfe; 70 ful greet repreef] B2D3FS2U grete esclaundre, Ad2BaTTr1 gret disclaundyr; vnto] Tr1 booþe to; 72 for2] D1D3 to; pitee] *H (*exc.* Tr1) vertu, Tr1 goode; it] Ad2BaB2D1D3FT *om.*; 73 hath] S2 *om.*; 74 and] D1 *adds* so; 75 shame] *H (*exc.* Tr1) sclaundre; 76 here] S2 *adds* a, Tr1 *adds* hye; 77 Þat] Tr1 whiche; in] Ad2 Ba *add* suche; neede] Tr1 *adds* þat; helpe can] S2 *trsp.*; 78 þat] Ba throw, B2FT *om.*, D1D3 of; by] B2D1D3FT thorgh; 79 ignorant] BaB2D1D3FT innocent; 80 Betraye] Tr1 *adds* sithe; is no wondir] S2 no wonder is; syn] Tr1 *om.*; 81 þat] BaB2D3FS2TTr1 *om.*; 82 was] D3 *om.*; the] B2D1D3Tr1 *om.*; 83 al] B2D3FT *om.*; 85 men nat] BaB2FS2T *trsp.*; remes] BaB2D1D3FT citees; grete and kynges] Ba and grit kingis; 86 is] BaB2D1D3FT *add* it; þat] Ba *om.*; a] BaB2D1D3FT *om.*; 87 false and hid] *H (*exc.* S2) falsly, S2 fals hid; 88 tho] *H suche; 89 wil] BaB2D1D3FT wytte; ay reedy is] BaB2D1D3FT is euer redy; 90 To] S2 In; hy] BaB2D1D3FT *om.*; 91 mennes sleighte] Ba fals men; 92 the] B2U this, BaD1D3FTTr1 these, S2 othir; 93 nat] TU *om.*; 94 as] S2 *adds* that; they] D1D3T *om.*; 95 procuren] S2 *adds* men; for] Tr1 *om.*; 96 He] S2 and; him] S2 thanne; cause] BaB2D1D3FTr1 *adds* to; 97 him qwytith] BaB2D1D3F guerdoneth he, S2 to guerdoun, TTr1U guerdoneth; 98 Smal] *H Lytell; hem] B2F *om.*; 99 To … wrecche] *H Anothir wreche vnto his felowe; 100 hath thee] *H *trsp.*; 101 and1] BaS2 *om.*; inconstant] D3 constant; 103 And] S2 That; day2] Ba *adds* sche; 105 Anothir comth] Ba *trsp.*; 106 ryde] S2 forth, Tr1 *adds* on; 107 ther] *H (*exc.* S2) *adds* for, S2 here for; 108 can] *H wol; no wight] Ba no thing, S2T not; withseye] S2 *adds* nay, Tr1 sey ney; 109 qwikly] *H smertly; 110 so] *H thus; faren] Tr1 blamed; the2] U be; 111 Whoso] Tr1 Who þat; hangid moot] Tr1 offt gyled shal; 112 Ay] S2 For ay, Tr1 For; desiren] S2 *adds* is; 114 ne wynne] Ba win na; 115 Repreef of here he spekth] B2D1D3FS2TTTr1U He speketh hir reprefe; 116 labbyng] Ba babbling, B2F babbyng, D1D3Tr1 blabbyng; 117 sundry] *H dyuers; often] S2 of will; 118 sundry] Tr1 many; 119 accheuen] D1D3 haue; 120 Ful] Ba *om.*, Tr1 For; a man] Ba one; eek wolde] D1D3S2Tr1 *trsp.*; 121 in loue spent his tyme] *H (*exc.* D1) in loue his tyme spent, D1 his tyme in love spent; 122 Men] U when he; wiste] BaS2Tr1U *add* that; his lady] S2 sche; 123 were] S2 *adds* planly; his lady] *H (*exc.* S2) hyr pleynly, S2 hir; 124 were] BaD1D3 *om.*; 126 But] T *adds* onely; 127 Euery] Tr1 For euery; 128 shee] S2 thai; 129 leiser han] F S2 *trsp.*; 130 ne] D1 *om.*; he] U *om.*; 131 on maddyng he] *H (*exc.* S2) he on maddyng (Ba madness), S2 on madding; 133 þat1] S2 And that, Tr1 which; louen] S2 *adds* nothing; þat2] BaD1D3S2U *om.*; 134 To] Tr1 And; 135 armen] S2 honour; 136 And in] Ba In, D1D3 And, Tr1 For þe; wommen] Ba *adds* and; 137 As þat] S2 And; 138 If þat] Tr1 And if; a] Ba *adds* gentill; 139 Al moot he flee] *H (*exc.* Ba) He moot flee al (S2 *adds* thing), Ba He most all eschew; is to it] *H ther to is; 140 therto] *H (*exc.*

Tr1) his grete, Tr1 mans gret; 141 A] Tr1 Right; foul] Tr1 *adds* it; vice] B2D1D3FU thinge, S2 voise, TTr1 *om.*; of] Tr1 a; tonge] S2 *adds* is for; to] U of; 142 gabbith] S2 and; 143 T hem; is] D1 *om.*; so2] F is; wight] T lighte; 144 wan] S2 *adds* þat; 145 it … and] Ba is schewin so slawly and; S2 is schewit so and so; 146 Þat] D3 *adds* is; him neuere] S2 *trsp.*; ouertake] Tr1 *adds* he; 149 or] S2 and; 150 or] BaB2 *om.*; 151 or] S2 in; and] S2 *om.*, Tr1 al; 152 and fals] B2 *om.*, BaU fals; 154 nat] *H *add* that; 155 the hy God] D1D3 God the hie, Tr1 hyeghe god; 156 was] Tr1 were; 158 Yis] BaB2D1D3FTTr1 *add* al, S2U This all; wel knowen] *H (*exc.* Ba) woot that, Ba watt; 159 from] BaS2 *add* the; 160 therfore] Ba *adds* gife; angels] B2 *adds* yeue; 161 he þat] Tr1 which; that2] BaF *om.*; is] Tr1 *adds* muche; 163 goode were] Tr1 of hem were goode; 164 thanne] Ba so; 165 is] BaS2Tr1 *om.*; good] BaS2Tr1 *adds* is; for] BaB2D1D3S2T *om.*; 166 deeme] Tr1 *adds* it; they been alle] Ba thay all þerfor be, S2 all ben; 167 see] S2 *adds* full, Tr1 *adds* it; wel] S2 *adds* þat; 168 truste] BaS2Tr1 *add* þe; 169 man] D1D3 *om.*; oghte] D1S2T *add* to; han] D3 haue haue; 171 eithir] BaTr1 *om.*; or] Tr1 *adds* ellys; 172 he be] Ba it be, D1 *trsp.*, D3 he, T she be; badde or good] Tr1 goode or badde; this] Ba it; 173 Euery man] Ba Every wight, Tr1 For ych wight; 175 is it] D3 *trsp.*, Tr1 haþe he; speke of hire] *H of hir to speke; 180 thow … be] Tr1 man shal honnour þee; 181 nat hire] Ba hir than not, B2D1D3FTU *trsp.*, S2Tr1 hir; 182 therthurgh] *H ther by; 184 Men seyn] Ba *om.*; foul] D3 fouler, Tr1 beest; is] Ba *adds* full; 185 Whatso it] BaS2 Quhat ever (S2 so) he, B2FD1D3TTr1U What that (B2F *om.*) he; 186 wont is] *H vseth; 187 of wommen wel] *H wel of wymen; is] D1D3S2U *add* the; 188 for] FS2 *om.*; to] D3 *om.*; 189 hem list] *H (*exc.* S2) they wol, S2 3e woald; 190 Ladyes] *H These (Ba The) ladyes; 191 bookes] Tr1 makynges; 192 whiche] U swich; they lakken] *H dispisen they (BaTr1 *trsp.*); 194 hem yeue] *H *trsp.*; 197 wikkid] *H sory; 198 they] Ba women, S2 *adds* haue; 200 oon] Ba *om.*; may rehercen al] Ba may reherse thame all, S2 reherson schall, Tr1 koude rehersen al; 201 and] Tr1 *adds* yit; shal] S2 all; 202 Who … malice] B2D1D3FTTr1 The world hir malice (B2 *adds* it) may not, S2 The warld may nat þer malice; 203 Nat the world] Ba As, B2FD1D3TTr1 as (S2 and) that (B2F *add* theys, S2TTr1 *add* the); seyn] Ba *adds* for; 204 callid] Tr1 cleped; 205 repreef] Tr1 vilannye; 206 I trowe] S2 of dede; 208 endytith] Ba wrytith; 209 it] S2 his; prose] FTTr1 *add* or; 212 bewaar sholde] S2 *trsp.*; 216 Namely] D1D3S2TTr1U And namely; 219 wrong] Ba *om.*; do we] *H I do; 220 labour and trauaille] B2D1D3FTTr1U trauayle and labour; 221 vs] *H me; my] S2 *om.*; 223 Clerkes] *H (*exc.* Ba) These (S2TU This) clerkys, Ba Thus theis clerkis; hire] D1 *om.*; outrageous] *H (*exc.* D1) cruel, D1 grete cruell; 225 ful] Ba for; our] *H my; 226 Tyd] S2 ycheyned; lo] *H *om.*; what] BaU *om.*; 227 for] Ba *om.*; atteyne] S2 susteyne; 229 for þat] BaS2 for, D3U *trsp.*; they] S2Tr1 *om.*; 230 by] S2 for; 231 For] S2 *om.*; rebelle] S2 reule; vs] *H me; our] *H my; 233 the] F *om.*; oure] *H myn; 234 we] *H I (Ba *adds* can); can] Ba *om.*; 238 vs] *H me; 239 in herte] Ba in hairt in hairt; 241 we] *H I; mennes] *H folkes; 242 vs] *H me; hem sende] Ba *trsp.*, Tr1 to sende hem; and2] *H or; 244 Our] *H my; sharp] *H (*exc.* S2) *adds* persyng (Ba persing persing); strokes] S2 *adds* persyng; sore] *H *om.*; 245 and2] BaD1D3Tr1 *om.*; they] Ba *adds* do, T the, S2 3e; kerue] S2 bern, Tr1 brest; 246 greet] Ba *om.*; 247 han deceyued] Ba *trsp.*; 248 it] Tr1 *adds* is; knowen is] Ba *trsp.*, D3 knowen þis; 250 þat] Ba *om.*; 251 kowde] Tr1 cane; so] Ba full; 252 aght] Ba oft þat, S2 *adds* þat; 253 trustith] Ba *adds* 3e; þat] S2 *om.*; 254 kneewen] S2 *adds* full; 255 wiste] Tr1 *adds* wel; 257 And] Ba *adds* thus, Tr1 *adds* so; clerkes] S2 *adds* haue; they] Ba *om.*; 258 venym] D1 women, D3 womman; was] Tr1 þey were; 259 the] *H (*exc.* BaS2) thise, S2 thir; clerkes] Tr1 *adds* wel; often were] BaS2 *trsp.*; 260 This] *H (*exc.* S2) These; ne] *H (*exc.* BaS2) *add* thise, BaS2 nor this; 261 Weren nat they] *H were noon of thoo; 262 þat] BaD1D3FTTr1U as; 264 To] F The; forthy] Ba *om.*, B2

for, D1 for they, T11 *adds* weel; may] Ba ou3t, U *adds* not; 266 honur] *H worship; gete noon]
D3 *trsp.*; 268 feithful goode] T *trsp.*; 269 and2] *H or (Ba *adds* to); 273 is] S2 *om.*; oon for] Ba
one, B2D1D3FS2TU a wight, T11 folkes for; 275 any] T11 *om.*; 276 They2] S2 that; wonne] T11
conquerd; 278 been so freel] S2 haue swich merci; mowe hem nat] S2 may no man; 279 But]
Ba That; whoso] D1D3 who; lykith] Ba *adds* thay; 281 de] S2 of; 282 occupacioun] T11
opynyoun; 288 we] *H I; ne in] Ba nor; our] *H my; 289 and1] Ba *om.*; peyne] S2 part; may]
*H (*exc.* F) shold, F holde; 292 soone also] S2 *trsp.*; 293 dar] Ba may; 295 moot it] Ba mote,
B2D1D3FT *trsp.*; 297 womman] D1D3 *add* be, S2T11 *add* for; what] Ba *adds* so, S2 qwho, T11
adds euer; 300 been] S2 *adds* richt, T11 *adds* alle; þat] BaS2T11 *om.*; 301 pitee] S2 bountee; 303
the1] Ad2BaS2 *om.*, D1D3 *add* grete; 304 falsly] T11 *adds* þane; he] T11 his; hire] Ad2Ba *add*
trewe, T11 *om.*; 305 hath] Ad2BaS2 *om.*; 307 falsen] Ad2 dysceve, T faylen; þat] D1 and; from]
*H (*exc.* T11) *adds* his, T11 *adds* þayre; 308 kepte] Ba saist, S2 helped; him] S2T11 *om.*, greet] S2
adds a; name] T11 fame; 309 traitour] D1D3 duke; 310 man] *H wrecche; hath] Ba *om.*; 312 him
releeued] S2 *trsp.*; greeues] *H (*exc.* S2) smertys, S2 herts; 316 our] *H (*exc.* S2T11) my, S2 *om.*,
T11 þe; may men] BaB2FS2 *trsp.*; 317 whoso] D1D3 who; for] D1D3 *om.*; 319 repreef ne of] *H
repreuable; 320 herte of man … dede] *H mannes hert trouthe hath (T11 *adds* nowe) no (S2:
neuir) stede; 321 naght] T11 barreine; trouthe] T11 feyth; 322 womman] BaB2D1D3FT *add*
namely it, S2 *adds* namely þat, T11 *adds* namely; hir vice] *H (*exc.* T11) *om.*, T11 þis; nat
vnknowe] T11 ful wel knowe; 323 also] T11 *adds* þat; 324 vnto] B2F *add* a, T11 *adds* þeos; crabbid
wikkidnesse] Ba wicket crabbitness; 327 Yee strah] *H (*exc.* Ba) No fors; foorth] S2 *adds* and;
noon] B2FS2 no, T11 lytel; Yee … heuynesse] Ba be war women of thair fikilness; 328 Keepe]
T11 *adds* wel; what] S2T11 *add* so; 335 Folk enpoysone] *H *trsp.*; or] Ba nor, B2D1D3FS2T ne;
337 loue] S2 *om.*; and] Ba *om.*; 340 ay] BaS2 euir; 342 discreet] D1D3S2 swete; 343 inward] Ba
adds thay; owtward] Ba *adds* by, T11 *adds* þe; 344 to] *H vn to; 347 and] T11 *adds* ful; 348 and]
B2F *om.*; hir] Ad2S2 *om.*; wordes] T *adds* ful; 349 nat] S2T11 *add* this; 350 Folwyth nothyng]
*H Ne (Ba *om.*) folweth nat; 351 oure] U her; 352 mankynde] S2T11 *add* to; his] T11 hir; 353
nakid it of ioie] Ba maid him without ioy; 355 to ete] B2FTT11U tasten, BaD3S2 to taist; 357
feend] BaB2D1D3FTU deuel; she] B2FTU *add* ne; 358 swellyng] T herte; 359 in] D3 *adds* his;
360 hire] B2D1D3FS2TT11U *add* for; 361 Eeue] T *om.*; welthe] *H (*exc.* Ba) helthe; 362 him]
S2 *om.*; by the feend] D1D3 *om.*; right] Ba *om.*, D1D3 *add* even; 363 nat knowyng] S2 *trsp.*;
the] Ba þat; 364 was it] S2 *trsp.*; 365 we] *H I; seyn] S2 *adds* that; this] T11 *adds* þe; 366 ne] Ba
om., T11 she; 367 may] T11 cane; a] Ba *om.*; 368 if] Ba *om.*; þat] S2TT11U *om.*; hir] Ba hairt and;
369 conpassid] S2 purposit; it was] Ba sche it; 370 impressioun] BaS2 intencioun; 371 deceit]
Ba *adds* of hir; 374 for] BaD1D3S2TT11U *om.*; 375 she sholde] Ba *om.*; þat gilt] Ba his harme
sche suld, *H (*exc.* Ba) this (D1 his) harme; 376 be the] S2 hie; 377 hire] T11 Eves; 378 brak] T11
adds þe; 379 Touchynge which] *H And touching that; 380 dar] U *om.*; we] *H I; 381 as]
B2FS2TT11U *add* that; 382 þat] D1D3 *om.*; 383 This haue] *H *trsp.*; sires] T11 goode sir; we] *H
I; 385 holde] S2 *adds* women, T11 *om.*; 389 on] *H me; 391 feend] T11 worme; 392 So] *H (*exc.*
T11) And so; Adam] Ba *om.*; 396 mankynde] Ba man, T11 *adds* hool; weighte] S2 plicht; 397
doun] Ba *om.*; from] BaB2D1D3FTU *add* the; 400 fro] *H to; 401 knowe had] Ba *trsp.*; 402
of hem recorde] Ba record of þame; 406 Endowid] T11 Hir endowed; hire] *H (*exc.* T11) *add*
to; 407 hepid] D1D3 happy; 408 weyk] *H (*exc.* S2) leene, S2 low; 410 laude] *H preysing;
put] U *om.*; 411 we witen] *H I sey; þat] U the; 412 Next] Ba So blissit of; God] B2 *adds* is; the]
T11 *om.*; is] B2 *om.*, D3 itt; þat] D3 *om.*; 414 wight] *H man; 415 cessyng] S2 wanting; it]
BaB2D1D3FS2T that; 416 Of] Ba And of; it is to] BaB2FS2TT11 now, D1D3 *om.*; taken]

BaB2FT *add* ryght good, D1D3 *add* nowe right good, S2 *adds* here gud, Tr1 *adds* goode; heede]
T kepe; 417 Shee] Ba He; 418 Honureth] Tr1 Worshipeþe; 419 And] S2 *adds* all; alle] S2 *om.*;
420 And] Tr1 For; shal] Tr1 *adds* offt; 421 gemme] *H *adds* o (Ba of); 422 Of] Ba That of;
blood] Tr1 *adds* heere; 423 ne] D1D3T *om.*; we] *H (*exc.* Ba) I; Thy ... foryete] Ba Thow luver
trew thow madin margiret; 424 O] *H thou; 427 of God] Ba of holy god, Tr1 þou goode; holy]
Ba thow; 428 vndirstondith] Ba *adds* this; we] *H (*exc.* Tr1) I (Ba *adds* only), Tr1 þat I; 430
right] Ba S2 *om.*; wel] Ba *om.*; nat] BaB2D1D3FS2T neuer; our] *H (*exc.* Ba) my, Ba to; 431
ay] *H euer; we] BaB2 *om.*, D1D3S2TTr1 I; 432 euere] D1D3 *add* I; but] S2 *om.*; 434 dryue]
Tr1 *om.*; of] B2D1D3FS2T *add* my; remembrance] Tr1 *adds* dryve; we nat] *H I ne; 435 also]
S2 *om.*; can yee] T *trsp.*; 441 him forsooken] B2D1D3FT *trsp.*; 444 for thus holy writ] Tr1 hooly
writte þus; 445 hardily] S2 redely; 446 it] *H I; 447 al the] *H (*exc.* S2) stable, S2 allway; 455
and] D1D3 *om.*; 457 noble] *H digne; worthy] *H so (Tr1 *om.*) noble; in] Tr1 of; 458 shee may]
*H he (S2 sche; Ba *adds* in fer) wol; nat] S2 *om.*; in feere] Ba *om.*; 459 Shee] *H He; vice] S2
om.; out] T *om.*; of] BaB2D1FTTr1 *add* his, S2 *adds* hir; 460 She1] *H He; she2] *H he;
leueth] S2 put; 463 thus we wolen] *H wol we (Ba I; Tr1 yee) thus; 464 yow commaunde] S2
trsp., Tr1 wol comande; 466 tho] *H thise fals (F *om.*); vntreewe] B2D1D3FS2TTr1 *om.*; 469
þat] D1D3 *add* here after; ne] D1D3S2 *om.*; come] Tr1 retourne; 471 Looke] S2Tr1 *add* that;
472 th'eir] BaD1D3 *om.*; 475 grace] S2 God; 476 MCCCC] *H a thousand and (D1D3 *om.*)
foure hondred (BaS2Tr1 hundrith; Tr1 *adds* yeres); and] Ba *adds* the, D1D3 the

LEARN TO DIE

Eight copies exist beyond H2: B, C, D, Ha, L, R, S, Y. D is also an autograph, Hoccleve's
'Durham' manuscript of the *Series* (which integrates the poem). D is used as copy text in this
edition from line 673, as H2 lacks the final leaves. BLY and CR comprise subgroups; S is an
early, independent, superior witness (lacks stanzas 1–3). (See further Ellis 2001: 276–7; Burrow
1999: x–xvii, xxii–xxv.)

2 konne] Ha *adds* and knowe, BCR knowe; 3 vniuersel] Ha *adds* kynge; 4 been] Ha *adds*
coueryde and; hid] L *om.*; alle] Ha *om.*; 6 al seest] Ha *trsp.*, Y seest; 8 the] Ha *om.*; 9 thow to]
Ha vn to; I] Ha *adds* the; 13 Sotile] Ha And sotylle; materes] *H *adds* right; 14 I feruently] CR
trsp.; desire] *H (*exc.* D) *adds* to; 15 sauoure] Ha *adds* thou; to] BCDHaL so; 16 and] Ha what;
teche] BLY tell; 18 yifte] Ha *adds* child þu; thow] Ha *om.*; 22 herkne] Ha *adds* well; 23 how]
Ha *adds* to; lerne] *H (*exc.* D) *add* to; die] Ha *adds* the; 24 a] Ha euery; lyue] Ha dye; 25 how]
S *adds* þat; a man] Ha pepulle; 26 me] Ha *adds* they; 27 how] Ha *adds* þat; with] B *om.*; an]
HaR *om.*; herte] Ha *adds* ryght; 28 That] R *om.*; loue me shal] BR me love shall, Ha shal loue
me trewly; 32 thyng] Ha happe; can] C can can; 33 this fayn] BCLRSY herof; heere] CR lere;
35 hauyng] B thyng; 37 Sone] Ha Childe; 38 swetnesse] *H (*exc.* D) rychesse; 39 rede] Ha *adds*
that; 41 ne] HaR *add* so; worthy] Ha *adds* for; 42 Preferred] Ha *adds* of; alle] Ha sothely; þat]
Ha *om.*; 45 Þat] Ha *om.*; ay heer] Ha euer, BCLRY ay, S *om.*; he] *H (*exc.* D) *adds* fulle; 46 at
al] Ha surely; 47 may] B *adds* þe; 48 But] Ha Ryght; þat] Ha þer be; 49 It ... may been] Ha
Whoo dyethe welle þe grace of god hathe hee; God] BCRSY *add* þe; 50 To] Ha *om.*; is to haue]
Ha and remembyr; 52 whan] S *om.*; deeth] C *om.*; cacche] Ha take; hir] CHaLRSY his; 54 And
hire] Ha Hym for, BCLRSY And him; and2] Ha *adds* to; 56 therof is] CDHaRSY *trsp.*, L is;
glad] Ha ryght gladde, L glad þerof; 57 oon] *H (*exc.* D) *om.*; 58 Þat] Ha *om.*; 60 thoght] C
though, Ha thynge; of] L *om.*; 63 they wolde] CHaR *trsp.*; in] R by; 64 mochil of hir tyme]

194 TEXTUAL VARIANTS

*H (*exc.* D) of her (B þer) tyme muche; 65 and] Ha *om.*; forthy] Ha for whye; whan] B *om.*;
67 And shal] Ha yett; hem] Ha *adds* he; 68 For shee] Ha Be cause; 72 thee] Ha *om.*; hire] Ha
adds hand þe, S *adds* han, BCLY *add* haue; led] R *om.*; away] R *adds* haue ledde; 74 right] *H
ful; 75 thow] L *om.*; wrappid were] S *trsp.*; 77 thow thee] S *trsp.*; 78 More to thee] Ha [G]rett,
BCLRSY Gretter; shal] CHaR *add* be to the, BLSY *add* to þe be; 83 To ... for to] Ha If thou
loue god þe bettyr shalt þu; 84 The misterie] Ha Mysteryes; I shal] CR *trsp.*; 85 inward] *H
(*exc.* Ha) now, Ha and see; and] CR *add* the; 87 good] BCLSY greet; 94 helthe] BCLRSY hele;
98 greet] R *om.*; 100 helle] Ha *adds* thus; 101 O] C R *om.*; 103 O] C R *om.*; 104 Nad I] CR That
I nade (C *adds* nat); 105 with2] BCLRS *om.*; 106 myn ende comth] *H (*exc.* D) negheth myn
ende; 109 an herte] Ha suche hartys; wont] B wounde; 110 And] Ha *adds* hathe be; 113 Litil]
Ha *adds* hadde; wende I] Ha *trsp.*; 117 Thyn hour] BDHaLSY Thy comynge vn to me, CR Thy
comyng; vnto me ful] BLY stole and me bounde, DHaS *om.*, CR to me; vncerteyn] BLY *om.*;
120 me with thee drawest] Ha draweste me forthe with þe; yren] Y þer; 121 wont is] C R *trsp.*,
Y wont it is; 124 wolde] Ha *adds* ryght; 125 place] BCHaRSY *add* now; for] R *om.*; 127 syde]
Ha *adds* fulle, BCLRSY *add* now full; 128 But] Ha *om.*; help] C *adds* there; is] BLRSY *add* þer;
129 sownyng] R comyng; 131 Thow die] Ha *trsp.*; Resoun noon] Ha noo resone; 132 ne noon
othir] Ha catell nee, BCLRSY catel nouþer; 133 may thee] BCHaLRS *trsp.*; dethes duresse] CR
duresse; 146 þat] Ha *om.*; nat] S *adds* þou; 150 wyse] *H (*exc.* Ha) *add* he; vnto] *H *om.*; 155
fauorable is] Ha *trsp.*; no] H2 *om.*; maner] B Ha *add* of; 156 hirself] Ha pepulle; 157 of greeth]
BCHaLRSY greet of, D of greet; 158 ne] Ha *om.*; and] B ne, R nor; yonge] Ha *adds* and
myddyle age; hath] Ha *adds* sche; 159 ryche] Ha *adds* also; eek] Ha *om.*; 160 right] CR *om.*; 161
chek is] R *trsp.* 162 shee] B he; 163 oon also] *H an (B one; Ha *om.*) othir eek; 164 til] B to þat,
Ha to the tyme þat, LSY *add* þat; right] *H (*exc.* D) *om.*; 165 been] *H (*exc.* D) stonde; 168
And] BC sethen, Ha Sythe, LRSY siþen; heerbeforn] BLY beforn; 169 answeryng] *H (*exc.* D)
and seyde; 174 Worthy] *H (*exc.* D) *add* to; þat] S *adds* þat; 175 ny] *H (*exc.* D) *add* þat; 177
Of] R Which of; 183 nat] Ha *adds* for; hennes] C *om.*; 185 with] CHaR *om.*; 187 helthe] B hele;
I dide] Ha *trsp.*; 195 nat] Ha nothynge, L no; 203 shee] BHa he; 205 way] *H preef; fownde is]
Ha *trsp.*; of] Ha by; his] BLY þis; 206 can it] Ha *trsp.*, BLY can; 208 with] *H by; 209 swich]
*H (*exc.* D) whiche; and] *H (*exc.* D) *om.*; 210] ther] BCLY ne, R *om.*; 212 foorthwith redily]
D þat continuelly; 214 the way sy] R seeth verrily; 216 Anoonrightes] D Continuelly; 218 my]
Y *om.*; 220 Which] BCLRSY by, H2 with, Ha þat; blowe away] D vp reisith; 222 as] BHa *om.*;
223 þat] Ha whiche only; 225 now] *H (*exc.* D) al; 230 beautee hadde] *H (*exc.* D) *trsp.*; 231
yeeres] *H dayes; 236 droof I] Ha *trsp.*; leet] *H (*exc.* D) *add* it; 241 hir precioustee] Ha what
goddis plesure shuld bee; 244 ouerblynd was] BCLRSY *trsp.*, Ha was euer more blynde; 245
wo] Ha *adds* and sorowe; 246 now] Ha *adds* ryght; 247 And] Ha *adds* semblablye; as þat] B
trsp., Ha as; 249 me makith] Ha makythe me ful; 253 þat1] *H the; 256 alle] Ha *adds* manere;
eerthely] CR other; 258 and] B but; 259 soule] Ha *adds* for; 260 angwissh] CR wo; and] Ha
adds for; 262 or] HaR ne; 266 care] Ha *adds* yett; it] Ha I; 267 my] C *om.*; 272 and] BCLRSY
þat; 273 That] Ha I, BCRSY *add* I; helthe] S *om.*; 276 me] Ha *adds* þe fowle, CR *add* many,
BLSY *add* many foule; 277 Wondirly] *H (*exc.* D) Wondyrful; 279 I leet] D *trsp.*; dayes] Ha
adds soo; 280 nat was] Ha *trsp.*; scourgid] *H beten; with] Ha *adds* þe; 286 why for] Ha R *trsp.*;
287 vndirstande] Ha *adds* for; 292 vnruly] Ha vnwarely; 295 your2] *H (*exc.* D) *om.*; 297 God]
C good; your dayes] *H (*exc.* D) youthe, D your youthe; 298 me] B be; 301 whil] D *adds* it;
your] D *om.*; 304 in] Ha the; þat] C D R *om.*; 307 fresshnesse] Ha *adds* helthe; 310 had I] Ha
trsp.; ful] *H ryght; 311 conseillid] BCHaLRS *add* me; 314 Entre] R There entre; 315 had I] Ha

trsp.; 316 dych] L *om.*; 318 than] BLY þat; had thus] D thus had it, *H (*exc.* D) *trsp.*; 319 han] *H (*exc.* D) to haue; 320 han] *H (*exc.* D) to haue; 322 lent to me] *H (*exc.* Ha) grantid me (LY *adds* for), Ha me grauntyde for; 323 To] C *adds* the; 328 it] BHaLSY *add* to, CR to; 332 seye and] *H to thee; 335 which] D þat; is] BLY *om.*; 336 this] *H it; 342 and] B *adds* so; 345 so] R sore; 346 is goon] CRS *trsp.*; 347 cleene] CR nye; 348 mynde] *H (*exc.* D) harte; ther] CR *om.*; 349 than] Ha to; serche] BHaRSY seche, CL such; deeth] BCLRSY *add* to; 350 I] BCLY *om.*; theraftir] BLY *add* I; looke] CR *add* I; gape] D cape; 352 ful] Ha so; 356 Whyles] CR *add* that; tyme] Ha *adds* and seson; 357 had] BY *om.*; 359 Whethir] Ha *adds* þat; or] Ha other; 362 I] Ha *adds* haue, CR Haue; 363 helthe] CR *adds* werreyed; haue I] Ha *trsp.*; werreied] CR *om.*; 364 it] Ha *adds* I; haue] CR *om.*; purueied] CR *add* haue I; 366 correccioun] R contricioun; 371 now] *H al; 373 whethir] Ha *adds* þat; 375 is it] Ha *trsp.*; 376 and1] Ha *om.*; him] D me; fostre] B suffir, Ha noryshe; 377 ny arn] BHaLSY all be, CR ben, D all arn; slipt] CR spilte; 378 yeer] BCLRSY wintir; away] C *om.*; been] Ha ys; 379 haue I] BDLHa *trsp.*; 380 is it] CHaLRY *trsp.*; 384 As þat] B And as; þat ... oghte] Ha hys seruaunde in word werke wyll and thought; haue] C *om.*; or] BCLS and; 387 and] *H (*exc.* D) *adds* thi; 389 Þat] *H (*exc.* D) What; 393 day more] *H hour gretter; ioie] Ha *adds* myrthe; 399 folyly] D synfully; this beforn] Ha *trsp.*; 408 help] CR helthe; 410 to] *H (exc. D) vnto; 412 tyme] Ha seson; fynde cowde I] *H (*exc.* D) cowde I fynde; 420 he] Y 3e; 430 seiden] Ha *adds* to thys; yeuen] BCLRSY to 3eue; 431 of] DLRSY *om.*; 434 Fynde] Ha That fynde; can I] Ha *trsp.*; ne] BCLRSY *add* no; 435 fadir] CR god; 438 That] Ha thowe; I] BLY *om.*; greetly haue] Ha *trsp.*; 439 remembrith] Ha *adds* nowe; 445 good] *H (*exc.* D) my; lord2] *H (*exc.* D) god; 446 is] CR were; 447 satisfaccion] Ha *adds* only; 448 it] Ha *adds* now; this] *H (*exc.* D) *add* grete; 449 leeste] C *adds* þe, Ha *om.*; crommes] *H (*exc.* D) *add* which; ther] Ha onlye, BCLRSY *om.*; 451 wolden] Ha myght I; right] D ful; 452 noon fynde I] Ha I fynde them, BCLRSY nowe finde I folke; 453 Þat] CR *add* me ne; me] Ha *adds* nott, CR *om.*; 456 eek] Ha *om.*; yee alle] Ha *trsp.*; 457 And] Ha *om.*; vigour] Ha strengthe present; 458 han eek tyme] D tyme han eek, BCLRSY time haue eke; be ny] Ha vnto, R go to, BCLSY to; 459 Into] Ha *adds* the; 460 Tresor celestial] Ha Tresours of hevene; 468 thy2] BLY *om.*; 470 by] C *adds* þe; 472 þat] C then; I hccraftir] *H *trsp.*; 473 may] CR me; 478 haan] *H (*exc.* D) to haue; verray contricioun] B *trsp.*; 479 hele] CR helth; 480 lyf] BCLRSY self; 483 heuenes blisse] *H the (D *adds* mighten) þe blysse of hevene; mighten] D *om.*; thee byreue] *H reue; 484 is it] CR is, DS *trsp.*; 485 þat thow] BLY *trsp.*, CHa thow; 487 Sholdest departe] *H (*exc.* D) *trsp.*; 489 As ... thynke] Ha Doo thy parte or þu come to the brynke; seyn] BL *add* and; 492 hadde] BLY *om.*; 493 X yeer] CR Than; 494 yeer] CR here; 498 thow] CR than; 499 Do to] B *trsp.*; 500 Þat] *H (*exc.* D) Which; 501 O] CR *om.*; 502 me] BCHaLRS *add* now; 503 That] S *adds* I; I] S *om.*; 505 cleene is] C clene, Ha *trsp.*; 506 am I] BCHaLR *trsp.*; I can] BCLR *trsp.*; 507 the] Ha me; 509 am] RS *add* and; in] BLY *add* þe; 510 wight] B frende, Ha mane; 511 or] R nor; 513 leuen me] *H (*exc.* Ha) *trsp.*, Ha me they leven; 515 with] Ha *adds* demure; cheere] Ha *adds* and; 516 Seide] CR *add* now; were] BHaLSY *add* now; 517 it hadde] B it, Ha *trsp.*; experience] B *adds* had; 518 I may] B I may yeve, CR *om.*; 519 stiryng] CHaR sterne; 520 auaille] D profyten; but] B *adds* a; 523 Yen they] B Then they, C Than thei, R *trsp.*; 524 Eres] *H And eres haue (Ha *om.*); may nat with hem] *H (*exc.* Ha) may nat, Ha yett þei wolle not; 525 weene] B truste; 526 vndisposid] B *adds* not; 527 han tho wrecches right] BCLRSY tho (C the) wrecches haue, D ne haan tho wrecches, Ha suche wrecchis þei haue; 528 þat] *H which; folwe] CR falle; 529 deemen] *H (*exc.* D) *adds* þei; a] BLY any; 530 by thee] S *om.*; 531 it] CR *om.*; 533 Whan] Ha Than; 535 in]

BCLRSY of; feeblesse] Ha dystresse, BCLRSY syknesse; 537 seek] CR *om.*; in thy bed now] Ha nowe in thy bedde, CR in thy bedde sike, Y in bede now; 539 For] Ha Dowtles; 540 bodyes] Ha menys; 546 die] Ha *adds* thus; 548 Tho] BLY To; 549 Nat list] Ha *trsp.*, BLY No list; hire peynes putte] Ha put here peynes; 552 yeuen] *H (*exc.* D) sett; 553 th'ymage thus] CR *trsp.*; 554 Forthy] Ha Forwhy; 555 Whan] C *adds* thei in, HaR And; hem shal] Ha *trsp.*; 557 shal vexe] BCHaRSY *trsp.*; 558 thereof] CR they shull; 559 For] Ha Because þat; 562 wole] Ha with; 563 stownde] B kynde; 564 Nat] C But, L No; auaille] C amende; 567 neuere had] R *trsp.*; 570 is so dryue] *H gooth so (C to) faste; 573 for] Ha *adds* to; of] Ha the; lyf] CR luste; 574 coueiten] CR couert; to disseuere] Ha wolle they nevyre; 575 on hem stelith] BL steleth on þem; hir] BHaLY his; 583 list to] D lyke; now] BLY not; 586 Eerthely] Ha To erthely, BLY Off erthly; 587 an herte] B a man; 588 folk] D men, Ha pepull; into] B *om.*; tho perils] BLY the (B they) periles, CR perels to; sterte] B se none can; 591 now] CR *om.*; 597 That] D *adds* nat; oonly] Ha *adds* for to, BCLRS *add* to; shal it] D *trsp.*; 598 But deeth eek as] *H (*exc.* DHa) But deeth is ende eke, Ha Dethe ys only; ende] CLRSY *om.*; 599 ay þat] BHaSY *trsp.*, CR that euer; 600 desire] Ha *adds* evyre; 603 Euery] BLY Have euery; haue] BCHaRSY *om.*; me] B men; 610 vpon me] *H (*exc.* D) on me well; 616 Wakyng] Ha And wakynge; 620 assaille and vexe] BCLRSY vexe and assaile (CR assay), Ha wex on hym and assayle; 621 good lyuere] *H rightwys (CR rightfull) man; 622 Howso] *H (*exc.* D) Or how (Ha *adds* þat); gooth vnto] *H shal go to; 625 to] CR and; 627 And led by citeins] BCLRSY And ledde by citezeins, Ha By the noble cytesyns; the hy] CR that; 628 of1] D to; the court] CR that contree; 630 Into] C *adds* the; blisse] Ha *adds* only; 632 become] Ha *adds* and; it] C I; 633 in] CR *om.*; 634 receyue it] CR *trsp.*; 635 it] B I; haue] *H (*exc.* D) fynde; 638 Wherfore] BLY Therfore; 640 in] *H (*exc.* D) *adds* full; habundance] *H (*exc.* D) foysone; 641 auaillith] *H (*exc.* D) *adds* it; 642 weepe and conpleyne and] *H (*exc.* D) to wepe conpleyne, D conpleyne weepe and; crie] CR *om.*; 647 al] CR *om.*; 648 God] CR *om.*; 649 of] L *adds* my; 652 othir] Ha *adds* wey; 654 See how] Ha Take heed; now] Ha se howe; 655 dim my look] D my look ful dym; as1] D *om.*; 660 elles] BCHaLSY other, R otherwise; 662 breeth] *H (*exc.* D) wynde; the] BCR my; 664 I now see] CR see I now; 665 and] Ha of hyer, BCLRSY *add* her; 670 Now of confort] Ha Of comforte nowe; haue I] *H (*exc.* D) *trsp.*; 671 feendes] H2 freendes; 677 therof] CR *om.*; 678 viserly] CR grisly; 679 Me putte] Ha *trsp.*; thoghtful] Ha dowtful; dreedes] C *om.*, R drede; 680 iuge] BLY *add* rightwise; 681 weyest] CR *add* me; 683 by] CR *add* hem; of] CR *om.*; or2] Ha to; 685 shee] CR eke; 688 thurgh] *H for; 690 freendes and felawes] B felows and frendes; 692 streight] CR right; as2] CHaL *add* a; 693 offenses] C *adds* and; ther] Ha *adds* for; 694 maad haue Y] CR I haue made; 704 in] BLY on; and] BLY *add* on; 708 haue] BCLRSY *add* ye; on] B of, C in; our] CS your; 709 namely] Ha *adds* nowe; 711 the] Ha *adds* fayre; 714 as1] BCHaLY *om.*; a] BLY any; 715 youre] Ha *adds* grete; 716 eek of othir] *H other folkys; 722 rewarded been] C *trsp.*; 726 Worldly] Ha The worldly; as1] Ha *om.*; 732 of] CR *add* the; 735 han] Ha suffryne; 736 kyndes of] Ha sowres troble and; 738 woful sent is] D *om.*, Ha the cause ys oure offence; 751 wite] B *om.*; Y can vnnethe] BCLRSY vnnethe (B *adds* wite) I can; in] CR no; soothfastnesse] Ha stedefastnes; 756 this] LY my; 757 Neuere] Ha *om.*; deeth] Ha *adds* nevyre; 758 lyf] *H selfe; do now] BCLSY *trsp.*; 760 picchid] *H ficchid (Ha fixede); 764 Dwellynge] *H No dwellynge; haue espyd and] CR haue I espied ne (C: me), Ha can preyve ne; see] CR *om.*; 765 Han we noon] BCLRSY Haue (CRS Han) we here, Ha That we haue; 767 nat may] *H *trsp.*; but] Ha *adds* hit; permanable] CR perdurable; 768 lord God] B *trsp.*; merciable] BCHaLSY myserable; 769 axe] CR *add* and; 770 al] BLY *om.*, Ha ful; 773 to] BCHaLY *om.*; wole Y] Ha *trsp.*; dispose] BLY purpose; 778 Now wole Y voide] *H O (Ha *om.*) fy vpon the; 779 materas] C *om.*; 782 al] *H *om.*; folie] *H *add* all; 783 eek fy] CR *trsp.*; 790 thanne] *H *om.*; certes] *H certeinly full; 800 souffre] *H let; 802 thee] Ha *adds* soo; the] Ha *om.*; 805 grante] BHaLSY *add* now (Ha nowe vnto); 808 place] Ha *adds* only; 809 heere] CHaR *om.*; 810 it] CR *om.*; þat] Y *om.*; 811 place] Ha *om.*; 813 how] BLY *om.*; 820 thurgh] Y *adds* a; 821 myndes] Ha *adds* my; yen] CR thenne; shit] C sette; 822 perils] C *adds* I; am] L *adds* I; 824 to] *H *om.*; it is greet wit] Ha thou shalt it fynde grete profytt; 825 yong art] Ha *trsp.*; 828 nat maist] CHaR *trsp.*; for thee noon] Ha none for þe; 831 þat nat] Ha *trsp.*; 832 putte eek] C eke, Ha *trsp.*; twixt] *H by twyxt; 833 neede is] R *trsp.*; adrad] Ha *adds* þat; 835 trust and hope of] CR hope and; 837 Now] Ha Be; restfullere] Ha *adds* nowe; be] Ha *om.*; 840 is] BHaLY *add* þe; dreede of God] CR to drede godde; 842 is it] HaR *trsp.*, BLY is; 845 and1] CR *om.*; 849 be] Ha *adds* alle; 850 Remembre] Ha *adds* welle; on] Ha *om.*; 852 Or] Ha *adds* the; 853 þat] Ha the; 854 wilt] CHaRS shalt; they] CR the; thee] CR *om.*; 857 spirit] Ha soul; 858 Retourne] CR *add* to; god] B *om.*, Ha *adds* chefely; al] B *adds* to god; 859 vnto] CR *om.*; 860 For he] Ha That lord; to] CRY vnto; 861 Wherthurgh] CR By (C *adds* þe) which; saued] BHaLSY *add* this, CR *add* it; 862 fewe] BL wele, Ha *adds* þer; ere] CR here; 864 konne of the] BLY conne of, Ha wolle of; 867 heuene] Ha *adds* þe; ay shal] *H *trsp.*; 868 at al] CR *om.*; 872 close and shitte] Ha shytt and close; 873 nat keepe] CHaR *trsp.*; in hir conceit] Ha only for to; and] CR ne; 876 for] B *adds* þi, Ha because, SY *add* þat; ne] *H *om.*; 877 how] *H *add* men; 878 it] Ha *adds* lye and; 880 That deeth] Ha *om.*; waar] Ha *adds* dethe; 885 thy wit] BLY þi will, Ha thou wolte; therto] BHaLSY to it; 892 Thee] B *om.*; leid been] CR be leide; 893 What] Ha *om.*; and] Ha *adds* many, Y a; 894 alle tho] Ha abowte allsoo; 897 with2] CRY *om.*; 898 to] CR vnto; 899 can see] BHaSY *trsp.*, L so can; 902 conseil] CR conceite; 905 Weel thee dispose] Ha Dyspose the welle; reedy] Ha *adds* thou; 907 þat] Ha *om.*; waar] BLY raft; no] Ha *adds* trewe; 914 it] R *om.*; 916 so] CR *om.*; 917 þat] Ha whiche

BIBLIOGRAPHY

❧

I. Printed Primary Sources

Barr, Helen, ed. 1993. *The Piers Plowman Tradition: A Critical Edition of Pierce the Ploughman's Crede, Richard the Redeless, Mum and the Sothsegger, and the Crowned King*. London: Everyman's Library.

Boethius. 1927. *Boethius: De Consolatione Philosophiae*. Edited by Mark Science. Translated by John Walton. London: Oxford University Press.

Chaucer, Geoffrey. 1987. *Riverside Chaucer*. Edited by Larry Benson. Oxford: Oxford University Press.

———. 2019. *The Norton Chaucer*. Edited by David Lawton. New York: WW Norton.

de Lorris, Guillaume, and Jean de Meun. 1965–1975. *Le Roman de la Rose*. Edited by Félix Lecoy. 3 vols. Classiques français du Moyen Âge, 92, 95, 98. Paris: Champion.

de Pizan, Christine. 1932. *Lavision-Christine*. Edited by Sister Mary Louis Towner. Washington, D.C.: Catholic University of America.

———. 1999. *Epistre Othea*. Edited by Gabriella Parussa. Geneva: Librarie Droz.

———. 2012. *The Vision of Christine de Pizan*. Translated by Glenda McLeod and Charity Cannon Willard. Cambridge: D.S. Brewer.

Deguileville, Guillaume. 1895. *Le Pèlerinage de l'Âme*. Edited by J.J. Stürzinger. London: Nichols and Sons.

———. 1897. *Le Pèlerinage Jhesucrist*. Edited by J.J. Stürzinger. London: Nichols and Sons.

Deschamps, Eustace. 1878–1903. *Œuvres complètes de Eustache Deschamps*. Edited by Auguste Queux de Saint-Hilaire and Gaston Raynaud. 11 vols. Paris: Firmin Didot.

Doyle, A.I., ed. 1987. *The Vernon Manuscript: A Facsimile*. Cambridge: D.S. Brewer.

Eusebius. 1999. *Werke 2.2 Die Kirchengeschichte*. Edited by Eduard Schwartz and Theodor Mommsen. Berlin: Akademie Verlag.

Fenster, Thelma S., and Mary Carpenter Erler, eds. 1990. *Poems of Cupid, God of Love*. Leiden: Brill.

Frier, Bruce W., ed. 2016. *The Codex of Justinian: a new annotated translation, with parallel Latin and Greek text, based on a translation by Justice Fred H. Blume*. Cambridge: Cambridge University Press.

Fulgentius. 1968. *Sancti Fulgentii Episcopi Ruspensis Opera*. Edited by J. Fraipont. Corpus Christianorum Series Latina 91A. Turnhout: Brepols.

Gregory the Great. 1990. *Forty Gospel Homilies*. Translated by Dom Hurst. Kalamazoo, MI: Cistercian Publications.

Herrtage, Sidney J.H. 1879. *The Early English Versions of the Gesta Romanorum*. London: Oxford University Press for the Early English Text Society.

Hoccleve, Thomas. 1796. *Poems by Thomas Hoccleve, Never before Printed*. Edited by George Mason. London: C. Roworth for Leigh and Sotheby.

———. 1965. *The Formulary of Thomas Hoccleve*. Edited by E.J.Y. Bentley. Atlanta, GA: Emory University.

———. 1970. *Hoccleve's Works: The Minor Poems*. Edited by Frederick J. Furnivall and I. Gollancz (1892; 1925). Rev. ed. J. Mitchell and A.I. Doyle. Early English Text Society Extra Series 61 & 73. London: Oxford University Press for the Early English Text Society.

———. 1981. *Selections from Hoccleve*. Edited by M.C. Seymour. Oxford: Clarendon Press.

———. 1982. *Selected Poems*. Edited by Bernard O'Donoghue. Manchester: Fyfield Books.

———. 1999. *The Regiment of Princes*. Edited by Charles R. Blyth. TEAMS Middle English Texts Series. Kalamazoo, MI: Medieval Institute Publications.

———. 1999. *Thomas Hoccleve's Complaint and Dialogue*. Edited by John Burrow. Early English Text Society Original Series 313. Oxford: Oxford University Press for the Early English Text Society.

———. 2001. *'My Compleinte' and Other Poems*. Edited by Roger Ellis. Exeter Medieval Texts and Studies. Exeter: Exeter University Press.

———. 2002. *A Facsimile of the Autograph Verse Manuscripts: Henry E. Huntington Library, San Marino (California), MSS HM III and HM 744; University Library, Durham (Library) MS Cosin V.III.9*. Edited by John Burrow and A.I. Doyle. Early English Text Society Second Series 19. Oxford: Oxford University Press for the Early English Text Society.

Langland, William. 1987. *The Vision of Piers Plowman: A Complete Edition of the B-Text*. Edited by A.V.C. Schmidt. London: Everyman's Library.

———. 2008. *Piers Plowman: A New Annotated Edition of the C-Text*. Edited by Derek Pearsall. Exeter Medieval Texts and Studies. Exeter: Exeter University Press.

Lydgate, John. 2019. *John Lydgate's Dance of Death and Related Works*. Edited by Megan L. Cook and Elizaveta Strakhov. Kalamazoo, MI: Medieval Institute Publications.

Seuse, Heinrich (Suso, Henry). 1977. *Horologium Sapientiae*. Edited by O.P. Freiburg and Piüs Kunzle. Freiburg: Universitätsverlag Freiburg Schweiz.

———. 1994. *Wisdom's Watch upon the Hours*. Translated by Edmund Colledge. Washington, D.C.: Catholic University of America Press.

Skeat, Walter W., ed. 1897. *Chaucerian and Other Pieces*. Vol. 7. Works of Geoffrey Chaucer. Oxford: Clarendon Press.

II. Secondary Sources

Adams, Jenny. 2006. *Power Play: The Literature and Politics of Chess in the Late Middle Ages*. Philadelphia: University of Pennsylvania Press.

Appleford, Amy. 2008. 'The Dance of Death in London: John Carpenter, John Lydgate, and the *Dance of Poulys*.' *Journal of Medieval and Early Modern Studies* 38 (2): 285–314.

————. 2015. *Learning to Die in London: 1380–1450*. Philadelphia: University of Pennsylvania Press.

Atkinson, Laurie. 2019. '"And to that ende, here is remembrance": Registers of Petition in Thomas Hoccleve's Devotional and Begging Poetry.' *Medium Ævum* 88 (2): 301–28.

Benson, C. David. 1975. 'Prudence, Othea and Lydgate's Death of Hector.' *The American Benedictine Review* 26: 115–23.

Blumenfeld-Kosinski, Renate. 2006. 'Jean Gerson and the Debate on the *Romance of the Rose*.' In *A Companion to Jean Gerson*, edited by Brian Patrick McGuire, 317–56. Leiden: Brill.

Blurton, Heather, and Hannah Johnson. 2015. 'Reading the *Prioress's Tale* in the Fifteenth Century: Lydgate, Hoccleve, and Marian Devotion.' *Chaucer Review* 50: 134–58.

Bowers, John. 1989. 'Hoccleve's Huntington Holographs: The First "Collected Poems" in English.' *Fifteenth-Century Studies* 15: 27–51.

————. 2002. 'Thomas Hoccleve and the Politics of Tradition.' *Chaucer Review* 36: 352–69.

Brandmüller, Walter. 1991. *Das Konzil von Konstanz, 1414–1418*. 2 vols. Paderborn: Schöningh.

Brown, A.L. 1971. 'The Privy Seal Clerks in the Early Fifteenth Century.' In *The Study of Medieval Records: Essays in Honor of Kathleen Major*, edited by D.A. Bullough and R.L. Storey, 253–79. Oxford: Clarendon Press.

Brown, Peter. 2014. 'Hoccleve in Canterbury.' In *New Directions in Medieval Manuscript Studies and Reading Practices: Essays in Honor of Derek Pearsall*, edited by Kerby-Fulton Kathryn et al., 406–24. Notre Dame, IN: University of Notre Dame Press.

Bryan, Jennifer E. 2002. 'Hoccleve, the Virgin, and the Politics of Complaint.' *PMLA* 117 (5): 1172–87.

Burrow, John. 1994. *Thomas Hoccleve*. Authors of the Middle Ages. Aldershot: Variorum.

————. 1997. 'Hoccleve and the Middle French Poets.' In *The Long Fifteenth Century: Essays for Douglas Gray*, edited by Helen Cooper and Sally Mapstone, 35–49. Oxford: Clarendon Press.

————. 2002. 'Hoccleve's Questions: Intonation and Punctuation.' *Notes and Queries* 49 (2): 184–88.

————. 2013. 'Intonation and Punctuation in the Hoccleve Holographs.' *Notes and Queries* 60 (1): 19–22.

Catto, Jeremy. 1993. 'Religious Change under Henry V.' In *Henry V: The Practice of Kingship*, edited by G.L. Harriss, 97–115. Stroud: Alan Sutton Publishing.

Cerquiglini, Jacqueline. 1980. 'Le clerc et l'écriture: Le *voir dit* de Guillaume de Machaut et la définition du *dit*.' In *Literatur in Der Gesellschaft des Spätmittelalters*, edited by Hans Ulrich Gumbrecht, 151–68. Heidelberg: C. Winter.

Cole, Andrew. 2008. *Literature and Heresy in the Age of Chaucer*. Cambridge Studies in Medieval Literature 71. Cambridge: Cambridge University Press.

Connolly, Margaret, and Raluca Radulescu, eds. 2018. *Editing and Interpretation of Middle English Texts*. Turnhout: Brepols.

Cré, Marleen. 2018. 'Hoccleve the Poet: A Miniature.' In Vol. 14 *The Medieval Translator*, edited by Catherine Batt and René Tixier, 411–25. Turnhout: Brepols.

Downes, Stephanie. 2009. 'A "French booke called the Pistill of Othea": Christine de Pizan's French in England.' In *Language and Culture in Medieval Britain: The French of England c. 1100–1500*, edited by Jocelyn Wogan-Browne et al., 457–68. York: York Medieval Press.

Doyle, A.I., and M.B. Parkes. 1979. 'Paleographical Introduction.' In *The Canterbury Tales: A Facsimile and Transcription of the Hengwrt Manuscript with Variants from the Ellesmere Manuscript*, edited by Paul A. Ruggiers, xix–xlix. Norman: University of Oklahoma Press.

———. 1991. 'The Production of Copies of the *Canterbury Tales* and the *Confessio Amantis* in the Early Fifteenth Century.' In *Scribes, Scripts, and Readers: Studies in the Communication, Presentation, and Dissemination of Medieval Texts*, edited by M.B. Parkes, 201–48. London: Hambledon Press.

Epstein, Robert. 2002. 'Literal Opposition: Deconstruction, History, and Lancaster.' *Texas Studies in Literature and Language* 44 (1): 16–33.

Farmer, David. 2011. *The Oxford Dictionary of Saints*. 5th ed. Oxford: Oxford University Press.

Gayk, Shannon. 2010. *Image, Text, and Religious Reform in Fifteenth-Century England*. Cambridge: Cambridge University Press.

Gillespie, Vincent. 2011. 'Chichele's Church: Vernacular Theology in England After Thomas Arundel.' In *After Arundel: Religious Writing in Fifteenth-Century England*, edited by Vincent Gillespie and Kantik Ghosh, 3–42. Turnhout: Brepols Publishers.

Green, R.F., and Ethan Knapp. 2008. 'Thomas Hoccleve's Seal.' *Medium Ævum* 77: 319–21.

Griffiths, Jane. 2017. '"In Bookes Thus Writen I Fynde": Hoccleve's Self-Glossing in the *Regiment of Princes* and the *Series*.' *Medium Ævum* 86 (1): 91–107.

Hoche, Dominique T. 2007. *The Reception of Christine de Pizan's Fais d'Armes in Fifteenth-Century England: Chivalric Self-Fashioning*. New York: Edwin Mellen Press.

Horobin, Simon. 2009. 'Adam Pinkhurst and the Copying of British Library, MS Additional 35287 of the B Version of *Piers Plowman*.' *Yearbook of Langland Studies* 23: 61–83.

———. 2015. 'Thomas Hoccleve: Chaucer's First Editor?' *The Chaucer Review* 50: 228–50.

Houghton, Josephine. 2013. 'Deguileville and Hoccleve Again.' *Medium Ævum* 82 (2): 260–68.

Kern, J.H. 1916. 'Der Schreiber Offorde.' *Anglia* 40: 374.

Killick, Helen. 2010. *Thomas Hoccleve as Poet and Clerk*. Ph.D. thesis. York: University of York.

Knapp, Ethan. 1999. 'Bureaucratic Identity and the Construction of the Self in Hoccleve's *Formulary* and *La male regle*.' *Speculum* 74 (2): 357–76.

———. 2001. *Bureaucratic Muse: Thomas Hoccleve and the Literature of Late Medieval England*. University Park, PA: Penn State University Press.

Laidlaw, J.C. 1982. 'Christine de Pizan, the Earl of Salisbury, and Henry IV.' *French Studies* 36 (2): 129–43.

Langdell, Sebastian J. 2012. 'A Study of Speech-Markers in the Early- to Mid-Fifteenth-Century Hocclevian Manuscript Tradition.' *Notes and Queries* 59 (3): 323–31.

———. 2018. *Thomas Hoccleve: Religious Reform, Transnational Poetics, and the Invention of Chaucer*. Exeter Medieval Texts and Studies. Liverpool: Liverpool University Press.

———. 2023. 'Thomas Hoccleve.' In *The Oxford History of Poetry in English*, vol. 3: *Poetry in English 1400–1500*, edited by Julia Boffey and A.S.G. Edwards. Oxford: Oxford University Press.

Lawton, David. 1987. 'Dullness and the Fifteenth Century.' *English Literary History* 54 (5): 761–99.

———. 2017. *Voice in Later Medieval English Literature: Public Interiorities.* Oxford: Oxford University Press.

McWebb, Christine, ed. 2007. *Debating the Roman de La Rose: A Critical Anthology.* London: Routledge.

Martin, Carl Grey. 2019. 'In Agincourt's Shadow: Hoccleve's "Au treshonorable conpaignie du larter" and the Domestication of Henry V.' *Studies in the Age of Chaucer* 41: 173–209.

Mooney, Linne R. 2006. 'Chaucer's Scribe.' *Speculum* 81: 97–138.

———. 2007. 'Some New Light on Thomas Hoccleve.' *Studies in the Age of Chaucer* 29: 293–340.

———. 2011. 'A Holograph Copy of Thomas Hoccleve's *Regiment of Princes.' Studies in the Age of Chaucer* 33: 263–96.

Mooney, Linne R., and Estelle Stubbs. 2011. 'A Record Identifying Thomas Hoccleve's Father'. *Journal of the Early Book Society* 14: 233–7.

———. 2013. *Scribes and the City: London Guildhall Clerks and the Dissemination of Middle English Literature, 1375–1425.* Woodbridge: York Medieval Press; Boydell Press.

Mundy, John Hine, and Kennerly M. Woody, eds. 1961. *The Council of Constance: The Unification of the Church.* New York and London: Columbia University Press.

Nall, Catherine. 2012. *Reading and War in Fifteenth-Century England: From Lydgate to Malory.* Cambridge: D.S. Brewer.

Nissé, Ruth. 1999. '"Our fadres olde and modres": Gender, Heresy, and Hoccleve's Literary Politics.' *Studies in the Age of Chaucer* 21: 275–99.

Nuttall, Jenni. 2007. *The Creation of Lancastrian Kingship: Literature, Language, and Politics in Late Medieval England.* Cambridge Studies in Medieval Literature 67. Cambridge: Cambridge University Press.

———. 2015. 'Thomas Hoccleve's Poems for Henry V: Anti-Occasional Verse and Ecclesiastical Reform.' Oxford Handbooks Online. doi: 10.1093/oxfordhb/9780199935338.013.61. Oxford: Oxford University Press.

———. 2016. 'The Vanishing English Virelai: French "Complainte" in English in the Fifteenth Century.' *Medium Ævum* 85 (1): 59–76.

Nuttall, Jenni, and David Watt, eds. 2022. *Thomas Hoccleve: New Approaches.* Cambridge: DS Brewer.

Parkes, M.B. 1969. *English Cursive Bookhands 1250–1500.* Oxford: Clarendon Press.

Patterson, Lee. 2001. 'Beinecke MS 493 and the Survival of Hoccleve's *Series.'* In *Old Books, New Learning: Essays on Medieval and Renaissance Books at Yale,* edited by Robert G. Babcock and Lee Patterson, 80–92. New Haven, CT: Beinecke Rare Book and Manuscript Library.

Pearsall, Derek. 1992. *The Life of Geoffrey Chaucer: A Critical Biography.* Oxford: Wiley-Blackwell.

———. 1997. *John Lydgate (1371–1449): A Bio-Bibliography.* English Literary Studies Monograph Series. Victoria: University of Victoria Department of English.

Perkins, Nicholas. 2001. *Hoccleve's Regiment of Princes: Counsel and Constraint*. Cambridge: D.S. Brewer.

———. 2018. '"Heer Y die in thy presence": The Rewriting of Martyrs in and after Hoccleve.' *The Review of English Studies* 69 (288): 13–31.

Perry, R.D. 2015. 'Lydgate's *Danse Macabre* and the Trauma of the Hundred Years War.' *Literature and Medicine* 33 (2): 326–47.

Peterson, Clifford, and Edward Wilson. 1977. 'Hoccleve, the Old Hall Manuscript, Cotton Nero A.x., and the Pearl-Poet.' *The Review of English Studies* 28: 49–56.

Porter, S., and I. Roy, eds. 1986. *Handbook of British Chronology*. 3rd ed. London: Royal Historical Society.

Richardson, Malcolm. 1986. 'Hoccleve in His Social Context.' *Chaucer Review* 20: 313–22.

Roberts, Jane. 2011. 'On Giving Scribe B a Name and a Clutch of London Manuscripts from c.1400.' *Medium Ævum* 80: 247–70.

Rozenski, Steven. 2008. '"Your Ensaumple and Your Mirour": Hoccleve's Amplification of the Imagery and Intimacy of Henry Suso's *Ars Moriendi*.' *Parergon* 25 (2): 1–16.

Sandison, Helen Estabrook, and Christabel F. Fiske. 1923. '"En mon déduit a moys de may": The Original of Hoccleve's "Balade to the Virgin and Christ".' In *Vassar Mediaeval Studies, by Members of the Faculty of Vassar College*, 233–45. New Haven, CT: Yale University Press.

Schieberle, Misty. 2019. 'A New Hoccleve Literary Manuscript: The Trilingual Miscellany in London, British Library, MS Harley 219.' *Review of English Studies* 70: 799–822.

Simpson, James. 2010. *Under the Hammer: Iconoclasm in the Anglo-American Tradition*. Clarendon Lectures in English. Oxford: Oxford University Press.

Smith, Toulmin L. 1882. 'Ballad By Thomas Occleve Addressed to Sir John Oldcastle, AD 1415.' *Anglia* 5: 9–42.

Sobecki, Sebastian. 2019. *Last Words: The Public Self and the Social Author in Late Medieval England*. Oxford: Oxford University Press.

———. 2021. 'The Handwriting of Fifteenth-Century Privy Seal and Council Clerks.' *Review of English Studies* 72 (304): 253–79.

———. 2022. 'Communities of Practice: Thomas Hoccleve, London Clerks, and Literary Production.' *Journal of the Early Book Society* 24: 51–106.

Spinka, Matthew, ed. 1965. *John Hus at the Council of Constance*. New York: Columbia University Press.

Stokes, Charity Scott. 1995. 'Thomas Hoccleve's "Mother of God" and "Balade to the Virgin and Christ": Latin and Anglo-Norman Sources.' *Medium Ævum* 64: 74–84.

Strohm, Paul. 1996. 'The Trouble with Richard: The Reburial of Richard II and Lancastrian Symbolic Strategy.' *Speculum* 71 (1): 87–111.

Trudgill, Marian, and John Burrow. 1998. 'A Hocclevean Balade.' *Notes and Queries* 45 (2): 178–80.

Turville-Petre, Thorlac, and Edward Wilson. 1975. 'Hoccleve, "Maistir Massy" and the Pearl Poet: Two Notes.' *The Review of English Studies* 26: 129–43.

Wakelin, Daniel. 2014. *Scribal Correction and Literary Craft*. Cambridge: Cambridge University Press.

Wallace, David. 2006. *Premodern Places: Calais to Surinam, Chaucer to Aphra Behn*. Oxford: Wiley.

Warner, Lawrence. 2015. 'Scribes, Misattributed: Hoccleve and Pinkhurst.' *Studies in the Age of Chaucer* 37: 55–100.

Watt, David. 2012. 'Thomas Hoccleve's La Male Regle in the Canterbury Cathedral Archives.' *Opuscula* 2 (4): 1–11.

———. 2013. *The Making of Thomas Hoccleve's Series*. Exeter Medieval Texts and Studies. Liverpool: Liverpool University Press.

Printed in the USA
CPSIA information can be obtained
at www.ICGtesting.com
CBHW080313091024
15594CB00008B/745

Printed in the USA
CPSIA information can be obtained
at www.ICGtesting.com
CBHW080313091024
15594CB00008B/745